D Meadows

January 2015

About the Author

Dr. John Robertson comes from a naval background; his father having been the gunnery officer in the famous British battle-cruiser HMS *Hood*. Dr Robertson joined the Royal Navy as a medical cadet and graduated from Edinburgh University in 1964, going on to serve a further six years as a doctor with the Royal Navy. Part of that time was spent as Staff Medical Officer to the Admiral of the British Western Fleet in his flagship HMS *London*, visiting many parts of the world.

Returning to civilian life, Dr Robertson specialised in Psychiatry working as a consultant in various London teaching hospitals where he took a special interest in post-graduate education. He also set up a trainee's exchange scheme with National University Hospital Singapore. He was made a Sub-Dean of the British Royal College of Psychiatrists in 1997.

Dr. Robertson retired in 2002 and spends the winter months in Penang, where he is a member of the Penang Heritage Trust. He is married with two sons.

Pubished by:

Éditions Intervalles
Editorial Direction: Armand de Saint Sauveur
80, Boulevard Haussmann, 75008, Paris, France
Tel: 331534383   Fax: 33153430595
www.editionsintervalles.com

Printed by:

Super Sonic One Stop Print
No. 67, Petani Road, 01050, George Town, Penang, Malaysia

First published in Kuala Lumpur, Malaysia in 2012 by:

Trafalgar Publishing House
Unit 15.07, Plaza 138, Jalan Ampang, Kuala Lumpur, Malaysia

ISBN 978-2-916355-97-9

THE BATTLE OF PENANG

World War One in the Far East

28th October 1914

J.R.Robertson

ÉDITIONS INTERVALLES

In memory of my father

Acknowledgements

In writing this book I am indebted to many people who have given me their time, advice and practical assistance. Below, I have listed the main contributors, although there were many others who played a part.

To Khoo Salma, Chair of the Penang Heritage Trust, for suggesting I should write this book and giving her valuable editorial advice. To Neil Khor for his practical assistance throughout. To Leslie James for his historical and local knowledge, and helping to correct the initial manuscript. To Chris Choo and Choy Koon Fatt for technical editing and graphic design. To Captain Ivan Stadchenko, Deputy Military and Naval Attaché at the Russian Embassy in Kuala Lumpur, for his kindness and enthusiasm, and for translating the Russian material. To Melvin Low, General Manager of the Russian Resources Office Penang for liaising with the Russian Embassy. To Captain Pierre Delbrel, Defense Attaché, French Embassy, Kuala Lumpur, for his support, encouragement and for liaising with Nouméa, New Caledonia. To Patrick Ung for his assistance with the Service Historique de la Défense, Paris. To Bernard and Donovan Yeoh, and Foo Han Piew for their advice and assistance. Finally to Kay Lyons for final proof-reading and the onerous task of compiling the index.

Contents

List of Illustrations

Key People in this Narrative

Chinese

Pu Yi. Child Emperor of China from 1908 to 1912
Yuan Shikai. First Prime Minister then President of Chinese Republic 1914
Sun Yat Sen, Dr. First President of Chinese Republic 1912
Cheong Fatt Tze. Mandarin of vast wealth, previously Penang's Chinese
    Consul

British

George V., King. Grandson of Queen Victoria
Churchill, Winston. First Lord of the Admiralty 1914
Battenberg, Prince Louis. First Sea Lord 1914
Grey, Sir Edward. Foreign Secretary 1914
Conyngham-Greene, Sir William. H.M. Ambassador in Tokyo 1914
Jordan, Sir John. H.M. Minister at Peking 1914
Jerram, Martyn. Vice Admiral. C-in-C China Station & Allied Flotilla.
    1913–1915
Young, Sir Arthur. Governor of Singapore during mutiny
Ridout, Brigadier General. General Officer Commanding Singapore 1915
Grant, H.W. Captain. In command of *Hampshire*
Cochrane, Captain. In command of *Yarmouth*
MacIntyre, Duncan. Commander Royal Navy Reserve. Port Intelligence
    Officer & Harbourmaster Penang
Maund, Guy. Lieutenant. British liaison officer in Russian cruiser *Zhemtchug*
Brown, William. Master-Mariner. Penang Pilot 1914
Ellis, Dr. W.G. Senior Officer, Singapore Volunteers, during mutiny
Cross, Reverend William. Minister of Penang's Presbyterian Kirk

French

Poincaré, Raymond. French President 1914
Augagneux, Victor. French Navy Minister 1915
Aubert, Monsieur. Head of Justice Division, Fleet Services, Paris. 1915
Huguet, Albert. Rear Admiral. C-in-C Far East Squadron. Flagship *Montcalm*
de Paris de Boisrouvray, Charles. Captain, Chief of Naval Division for
        Indo-China, Saigon. 1914
Couraye du Parc, Commander. Acting Chief of Naval Division for Indo-
        China after de Paris de Boisrouvray's death. Jan. 1915
Fatou, Captain. Substantive Chief of Naval Division for Indo-China after
        de Paris de Boisrouvray's death. Feb. 1915
Le Coispellier, Captain. French Naval Reserve, Commissioner, Saigon
        enquiry, from 5th Feb. 1915
Daveluy, Captain. In command of *Dupleix*
Audemard, Louis Théophile. Commander. In command of *d'Iberville* &
        destroyer squadron, Saigon
Pochard, Lieutenant. Audemard's second-in-command. Acting commandant
        of *d'Iberville* during Saigon enquiry
Tavera, Charles. Enseigne. *d'Iberville.* Wrote the report on loss of *Mousquet*
Baule, Lieutenant. In command of *Fronde*
Castagné, Victor. Commander. In command of *Pistolet*
Théroinne, Félix. Lieutenant. In command of *Mousquet*. Went down with
        his ship
Carissan, Léon Jaques. Enseigne *Mousquet*. Died at Sabang
Bourçier. First Engineering Officer *Mousquet*. Killed in action
Hamon, Matelot. Bugler. *Mousquet.* Died on board *Newburn*
Calloch, Matelot. Gunner, *Mousquet*. Rescued Carissan. Survived

Germans

Wilhelm II, Kaiser. King, and grandson of Queen Victoria
von Bismark, Otto. Previous Chancellor to Kaiser Wilhelm II. Retired
von Tirpitz, Alfred. Admiral. Navy Minisiter. 1914

von Spee, Maximillian. Reichsgraf. Rear Admiral. East Asiatic Squadron.
    Flagship *Scharnhorst*
von Müller, Karl. Commander. In command of *Emden*
von Mücke, Hellmuth. First Lieutenant, *Emden*
Lauterbach, Julius. Master, *Staatssekretär Kratke*. Lieutenant, Imperial Navy
    Reserve & Prize Officer *Emden*
von Hohenzollern, Prinz Franz Joseph. Second Torpedo Officer. *Emden*
Diehn, Herr. Manager of Behn, Meyer & Co in Singapore 1914

Russians

Nicholas II. Romanov. Russian Tsar (Emperor). His wife, Alexandra,
    Tsarina, granddaughter of Queen Victoria
Grigorovich, Ivan Konstantinovich. Navy Minister 1915
Rimsky-Korsakov, Rear Admiral. C-in-C Vladivostok & Pacific Fleet 1914
Cherkasov, Baron Ivan Alexandrovich. Captain, in command of *Zhemtchug*
Cherkasova, Baroness Varvara. Cherkasov's wife
Kulibin, Lieutenant Commander. Second-in-Command *Zhemtchug*

Japanese

Yoshihito, Emperor. 1914
Yamamoto Gonbee. Admiral. Japanese Prime Minister 1914
Tochinai. Vice Admiral. Commander of Allied naval patrols Indian Ocean
    following Jerram's departure, early 1915

Australians

Glossop, Captain RN (seconded to the RAN). In command. HMAS *Sydney*

Preface and Notes on References

The discovery of a grave by a beach on a small island off the east coast of Penang led me to investigate this story. The grave was all but obliterated, but a rough inscription identified it as the resting place of two Russian sailors. Their bodies had presumably been washed up on that isolated shore and been buried by local fishermen. They came from the Russian ship *Zhemtchug*, sunk by the German cruiser *Emden* in Penang harbour almost 100 years ago. I discovered that a French ship *Mousquet* was also sunk outside the harbour at the same time. A talk and a magazine article that I wrote around this story created some renewed interest amongst people in Penang, but my sources were mostly secondary.

When it was suggested that I might write this book, I had to do much more research, and this drew me to the unexpected and rather uncomfortable conclusion that the British harbour authorities in Penang were guilty of a reckless disregard for security and, quite without justification, passed the blame for the ensuing tragedy onto the French and the Russians. Nevertheless, the British version of events seems to have shaped prevailing beliefs ever since, and I hope that this book will do something to set the record straight.

The French Internet website 'Forum: Pages d'Histoire: Marine', under the heading *Mousquet,* was an important source of information regarding *Mousquet*'s survivors. It also included some useful references. It has contributions from relatives, including a photograph of *Mousquet*'s survivors. I posted a request, seeking information regarding some remains of *Mousquet*'s crew that were brought ashore by Malaysian divers in late 1969. It elicited an immediate response directing me to Nouméa in New Caledonia. This information was not known to the French naval authorities in Kuala Lumpur and they rendered invaluable assistance in obtaining photographs of the memorial at Nouméa Naval Base.

Fearing that the grave of *Mousquet*'s Enseigne Carissan at Sabang had been destroyed by the recent tsunami, I paid a visit and was happy to find the grave intact and well-tended.

Epilogue

At the end of the book I have added an epilogue. It belongs to the narrative, but lies to one side of it. Reverend William Cross, one of the main personalities in this book, gave a lecture to the Penang Athenaeum some months after the battle. He reflected upon the German philosopher Nietzsche, considering the consequences of that philosophy for the German people and rejecting it as an ideology. He makes rather chilling predictions that did not come true for another two decades. Some excerpts from his lecture are reprinted here. It provides an insight into the prevailing beliefs in Europe at that time, as well as his own. On reflection, it also gives pointers to many of the ideological tensions that affect the world today.

References

It was clear that if I was going to add anything to the body of literature surrounding this story, it would mean going back, as closely as possible, to primary sources. Numerous books have been written about *Emden* in English, as well as in German, and I have not attempted to give a comprehensive review of all those books. Suffice it to say that the ones published in English are, in the words of Prinz Hohenzollern, generally 'more zealous than accurate', although Van der Vat's book *The Last Corsair* is excellent.

After some persistence, I happened upon a file held in the Paris naval archives at the Château de Vincennes. This contained a large amount of material from an enquiry that was held in Saigon following the loss of *Zhemtchug* and *Mousquet*. It is officially described as the 'Penang' Enquiry, but for the purposes of this book I have referred to it as the 'Saigon' Enquiry, because that is where it was held. It was the only formal enquiry that was carried out covering *Emden*'s raid on Penang harbour. It was conducted with due legal process and many witnesses were called. For this reason I rate that material as very reliable. I am not aware of any books published in English that used this material; perhaps because it was conducted in French.

The German primary sources rest on the report that was submitted by Commander von Müller to the German authorities. Included in that were the charts of *Emden*'s movements in Penang harbour, copies of which are in the Penang Museum today and reproduced here. Unfortunately, all of *Emden*'s documents were destroyed, apart from a fragment of the signal log.

Whilst the events were still fresh in their minds, Commander von Müller and the rest of his officers spent their first few weeks in captivity putting together their best recollections of what had happened during *Emden*'s voyage in the Indian Ocean. Doubtless Lauterbach, the prize officer, and von Mücke, the Second Lieutenant, added to it when they returned to Germany after their escape.

Von Müller chose Lieutenant Prinz Franz Joseph von Hohenzollern, his second torpedo officer, as his writer, and that report formed the basis of the book that Prinz Hohenzollern later published: *'My Experiences in* SMS *Emden'*. I have taken this book as a 'virtual' primary source because it is based upon his own copy of von Müller's official report. But it has the advantage of many fascinating anecdotes which bring the whole story to life. He was the nephew of the Kaiser and writes in an amusing and very engaging way. His account tallies remarkably faithfully with the British archives. It is probably the most reliable source there is, from the German side. It is remarkable that the positions he quotes for *Emden* on particular days tally so closely with independent sources. Perhaps one, or some, of *Emden*'s officers kept their own pocket journals which survived and may have been used for reference, but that is mere speculation.

The only substantial difference from the British archives lies in the movements of *Emden* in Penang harbour. Here, the German accounts tally very closely with local eye-witnesses, the French enquiry and the Russian accounts, but not with the British. It becomes clear in this instance that the British accounts were the least reliable, based as they were upon a single report by *Zhemtchug*'s British liaison officer Lieutenant Maund, who was actually ashore at the time. It was forwarded to the Admiralty by Vice Admiral Jerram and, because the British held no enquiry, it became the official British version for ever after.

Nearly all the relevant Admiralty correspondence survives in the British National Archives at Kew, together with some unedifying material surrounding the feverish diplomacy which brought Japan into the war on the side of the Allies. The Admiralty Monograph collates material taken from the logs of the British ships involved in the *Emden* hunt, plus the log of *Markomannia*, *Emden*'s tender. Again it is very thorough, except for the movements of *Emden* in Penang harbour, where it relies, once again, upon the single source of Lieutenant Maund's report.

Access to the Russian Navy archives was obtained through the Internet organisation 'Blitz'. The archives are extensive, but many papers are missing from the service file of Baron Cherkasov, Captain of *Zhemtchug*. Those that remain show that his court martial did not seek to consider evidence that lay beyond his competence as *Zhemtchug*'s commander, such as the security measures taken by the British in Penang harbour. Nevertheless, copies of letters from Baron Cherkasov and his wife Varvara are still in the file and add much of human interest to the general picture.

The ministerial file of the Reverend William Cross proved elusive because the Free Presbyterian Church of England no longer exists. But when it was finally run to earth in Cambridge, it revealed an unexpectedly large collection of contemporary cuttings, photos and papers, many written is his small neat handwriting, and some written the day after the attack. His analysis of the issues is very searching and provides a clear account of what happened. In his file, carefully wrapped in an envelope, was a piece of shrapnel from one of *Emden*'s shells. He also wrote an account of the Singapore mutiny.

It amused me to bring in as references some excerpts from a nearly 100-year-old book that I inherited from my father, who was a naval gunnery officer in World War II. It is called *The Wonder Book of the Navy*. It was published during World War I in 1917, and presented to my father the same year by his grand-parents when he was nine years old. It is almost exactly contemporary with this story. It is full of illustrations and fascinating technical insights into warship-building, weaponry, propulsion, communications, naval training and contemporary attitudes: particularly their admiration for the Japanese Navy.

Naval Ranks

Throughout the book I have used the equivalent Royal Navy convention for officers' ranks to allow more-or-less direct comparisons of seniority. This is an approximation, because although it works fairly well for the German navy, with exactly equivalent 'rings' on their sleeves, in the case of the French navy it works rather less well. For example, Capitaine de Vaisseau de Paris de Boisrouvray, the Commandant in Saigon, would almost certainly have been designated a Commodore in the Royal Navy, being the senior Captain on the base; but I have referred1 to him as 'Captain'. Lieutenant de Vaisseau Théroine, Commander of *Mousquet*, would probably have been a Lieutenant Commander in the Royal Navy, given his seniority, but here he is referred to as 'Lieutenant'. In the case of the French rank of Enseigne Première Classe, the Royal Navy equivalent is a Sub Lieutenant but the French Enseignes Première

Classe in this narrative were given a degree of responsibility considerably above that of a Sub Lieutenant in the Royal Navy. The mismatch in this case I considered too wide and, accordingly, I have retained the designation of 'Enseigne' for those French officers.

The commanding officer of a ship or an establishment can be almost any rank, depending on its size. In the French convention, a commanding officer is generally referred to as 'Commandant', regardless of his actual rank. This can be seen in some of the quoted correspondence.

Metric Equivalents

I have expressed most of the weaponry, as well as distances, in metric equivalents, although the British armaments were normally measured in inches. The exception is nautical miles, or nautical miles-per-hour; 'knots', which are used universally by everyone at sea. One nautical mile is 2,000 yards, which is 1829 metres; almost 2 kilometres.

Place-names

I have used the place names that were current at the time, although I have sometimes added the modern equivalent in brackets to save the reader the bother of looking it up. That vast archipelago we now call Indonesia was called the Dutch East Indies in those days, with Batavia (Jakarta) its capital. These islands are at the heart of the narrative covering *Emden*'s voyage. Weh Island, with its important port of Sabang, is generally referred to in contemporary references and charts as 'Pulo' or 'Pulau' Weh. That is the local word for 'Island'. For that reason, I have retained the name Pulau Weh.

The Text

Certain conventions have been employed to assist the reader. Ships' names are written in italics, such as *Mousquet,* and square brackets [ ] denote comments I have inserted into quotations from others. Quotations from documents are not given in full, to avoid undue discursiveness. In certain cases however, I have copied extended quotations, in order to give the reader the true flavour of the piece. An important instance is the infamous article from the *New York Times* quoted in Chapter 11.

JRR February 2012

Second edition

Since the first edition was published some corrections have been made and some new material has been added. This includes the photograph of *Zhemtchug's* survivors in Penang Hospital which was originally taken from a Russian magazine, plus a contemporanious tinted postcard of Penang's Esplanade. Interestingly the tree shown opposite Fort Cornwallis is still there today.

JRR November 2013

Chapter 1

Penang: 1914

Just before dawn on 28th October 1914, a sinister silhouette could be made out against the night sky. It was a warship with four funnels inching slowly into Penang's outer harbour; silent, unchallenged. A Russian cruiser *Zhemtchug* lay there at anchor; immobile, unsuspecting. Her boilers were shut down for cleaning and the warship had emergency power only. She was unable to manoeuvre. Then the mysterious intruder suddenly open fire at close range. Through singular misfortune, the harbour launch and the Russian ship had mistaken the intruder for an allied cruiser. Thus *Zhemtchug* failed to open fire till it was too late. In one almighty eruption the Russian cruiser blew up like a volcano. Her magazine had exploded and inside that great jet of fire, massive chunks of metal were thrown high up into the air and scattered far and wide. She then sank in a few seconds, trapping many of her crew between-decks. Of those who survived, many were seriously burned and mutilated.

As dawn was breaking the intruder, which was the German light cruiser SMS *Emden,* left the harbour and made off, lest any other warships in the harbour should try to retaliate.

Unhappily a French destroyer *Mousquet* was out on a routine patrol to the north-west of Penang Island. That morning she was returning to Penang without any knowledge that an enemy warship was in the vicinity. When the crew sighted *Emden* steaming towards them, they also mistook her for a friendly cruiser. Only when *Emden* opened fire did they realise that they were in the presence of an enemy warship. *Mousquet* made a valiant attempt to counter-attack with her light-weight guns and even loosed off a torpedo, but the German captain kept his ship out of range of *Mousquet's* torpedoes and quickly crushed her with *Emden's* overwhelming fire-power.

That morning, Penang's hospital was overwhelmed with Russian casualties from *Zhemtchug*. Many more had died and the Russian memorial in the Western Road cemetery bears silent witness to their sacrifice. Today, a large anchor rests by their tombstone. A list of eighty-nine Russian dead is inscribed there: crewmen of *Zhemtchug* who lost their lives. On Jerejak Island nearby, beside a quiet stretch of beach, lies another grave where the bodies of two Russian sailors from *Zhemtchug* were washed up and later buried. Penang is sometimes called the Pearl of the Orient; by a strange coincidence, *Zhemtchug* also means 'pearl'.

Just outside the Penang Museum is an anchor on display which most visitors pass by without noticing.[1] It stands as a memorial to *Mousquet* (which means 'musket'). Few looking at that anchor today could imagine the dreadful carnage that lies behind it.

This is the story of those two ships and the men who commanded them, and the German cruiser *Emden* which sank them.

It is one hundred years since those tragic events took place and the reason why German, French and Russian ships were fighting each other in Penang is no longer common knowledge. It happened in the early weeks of World War 1, when the global forces of imperialism were at their height, not just in Europe, but also in the Far East. A naval confrontation was then being fought by the imperial powers of the day, right across the Far East and the Pacific, with the Germans standing alone against the rest. The allied powers of Britain, Australia, New Zealand, France, Russia and Japan were all ranged against them.

Of these, Britain and Japan had by far the most powerful fleets, and all of them had a deep involvement in protecting their interests in the Far East, especially China, which held vast commercial investments on behalf of the imperial powers. At that time the French Empire encompassed Indo-China (present-day Cambodia, Laos and Vietnam) with additional treaty-port rights in Shanghai on the Yangtze.

The Netherlands remained neutral in this war, but their territory covered the wide archipelago of the Dutch East Indies; now known as Indonesia. One of their key bases was Sabang on Pulau Weh, at the northern tip of Sumatra. This base lay close to Penang and was soon to assume great importance for *Mousquet* and her crew.

An eye-witness to those tragic events was the Minister[2] of the local Scottish Presbyterian Kirk[3] in Penang. The Sunday after the battle, in a sermon filled with anger and outrage, he denounced those responsible for the security of Penang harbour from the pulpit of his church. He accused them of a dereliction of duty. So far as we know, he was the only one who dared to do so. Was there something special about this man that made him do this? Why would he dare to challenge British authority and run the risk of being called unpatriotic or, worse, a traitor? Yet there can be no doubt that he was a thoroughly credible witness; a key witness in fact to the story that was unfolding. He was outspoken, independent-minded and, above all, had a strong sense of moral purpose. His past history testified to all of those traits.

In his previous ministry in London he was a fearless debater, organising open discussions in his church hall to which sceptics, atheists and people loitering about with nothing better to do were invited. He called them 'conferences'. These were rowdy affairs, but he relished the challenge.[4]

These meetings would frequently turn to European politics, because an influential segment of German society at that time subscribed to some of the ideas of Nietzsche, especially the apparent belief in a 'master race'. Anti-Semitism was on the ascendant throughout Europe, especially in certain parts of London which housed large Jewish populations. Cross thought about these things seriously. Racial prejudice was anathema to him and he was very pessimistic about Germany. Even in 1912, he believed that war with Germany was inevitable.

This was quite shocking for most people in Britain. The German king, Kaiser Wilhelm II, was Victoria's eldest and favourite grandson. Queen Victoria herself came from a German family and spoke German with her husband, Prince Albert of Saxe-Coburg-Gotha. When the Kaiser was only 30 years old, Queen Victoria bestowed on him the honorary rank of Admiral of the British Navy and had a full-length portrait painted of him in a British admiral's uniform, which now resides in the Queen's collection.

For many years Otto von Bismarck had been Chancellor to Kaiser Wilhelm II, and to his father before him. 'I want no colonies,' said Bismarck, 'they are only good for providing offices.'[5] Instead, he pursued a policy of friendly relations, paying other countries to provide the necessary protection and facilities for his ships; this was mostly Great Britain. But now he had retired and a spirit of militaristic, national fervour had gathered pace in Germany with the rapid acquisition of colonies. These were mainly in Africa, but included a part of New Guinea, together with many islands in the western Pacific, including Samoa and the Bismarck Archipelago. In China, Germany

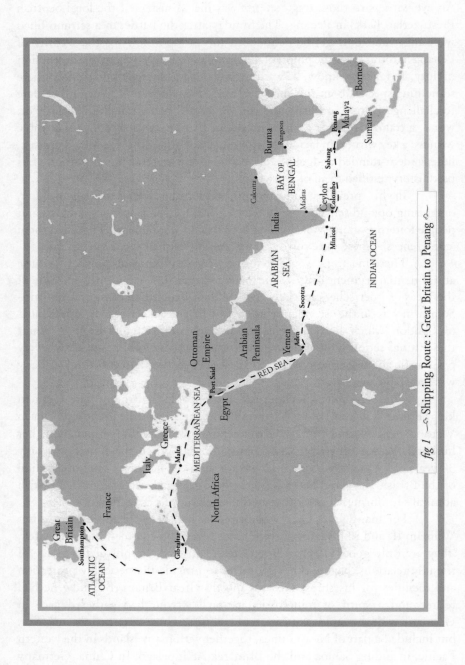

fig 1 ❧ Shipping Route : Great Britain to Penang ❧

occupied a well-developed naval base in Tsing Tao, which, like the British in Hong Kong, they had acquired on a 99-year lease.

In 1912, twenty years after that portrait of the young Kaiser was made, things were looking very different. Queen Victoria was dead and there were serious tensions in Europe. It is a curious fact that at the outbreak of World War 1, the British King George V, Tsarina Alexandra wife of the Russian Tsar, and the German Kaiser Wilhelm II were all Queen Victoria's grandchildren. At this distance in time, it is easy to forget the complex interwoven nature of the European aristocracy and its elites.

The threat of war was now on everybody's mind, none more so than the French, who had only recently been roundly defeated in the Franco-Prussian War. Prime Minister Raymond Poincaré was thoroughly pessimistic.

Two years before World War 1, Reverend Cross decided he was going to Penang,[6] and his voyage followed the well-trodden trade-route between Europe and the Far East. His journey provides a convenient illustration of the way Great Britain managed her vast maritime empire. Britain had a large fleet of merchant ships and a powerful navy to protect them. They also needed a string of suitable bases to connect up the dots.

The trade-route (Fig. 1) passed through the Mediterranean via Malta, where most of the survivors from *Emden's* eventual demise were later imprisoned. The route then passed through the Suez Canal and out into the Red Sea, where the British presence suddenly ceased, because the west coast of Arabia belonged to the Turkish Ottoman Empire. But at the foot of the Red Sea, in Yemen, the British had another base, Aden. These factors were soon to became crucial to the survival of a small group of German sailors who escaped from *Emden's* eventual destruction.

Socotra Island and then Minicoi Island would have been passed to port, as merchant ships headed for Colombo on the southern tip of Ceylon (Sri Lanka). Colombo was a bustling trading hub, one of the busiest in the world because all the trade across the Indian Ocean and the Bay of Bengal stopped there. That is why these places became the focus for *Emden's* later, daring, exploits.

The final lap crossed the Bay of Bengal to Penang, which was then, along with Malacca and Singapore, a part of the British Straits Settlements. George Town, the capital, was a bustling port where ships passing up and down the Malacca Straits could discharge and load fresh cargoes and refuel. Penang also served as a transoceanic coaling station, connecting the Indian Ocean with the eastern China trade.

Cross was 44 years old when he arrived in George Town, with his wife and son, and his descriptions of Penang in that era paint a useful picture of the place as seen through the eyes of a foreigner.

By that time the town had grown very prosperous, with the development of tin mining and rubber plantations on the mainland. Indian Muslims known as Chulias had long-established trading connections, but the largest elite were the Chinese with elaborate trading networks throughout the region. In contrast, the native Malays were generally farmers and fishermen around the rural parts of the island.

After finally settling into a new house in Logan Road, Cross wrote an upbeat letter dated 9th May 1913, to a friend in London.

> ... Everything is utterly different from home. So far we have kept (apart from sporadic gymnastics of the germs) fairly well, and we get to like the place very well. The population of the town is about 200,000, chiefly Malays and Chinese, but our work is entirely among the European population, and the European population needs the Church. The influences of evil here are very bold and strong, the religious forces weak. But on many sides there are signs that the Good Spirit is with us, and we are encouraged in our outpost to stand firm with a good heart.[7]

The local people would have found Cross a very strange man indeed because of his lack of interest in the comforts of life. In his austere mind, such things were of little account. Penang, he believed, was in dire need of spiritual cleansing. George Town was packed with unattached men. Just one year before Cross arrived, the ratio of Chinese men to women was more than two to one.[8] Campbell Street and Cintra Street were designated as 'red-light' districts and in 1908 Campbell Street had some 800 women working as prostitutes.[9] There was a lot of sin about.

Cross soon established himself as a leading member of the community and later, when he went to Singapore, it was said of him that 'he emerged as the acknowledged leader of our Malayan Churches'.[10] Because of this, his accounts of the battle in Penang harbour, and the opinions he expressed afterwards, carry much authority and can be respected.

He might have been surprised to find so many Germans freely mingling with the British in such a friendly way; indeed, some German merchants had become virtually naturalised Englishmen. Out east, British and German interests had evolved together with German commercial activity depending upon a certain ideological benevolence from Britain and the Netherlands, whose governments believed in the principles of free trade.[11]

Giant German shipping lines had emerged, with North German Lloyd the largest. Behn, Meyer & Co which managed all North German Lloyd's coastal shipping, had their main offices in Singapore, with Herr Diehn (whose name crops up again in Chapter 13) holding the position of senior manager. Many locally owned shipping companies were also carrying freight and migrant labour from Penang to other regional ports in Sumatra, northern Malaya, Siam and Burma.

The Chinese communities around the Malacca Straits, the Dutch East Indies and Siam had prospered mightily. The wealthy Chinese elite must have been an awesome sight, living in great mansions with vast families, multiple wives and dozens of servants. On special occasions they could be seen in public, dressed in their rich, flowing Chinese robes, their wives and daughters glittering with jewellery. One of the most prominent of these was Cheong Fatt Tze, a mandarin of vast wealth and Penang's Chinese Consul back in the imperial days. At that time, the Imperial Court in Peking was in dire need of funds and wealthy overseas Chinese could buy such titles, which previously had depended on passing the difficult imperial examinations. When he was in Penang, Cheong occupied his fine Blue Mansion in Leith Street.

It is hard to imagine what China must have been like in those days. Despite her political weakness and the poverty of her people, China had immense wealth; its huge export trade was principally in tea, silks and ceramics. The imperial powers, soon to be precipitated into a state of war, had vast trading commitments in China. To balance their massive trade deficit with China, the British relied upon opium, produced in Bengal.

In the past, the Chinese government had tried to put a stop to foreign trading altogether because opium was having such a ruinous effect on the Chinese coastal population. Seeing the decimation of their China trade looming, the British government declared war – the Opium War. It was a scandalous act of aggression to counter the Chinese government's efforts to stamp out the pernicious opium trade, and the Chinese lost.

Britain emerged at the end of the Opium War even more powerful, with Hong Kong and five other ports – Canton, Amoy, Foochow, Ningpo and Shanghai – wide open to British residents. Soon there was a string of towns, like Nangking, stretching for hundreds of miles up the Yangtze, where British subjects had the right of 'extraterritoriality'. This gave them the right govern these ports however they pleased, under British, rather than Chinese, law.[12] In 1900 a tragic attempt was made to throw off the colonial yoke in the Boxer Rebellion. It failed, and unrest in China rumbled on for years.

One leader, however, had emerged from the Boxer Rebellion and grew ever more powerful. This was the wily and ambitious warlord, Yuan Shikai.

Britain now had virtual control of the entire Yangtze Valley and the whole hinterland of Shanghai. This accounted for half of the Chinese export market. The German merchant fleet used many of the same ports as the British, with full British government encouragement. It was into this complicated network of trade and politics that the British Navy Commander-in-Chief, Vice Admiral Martyn Jerram, was precipitated early in 1913, just a year before Word War One broke out.

Up north the Japanese had their eye on considerable territorial expansion into China. The Russians had once occupied Manchuria in northern China, bringing the Trans-Siberian railway right down to the tip of the peninsula at Port Arthur[13] on the Po Hai Sea (Fig. 4). However, in February 1904, during the Russo-Japanese War, the Japanese seized Port Arthur, destroying many Russian ships under cover of darkness using fast torpedo boats. In May 1905 they destroyed the bulk of the Russian fleet in the Battle of Tsushima although one of the cruisers, *Zhemtchug,* survived. Ten years later she achieved lasting fame by being sunk in Penang harbour.

In 1912 the Japanese controlled much of the northern Chinese seaboard – but not quite all. Britain had a base at Wei Hai Wei, on the southern side of the Po Hai Sea, whilst in Germany's well-fortified base in Tsing Tao, lay the powerful German East Asiatic Squadron.

In the Chinese coastal ports the local merchants may have grown very rich but, politically and militarily, China was now on her knees. The expansion of foreign powers into Chinese territory dominated the political landscape. Indeed, many commentators of the day saw war as far more likely in the Far East than anywhere in Europe. Despite these difficult circumstances, the European powers somehow settled their differences, whilst endeavouring to maintain some control over Japan.

When the Empress Dowager died in 1908, she left the young prince Pu Yi, who was just a child, to take over as emperor, surrounded by useless advisers and eunuchs. This could not last. Outside China, various reform movements were being established. Not all were dedicated to the overthrow of the Qing dynasty, but simply sought government reforms. With its large

Chinese population, Penang was deeply embroiled in the politics of the Far East, and Cheong Fatt Tze, with his immense wealth, attracted regular visits from such reformists. Besides them however, there were the out-and-out revolutionaries, particularly Dr Sun Yat Sen.

By 1910 Sun Yat Sen was travelling extensively, including trips to Singapore and Penang. In Penang he was mainly based in 120 Armenian Street, and during a four-month period he convened his famous Penang Conference, which planned an uprising in April 1911. It is an interesting fact that Sun Yat Sen and other Chinese revolutionaries of the day had strong links with Japan. 'Republican China went to school in Tokyo.'[14] They aspired to the kind of transformation and modernisation that Japan had undergone in the latter part of the 19th century. For Japan, modernisation, followed by industrialisation had been swift and bloodless because it came from the top.[15] Japan now had a very powerful navy. Their early warships were mostly British-built, but within a few years, the Japanese could design and build their own warships, often to superior specifications.[16]

On 10th October 1911 a new Chinese Republic was created, with a revolutionary government set up in Nangking and Sun Yat Sen provisionally at its head. But the warlord Yuan Shikai had by now become Prime Minister, with his own power-base in the north. He soon took over as president from Sun Yat Sen, and moved the capital from Nangking to Peking.

When China's first democratic elections were held, the Kuomintang party won, but their leader was assassinated and the party crushed. Yuan Shikai wanted complete control. However, the southern Chinese, including many of those in Penang, never accepted Yuan's leadership, and China descended into civil war with Sun Yat Sen leading the Second Chinese Revolution from the south.

However, Yuan Shikai was still the president of China, and with the outbreak of World War 1 he was the man the foreign powers had to do business with. This was the reality of the situation for the British, who liked to style themselves as the 'protectors' of Chinese interests. Although the Qing dynasty had been overthrown and a republic declared, everyone thought it was just a matter of time before China finally disintegrated, with the imperial hyenas, especially the Japanese, moving in on the corpse. But it takes a huge iceberg an awful long time to melt. The vastness of China gave her the time to begin the long drawn-out revolution that ultimately saved the Chinese empire from dismemberment.

To grasp the state of play between the imperial powers in the Far East at the outbreak of World War 1, the situation in China is the key. China was already in a state of civil war. The imperial powers protected their interests with powerful naval forces deployed in bases around China's coast. The French navy-base was further south in Saigon. (Fig 2), but foreign warships including the French were particularly active around the Yangtze, where local armed insurgents were posing a threat to trade.

Penang was not at the centre of things yet, so the narrative now leaves Penang and moves to China. First to Tsing Tao and then to the British navy's China Station in Hong Kong, where Vice-Admiral Martyn Jerram was settling in.

Chapter 2

Saigon and the China Station

Germany held the balance of power in the Far East for ten years before the outbreak of World War I. Ever since the First Sino-Japanese War and the later Russo-Japanese War, Japanese attempts to occupy Manchuria and key areas around the Po Hai Sea had been frustrated by the Germans who, to the fury of the Japanese, installed themselves comfortably in Tsing Tao. For the time being the Japanese had to content themselves with occupying Korea and Port Arthur.

Germany invested a great deal of effort developing Tsing Tao, which they hoped would match Britain's Hong Kong. They spent a fortune building a well-equipped dockyard and support services in the hinterland, extending thirty miles into the adjacent Kiao Chow Peninsula.[1] They even built a brewery making Tsing Tao lager, which is still in production today. A garrison was posted in the base with great gun emplacements installed to ward off attacks from the sea.

Japan and Britain had forged an alliance in 1902. At the time it was aimed at countering Russian power, but although Russia's influence had since waned, the alliance still remained. Thus Great Britain's relations with Japan were generally much more friendly than Germany's, and over the next ten years Britain endeavoured to remain on good terms with both.

When Jerram arrived at the China Station in 1913, his headquarters was at Britain's fortified base in Hong Kong, but he had other bases including Wei Hai Wei in northern China, and far to the south-west he had Penang and Singapore (Figs 2 & 4). Those two were not fortified,[2] but like Hong

Kong they were connected to all the major parts of the British empire through underwater telegraph cables, which emerged on land as cable stations.

Jerram had a daunting task. The politics in that part of the world were fiendishly complicated and involved everything he touched. He must have been a genial, tactful and diplomatic man, or he could never have achieved such seniority. A contemporary photograph shows a stout man in his mid-fifties, with a big head and a plethoric countenance, doubtless soaked in the pink gin that was the essential lubricant to socialising in those days. The late American professor and naval historian Arthur J. Marder described him as 'colourless, not possessing much initiative or dash, a reliable, reasonably competent officer with no frills'.[3]

Jerram had to maintain good diplomatic relations with both Japan and Germany, whilst protecting British commercial interests from pirates, bandits and the warring factions in China. Things were especially hot around the Yangtze where so many European 'treaty' towns and ports were concentrated.

One British gunboat patrolling the Yangtze was *Thistle*;[4] and on board was the young 23-year-old Sub-Lieutenant Guy Maund. He was educated at Osborne Royal Navy College on the Isle of Wight, off the south coast of England, and from there, aged fifteen, he progressed on to Dartmouth Royal Naval College.[5] Once taken into active service in 1913, he was soon out on the China Station on the Yangtze. Later, he was promoted to Lieutenant and given command of the gunboat *Kinsha*.[6] He was a capable officer in all respects. He was proficient in French and German[7] and was even recommended for accelerated promotion. His language skills were soon put to use when he was appointed as the British liaison officer on board the ill-fated Russian cruiser *Zhemtchug,* which was sunk in the Penang harbour battle. His subsequent report to Jerram describing that action had far-reaching consequences.

Unfortunately for Jerram, the patience and diplomatic skills of peace-time work are not always ideal character-traits in time of war. His management of events following the outbreak of World War I revealed a distinct lack of imagination and flair.

France was Britain's principal ally in the Far East. Admiral Jerram's first sight of the French navy was when he spotted their two massive armoured cruisers, *Montcalm* and *Dupleix,* on patrol on the Yangtze.[8]

The French had a large enclave in Shanghai and French warships were often seen on the Yangtze. Back in their main naval base in Saigon, *Mousquet,* which was soon to be sunk outside Penang harbour, was one of

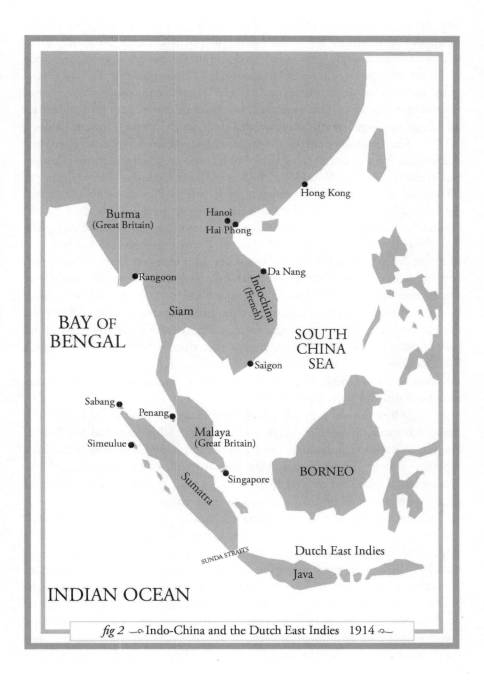

fig 2 ❧ Indo-China and the Dutch East Indies 1914 ❧

four French destroyers forming a squadron. She was built in Nantes on the Loire and launched in 1902. *Mousquet* was not large, only 56 metres long, with a shallow draught.[9] She was fast, doing up to twenty-eight knots, which could out-pace most other ships in those days. For armaments she had several guns and two on-deck torpedo tubes. Her biggest gun was a single 65mm (9-pounder) cannon on the forecastle, but it would have a very limited impact on a large warship. For that, they needed their best weapons – their torpedoes.

The Commandant of the destroyer squadron was Louis Théophile Audemard. He was not a young man – at least not young by naval standards – but in the year before World War I he was given command of the old destroyer *d'Iberville,* with the young Lieutenant Pochard as his second-in-command. Audemard had been out in the Far East for many years and by 1914 he was almost 50, having spent most of his naval career in Saigon as a hydrographer. But Audemard was not a healthy man. Recurring bouts of malaria and frequent periods of sick leave had weakened him over the years.[10] Promotion had only come slowly and he must have known that he would be unlikely to progress further, at his age. As events over the next few months unfolded, he showed himself to be a compassionate, mild-mannered man with a great deal of patience. He did his best to make life bearable for the men under his command who were struggling in a very uncomfortable environment.[11] His character was in stark contrast to the commanding officer of the Naval Division of Indo-China, Captain de Paris de Boisrouvray,[12] an old sea dog with little time for such sentiments.

D'Iberville was a peculiar looking ship: stubby, with a rounded hull. Rapid advances in warship design and weapons technology had left her far behind. She could barely make twenty knots and had only one big weapon, a 100mm (4-inch) gun mounted on the forecastle; she had no torpedoes.[13] The French had a powerful navy at that time, but their policy – for a number of reasons – was to send out-of-date ships to Indo-China.

France, like the Germans and the British, was in a naval arms race, constructing vastly expensive battleships of the Dreadnought design. These ships were oil-fired and driven by steam turbines. Huge 300mm guns could hurl a 385kilogram projectile over 25 kilometres with quite extraordinary accuracy. But the French ships in Indo-China were generally older and coal-burning, with reciprocating engines subject to chronic wear in their engine bearings owing to primitive lubrication. If cranes were not available, refuelling a ship meant man-handling hundreds of bags of coal onto the deck and into the hoppers, leading to the coal bunkers. Coaling was hot, filthy work, a nightmare in the tropics, and cleaning up the ship – as well as the men – afterwards was a major chore. Such was the inefficiency of the bigger warships that, unless they kept their speed below ten knots, in just a week they could eat their way through a full load of coal, shovelled manually into the furnaces by dozens of men in the stoke-holds.

Another serious drawback of these old ships was their boilers. Boiler-cleaning had to be done very regularly, or the already inefficient engines would suffer a serious drop-off in power. Essential, regular maintenance could take several days, and during that time the boilers were shut down and the ship had to make do on a minimum of residual power, sometimes relying on electrical accumulators. Furthermore, they could not start up instantly like a modern ship. It could take an hour to get up steam before they were ready to move.

All of these technicalities were of crucial importance in the Battle of Penang, and were a major contribution to the disasters that befell *Zhemtchug* and *Mousquet*.

Of the remaining three destroyers, *Fronde*[14] was commanded by Lieutenant Baule, *Pistolet*[15] by Commander Castagné, and *Mousquet*[16] by Lieutenant Théroinne.[17] These destroyers could be very effective around inshore waters, especially at night, but just one of them out on its own in daylight was no match for a cruiser like *Emden*. Furthermore, their antiquated torpedoes had an abysmal range of only 600 metres.[18]

By way of contrast, Germany had a powerful squadron in Tsing Tao. Jerram's opposite number there was a very distinguished, aristocratic Prussian: the 51-year-old Rear Admiral Maximillian Reichsgraf (Count) von Spee. He had an extraordinary presence and Jerram was completely smitten from the moment he first met Graf Spee.

One of his contemporaries wrote:

> He was a favourite of the wardroom.[19] He made everybody his friend with his invariable kindness, his unaffected and engaging nature and his dry sense of humour.'

In his later years, a fellow admiral wrote very warmly of Graf Spee:

> ... [with] his simple, unaffected personality, and the brave manner in which he faced the many formal occasions at which he had to be present, and which he found so distasteful. In appearance

he held himself as erectly as he had always done and his great height made him immediately distinguishable on the bridge of his flagship. His hair, his short beard, his moustache and even his bushy eyebrows had all turned a steel grey; his deep-set blue eyes suggested a fit man with instant reactions, and a decisive mind.[20]

The German High Command, under the Navy Minister Admiral Tirpitz, regarded their East Asiatic Squadron as worthy of powerful armoured cruisers for protecting trade and their colonial possessions. Graf Spee was in *Scharnhorst*, a magnificent ship, together with his two sons who were serving alongside him. *Gneisenau* was another large armoured cruiser. Four more light cruisers made up the rest of the squadron; and one of these was Seiner Majestät Schiff (SMS) *Emden*.[21]

In addition, Graf Spee had various supply ships; one of these was the fast, British-built collier[22] *Markomannia*. *Emden*, with *Markomannia* as her tender, were soon destined to make history.

The commander of *Emden*, Karl von Müller, became a key player in the early weeks of World War I by decimating British merchant shipping in the Bay of Bengal, finally sinking *Mousquet* and *Zhemtchug* in Penang. Von Müller came from Hanover, the son of a colonel in the Prussian army and a French mother. Von Müller never married and seems to have been a very reserved man, yet he was extremely courteous. In the spring of 1913 he was promoted to Commander[23] and given charge of *Emden*. He was 40 years old, and in the year before the war he carried out patrol duties up the Yangtze, working alongside the British cruisers and river-gunboats, protecting German commerce from pirates and raiders.

Von Müller soon become well known because of his daring. He ran the gauntlet of bombardment from Chinese shore batteries and successfully shelled several rebel forts along the Yangtze. *Emden* even won the squadron gunnery prize. For his sterling service on the Yangtze, von Müller was awarded the Order of the Royal Crown Third Class with Crossed Swords.[24] Like many German naval officers in his day, von Müller had a great admiration for the British Royal Navy and when the opportunity arose he befriended several Royal Navy officers, including Captain Grant of the cruiser *Hampshire*.

The second torpedo officer in *Emden* was Lieutenant Prinz Franz Joseph von Hohenzollern, the Kaiser's nephew. He eventually became von Müller's chosen narrator for *Emden*'s voyage. In a surprisingly self-effacing tribute to von Müller, Prinz Hohenzollern wrote:

This truly noble man had greatness of character and goodness of heart. He was a friendly captain, always ready with help, and, to those who had the privilege of knowing him more closely, an excellent and steadfast friend. In the *Emden* I was a mere Lieutenant and I had no proper opportunity to come into prolonged and active contact with him. For so long as he was with us in captivity at Malta [*see* Chapter 16], he was, in the truest sense, a good counsellor to me and I may also say, a faithful comrade.[25]

Just before the war, Mr Sydney-Smith, a planter from Ceylon had accompanied von Müller on a voyage across the Pacific and observed that:

Captain von Müller was one of the most charming men one could meet and immediately impressed himself on a new acquaintance as one of the best. Slightly above average height and build, he is a powerful man, clean-shaven and fair. Every inch of him was a sailor and his blue eyes had the far-away penetrative look that one is accustomed to associate with sailors. He spoke English excellently and in all respects might easily have passed as an Englishman, but for his occasional peculiar phraseology. French I believe he spoke better. His favourite pass time was playing with the many children on board, with whom we had many a romp together and listening to the Filipino band by the hour. Well-informed on all subjects, he was a most interesting and tolerant-minded man. He was an ardent admirer of the British Navy – second to none – and his own, and had no use for any other except the Japanese, a people, however, he did not love.

The idea of being opposed to his pals in the British Navy he said, was too cruel to think of, and he hoped for a better understanding between Britain and Germany, and counted many friends in England. His charming personality, genial smile and ways covered, one felt, a character as transparently honest and straightforward. His life however was tinged by sorrow. He confided in me the knowledge of a weak heart and that his days were numbered.[26]

Turning to British commitments at the time, Jerram's first task was to make official visits to Yokohama and Tokyo to pay his respects to the Japanese government.

Japan was an important ally to be sure, but one whose territorial ambitions in China remained undiminished – contrary to Britain's own commercial interests. The Japanese Prime Minister was Admiral Gonbee [Count] Yamamoto who for years had been Chief of the Imperial Japanese Navy. He even wrote their definitive gunnery manual. It was he who had done much to push for the modernisation of the Japanese Navy and presided over the Russo-Japanese War. Jerram must have been in considerable awe of this man.

Whilst he was visiting Tokyo, Jerram also met Graf Spee in his flagship *Scharnhorst*. With characteristic politeness, Graf Spee postponed sailing till Jerram's arrival. Graf Spee's reception by the Japanese would have been altogether less cordial than Jerram's!

Jerram also met the British Ambassador in Tokyo, Sir William Conyngham-Greene who, at the outbreak of war, became involved in frantic diplomatic activity to ensure that the mighty Japanese Navy came into the war on the side of the Allies. In his telegraph to the Admiralty, Jerram reported that:

> H.M. Ambassador Sir Conyngham-Greene informed me that owing to the court being in mourning [the Empress Dowager had died], there would be no great amount of entertaining, but nevertheless my time was fully occupied with it, including a luncheon given by Admiral Saito (Minister of Marine) and a dinner by Admiral Ijuin (Chief of the Naval General Staff); I also gave an official luncheon on board *Minotaur*. Our reception by all, was most kind and cordial, and on sailing I requested that my thanks might be conveyed in the proper quarter.
>
> I was received in audience by His Majesty the Emperor, together with my staff, and the Captains of Ships being presented by the Ambassador: and was subsequently received by H.M. the Empress. I also visited the Princes Higashi Fushimi and Hiroyasu Fushimi, the latter of whom had been with me in the *Goliath* for the manoeuvres of 1909.[27]

What Jerram made of Emperor Yoshihito we do not know because he was a man with physical and psychological disabilities resulting from an attack of meningitis in childhood. But his wife the Empress was, by all accounts, an engaging person. The link with Prince Hiroyasu is interesting, revealing the close ties that existed in those days between the British and the Japanese navies.

Further visits however, were soon curtailed because problems were brewing on the Yangtze. Jerram immediately contacted H.M. Minister at Peking, Sir John Jordan, asking if he should visit the Yangtze straight away? The immediate answer was 'yes'. Apparently Sir John thought it highly desirable because the Japanese, German, French and American admirals were already there. Today we might think that five admirals on one river constituted rather a crowd!

Alongside a large British force of cruisers and gunboats on the Yangtze there was an additional French cruiser, three American ships, one Japanese, four German and one Austrian:[28] quite a collection. All were endeavouring to protect their merchantmen in an increasingly hostile environment. Maund was also there, patrolling the Yangtze in the gunboat *Thistle*. He would certainly have known *Emden* and the reputation of her daring commander von Müller.

Jerram was now faced with a fresh problem caused by intensive fighting on shore. Communications via the shore stations were appalling. At this point *Thistle,* with Lieutenant Maund, was at Hankow.[29] The distance from Hankow to Shanghai was huge – over 1000 kilometres down-river. Jerram therefore decided to set up a chain of eight ships down the Yangtze, from Chungking to Shanghai. Each was in radio contact with the next, so messages could be passed right down to Shanghai. By mid-July Jerram's arrangement of radio-ships down the Yangtze had become something of an administrative nightmare, because everyone wanted to use them. (Fig 3).

> Although I now have a wireless chain from Hankow to Shanghai, the wireless work is found to be very difficult: the Chinese shore stations still accept telegrams but it is quite problematical whether they send them through, and in any case a delay of some days is to be expected. Consequently everything has to be done by wireless, and the consular authorities in all the ports look to our ships to transmit their messages, besides the large amount of naval work going on. With the ships of five nations: British, American, German Japanese and French, thus competing against each other, the result was confusion. I have arranged with the other nations that the 12 hours of day and night shall be allotted, two [hours] to each nation exclusively, and the remaining two for general use.[30]

This anecdote illustrates the difficulties in those days with primitive radio-communication. This problem was crucial to the later sinking of

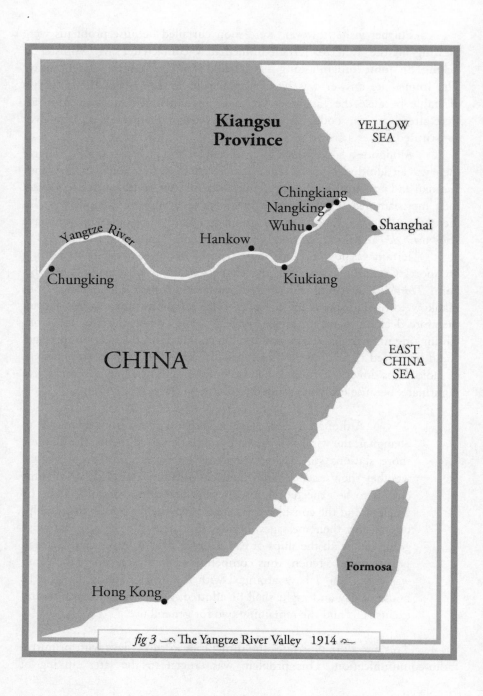

fig 3 ⤳ The Yangtze River Valley 1914 ⤳

Mousquet outside Penang harbour.

However, the protection of ex-patriots in their enclaves in Nangking and Shanghai was Jerram's current difficulty. The northern forces of Yuan Shikai were pushing the rebels southwards and a rout was likely to follow. This meant thousands of southern troops arriving in Nangking; unpaid, unfed and ready to start looting. Yuan Shikai's forces soon followed after them, adding to the general chaos. Sir John Jordan reported: 'The Northerners have now obtained possession of Nangking and have been looting, burning and committing every excess without restraint.'

Down the Yangtze in Shanghai, the weapons arsenal was under attack, and an international corps of volunteers had to be mobilised. In his rather dry style, Jerram gave the following description of Shanghai when the heat was on.

> The Southern troops are on the whole undisciplined, and lately they got very much out of hand, straggling into various suburbs round the [European] settlement, which are also used for secret meetings and intrigues. This constitutes a distinct menace to outlying portions of the settlement and on 26th [July], the consular body and the municipal Council asked the Japanese Vice Admiral, as the senior naval officer present, to authorise the landing of forces of seamen and marines, of various nationalities, for patrol purposes. A force of 500 were landed including 120 men and 4 Maxim guns from *Newcastle*.
>
> There are in all, about 900 seamen and marines landed from the men-of-war, for the protection of the settlement, under the command of the Japanese Vice Admiral Nawa.[31]

It was clearly British policy to allow the Japanese this opportunity to control the Chinese insurgents. This would have pleased the Japanese mightily and it was done with great efficiency. Jerram would have been left in no doubt that in this part of the world, Japanese ambitions had to be both feared and controlled. But it must be said that the Japanese proved remarkably efficient at maintaining law and order around the suburbs of Shanghai.

Jerram was clearly deeply impressed by the Japanese, and as events unfolded, he was hugely relieved when they entered the War on his side, going on to capture Tsing Tao. He could not have managed without them. Furthermore this Japanese efficiency was again deployed on his behalf in quelling the Singapore Mutiny.

Returning to events that were unfolding in China, order was eventually restored and life began to settle down once more, but Sir John Jordan added a note of caution about Japanese intentions.

> There has undoubtedly been a considerable growth of Japanese power and prestige in the Yangtze Valley – a growth deliberately fostered by the Japanese government. Numbers of [Japanese] claims, commercial and political, have been 'staked out' in that region and their owners only await the disruption of China before entering into full proprietorship. A majority of Japanese are, it is certain, confident that the period of waiting will not be protracted. Japanese action in this direction has been so strong, as to arouse Chinese fear and hatred. The Japanese doubtless trust to overcome this by force, as they have done in Korea, where they have reduced the populace to a condition of helpless and 'sheep-like' inactivity.[32]

In the space of the next few months, revolutionary activity in China began to simmer down, largely it seems for want of money, but Jerram remained vigilant.

> This great waterway [the Yangtze] is the most important part of China, and its importance will increase with the development of the country. There are now daily services of river steamers from Shanghai to Hankow (700 miles)[33] and great competition between British, Chinese, German and Japanese steamship and mercantile companies, exists.[34]

This lull enabled Jerram to return to his base in Hong Kong. It was not long before he received a visit from Graf Spee. Jerram remarked that to everyone's dismay, Graf Spee was retiring from the German East Asiatic Squadron.

> On 19th December [1913] the German Cruiser *Scharnhorst* (Flagship of Vice Admiral Graf von Spee) arrived at Hong Kong and remained till the 3rd January. Our relations with the German Admiral and his officers are always of a cordial nature.[35]

Jerram now turned his attentions to the French, who were increasingly apprehensive about a war in Europe and kept in close contact with their allies. On 15ᵗʰ December 1913, aboard his flagship *Montcalm*, Admiral de Kerrilis, Commander-in-Chief of the French Naval Division for the Far East (Division Navale de l'Extrême-Orient), had visited Jerram. Also on board was the Governor of French Indo-China, who had business in Canton, whatever business that might have been. Soon afterwards, a new French admiral was appointed to replace de Kerrilis; he was Rear Admiral Albert Huguet.

Huguet, a native of Boulogne in Pas-de-Calais, was 57 years old.[36] He was a small man with open sensitive features, thinning hair, a light beard and an upturned moustache in the French style. He had entered naval college just four years after the Franco-Prussian War and was exceedingly wary of German military power. His concern was shared by the French Prime Minister Raymond Poincaré.

Some weeks later in early 1914, the newly appointed Admiral Huguet duly visited Jerram, carrying proposals from the French government.[37] At this crucial meeting in Hong Kong, it was decided that should hostilities with Germany break out, Saigon would provide their destroyer squadron – *d'Iberville, Mousquet, Pistolet* and *Fronde* – to patrol the northern shipping lanes of the Malacca Straits, using Penang as their base. At the same time the French cruiser *Dupleix,* under Captain Daveluy, would be redeployed to join Jerram's squadron in Hong Kong. That meeting between Jerram and Huguet was the moment when *Mousquet*'s fate was sealed.

Early in 1914 a major earthquake hit Japan, and this required a friendly response from Admiral Jerram. He offered assistance from the light cruiser *Yarmouth* to the Japanese Prime Minister. His offer was appreciated but politely declined, although the Japanese Vice Admiral Nawa paid Jerram a visit.[38] So relations between the British and the Japanese were being carefully nurtured on the political front. *Yarmouth* was yet another ship destined for a more dramatic role in Penang.

Meanwhile, Jerram was having increasing problems with piracy around Canton, where embarked passengers were now hijacking ships on the high seas. In some cases guards were posted on the bridge behind iron and barbed wire grilles and bulletproof shields, to repel attacks.[39] Jerram had to do something drastic, and on 5ᵗʰ May he took off with no fewer than fourteen British warships to the northern waters of the Yellow Sea and the British base in Wei Hai Wei, ostensibly for a spot of gunnery practice, but also to be closer to Peking.

There he had a personal meeting with Yuan Shikai. If these southern pirates could not be controlled, then he, Jerram, would call upon the ever-belligerent Japanese to help out. We do not know the details of what was discussed at that meeting, but it is unlikely to have been anything but frosty. Yuan Shikai was less than sympathetic and Admiral Liu, the Minister of Marine, could only advise the foreigners to be more vigilant.[40]

The political climate in Europe was now growing a whole lot worse, and the Germans and the British on the China Station could only look on with dismay. With Jerram and his ships close by in Wei Hai Wei, the Germans and the British held a memorable party in Tsing Tao, which has gone down in history. It highlights the rift that sometimes exists between fighting men and their politicians. Jerram reported that:

> In the middle of June, I visited Tsing Tao in *Minotaur*[41] on the invitation of the German Commander-in-Chief, Graf von Spee, and remained there four days. Marked and genuine hospitality was shown to myself and the officers and men. A very friendly feeling exists between the British and the German ships on the China Station and I regret that Graf von Spee is shortly to be relieved on the termination of his appointment.[42]

The two squadrons played football together, with the British winning, whilst the Germans won at gymnastics. Commander von Müller of *Emden* met up with his pal Captain Grant of the cruiser *Hampshire*. In a fog of beer and good cheer, accompanied by the oom-pah of a German brass band, both sides agreed that they would never fight each other. Looking back at it now, that declaration is rather sad.

However, getting back in the world of realpolitik and trying to keep in with everybody, Jerram now visited Vladivostok.

> The visit of the Squadron to Vladivostok, which has just terminated, has been marked by great cordiality and hospitality on the part of the Russian naval and municipal authorities, which was suitably returned by the British ships.
>
> A very full programme of entertainment had been arranged for officers and men and nothing could exceed the courteous attention which was received. Rear-Admiral Schultz, formerly Captain of the *Novic*, provided an escort of destroyers when we sailed and both he and Rear-Admiral Rimski-Korsakov,[43] placed all the resources of the

port at our disposal.[44]

Whilst he was there, Jerram noticed that there were obvious tensions between the Russian Army and Navy:

> It was the subject of frequent remarks that the relations between the naval and the military officers at Vladivostok are very strained, so much so, that they know little of each other, either socially or officially.[45]

After the seriously embarrassing defeat of the Russian Navy by the Japanese at Tsushima, the Russian military's resentment against their own navy was still smouldering beneath the surface. The loss of *Zhemtchug* that was soon to follow must have rubbed salt into that wound and goes some way to explain the savage treatment meted out to *Zhemtchug's* captain at his court-martial.

By now it was June 1914 and events on the political front were moving fast. The French were more than ever convinced that war with Germany was inevitable. Admiral Huguet mobilised his destroyer squadron in Saigon, preparing them to make for Singapore and the Malacca Straits should war break out. The French destroyers may have been no match for German cruisers in open waters, but inshore they were a force to be reckoned with, even with their short-range torpedoes.

There was an intriguing contrast between the personalities of the four French commanders. In overall command was the kindly Commander Louis Audemard in the old, slow, *d'Iberville.* Second-in-command was Commander Victor Castagné of *Pistolet,* an energetic, zealous officer in his early thirties. Next came *Mousquet,* commanded by the 43-year-old Lieutenant Félix Théroinne. He was much older than Castagné, but junior in rank. His photograph shows a dark man with a full beard and a serious, rather commanding expression. He was a solid commander, although lacking imagination. Born in Brest, he entered the navy aged 18 and his promotion had been slow.[46] But Audemard observed that he had served well in submarines for ten years – dangerous craft in those days – where he displayed an unflappable, quiet, calm.[47] Finally there was Lieutenant Baule of *Fronde.* We know rather less about him because his ship was hardly involved in the battle in Penang harbour.

The following anecdote shows the contrast between Commander Castagné and Lieutenant Théroinne, although the story requires some technical details by way of introduction.

With 6,300-horsepower engines, *Mousquet* had a top speed of twenty-eight knots, which was very fast, but her bunkers could only hold 100 metric tons of coal. At ten knots this would keep her going for nine days, or 2,900 nautical miles, but only five days or 1,700 miles, at fourteen knots.[48] At full power that amount of coal could easily be expended in a day. The point is that fuel consumption was immensely variable, depending on speed. But it also depended very much on the type of coal used. The quality of coal varied tremendously, according to the sources that supplied various coaling stations.

Pistolet, *Mousquet* and *Fronde* had been carrying out patrolling exercises up the Malacca Straits, stopping at Penang for coaling and provisions. In the absence of *d'Iberville*, Castagné was in overall command. They were using low-quality 'roche' coal, and Castagné was unimpressed with *Mousquet's* performance in terms of coal consumption. He even brought their engineering officer, Bourçier, aboard his own ship to demonstrate how to economise. Despite this, *Mousquet* ran into trouble with her coal bunkers nearly empty before they got back to Singapore. Whether Bourçier had been using the wrong technique, or whether Théroinne had taken on insufficient coal in Penang is unclear, but Castagné was livid. He sent off a very stiff letter to his immediate superior, Commander Audemard, insisting that it be forwarded to the Commandant in Saigon, Captain de Paris de Boisrouvray.

> I am sending a report regarding Lieut. de Vaisseau, Commander of *Mousquet,* about a shortage of coal that took place aboard his ship on 17th June, during the trip from Penang to Singapore. I believe that he had some empty space in the bunkers of *Mousquet* on arrival in Penang. What did they do? Nothing.
>
> Théroinne knew exactly what he had in his bunkers, so he knew that if his consumption continued to rise, when he only had 'roche' coal, he could not have reached Singapore. He did nothing. He did not request the loading of coal [in Penang] and got under way in a state that would oblige him to stop in the open sea without fuel. For the whole of the 16th he proceeded with an enormous consumption. He signalled nothing till the morning of 17th, when he was obliged to signal his condition; that he would not be able to reach Singapore.[49]

Continuing his rant, Castagné clearly thought that some formal disciplinary action should be brought, adding:

I insist especially, that a severe reprimand should be given, because it was the second time that problems arose on *Mousquet*. A month ago, this ship needed to turn her furnaces low 100 nautical miles from Cam-Pauh, or else she would have completely used up her supply of water and would have been unable to continue the journey except with help from *Pistolet*.

The first mistake can be excused, but this one today requires severe punishment.[50]

It is amusing that Castagné, in his rage, referred to Bourçier as an engineer 2nd class'. In fact his designation was 1st class. Tragically, Bourçier was killed a few weeks later when *Mousquet* was sunk by *Emden*.

The complaint was duly passed on to Captain de Paris de Boisrouvray in Saigon. He gave Théroinne an official warning the very next day purely on the basis of that one letter but after some calmer reflection he amended it, crossing out the word 'official' and substituting 'verbal' scrawled in his own handwriting.[51] This was typical of the man. His impulsive character had much more serious consequences for Audemard after *Mousquet* was sunk.

In truth, the French were very tense. They were quite certain that a war was just round the corner, and the ships from the French Naval Division for the Far East would soon be called to action. Germany, they feared, had long nurtured a desire to seize Cochin-China. The French alliance with Britain was essential, and they could not allow their credibility as an efficient fighting force to be compromised.

This incident also establishes Castagné's as a stickler for discipline and efficiency. This is important because it gives the lie to an article later published in the *New York Times* accusing him of irresponsible conduct and ill-discipline aboard his ship. There is no evidence whatever to support that accusation.

Chapter 3

War: The Dominoes Fall and Japan Steps In

Jerram's main task was to protect the China trade, but he also needed to cover Malaya and the Straits Settlements, including the all-important Malacca Straits. Added to that, he had to cover the whole of the Bay of Bengal and the Indian Ocean as far west as Ceylon. The shipping routes that passed through the Bay of Bengal came not just from the Malacca Straits, but from Rangoon and the Irrawaddy, Calcutta and Madras. Altogether these shipping routes accounted for a major part of world trade.

In the event of war, the area Jerram had to cover was even greater. His jurisdiction extended far into the south-western Pacific, although with added support from the Australian and New Zealand navies. The waters to the west of Ceylon were covered by the British East African Squadron, but everything that lay to the east was Jerram's responsibility.

Should the Dutch enter a war against Britain, their warships in the Dutch East Indies would constitute a substantial threat. Further north, around the Yellow Sea and the western Pacific, the Japanese also had a very powerful navy; more than a match for Jerram's squadron. It was vital for Britain to remain allied to Japan despite the Japanese appetite for adding bits of territory to their burgeoning empire.

The German East Asiatic Squadron had some powerful ships, but hitherto they had always co-operated with the British Royal Navy. In the event of war with Germany, Jerram's Far East Squadron would be the greater force. Even so, Jerram's round of diplomatic visits served a vital purpose, especially his visit to Japan.

Early in 1914, even though the threat of a European war was looming, Jerram's main concern was still China. *Yarmouth* was keeping the peace on the Yangtze, whilst Jerram himself was in Wei Hai Wei, close to Tsing Tao and also China's President Yuan Shikai in Peking. Anticipating a possible outbreak of war with Germany, he was rushing to get his battleship *Triumph,* which was in Hong Kong, ready for sea.

Reminded of his earlier discussions with the newly arrived French Admiral Huguet, he contacted the Admiralty in London:

> *Montcalm* is in the South Seas and *Dupleix* is on passage to Nagasaki. I have not yet received instructions to cooperate, but if you authorise me doing so, I propose to ask for them to join with me and carry out arrangements already sanctioned by the Admiralty.[1]

The French destroyer squadron in Saigon was then alerted. Three additional mercantile cruisers in Hong Kong were requisitioned and fitted out with guns. These were *Empress of Russia, Empress of Japan* and *Empress of Asia.*[2] The latter very nearly caught the *Emden* some weeks later, and *Empress of Japan* eventually captured *Exford,* one of *Emden's* colliers, with Lauterbach, *Emden's* prize officer, aboard.

Since 1907 Britain, France and Russia had been bound together in the Triple Entente, whilst Austria-Hungary, Germany and Italy were bound by a treaty called the Triple Alliance. This made two opposing factions: Britain, France and Russia on one side, and Germany, Austria-Hungary and Italy on the other. These treaties were intended as a deterrent, but the actual consequence was mutually assured destruction. Everyone, including Jerram, was just waiting for someone to set the thing off.

The trigger was pulled, in more ways than one, on June 28th 1914 in Sarajevo the capital of Bosnia which was then under Austro-Hungarian rule. Some Bosnian nationalists managed to shoot Archduke Ferdinand, who was heir to the Austrian throne. Neighbouring Serbia supported the Bosnian nationalists and political tensions rose rapidly over the next four weeks. This so enraged the Austro-Hungarian government that they decided to attack Serbia. This precipitated a chain reaction. Russia went to Serbia's defence, Germany attacked Russia and, in doing so, marched through neutral Belgium. France was bound to defend Belgium and thus attacked Germany. Britain was allied to France and entered the war on their side. All this happened within a week, at the beginning of August 1914.

The British Queen Mary showed an unusual flash of wit by remarking, 'There must be reasons for going to war – but for Serbia? Words fail me!'

Then came the opportunists. The first of these was Japan. They had not come into the war just yet, but soon would. The other was Ottoman Turkey. The Balkans had a sizeable Muslim population, especially in Bosnia, so Turkey sided with the rest of the Balkan states with Germany, and against Serbia. It also gave the Turks a renewed chance to have a crack at their traditional enemy, Russia, in the Caucasus. Turkey had a secret alliance with Germany from July 1914, but their formal entry into the war did not take place till 28th October, the same day as the battle in Penang harbour. Their timely entry into the war on the side of Germany was to have fortunate consequences for the crew of the *Emden*.

As soon as it was announced that Britain was at war, there was great enthusiasm in the dominions to offer assistance, none more so than Australia and New Zealand. Australia offered 20,000 men, whilst New Zealand offered 8,270 men and 3,838 horses, ready to go in four weeks' time. The troops were to be transported in ships used for the frozen meat trade, so they were going to bring a vast quantity of frozen mutton with them.

All these ships needed an armed escort and it fell to Jerram to organise it. Jerram was now Commander-in-Chief of a multinational naval force: adding French, Russian, Australian and New Zealand warships to his British Far East Squadron. All these ships now came directly under his orders. The Australian navy were to seize the German territories around New Guinea, while New Zealand was to seize German Samoa.[3]

Jerram had to keep an eye on Tsing Tao where Graf Spee's impending retirement was now on indefinite hold. Jerram knew that Graf Spee's big cruisers were not in port, but the light cruiser *Emden* had already sprung into action, capturing the Russian ship *Rjäsan* in the Tsushima Straits, bringing her back to Tsing Tao to be refitted as an armed auxiliary. This was done by the Tsing Tao dockyard at lightning speed before being added to the German squadron, renamed *Kormoran*.

There were several merchant ships in Tsing Tao and one of them was *Staatssekretär Krätke*. Her master was Julius Lauterbach, who was to become a central figure in the story that was unfolding. As a Lieutenant in the German Imperial Navy Reserve, Lauterbach was doing his annual stint for the Kaiser aboard *Emden*. He had a prodigious knowledge of local merchant shipping and their trading routes and knew many of their captains.

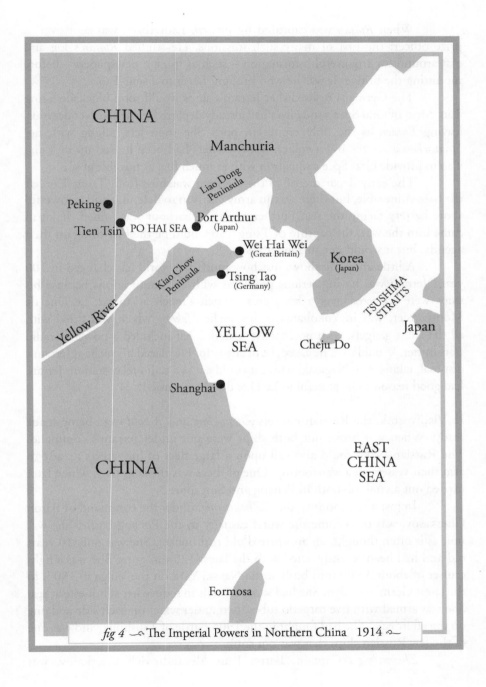

fig 4 ❧ The Imperial Powers in Northern China 1914 ❧

When *Rjäsan* was captured by *Emden*, Lauterbach was sent over as prize officer; the first of many such missions. He studied *Rjäsan*'s log and cast around for any useful information – such as foreign newspapers – before mounting the bridge. It was he who brought her into Tsing Tao.

The Germans realised that Jerram's ships would soon blockade Tsing Tao. Most of Graf Spee's squadron had already departed for a secret rendezvous, leaving *Emden* as the only cruiser in port. She soon left, taking with her *Staatssekretär Krätke* and a collier. Many colliers had been loaded up in Tsing Tao to provide Graf Spee's squadron with as much fuel as possible at sea.

The early departure of all the German warships from Tsing Tao left the base vulnerable, but there was an army garrison to defend it and a powerful shore battery facing the sea. Furthermore, the harbour was mined. If Japan came into the war, the capture of Tsing Tao would be the first thing on their agenda, but it would not surrender easily.

A little anecdote shows just how much the world has changed in 100 years. Jerram was having serious problems with communications because his ships were scattered over a huge area. A rich French aristocrat, Le Duc de Montpensier, was in Yokohama in his yacht *Mekong* which was fitted with all the latest gadgets, with no expense spared. That included a powerful radio transmitter. Would that, he asked, be of any help? He placed his yacht at Jerram's disposal, taking it to Nagasaki where it could act as a radio relay station. Jerram had good reason to be grateful to Le Duc de Montpensier![4]

In Vladivostok, the Russian cruisers *Zhemtchug* and *Askold* were being made ready. When war broke out both ships were put under Jerram's command. The Russian Navy could also call upon a large fleet of 'privateers', ready to arm their vessels on a war-footing. One of these was the ship *Orel*, which later carried out a vital job both in Penang and Singapore.[5]

In just a few months' time, *Zhemtchug,* under the command of Baron Cherkasov, was to become the worst casualty in the Penang battle. She was not, as is often thought, an antiquated old rust bucket. She was only 10 years old and had been recently fitted with the latest 120mm guns. She was a light cruiser of about 3,000 tons built at the Nevski Yard on the Volga in 1903, to the latest German design. She had short funnels to reduce her silhouette at sea. She was armed with five torpedo tubes, two under water on each side and one on the afterdeck.[6] She had fought in the 1905 Battle of Tsushima, and was one of the few Russian ships that was not sunk.

Zhemtchug's Captain, Baron Ivan Alexandrovich Cherkasov, was born in Moscow on 26th October 1875 and educated in the Russian Navy Cadet Corps, but he never attended the Russian Navy Academy. In such an aristocratic family he was presumably educated by private tutors. He specialised in gunnery; this skill was put to good use, many years later, in the Caucasus. He was promoted to Lieutenant at the age of 24, and two years later, in November 1902, he was given a medal for his services in China. In the Russo-Japanese War he was in the cruisers *Russia* and *Gromoboy*, but he apparently avoided action and did not participate in the Battle of Tsushima at all. He was given command of *Zhemtchug* in May 1914, just before World War I broke out.[7]

The other Russian cruiser to be attached to Jerram's squadron was *Askold*. She was four years older than *Zhemtchug*, but very much bigger at 6,000 tons. She, too, escaped the Battle of Tsushima by being interned in Shanghai.[8] She absolutely bristled with armaments: twenty-eight guns altogether, six of them 150mm, which had a long range. She also had six torpedo tubes. She was built in Germany to a German design, with five immensely tall, thin, funnels which made her quite unmistakable at any distance.

Askold was later seized by the British after the Russian revolution. The British sailors dubbed her the 'packet of Woodbines', named after a brand of cheap cigarettes sold in fives. She survived World War I unscathed after giving sterling service to Jerram and the Allies.

The Expeditionary Force from Australia and New Zealand was going to be vast. There were also many other transports bound for Europe, from Hong Kong, Calcutta and French Indo-China. All of these had to be escorted via Singapore up the Malacca Straits and over to Colombo. Jerram's task was to protect all of these transports from any possible attack by Graf Spee's cruisers.

Jerram reasoned that Graf Spee's two vital needs were fuel and communication. On Yap Island, in the German Carolines, there was an important radio station. Jerram had received information that Graf Spee's squadron had gone east, and he felt sure that they must be at Yap Island. The island was connected to undersea telegraph cables which Graf Spee could use with a reasonable degree of security. So on 6th August, Jerram set out for Yap Island in his flagship *Minotaur*, with a veritable armada of warships, including the French cruiser *Dupleix*, ready for the mother of all battles. But when he arrived there, there was absolutely no sign of Graf Spee or his squadron. So Jerram contented himself with demolishing the radio station. The wireless station was:-

... conspicuous in a small clearing, surrounded by dense palm groves about two miles S.W. from the settlement, on rising ground, about 1/4 mile from the beach. It appeared to be entirely isolated, and consisted of one strong steel, or iron, trellis-work mast, about 200 feet high, close to the foot of which were buildings, evidently the power plant, offices, etc. whilst about 1/4 mile distant were what looked like the dwelling house of the operators.[9]

Jerram's ships steamed up and down for a while, but saw no sign of life. There must have been operators there because the radio station started to jam Jerram's radio signals, so he responded with a flashing Morse lamp, saying 'move out of the way, because we are going to demolish your wireless installation' or, as his wireless operators put it in rather bad German:

Punkt 9 Uhr v.m. Wir auf die Funkentelegraphieanlage mit schwaren Geschützen geshossen. Jedermann sollte sich von der Nähe der F/T Station entfernan. Bestätigen Sie Empfang diesen Mitteilung.[10]

There was no response, so they opened fire and reduced the place to rubble. It was the only time that Jerram would personally see action till the Battle of Jutland, exactly two years later. Jerram had no idea where to look next so he returned to Hong Kong, taking *Dupleix* and the other cruisers with him.

Meanwhile, the French were moving fast. On 12th August the French Admiralty radioed Huguet, who was then with *Montcalm* at Suva, capital of Fiji. Huguet was asked to await a military expedition, which included two cruisers, that was coming from New Zealand. Their plan was to go and capture German Samoa as quickly as possible, before the Japanese got there. The Americans much preferred that solution.[11]

D'Iberville, Fronde, Pistolet and *Mousquet* had duly arrived in Singapore from Saigon, ready to take on patrolling duties wherever they were needed.[12] Jerram decided not to send the French destroyers up the Malacca Straits just yet. Instead, he kept them back to patrol the Java Sea, well to the south of Singapore. Graf Spee's cruisers could have been lurking there, slipping out southwards into the Indian Ocean, ready to pounce on any ships coming from Australia.[13]

Shifting the scene over to Graf Spee's squadron, we can now recapitulate what they had really been up to during those two weeks. The German squadron was miles away from Yap Island. They were at Pagan Island in the Marianas group, on roughly the same latitude as Formosa. Pagan Island was almost completely uninhabited and nobody would think of looking for them there.

On the way to Pagan Island, the last of the creature comforts were jettisoned from *Emden*. Warships are very crowded and uncomfortable at the best of times, but when they are stripped down for war, everything that might burn or create a hazard has to be removed. The last remains of her peacetime amenities were sacrificed. Prinz Hohenzollern later wrote that he particularly disliked the 'poisonous' green paint on the wardroom bulkheads, after the wood-panelling had been stripped off.[14]

As *Emden* steamed into the harbour at Pagan Island, the whole of Graf Spee's East Asiatic Squadron was there, with their colliers and supply ships, including Lauterbach's own ship, *Staatssekretär Krätke*.

Graf Spee then called all his commanders together in *Scharnhorst*, expressing the view that the cruiser squadron should be kept back in reserve. He hoped that they could tie up Allied warships searching for them over a longish time. His big armoured cruisers *Scharnhorst* and *Gneisenau* used up vast quantities of coal and were more conspicuous, so rather than cruising around in circles for too long, he decided to head for South America, passing Samoa on the way. This was an interesting decision because it meant that he was taking his squadron out of action for many weeks. However, there was another reason: he feared that Japan would come into the war on the side of the Allies, and Japan had a very powerful navy – more than a match for the German ships.

Von Müller of *Emden* took an entirely different view about the best use of the light cruisers. The sheer volume of merchant shipping around the Indian Ocean would especially favour cruiser warfare [Kreuzer Krieg], and the appearance of German warships off the Indian coast, von Müller argued, would have a marked influence on the morale of the Indian people.[15] Besides that, Britain depended on merchant ships to maintain its empire, and he believed that light cruisers would be excellent commerce-raiders. After all, he argued, not all ships could be protected in convoys and many ships would be unescorted. Such ships would be vulnerable to attack from a lone wolf. This way of thinking had been argued by naval strategists for years, especially the French. This group was called the *jeune école*.[16]

These two competing schools of thought had split the top brass of the German Navy since the 1890s. Cruiser warfare (Kreuzer Krieg) was compared with battle-fleet warfare (Flotten Krieg). The latter was favoured by the Navy

Minister, Alfred von Tirpitz, but von Müller clearly took the opposite view.

It is interesting that in both world wars, the war at sea was at its most effective when the strategy of commerce-raiding was used, although that task would soon pass to submarines. *Emden* and *Karslühe*, another unattached German cruiser in the Caribbean, were the first to demonstrate the great effectiveness of this kind of guerrilla warfare at sea, although a third lone cruiser, *Königsberg*, which was operating out of Dar es Salaam, proved much less successful.

Von Müller argued that *Emden* could live off her wits and whatever supplies and fuel she could capture. If they ran out of luck, they could head for a neutral port and sit out the rest of the war. It is important to remember that at that time, people believed that the war would be over by Christmas. Indeed the war in the East was over pretty quickly, thanks to the entry of Japan.

Graf Spee listened carefully to what von Müller had to say and said he would sleep on it. That night the entire squadron weighed anchor and headed out into the Pacific. But early next morning, Graf Spee signalled *Emden* to detach from the main squadron and head for the Indian Ocean, with the new British-built and comparatively fast *Markomannia*, acting as her supply ship.

It was now 15th August, and Von Müller immediately set a course for Angaur in the Palau Islands. They could occasionally pick up radio transmissions from Tsing Tao, especially at night, and they were well aware that Japan, though not yet in the war, was very determined to capture the Germans' one and only base at Tsing Tao.

When *Emden* and her tender *Markomannia* got to Angaur, the news was bleak. Tokyo had issued an ultimatum to the Germans to quit Tsing Tao by 23rd August, or they would declare war. That was in just a few days' time.

The Germans were not the only ones to be concerned about the Japanese. Back in Peking, Yuan Shikai had already announced that China would remain neutral in this war, hoping thereby to avoid any formal hostilities with the European powers or with Japan. He followed this announcement with immediate action. On the Yangtze River, both Britain and Germany agreed to remove or dismantle their vessels. This included Lieutenant Maund's gunboat *Kinsha*. The Chinese also impounded *Thistle*, Maund's old ship, but allowed the crew to go free with their small arms. Thus the Germans and the British were unable to fight each other on the river; nor could they engage in any hostilities against the Chinese.[17]

The Chinese were hoping that if the Germans were squeezed out of the Kiao Chow Peninsula, Tsing Tao would be returned to them, or at least have it held in trust till the end of the war. Yuan Shikai looked to the British for support in this matter, but sadly it was not to be. The diplomatic pressures on the British were very great and what follows relates the grizzly details of just what happened next.

The Japanese still had not declared war. In fact on 5th August, off the Korean Peninsula, two Japanese warships even dipped their colours to *Emden*![18] It is quite possible that this incident was the origin of later stories that *Emden* tricked a Japanese cruiser into dipping its colours. Nevertheless, the Japanese desire to take up arms against the Germans was very great, backed by Japanese public opinion.

There was really no reason why the Japanese should make war on Germany, apart from her 1902 treaty with Britain. Germany had not violated any treaty nor encroached on Japanese territory. The only justification, from Japan's point of view, was their 'moral' right to Tsing Tao and the adjoining Kiao Chow Peninsula. Germany had forced Japan to abandon its plans to occupy Tsing Tao after the first Sino-Japanese War. Not long after, Germany herself leased the base from the Chinese. This inflamed the Japanese people with burning hatred.[19] Now it was only diplomatic pressures that were stalling Japanese plans to invade. Without Germany's presence, Japan saw the door to Tsing Tao, and thence to China, wide open. Only the British were standing in the way.

German possessions in the Pacific – all those islands – were also a tempting target for the Japanese, and that posed a threat to the Americans in the Pacific. The American public was very anxious that Japan should not seize these islands. The islands of Samoa were split between America and Germany, and hitherto this arrangement had been satisfactory. So long as Japan could be stalled, the Allies might get to Samoa first. But if Japan declared war straight away, all the German territories in the Pacific would be up for grabs.[20]

Now it was the time for 'diplomacy'. The negotiations were co-ordinated by three men: Sir Edward Grey, the Foreign Secretary in London, Sir John Jordan, the British Minister in Peking and Sir William Conyngham-Greene, the British Ambassador in Tokyo.

The Japanese, it seemed, were determined to seize Tsing Tao, come what may, with no intention of giving it back to China. Japanese public opinion, they said, would allow nothing less. But they grudgingly conceded that they might leave the rest of China alone.[21] Britain believed that unless she continued to act alongside Japan, she would lose all future influence in the region. This was probably correct.

The central problem was the need to send troops across neutral Chinese territory in order to attack Tsing Tao from behind. This was exactly what Germany had done in Belgium, which brought France and then Britain into the war, and it would certainly invite international condemnation. Yet the Japanese Foreign Minister was adamant that this had to be done. Sir Conyngham-Greene reported:

> As regards foreign territory, His Excellency pointed out that it is indispensable to cross a small tract of Chinese territory in order to attack Tsing Tao from behind, as the sea approaches were mined, which would make it impossible to reduce the place from the sea alone. In this connection he was ready to give an assurance to the Chinese Government before taking action, that the Chinese forces should immediately evacuate the territory thus crossed. It seems to me that these reservations are reasonable.[22]

In other words, the Japanese were determined to cross neutral Chinese sovereign territory whether the Chinese liked it or not, and the Japanese forces would expect the Chinese to clear out whilst they were at it. This, they added outrageously, was 'reasonable'. Sir Edward Grey saw that he had no alternative but to sell this humiliating demand to the Chinese if the Japanese were to be prevented from simply going it alone. Sir John Jordan in Peking had to find some way of preventing Chinese military resistance to any violation of their territory without inflaming Chinese public opinion.

The deal that Sir John Jordan finally reached with Yuan Shikai was this: the invading Allied armies should be allowed into the hinterland behind Tsing Tao, whilst the local Chinese commanders would be ordered to withdraw to a safe distance. Yuan Shikai could arrange this because he controlled the Chinese commanders in the north. In return, Britain would guarantee that the Japanese would make no further encroachment on Chinese territory, with the tacit understanding that Tsing Tao would be restored to the Chinese at the end of the war.

This agreement with Yuan Shikai had to be secret and nothing was to be put in writing. From the Chinese perspective, such a secret deal by Yuan Shikai could have been construed as an act of treachery against his own people, but he saw no alternative. Once the invasion had taken place, the Chinese Government would, of course, publicly put up a formal protest, but no further action would be taken.

Whilst these negotiations with Peking were going on, the British managed to hold the Japanese back from any formal declaration of war. They were determined to allow the Australians, the New Zealanders and the French a head-start in the race to grab German possessions in the Pacific. In this they succeeded, and the grumpy Japanese finally agreed to postpone their declaration of war on Germany till 23rd August. This was the ultimatum that the *Emden* officers learned about upon their arrival at Angaur.

Meanwhile, Jerram was becoming almost as impatient as the Japanese. He sent an irritated note to the Admiralty – rather like banging on the bathroom door – asking them to hurry up. He was, he said, doing his best to cover a huge area with too few ships. From his base in Hong Kong he was watching Tsing Tao, besides patrolling the waters around the Dutch East Indies and the south-western Pacific. He said that Graf Spee's squadron was out there somewhere, with 20,000 tons of coal afloat in various colliers, and might pop up anywhere. They might go to the Dutch East Indies or even to South America. He went on to say that he was in the dark about Japan's intentions and would welcome some information. Were they going to declare war or weren't they? But Sir William, in Tokyo, now had the American press to contend with; they were accusing Britain of being Japan's patsy.

Peking was also not convinced that Britain could prevent any further violation of Chinese territory. They feared that Britain would simply duck out of their responsibilities towards China once the Japanese were allowed in. In the end, Britain's promise to Yuan Shikai was actually honoured, although the Japanese never let go of Tsing Tao till they were defeated at the end of World War II. There was an added caveat, that it would be British soldiers, not Japanese, who would cross Chinese territory to attack Tsing Tao.

On 21st August, just two days ahead of the Japanese deadline, Sir John Jordan in Peking sent the following telegram to London stating that Yuan Shikai had allowed a verbal assurance and:

> The President would ask that this arrangement should be regarded as a private understanding between Great Britain and China. China has no objection to a breach of neutrality, *which has for one of its objects the restoration of Kiao Chow to China*. [Author's italics].[23]

It was a shabby deal, and Yuan Shikai himself probably did not believe a word of it. But unilateral action by Japan would have been worse and the compromise probably postponed further Japanese territorial expansion in

China for the next two decades. Japan declared war on Germany and Jerram's wish had finally come true. The negotiations had lasted only ten days. At last the Admiralty sent Jerram a reassuring telegram stating:

> You may now leave the whole protection of British trade north of Hong Kong to the Japanese, concentrating your attention, in concert with the Australian squadron, on destroying the German cruisers.[24]

It must have come to Jerram as a huge relief. He had never shown very much sympathy for the Chinese, but he respected the Japanese. They had really good ships and were very professional.

The last word on Royal Navy attitudes towards the Japanese Navy in those days has to go to the *Wonder Book of the Navy*, a book suitable for English boys wishing to join the Royal Navy which was published in Britain in 1917 during World War I.

> The Navy of Japan is the newest of the great Powers, but second to none in the bravery and efficiency of its men.
>
> The Japanese Navy is modelled on the British, and most of the ships in the Japanese Navy were built in Great Britain, until after the war with Russia, but the Japanese now build for themselves. It is said that they have a quantity of material all ready to build many other ships with, and that if their country needed the ships, multitudes of Japanese workmen would go and build them asking no pay, but simply their food. That is the wonderful patriotic spirit of the Japanese.[25]

Chapter 4

The Hunt for Graf Spee

Emden Slips Unseen into the Indian Ocean

After the Japanese ultimatum was delivered to Peking, the German Chargé d'Affaires sent a rather wacky telegram in English to the German Minister of Foreign Affairs:

'Engagement with *Miss Butterfly* very probable.'[1]

Japan was now entering the war on the side of the Allies, determined to 'wipe out Germany from their part of the world for ever'.[2] This effectively cut off Admiral Graf Spee's squadron from any hope of survival in those waters, and made life for the British Navy a great deal easier. Winston Churchill, the First Lord of the Admiralty, made a famous comment about Graf Spee's East Asiatic Squadron. Without access to a secure supply of coal and with limited communications, Graf Spee's squadron was 'like a cut flower in a vase, fair to see, yet bound to die'.[3]

But so long as Graf Spee was still at large, the Royal Navy had to account for his ships. The big question was strategy. Would it be better to concentrate on defending Allied shipping lanes, or should Jerram go all out to find Graf Spee's biggest ships and sink them?

The Royal Navy's First Sea Lord (not to be confused with the political appointee Churchill, who was First Lord of the Admiralty) at that time was a German, His Highness, Prince Louis of Battenberg, who was married to yet another of Queen Victoria's grandchildren, and was in turn grandfather to Prince Philip, the husband of Queen Elizabeth II. Although he held British citizenship, his German origins were soon to act against him and his thick German accent was definitely a problem! But he had done much to bring the fleet up to a state of war-readiness and he loved mighty battleships. By the end of October 1914 he was replaced by Admiral Sir John Fisher, but for the moment it was Prince Louis of Battenberg who was managing Admiral Jerram.

With the Japanese joining the Allies, they now controlled all northern Chinese waters and Jerram must have passed over that responsibility with alacrity. The Japanese then made ready to take Tsing Tao. The British battleship *Triumph* was by now at Wei Hai Wei, and Jerram ordered them to escort the British troop transports from their base in Tien Tsin, near the mouth of the Yellow River, to the Kiao Chow Peninsula. There they were to 'assist' the Japanese in taking Tsing Tao from the land. In return, the Japanese offered three of their cruisers to help Jerram patrol the remainder of his sphere of activity.

With the powerful Japanese navy patrolling Chinese waters to the north, as well as the seas far out into the north-western Pacific, Jerram figured that Graf Spee would be most unlikely to risk a confrontation. The safety of Allied trade in that part of the world, therefore, seemed pretty certain.

Foreign treaty ports and autonomous enclaves in China, especially those around Shanghai, were not re-occupied by the Chinese; this included the all-important French radio station with its tall mast, which could still be used for vital communications.[4] The Chinese warring factions were, for the first time, allowed to pursue their own agenda without foreign interference. But for Yuan Shikai, the forthcoming Japanese attack on Tsing Tao was still a concern.

In Vladivostok, the Russian Admiral Rimsky-Korsakov had prepared the cruisers *Zhemtchug* and *Askold* to be added to Jerram's squadron.[5] They sailed for Hong Kong on 10th August with *Askold* stopping in Japan en route to pick up a consignment of mines, and *Zhemtchug* ordered to check for German merchantmen around the Philippines, before escorting some French transports south from Saigon.

The Australian and New Zealand Navy ships were already under Jerram's command and their first objective, in company with the French flagship *Montcalm,* was to seize German possessions in the Pacific, including German Samoa, well ahead of the Japanese. That would keep them tied up at least until the middle of September.

That left Jerram with the task of protecting the main trade routes around Indochina from possible attack. Hurrying back to Hong Kong from Yap Island, Jerram contemplated bombarding the radio station at Angaur, but thought better of it. That was on 16th August and, ironically, *Emden* – now detached from Graf Spee's squadron – arrived at Angaur just two days later![5] It was the first of many near-misses.

A large number of transports destined for Europe were now assembling in various ports, all within Jerram's area of responsibility. The provision of armed escorts required many ships and careful co-ordination. The Australian Admiral Patey was very concerned about the safety of the trade routes, particularly those coming north from Fremantle and passing to the south of Java. His Australian transports would be going that way very soon. If Graf Spee's squadron was lurking somewhere around the Bismarck Archipelago so close to Australia, that could be very serious. But Jerram did not think it likely. He informed the Admiralty that:

> Probably *Scharnhorst, Gneisenau, Emden* and *Nürnberg* are now together but their position is still unknown, though the Marshall Islands seem likely. They have more than 20,000 tons of coal afloat. [6]

What was happening far out in the Pacific, he thought, really did not matter, if Graf Spee's squadron was indeed out there. Plodding around the Marshall Islands looking for them, miles out in the middle of the Pacific, was a hopeless idea. The distances were simply too great.

The Admiralty – or at least Louis Battenberg – thought differently. They were completely fixated on large capital ships and less concerned about light cruisers. The Admiralty wanted big prizes. They wanted Jerram to concentrate on finding *Scharnhorst* and *Gneisenau* and sink them. Fortunately for Jerram, the Admiralty allowed him to make his own decisions locally. He reckoned that, given the huge coal consumption of those large armoured cruisers, Graf Spee would probably take them straight over to South America to cover the busy trade routes from Cape Horn, which funnelled into a narrow space. On the other hand, Graf Spee's squadron could also be much closer to home, so Jerram had to plan for that possibility as well.

Clearly, Jerram had absolutely no idea that *Emden* was well on her way to wreaking havoc in the Bay of Bengal. But he had been alerted. Some days previously, mail bags seized from a German ship coming out of Tsing

Tao led him to suppose that Graf Spee might be heading for the west coast of Sumatra, and that was precisely where *Emden* was heading at that moment. This was one of the main reasons why Jerram decided to quit Hong Kong and head for Singapore, which was much further south, and closer to the area he needed to watch. The auxiliary cruisers that had been requisitioned and refitted in Hong Kong were already patrolling the area between Hong Kong and Singapore.[7]

Jerram needed a lot of ships, and to get sufficient men to crew them had been a nightmare; scraping the bottom of the barrel, so to speak. By the time the last of them, the *Empress of Russia*, was got ready, there were practically no naval ratings left in his part of the world. All the merchant navy crew who were already in the ship, including the Chinese, were signed on, assisted by the Wei Hai Wei Island Guard of Marines. To them were added French sailors from their decommissioned gunboats on the Yangtze, commanded by the French intelligence officer from Shanghai, plus a French surgeon. The Royal Garrison Artillery provided some more men and some Pathans, 'kindly lent by the General Officer Commanding the troops in South China'. With this very mixed international crew, the ship apparently worked fine and in 'perfect – although occasionally vociferous – harmony'.[8]

On 30th August Admiral Jerram duly arrived in Singapore in his flagship *Minotaur*. The French destroyer squadron was there when Jerram arrived. The plan that Admiral Huguet had discussed with Jerram in Hong Kong before the war had now been put into effect. The French had already been patrolling around the Java Sea but had found nothing.

Next came *Hampshire, Yarmouth* and the French cruiser *Dupleix*. In command of *Hampshire* was Captain Grant, the old pal of *Emden*'s commander von Müller. They had last seen each other at that party in Tsing Tao just a few weeks before and, though neither of them knew it, they were destined to play a cat-and-mouse game over the next two months.

All three of these cruisers were soon to be caught up in the hunt for *Emden* and became a very familiar sight in Penang. Next, *Cadmus*, a sloop from the Yangtze, arrived in Singapore. Two Japanese cruisers, *Ibuki* and *Chikuma*, were on their way south to Hong Kong and were expected on 31st August. *Ibuki* was a powerful battle cruiser with four long-range 305mm guns and eight 203mm medium-range guns. *Chikuma* was faster and lighter, with eight 152mm guns and four 78mm guns.[9] *Chikuma* soon became a regular sight in Penang, known colloquially as 'The Jap'.

So far, Jerram's ships had found nothing. There had been no sightings of German warships around the waters of the Dutch East Indies; at least nothing that was reported to him. Meanwhile, a detachment of sailors from the Yangtze riverboats had been brought to Hong Kong and among them was the British officer Lieutenant Maund, from *Kinsha*.

Jerram had selected Maund for an unusual posting. *Askold* and *Zhemtchug* were stopping in Hong Kong before proceeding to Singapore. Because he spoke good French, Lieutenant Maund was to be the liaison officer for *Zhemtchug*. All educated Russians, especially the aristocracy, spoke French; indeed, it was considered chic to speak it amongst themselves and Captain Baron Cherkasov, commander of *Zhemtchug*, would have spoken French fluently.

So, what had been happening on board *Emden* during that week? They got the news that Japan had finally declared war by radio when they were in Angaur. Morale must have been low. *Emden*'s wireless operators were on duty twenty-four hours a day and picked up news broadcasts on many wavelengths, especially Tsing Tao, which they could often hear at night when conditions were better.

Germany had advanced wireless technology because they depended less on undersea telegraph cable networks than the British. German ships were equipped with powerful Telefünken sets, but the disadvantage was that messages had to be in cipher rather than 'en clair'. *Emden* was, of course, subject to strict self-imposed radio silence. Any transmission on her part would instantly give away her position. But she could listen, and she did – all the time. Sometimes the officers got hold of newspapers, which were also a valuable source of information.

Despite the bad news from Japan, *Emden*'s First Lieutenant, von Mücke, tried to keep the crew's spirits up. He was a very tall man with a distinguished air, which complimented the quiet, self-effacing, rather distant character of Commander von Müller.

Von Mücke was not in the least self-effacing and he had good leadership qualities. He was also said to have a good sense of humour, but he was a strict disciplinarian. This was not resented by the crew; on the contrary he was popular, so he must have been a fair man. Every Sunday he set up maps and delivered a talk on the current state of affairs in Europe; he took care to dwell on the good news.[10]

It was generally believed that the war 'would be over by Christmas', and many of *Emden*'s crew must have assumed that they would not need to hang on by themselves for too long. An article in the *Penang Gazette* said 'even the Kaiser has begun to repent the challenge he threw out.'[11] It was generally agreed that the cost of the war to Germany was unsustainable and she would have to sue for peace very soon. Others were not so sure. Much later on, at the end of November, the *Straits Times* had become more pessimistic.

> ... the possible duration of the war is not minimised. The 'all over by Christmas' lot are at longer odds than any Derby winner ever started at. The 'finished in another 6 months' division are also outsiders. 'Another 9 months' prophets can have odds approaching double figures. '1916' is the most probable ... The thought that the war has not really begun is far more likely and this is the thought at the back of the minds of the most sagacious.[12]

In fact, the war would drag on till November 1918, but nobody would have believed that at the time.

Captain von Müller's destination, as he had explained to Graf Spee, was the Indian Ocean, because there was plenty of space to get lost in. There were also busy shipping routes around the Bay of Bengal, all connecting with the great shipping hub of Colombo.

First von Müller had to get there unseen. He had to keep away from all the main shipping lanes and tiptoe through dozens of islands in the Dutch East Indies. Being neutral, they would be unlikely to give away his position or inform the enemy. So, after leaving Angaur they headed for the Moluccas (the 'Spice Islands'), and thence southwards, through the Molucca Straits, leaving Sulawesi to westward. From there *Emden* continued on southwards as far as East Timor, visiting a sheltered bay on the south side of the island of Tanah Jampeia. *Emden* was supposed to be meeting a German collier there, but it never turned up. Nearly all German ships had, by then, been impounded in neutral harbours. What did turn up was the Dutch battleship *Tromp,* whose captain advised *Emden* of the rules governing strict neutrality and insisted she move on after coaling from her tender *Markomannia*.[13] There is no evidence that *Tromp* ever passed the information of *Emden*'s whereabouts on to the Allies.[14]

Coaling at sea was back-breaking, filthy work. The two ships had to come alongside one another; therefore it was best done in a sheltered harbour where the sea was flat calm with no current running. The heavy bags of coal had to be passed from one ship to the other, tearing up the decking, making dents and rubbing the paint off the ship's side. Von Mücke used old stuffed hammocks as fenders. Then, the ship, the men and their clothes had to be cleaned. For that, a plentiful supply of soap was needed, which led to an amusing anecdote later.

Now, with her coal bunkers full, *Emden* steamed westwards, hugging the north coast of Flores Island till they reached Lombok and the Lombok Straits, which separates it from the island of Bali. One thing that would have raised the spirits of the crew was the fine weather, and the beautiful scenery as they passed close to various islands. They saw many sailing schooners in those parts, plying to and from Batavia (Jakarta). Even today *phinisi*, traditional Indonesian sailing schooners, still ply their trade between the myriad islands of Indonesia.

It was at this point that *Emden* first made use of a dummy fourth funnel which the crew erected just abaft the bridge, making her look, at a distance, a little like the British cruiser *Yarmouth*. *Emden*'s famous fourth funnel fooled many ships over the next few weeks and also in Penang harbour.[15]

The dummy funnel was Lieutenant von Mücke's brainwave. It had a wooden frame covered in canvas and painted to match *Emden*'s other funnels. At first it was flat, but later the crew made it oval with internal struts to stiffen it. They used it regularly from then on as a disguise, although it eventually became rather discoloured and battered. In those days, ships had to be recognised at a distance by their silhouette and the configuration of the funnels was the key.

Once through the Lombok Straits, *Emden* was at last in the Indian Ocean and, as luck would have it, she had not been spotted by the Allies. She now sailed north-west in a wide arc, following the south coast of Java and then Sumatra, heading for the island of Simeulue (pronounced Simmer-loo-er). The west coast of Sumatra is lined with a string of islands, and in later weeks these were to prove invaluable when *Emden* or her tenders needed somewhere to hide or to keep a rendezvous.

Meanwhile, Jerram had some unwelcome news from the same area that *Emden* had just entered. A British merchant ship, *City of Winchester,* was sunk off the Arabian coast by another lone German cruiser, *Königsberg,* operating out of Dar-es-Salaam and lurking off the east coast of Africa. The first Jerram knew about it was when *Königsberg*'s tender, *Goldenfels,* disembarked the merchantman's British crew at the neutral Dutch port of Sabang, off the northern tip of Sumatra.[16] Jerram had to act immediately, and sent *Hampshire*

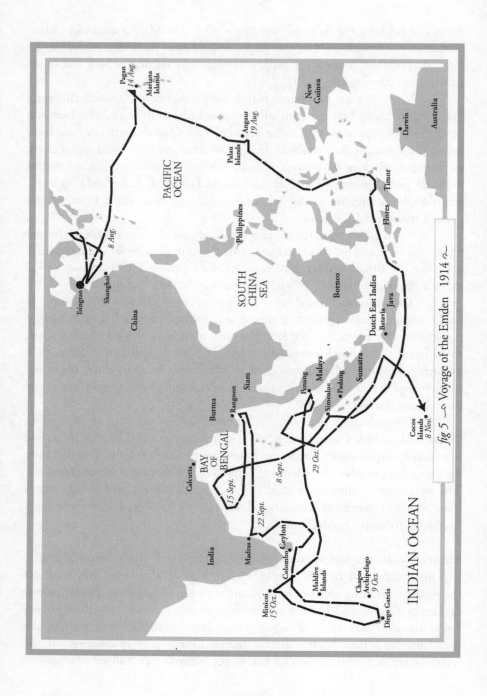

fig 5 ~ Voyage of the Emden 1914 ~

with the French destroyer squadron up the Malacca Straits to carry out a search. Once they reached Penang, *Hampshire* dropped off the French destroyers before going on to Sabang.

Hampshire arrived at Sabang on 1st September. International rules allowed her a brief visit to a neutral port, provided no supplies were taken on board, and the visit lasted less than a day. There was no sign of *Königsberg*. So, between 2nd and 10th September, *Hampshire* worked her way down the west coast of Sumatra, including the island of Simeulue,[17] but still no sign of *Königsberg*.

At that point *Emden* came perilously close to capture even before her campaign had begun. Whilst *Emden* had been sailing up the west coast of Sumatra, *Hampshire*, along with the French destroyers, was cruising up the east side. The two almost met at the island of Simeulue. The British only realised this many months later when *Markomannia* was captured. They studied her log and put two and two together.

Admiral Jerram's expectation that a search of the Dutch East Indies would yield some result was very nearly realised, for on September 4th the *Emden* was coaling at Langeni, or Telok Delam, on the east side of Simeulue Island. The *Hampshire* in the course of her search of the west coast of Sumatra must have passed close to her. In fact she had searched that very anchorage the previous day.

Equally unconscious of what had so nearly been a meeting, the ships proceeded in opposite directions, the *Hampshire* to rejoin the Admiral in Singapore and the *Emden* into the Bay of Bengal. She was the first warship of any nation to enter that peaceful spot since the outbreak of war.[18]

In fact, that Admiralty account is not quite right. Luckily, *Emden* had some warning, with loud radio transmissions coming from somewhere very close. It was the repeated call-sign Q.M.D. and *Emden* concluded that it had to be *Hampshire* or *Minotaur*.[19] That evening *Emden* remained below the horizon and did not sail into Simeulue harbour till late the next day, when the radio transmissions had died away. *Hampshire* had left that very same morning, without ever seeing *Emden*.

Von Müller chose the island's fine sheltered bay for coaling because it was hidden from view from the open sea and was something of a tropical paradise. *Emden*'s chronicler, Prinz Hohenzollern, was entranced with the place:

At six o'clock in the morning we ran into the quiet bay. It looked heavenly. The narrow entrance thickly framed in mangroves and behind them the primeval forest, in all the magnificence of the tropics, was the most superb sight I have ever seen. New and beautiful pictures greeted our delighted eyes as we passed further in and after a long sea voyage the impression was unforgettable. A fairy land indeed.[20]

They had been led to expect that a German collier would be there to greet them, but it never appeared. So they had to take more coal from *Markomannia*. They also took the opportunity to clean the ship and make minor repairs. As with all ships, *Emden* quickly developed rusty areas which had to be painted over, covering her hull with various paint patches.[21] She also carried some livestock on deck, which was looked after by farm boys amongst the crew. *Markomannia* even had a cow and, when the chance arose, crew members went ashore to get some fresh grass.[22]

Just as at Tanah Jampeia, they were soon spotted by the Dutch, and a government boat came into the anchorage to remind them of international law. Their twenty-four hours had passed long since and they would have to leave straight away. But sitting with a glass of iced whiskey-and-soda within easy reach, the Dutch official allowed them to complete the task of coaling before they sailed. As with the *Tromp*, no word of this was ever passed to the Allies, with the Dutch sticking rigidly to their neutrality. It is curious to reflect that the Dutch and the local Achehnese were fully aware of *Emden*'s location, and where she was likely to be heading, yet absolutely nothing of this ever got to the ears of the British. To be on the safe side, von Müller ordered *Emden* to steer a south-easterly course to create the impression that they were going that way.[23] But they were not, and once out of sight of land they doubled back, steering north-west under cover of darkness.[24]

Jerram, for his part, was satisfied that nothing could slip through his fingers. *Chikuma* now returned to Singapore and one of her officers, Commander Yamanashi, was seconded to *Minotaur* from the Imperial Japanese Navy to act as his liaison officer.

On 5th September Jerram commenced another search in *Minotaur*, covering the north coast of Java, with *Yarmouth* sweeping to the south. They met up at the Bali Straits, having found nothing. *Ibuki* hung around Java for longer, but hearing nothing from *Hampshire*, Jerram concluded wrongly that: 'I was by this time convinced that it was most unlikely that any German armed ships were anywhere in the neighbourhood of Java or Sumatra.'[25]

Jerram was hoping that the Bay of Bengal would remain a peaceful spot. Almost the entire coastline was under British rule and, without German competition, business for merchant ships had never been better. As Napoleon once said, 'Britain is a nation of shop-keepers.' Indeed; trade was everything. Right at the beginning of the war, on 9th August, the intelligence officer in Singapore blocked the nearby routes to ports north of Java, but the Admiralty immediately countermanded that order with this telegram:

> Constant complaints received from ship-owners' vessels being detained, especially in Far Eastern and Australian waters. A Government scheme for war insurance had been designed to keep ships running in spite of some losses.
>
> Essential trade of Empire should continue uninterrupted. If vessels sail after dark, make good offing [sic] and avoid regular track. Danger of capture small.
>
> Most essential impress this on all concerned. No ships should ever be detained unless definite news of presence of enemy cruisers in immediate vicinity.[26]

The precautions introduced at the beginning of the war were soon abandoned. The war had been going on for a month and nothing ever seemed to happen in the Indian Ocean, and this perception seemed to be encouraged by the Admiralty. This was *Emden*'s good fortune because, by that time, merchant shipping in their area took few precautions and was ripe for commerce-raiding. The shipping in the Bay of Bengal was now carrying on as if it was peace time, neglecting even the most elementary precautions such as avoiding regular routes and obscuring ships' lights. Avoiding the usual routes meant longer distances, and that cost money for extra fuel. To obscure their lights meant a greater danger of collision. All of these risks were repugnant to owners and masters. Not only that, but the local English-language newspapers continued to publish exact details of ships' cargoes, dates of arrivals and sailing, and their destinations. These newspapers were, of course, on board the ships that *Emden* subsequently captured.[27]

Emden was now heading towards the Bay of Bengal. The only Allied warships anywhere near them were the French destroyers in Penang. The destroyers were not well prepared. Since the outbreak of war the squadron had had no time to carry out their normal schedule of maintenance, or even get themselves into battle-readiness. From early August they had been in continuous service, and routine attention to their boilers and engine-bearings had been neglected.

These fast little ships depended on being lightweight, so their engines did not have the long-distance endurance of cruisers. They were shallow-draught metal boxes with little insulation, hot as an oven during the daytime, especially if the sun was out. There was no air-conditioning, only electric fans which depended on electrical generators, which only worked when the boilers had steam up. Even in the more northerly waters of Saigon, the crewmen would sometimes sleep on deck, rather than in their quarters, because of the heat. Larger ships lay deeper in the water, had better insulation and more powerful ventilation systems. But these destroyers were not designed for comfort in the equatorial heat. Only when they were under way did things improve, with a cooling breeze passing through the ship.

Since arriving in Singapore, various makeshift arrangements had been made to allow the crew to sleep regularly under awnings on deck, some in hammocks and some flat on the decks, only partly protected from the heavy rains. In Penang the rains were even worse. Storms were frequent at that time of year, with violent and torrential downpours. The sailors also described an enervating 'electrical tension' in the atmosphere, which was probably due to the extreme humidity. Paradoxically, *Emden*, a larger ship comfortably on the move, would deliberately steer into a rain squall to cool off, replenish her fresh water, and allow the crew a natural shower![28]

It is certain that if they were sleeping on deck in harbour, the French sailors would have been plagued by mosquitoes unless they used nets. Throughout all this, they had to do their best to keep a state of alertness, maintaining lookouts and regular watch-keeping. It was essential, therefore, that they were given shore leave whenever possible to allow them some brief respite. Over the ensuing weeks, French sailors became a common sight in George Town. Being Catholics, they would have attended the Church of the Assumption, officiated by Father L.M. Duvelle.

But all that came later on. It was early days yet, as they settled into Penang. After the French destroyers had left the waters of Java in August, Jerram assured them that they would have the services of a cruiser in company with them, but this proved to be sporadic. In the beginning, *Hampshire* was assigned to accompany them, but as soon as they reached Penang she was detached to search the west coast of Sumatra. She then passed through the Sunda Straits to be reunited with Jerram's squadron back in Singapore.

The French destroyers were now on their own. They were given a line of patrol 340 nautical miles long, between Penang and Diamond Point off Acheh Head. This was right by Pulau Weh, where Sabang was situated (Fig. 6). Two ships out of four had to patrol that line, whilst the other two remained at anchor in Penang, one of them being at one hour's notice to raise steam. This left no time for cleaning their boilers or servicing their machinery.[29] In addition, they quickly discovered that they were getting precious little information, or even co-operation, from the Penang harbourmaster.

Besides that near-miss with *Hampshire*, *Emden* probably came very close to an encounter with the French destroyer *Fronde*. This happened just after *Emden* left Simeulue, on the night of 4th September, when *Fronde* was out on one of her first patrols off Diamond Point. By and by *Fronde's* lookouts spotted the silhouette of a cruiser without lights, which seemed to be pursuing them. The identity of the cruiser remained a mystery and *Fronde* had great difficulty putting on sufficient speed to get safely out of the way.[30]

Fronde immediately reported the sighting to Jerram's headquarters in Singapore, which duly passed it on to the Admiralty.[31] But although the cruiser had not been identified, Jerram decided to take no action. It now seems very likely that she was indeed *Emden,* yet the trade routes in the area remained open. Commerce had to keep going at all cost.

Unseen, *Emden* now steamed northwards, past the Nicobar Islands, and on towards the busy shipping lanes in the Bay of Bengal. As she entered the Bay she ran into a heavy rain squall. As was their habit, the crew quickly replenished their fresh water supply and took a free shower. But now they were running out of soap, so they had to capture fresh supplies of that essential commodity very soon!

Chapter 5

Admiral Jerram Hunts for *Emden*

It was 7th September, and three weeks since *Emden* had set out on her own with *Markomannia* to try some commerce-raiding around the Indian Ocean. Admiral Jerram had heard nothing. On board *Emden*, however, the crew had been very busy. Lieutenant von Mücke had insisted upon daily drill to ensure that *Emden*'s crew regularly practised their seamanship skills, especially gunnery. They had become a very professional fighting team.

After leaving Simeulue, *Emden* entered the Bay of Bengal, intent on intersecting the shipping lanes between Rangoon and Colombo. The weather was fairly rough and on the first day they sighted nothing. But on the night of 8th September, around 11.00 p.m., they spotted a ship's lights and went after her, signalling her to stop. They fired a couple of shots across the bow for good measure. A prize crew was then sent over, commanded by Lieutenant Lauterbach. Prinz Hohenzollern described the scene:

> Armed to the teeth they rowed over and went aboard the stranger. At last the Morse lamp blinked out the message[1] 'Greek Steamship *Pontoporos* carrying 6,500 tons of coal for English Government, on her way to Bombay'.[2]

Although Greece was a neutral country, the cargo was British, so *Emden* had the right to seize it. The coal was from Bengal and of inferior quality, but *Emden* needed additional coal badly, so von Müller decided to keep *Pontoporos* as an extra coal tender. Prinz Hohenzollern went on:

The captain of the *Emden* asked the Greek captain if he would be willing on receipt of proper payment, to do service to Germany as represented by *Emden*. … both he and his command were ready to do so. It was the same to him he said, whether he served England or Germany. The main point was the payment.

Not long after, some of the crew of *Pontoporos* were landed at Calcutta and *Pontoporos'* chief engineer, Mr Forbester, described what happened. It shows von Müller's chivalrous treatment of prisoners and explains why the Germans were so careful. They realised that one day the boot would surely be on the other foot. Many weeks later, when he was captured himself, von Müller did not always get such good treatment at the hands of the British. But by then, the war had become a very brutal affair.

Mr Forbester, the only Englishman on board *Pontoporos*, was taken across to *Emden*.

As I stepped on deck the German Chief Engineer came forward and shook hands saying: 'Mr. Chief, you will be treated like a gentlemen. We can never tell, but we may be prisoners next'. All the crew raised their caps to me and the Skipper came down from the bridge and shook hands. He assured me that I would be treated well.[3]

So *Pontoporos* was taken on as a second tender along with *Markomannia*, hampered only by the fact that she could only make nine knots. It says much for Lauterbach's negotiating skills that the deal went ahead so smoothly and so fast. His intimate knowledge of all the shipping in that part of the world, coupled with his irrepressible good humour, gave him an immediate rapport with other ships' masters. A few engine-room ratings[4] came over from the *Emden,* and Lauterbach took temporary command. From then on, *Pontoporos* followed *Emden*'s orders.

The next ship they captured was a British merchant ship, *Indus*. She was on her way from Calcutta to Bombay, fitted out as a transporter ready to carry troops and horses. She had a mixed cargo of supplies for the troops, including a huge consignment of soap. This was a godsend for *Emden* because she had almost run out! Later, *Emden*'s officers were tickled to see this advertisement in a Calcutta newspaper which they took from another ship.[5]

Indus was carrying 150 cases of North West Soap Company's celebrated ELYSIUM soap and hence the pursuit. The men on the *Emden* and their clothes are now clean and sweet, thanks to Elysium soap!

The *Indus* crew were transferred to *Markomannia*, and after *Emden* had taken what she needed, including some good wireless equipment, she was sunk. The wireless was to come in very handy later on.

Our upper deck looked like a colossal warehouse. There were stocks, or at least samples, of everything. There were towels, soap, linen, tinned foods, fresh meat, live hens and ducks, drinks, nautical instruments, charts, pencils and some very welcome oilskins.[6]

Emden then started picking off ships at an alarming rate. There followed *Lovat, Kabinga, Killin* and *Diplomat,* all captured in the shipping lanes close to Calcutta. *Diplomat* went to the bottom with 30,000 chests of tea. The loss was estimated at £82,000, which must be over £1 million at present-day values. *Killin* was also a collier. Von Müller was most reluctant to sink her, but he did not have the resources to crew an extra ship.

Emden then caught up with an Italian ship, *Loredano.* As Italy was supposed to be Germany's ally through the Triple Alliance, von Müller hoped that the captain would take their prisoners to Calcutta. Captain Giacopolo refused, and was generally surly and unhelpful. Von Müller did not trust him, and his instincts were proven right. As soon as he could, after taking leave of *Emden*, Giacopolo warned a British freighter to steer clear and informed Calcutta of *Emden*'s whereabouts. This was in stark contrast to the Dutch, who maintained a strictly neutral stance throughout the war and passed nothing to either side.[7] Perhaps Giacopolo just hated Germans.

Kabinga was finally chosen to transport the prisoners. She was packed off to Calcutta with her wireless out of action. *Emden*'s crew dubbed *Kabinga* the *Lumpensammler* (the rag-bin), although the crew of all the captured ships were treated with great courtesy. The rest of the captured ships were sunk.

Kabinga's Captain Robinson had his wife and child aboard. As *Emden* sailed away, they and the other prisoners lined the guard rails, and gave *Emden* three hearty cheers because of the kindly way they had been treated.[8] On this, as on future occasions, the prisoners were released only after swearing they would not make war on Germany in the future.

Time was short. As soon as Calcutta was alerted, von Müller knew he might be captured. He therefore set *Emden* on an easterly course towards Rangoon, to get away from the immediate vicinity of Calcutta.

In the Madras–Rangoon sea lane *Emden* captured another steamer, the *Trabboch,* which was sunk by shelling her. This was accompanied by violent explosions and flames as the coal dust in her hold ignited. It was dark and the explosions must have been visible for miles around. A British ship, *Clan Matheson*, was nearby and saw the horizon light up. She made off in the opposite direction, but her lights were spotted and *Emden* gave chase. The ship was eventually stopped and, as usual, Lieutenant Lauterbach went aboard as prize officer. He found to his surprise that she had a very valuable cargo. Motor cars, locomotives, bicycles, typewriters and many fine things. The most valuable item was a racehorse which had been entered for the Calcutta races.

The part played by Julius Lauterbach as prize officer was of great significance. Each time a British merchant ship was seized, he would heave his great bulk aboard and speak to the master. In many cases he would bluff, pretending he knew more than he did. The conversation might go like this: 'Hello George, me ol' pal, – ages since I saw you last! – where have you been? We were expecting you yesterday!' The crews never gave him trouble and meekly handed him their ship's log and any newspapers, so that he could check on their recent movements and any other ships mentioned in the newspapers. Then he would settle down with the officers, a glass of beer to hand, and gossip. In this way he found out all sorts of valuable information.

Perusal of a fragment of *Emden's* signal log that survived reveals quite an amazing frankness from these merchant seamen regarding other ships' movements. *Emden's* wireless operators listened attentively to any transmissions in the area, whilst observing radio silence themselves, using only the signal lamp to flash Morse signals to other ships she was in company with. British merchant ships were very lax in taking precautions. They usually transmitted wireless signals 'en clair'[9] and stuck to the shipping lanes that both they and Lauterbach knew.[10]

It was not long before *Emden* heard a signal from Calcutta: "*Emden* position 16 miles south-east of False Point, Bay of Bengal, 11.30 p.m., 14th September.' The unfriendly Captain Giacopolo had done the dirty on them and given away *Emden's* position. Spitting with rage at what he saw as an act of inexcusable treachery, Prinz Hohenzollern had this to say:

A breach of faith and rank betrayal of an ally could not

have been expected or foreseen. We heard later that this betrayal was rewarded by the Indian Government. The captain received a gold watch and chain – the reward of Judas.[11]

The *Penang Gazette* reported that a grant of 25,000 rupees had been made out of the Bengal Imperial Relief Fund for distribution among the officers and crews of the vessels sunk by the *Emden,* whilst the Bengal government had given a sovereign each to the lascars[12] of the sunken vessels to cover the loss of personal effects. *Emden*'s exploits had caused British owners an estimated loss of three-quarters of a million sterling, which was a huge sum in those days.

As already mentioned, one the ships captured was *Diplomat.* This must have been a terrible shock for one passenger, the former traffic manager of the Calcutta Port Commission, Mr Windle, on his way to retirement in England.[13] He was carrying with him his large collection of Indian artistic objects, which went to the bottom.[14]

The Allied ships hunting for *Emden* from the direction of the Malacca Straits were hot on her tracks. Now that her rough whereabouts was known, *Emden* had to disappear. She made for a quiet spot in the Andaman Islands to take on as much coal as possible from *Pontoporos*. The crew were unused to Indian 'brown' coal, which is soft and powdery and much harder to shovel. In that tropical heat, progress was slow and the men had to rest more often. But they got some help from Indian coolies captured from *Clan Matheson,* now held prisoner on *Markomannia*. Prinz Hohenzollern described how quickly a ship's boiler tubes could get clogged up when she used that kind of coal. It was the same problem that had affected *Mousquet* before, in the Malacca Straits, with high fuel consumption and falling power output.

The main defects were revealed when the coal was used in the furnaces. There was no more steaming without smoke and the cloud of smoke betrays a ship for miles. Further, our coal consumption was far greater and the boilers and boiler tubes became so dirty that boiler cleaning, usually necessary every ten days, was now needed much more often[15]

In the event, Captain von Müller decided to keep the remainder of *Pontoporos*' coal in reserve, asking her to bide her time at a rendezvous to the west of Simeulue till *Emden* returned. Von Müller clearly hoped that other colliers would come his way, which indeed they did. So the slow

Pontoporos, with coal in reserve, detached herself from *Emden* and, with two of *Emden*'s officers on board to keep guard, made her way south, past the Nicobar Islands. Arriving off Simeulue, she cruised around very slowly, just over the horizon, so she could not be spotted from land and outside Dutch territorial waters. There *Pontoporos* waited for *Emden*'s return. In fact the crew never saw *Emden* again.

After she detached from *Pontoporos, Emden* headed off towards Rangoon for one last shot before disappearing.

While all this was going on, Jerram was in Singapore in his flagship *Minotaur*. He had news from the commodore in Hong Kong that the Russian heavy cruiser *Askold* had duly arrived from Vladivostok with her shipment of mines from Japan. She was now awaiting further escort duties to Colombo via Singapore. The light cruiser *Zhemtchug* was following later.

Up till 15th September Jerram still thought that *Emden* was out in the Pacific somewhere, with the rest of Graf Spee's squadron, so he never gave her a second thought. But the Dutch knew all along about *Emden*'s whereabouts – first, when she passed to the south of Java, and then later when she stopped at Simeulue. But they were careful to remain neutral.

Jerram still knew nothing. In fact he was fretting about his communications, trying to keep in touch with numerous ships scattered over a vast area. Singapore proved to be the worst possible place to be. In those days, with primitive wireless equipment, local thunderstorms and atmospherics made the task of reliable radio communication very difficult, a problem that was also affecting the French ships in Penang. He therefore decided to set up his headquarters ashore at Fort Canning.

Fort Canning was the military headquarters in Singapore and stood at the top of a hill, which, in those days, overlooked the harbour. Besides the fort, there was a light-house and a flag-staff for signalling to ships in harbour. Fort Canning's signal station was connected to the transoceanic telegraph cable network, besides having a radio-station with a tall mast. At Fort Canning, Jerram could communicate via telegraph and use the powerful wireless equipment provided by the radio-station. A nearby hotel was requisitioned as a billet for Jerram and his staff.

Penang, being an important commercial hub, also had a cable-station which allowed reliable communications with Singapore, although in reality that link was never fully employed.

Jerram was under great pressure to get the transports from New

Zealand and Australia safely across to Colombo. The Australians and New Zealanders had been steadfastly refusing to move for fear of an attack from Graf Spee's squadron. They knew that on 14th September Graf Spee and his squadron had arrived at German Samoa, only to discover that the island had been captured and was now under Allied occupation. Graf Spee had no chance of putting together a sufficiently large landing party to re-take it, so his squadron steamed off into the blue – nobody knew where. It was the first time that Graf Spee's squadron had been seen since the outbreak of war.

Samoa was far away to the north-east of Australia and New Zealand, so Jerram figured that Graf Spee's squadron was not much of a threat. There was no need, he reasoned, to commit too many of his precious cruisers to provide the Australians and New Zealanders with an escort. Putting himself in Graf Spee's shoes, Jerram realised that the German Admiral would have to keep his squadron together. They could not give away their position by using wireless, except in an emergency. Graf Spee had a lot of coal with him, but various other German colliers had been apprehended and impounded in neutral ports, so he would have to conserve his stocks. The distances involved in the Pacific were immense and Graf Spee could not afford to cruise around for too long. The Japanese Navy had their best ships, and lots of them, guarding the western Pacific. Quite correctly, Jerram predicted that Graf Spee had little alternative but to go east to the South American coast.

But the Australian Government, unversed in Jerram's inscrutable lore of the sea, disagreed. A rumour that Graf Spee might be heading towards Fiji,[16] and thus directly towards the New Zealand convoy route, was very alarming. *Scharnhorst, Gneisenau* and the other German cruisers, it seemed, could easily move to an area within striking distance of their convoys. They were not reassured that the British Navy knew its business. The New Zealand government therefore felt that it could not allow its troops to sail as arranged, and the concentration of troops in Wellington was stopped.[17]

The assembled Australian convoy now numbered forty-one ships, and the Australian Cabinet also perceived Graf Spee's squadron as a grave threat. They were not going to move unless a powerful armed escort of cruisers accompanied them. Jerram was impatient with this insistence. He had many tasks to perform over a huge area, patrolling the seas for German merchant ships, watching neutral ports and harbours in the Philippines and the Dutch East Indies, besides escorting many other transports. The French had transports from Indochina, and more were assembled in Calcutta; all of these were in Jerram's area of responsibility.

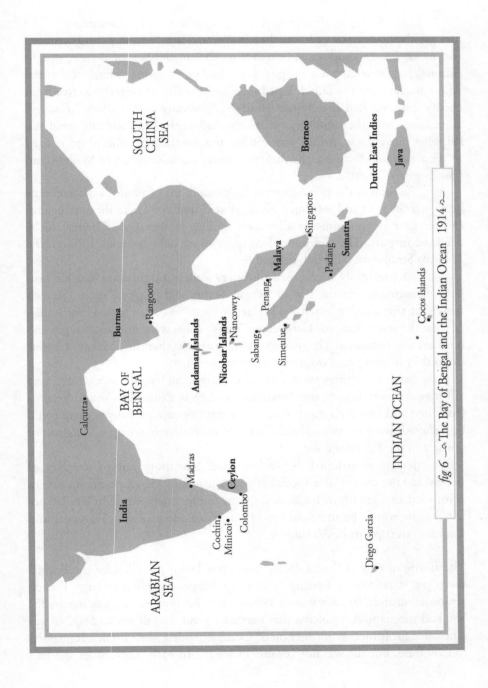

fig 6 ∼ The Bay of Bengal and the Indian Ocean 1914 ∼

On 15th September, Jerram was in his office in Fort Canning when he first got the news from Calcutta that *Emden* had sunk five ships and captured two more. *Emden*'s sudden appearance nearby, in the Bay of Bengal, caught Admiral Jerram completely off-guard. He had just convinced himself that the whole area around the Dutch East Indies and the Bay of Bengal was free from enemy ships. He had already written to the Admiralty to that effect.[18] *Emden*'s appearance, and the number of ships she had sunk, had suddenly paralysed shipping movements. And it was not just the Australians; other ships needed to get across the Bay using the shipping routes from Rangoon to Madras, and Singapore to Calcutta.

As soon as the port officer in Calcutta heard of *Emden*'s whereabouts he closed the port and informed his chief at Colombo. There the Intelligence Officer gave instructions for all vessels trading in the Bay of Bengal to be detained in port. The Colombo–Singapore route, which passed through the Malacca Straits, was also to be closed.[19]

As previously mentioned, ordinary British cargo ships had hitherto been chugging across the Bay of Bengal as they did in peace time. German merchant shipping, so extensive before the war, was now halted, with most of their ships impounded. Cargoes for British ships were now easy to get and business was booming. The owners, at any rate, felt that the chances of a lone cargo ship running into trouble were pretty small.[20]

But now things were different. Jerram had to do something very effective and very fast, or the Australians and New Zealanders would become frustrated and lose their motivation. If he did not capture *Emden* there could be a showdown with two valued allies. He immediately set up a squadron of cruisers to hunt *Emden* down.

Jerram dispatched *Hampshire* from Singapore out to the Bay of Bengal to take charge of a special cruiser squadron. He chose *Hampshire* to command the squadron because Captain Grant knew von Müller. Jerram felt that he would be the right man for the job. He also sent *Yarmouth* and *Chikuma* in support of *Hampshire*.

The northern end of the Malacca Straits was being patrolled by the French destroyer squadron in Penang, and it so happened that the large French armoured cruiser *Dupleix* was in Penang too, having her engines repaired.[21] She had mechanical problems that needed a great deal of work. *Dupleix* was scheduled for future escort duty on 6th October, taking some French transports to Colombo, but she was not yet in a fit state.[22] In early September she had crept up the Malacca Straits to Penang, well ahead of the convoy, to undergo repairs. Although she was immobilised for some time, she reinforced the French destroyer squadron with her big guns. When the transports caught up with her in four weeks' time, she would be ready to take them across to Colombo.

Hitherto, the British harbour authorities in Penang had been uncooperative with the French officers to the point of rudeness, and simply disregarded almost everything that Audemard suggested. But Captain Daveluy of *Dupleix* had been attached to Jerram's squadron and had developed a good relationship with him, so he hoped that the harbourmaster would listen to him; even if he did not listen to Audemard.

Once he had seen what was going on in Penang, Daveluy set about trying to improve the arrangements for the four French destroyers. Apart from improving communications with the harbour authorities, he also saw that the ships were badly in need of servicing. Soon it would be quite impractical for them to keep two out of four destroyers on continuous patrol.

Commander Duncan MacIntyre of the Royal Navy Reserve was the port Intelligence Officer in Penang. He was also the Harbourmaster. His background was in the merchant service, hence all his energies were concentrated on maintaining the movements of merchant shipping in and out of Penang harbour, just as if it was peace time. He reacted in completely the opposite way to his colleagues in Calcutta and Colombo. When *Emden* was known to be prowling around the Bay of Bengal, his colleagues had shown some prudence, closing their respective ports – for a short time, anyway. The harbourmaster in Penang showed a total disregard for *Emden* and the danger she posed. He did nothing at all.

It was impossible for Audemard alone to wield any kind of authority. MacIntyre was supposed to be liaising between Admiral Jerram and the warships in Penang. It was his job to keep the French commanders fully informed, particularly about ships' movements, but all the evidence shows that he was unprepared to do this.[23]

If warships were due in to Penang harbour, the French destroyer squadron was the last to know about it. These difficulties became all the more serious after *Emden* appeared in the Bay of Bengal, sinking ships with apparent impunity. An attack on Penang harbour was more than a remote possibility. Without MacIntyre's assistance, how were the French to know which ships were expected, especially at night? The people living in Penang talked about it all the time. One of them was Reverend Cross, who wrote a letter the day after

Penang harbour was attacked, remarking: 'Everyone knew that such a danger was imminent'.[24]

It seems that the only people to remain totally unconcerned were the harbourmaster and his staff. He insisted, against explicit written advice from Audemard,[25] that Penang harbour should be fully lit every night, including the harbour roads. No restrictions whatever should be placed upon the movements of ships during the hours of darkness. The French would only be told who was coming in and out 'if he had time'.

This was mid-September and Captain Daveluy of *Dupleix* had been in command of the French squadron in Penang for about ten days. Unfortunately, he had little more success than Audemard in instilling some kind of sense into the harbour authorities, so the harbour and its roads remained lit up at night throughout September.

Whilst in Penang, Daveluy had a chance to step ashore. Like Audemard, he was dismayed to find further evidence of lax security. This time it was the sloppy management of German nationals. It worried him a great deal. All this was to come out later in an exasperated letter that Captain Daveluy sent to Jerram after the attack on Penang harbour had taken place.

At Penang, as well as in Singapore and Hong Kong, the English Civilian Authorities did not believe in expelling all German subjects. The bosses of German companies and likewise their employees are left at liberty on parole and continue to conduct their affairs. Likewise at Singapore you could see the Belgian flag floating above the door of a German merchant who is the consular agent of Belgium, and whose agency has doubtless never been revoked.

Right now, Penang is linked with the Dutch port of Sabang with frequent services. Several Dutch lines serve the two ports. It would therefore be easy for numerous Germans residing on the Island, to regularly reach a German agent at Sabang, with the most up to date information about movements within the port.[26]

In retrospect, there is no documentary evidence that *Emden* received any information relayed to them by 'spies', even though the British media were convinced of it. German nationals in both Penang and Singapore could have passed a good deal of information to Germany. But it seems they never did – or nothing of significance at any rate.

Meanwhile, Jerram's hard-worked ships were in need of attention and

Yarmouth was also consuming vast amounts of coal. On 18ᵗʰ September she had to dock in Penang with both her condensers leaking. Steamships had to recycle water from their engines using condensers, and these were topped up from the sea. Without regular cleaning the salty residue could cause damage and rusting. Hence the leaks. Four days were needed for repairs.[27]

For the moment, *Chikuma* was sent to patrol the west side of the Bay of Bengal, while *Hampshire* remained on the Penang side to search the Andaman and Nicobar Islands as far north as Rangoon. The northern waters of the Malacca Straits were, of course, regularly patrolled by the French.

The seas around Java were now being patrolled by a Japanese squadron under independent Japanese command.

Admiral Jerram was convinced that *Emden* would soon attack Direction Island in the Cocos. These islands lay way to the south-west of Sumatra, on the direct telegraph cable route from Australia to Colombo. Direction Island was a large communication hub where several trans-oceanic telegraph cables met. There was also a big radio mast there. Just as he, Jerram, had gone straight to Yap Island and destroyed the German radio station there, he expected von Müller to do the same on Direction Island. Anticipating an attack, he sent his two most powerful ships, *Ibuki* and *Minotaur*, to guard the island.[28]

Back on board *Emden*, however, von Müller had quite different ideas. Avoiding the Calcutta shipping lanes he decided to have a quick reconnoitre around Rangoon, before leaving that part of the Bay of Bengal entirely. He was now running a grave risk of capture, yet on 17ᵗʰ September, he put *Emden* right across the sea-lane in the Gulf of Martaban at the mouth of the Irrawaddy, as close to Rangoon harbour as he dared go. *Emden* saw nothing all day, but at nightfall she spotted a ship and intercepted her. She turned out to be a Norwegian ship *Dovre*. The captain spoke good German and some time was spent in conversation with him. He agreed to take *Emden*'s prisoners from *Clan Matheson* and *Trabboch* to Rangoon. *Dovre* had just come up the Malacca Straits and was able to inform von Müller that one of the armoured French cruisers, either *Montcalm* or *Dupleix*, was in Penang. He was wrong about *Montcalm* but quite right about *Dupleix* which was there at that very moment. After a cordial chat on board *Dovre*, Lauterbach made his way back to *Emden*.

Perhaps it was then, that the seed of an idea took root in von Müller's mind. What about an attack on Penang harbour? Perhaps he was fed up with sinking unarmed merchant ships and wanted to have a go at a French cruiser.

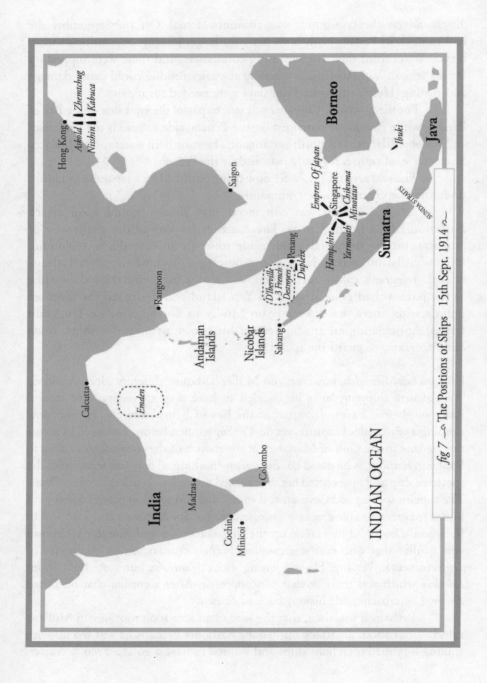

fig 7 ∼ The Positions of Ships 15th Sept. 1914 ∼

They were more powerful than *Emden*, but if he planned a surprise attack, he might get away with it. It is very likely that he also came by the information that French destroyers were there too, because when he finally arrived, he was looking for them. As his reputation for daring was already established when he was on the Yangtze, such an attack would be quite in character. But this was not the time. Right now he had another plan. He was going to cross the Bay of Bengal to attack Madras. But just before he left the Nicobars, *Emden*'s wireless picked up the same call sign that she had heard off Simeulue – 'Q.M.D'.

Just how easy it was to get a hold of vital information on ships and ship's movements, and learn about British reactions to their own exploits, was revealed by Prinz Hohenzollern:

> Lauterbach had brought fresh newspapers with him with the latest news from the theatres of war. The news of the greatest interest was of course the doings of the *Emden* in the Bay of Bengal. The English newspapers did not indeed belie our exploits but they attempted to quiet the anxious shipping and commercial circles with the assurance that the *Emden* would shortly disappear, even if she had not already been sunk by the allied warships.
>
> This piece of boasting made us laugh. We were still undestroyed in spite of the innumerable allied warships. Without meaning to, the various wireless stations also gave us useful news.

Once again, *Emden* was uncomfortably close to *Hampshire*, which was patrolling the Nicobar islands nearby. Just like before, *Emden* started picking up strong radio signals from a warship nearby. Again, the call sign was Q.M.D. Prinz Hohenzollern related what happened next:

> Another intercepted message was pathetically harmless and came to us as follows. Our friend 'Q.M.D.' had probably been in communication with some land station. Another land station had intercepted the message and wished to know who 'Q.M.D.' might be? A third station broke in with the answer: "Q.M.D.' is the armoured cruiser *Hampshire!*' The news was flattering to us because it confirmed our suspicions that it might be *Hampshire*.[29]

From then on *Emden* could easily recognise *Hampshire* and knew that she was one of the cruisers hunting for them.

On 18th September *Dovre* put the crew of *Clan Matheson* ashore in Rangoon, who duly relayed the message that *Emden* was nearby. That was the same day that *Yarmouth* and her captain, Cochrane, had put in to Penang for repairs to her condensers, so Cochrane received the worrying news right away.

Meanwhile, Grant in *Hampshire* was working his way north up the Andaman Sea, really close to *Emden*, as the latter well knew. Grant was deeply irritated to discover that the Indian colonial authorities were sending messages 'en clair'. This practice seemed to him so careless that on 19th September, he went into Port Blair on the Andaman Islands to tell them to stop doing it. He then continued his way north towards Rangoon. At about 4.00 a.m. on 20th September, he passed through the exact position where *Emden* had been at noon the previous day.[30] What he did not yet know was that wireless operators on the Andaman Islands were not only transmitting 'en clair', but had graciously identified his call-sign as that of *Hampshire*! Grant had missed *Emden* by only sixteen hours. *Chikuma,* which had been patrolling the western side of the Bay, then steamed off back towards Colombo. Later on she too had a very near miss.

In spite of all the drama around Rangoon, Admiral Jerram still felt that it was safe for the Australian convoy of transports to depart from Fremantle with only a modest armed escort – which was all he could spare, because three of his available cruisers were now taken up hunting for *Emden* around the Bay of Bengal. The Australian convoy would be heading far to the south of Sumatra and past the Cocos Islands on its way to Colombo. *Emden*, he thought, would present little challenge on her own, and Graf Spee's powerful squadron was miles away. But the Australians still disagreed.

Emden now disappeared for almost a week and on 22nd September, the Port Officer in Calcutta breathed a sigh of relief and declared the Colombo-Calcutta trade route open again. This proved to be very premature.[31] Back on board *Emden*, after all her activity around Rangoon, von Müller had indeed decided to make himself scarce. *Emden*'s presence around Rangoon was known and things were getting much too hot for comfort:

> Towards evening we passed through Preparis South Channel between the Andaman Islands. In the night the *Hampshire*'s wireless was so loud that our wireless staff estimated she could not be more than ten sea miles distant. After midnight we were through the southern straits and altered our course for Madras.[32]

Von Müller then steamed very slowly, right across the Bay of Bengal to Madras, avoiding the shipping lanes and without meeting anyone. He had decided to attack the oil installation.

Prinz Hohenzollern explained von Müller's reasoning, which proved to be quite correct:

> Madras is the third biggest port of India with 517,335 inhabitants. On the beach in the middle of the town lies the old Fort St. George and at the south end of the harbour lie the oil and petroleum tanks of the Burmah Oil Company.
>
> The principal object of our visit was to unsettle the Indian inhabitants. In addition we wished to destroy the oil tanks and if possible the shipping lying in the harbour.

Way back in early August, when he had conferred with Graf Spee at Pagan Island, von Müller had expressed the view that unsettling the local population would reduce their willingness to fight for Britain. There was some truth in that theory, which was born out later in the Singapore Mutiny.

Von Müller expected to be bombarded with the powerful 150mm guns of the Madras shore battery, They had a much longer range than *Emden*'s 105mm guns and knowing this, *Emden*'s gunnery crews had been practising all the way across the Bay of Bengal. To save valuable ammunition, small-bore rifles were inserted into the guns to shoot a target at comparatively short range, but using the big gun's control systems. In this case the guns' crews used *Markomannia* to tow the target.

The day of their intended attack was 22nd September, and the close attention to detail that characterised *Emden*'s preparations was vividly described by Prinz Hohenzollern:

> First of all the inflammable articles were transferred below the armoured deck. After lunch an officer's council took place held by the First Officer. It was necessary to go over once more all the points of our duties in the ship and to give every officer instructions, in case the Captain and First Officer should fall in the attack on Madras.
>
> Every possibility must be reckoned with. The men were given the opportunity of bathing in fresh water and were ordered to put on clean clothes. These measures were purely hygienic, designed to ensure that the men should be clean so that in case of a wound there

should be no complications. This foresight is doubly necessary in the tropics as in these hot zones the danger of gangrene is far greater than in European or continental climates.

Emden arrived under cover of darkness on the evening of 22nd September and found the whole place lit up, including the lighthouse.

> We were astounded that this was still burning, proving the unwatchfulness of the British authorities. The harbour lights were all burning and the whole town was a sea of light. How different it was in Germany and on German coasts where at the beginning of war all lights and light-houses were extinguished and no coastal town showed a light towards the sea. Here, however the opposite was the case.
>
> We rushed towards the harbour at a speed of 17 knots, steering thanks to their lights so that at the order 'open fire', the oil-tanks and the battery would be in line.
>
> At a quarter to ten we were still about 3,000 metres from the land. The *Emden* then turned to port and stopped.
>
> Immediately afterwards, followed the orders 'Switch on fore-mast searchlight. Open fire!' A few seconds later the first salvo blazed out and salvo after salvo followed. Tongues of flame went up from the oil tanks. I was very anxious about the return fire from the English battery but to our astonishment not a shot was fired.

He went on to explain that the only gun that fired back was a small one mounted on the harbour mole.[33] A steamer in the harbour was damaged with some casualties, and three of the towns-people were killed by stray shells. A large number of the inhabitants left town the next day by rail.[34]

5,000 tons of Burmah Oil had gone up in smoke. This did nothing for the morale of the local Indian population who took a very dim view of evident British vulnerability. It was quite some time before the British authorities could reassure the locals that the Germans were not about to invade. This was exactly the effect that von Müller had predicted.

Emden escaped without a scratch and vanished into the night. The reaction of the English newspapers was mixed. Hitherto their stories about *Emden* had been the tale of a plucky underdog, but now some people had been killed and a whole town had been reduced to a state of fear. This was serious. On 25th September the *Penang Gazette* carried several articles. One of them gave a brief description of *Emden* and then added: 'It is possibly quite correct [to] surmise that assistance received by the raider is afforded by persons with an eye to making money.'[35]

The conspiracy theorists would henceforward come out in strength. Nobody seemed willing to face the fact that British security precautions were abysmal, whilst the Germans were scrupulous in their planning and attention to detail. There was more than a touch of arrogance in the failure of the British harbour authorities to do their job properly. In mitigation it can only be said that nothing was allowed to interfere with trade, and that was Admiralty policy. Ship owners were happy to bear a few losses, so long as they had insurance cover.

A delightful piece of journalistic hauteur appeared in the *Penang Gazette & Straits Chronicle* just after the attack, emphasising the sinister underhand ways of *Emden*, as opposed to the pluckiness of the locals. Civilian casualties were emphasised.

> *Emden* fired nine shots into the city and hit the telegraph offices, seamen's clubhouse, trucks in the harbour and two oil tanks which are ablaze.
>
> On our guns replying, the *Emden* disappeared with lights out. Two Indians and a boy were killed. The public were perfectly calm and their attitude was admirable.[36]

The paper added, in an adjoining article, that they had "quiet confidence" that Germany would soon be unable to continue the conflict, because of severe economic constraints.[37]

The killing of civilians was the main message. In fact *Emden* had fired 125 rounds,[38] and yes, the first few rounds went high and landed in the town behind the oil depot, but the shore battery did not reply. The *Emden* was firing for about half an hour, which should have given them ample time to respond. Why they did not, is a mystery. One shell exploded aboard the passenger steamer *Chupra* which was in the harbour, causing altogether 26 casualties. The whole incident, its unexpectedness, the glare of the burning oil-tanks at night time, and the ineffectiveness of the defence, made a deep impression on the local population.[39]

When *Emden* finally steamed away, the crew deliberately kept her lights on, so she would appear to be travelling on a northerly course.[40] Once over the horizon she turned about and headed south. The towns people, especially the Indian population, were anything but calm, and great damage was done to the illusion of British invincibility.

Back in London, Lord Portland, a member of the government, reassured the press and the public, with extraordinary insensitivity and pompousness, that Madras was 'not important'.[41] There followed a slightly more thoughtful article in the *Straits Times,* written shortly after, but not published till 5th October, in which the total lack of security precautions was tacitly acknowledged.

> That the visit was unexpected may be judged by the fact that the lighthouse was working as usual and probably helped the cruiser to take her bearings and fire, with the accuracy with which it did. This, however would not have been impossible even if the Madras light had been extinguished, if it is true that one of the cruiser's officers is a master of a Hansa liner which called at all the Bay ports including Madras. The visit to Madras was paid early enough [in the evening] to find the shore lights all ablaze, the trams working and all the business of the town as usual, at that time of night, going on. [42]

It is quite likely that the ship's master in question was Lieutenant Lauterbach, who did indeed have knowledge of the Bay ports and Penang harbour as well. The article went on to report that fragments of a shell-burst missed their mark and were found:

> On the verandah of the Madras Mail office and in front of the Old Bank of Burma, the only occupants of which latter were Mr. and Mrs. Wynne-Cole, who had a very alarming experience when fragments spattered against the upper story of their premises and even entered the drawing-room.

But now the spectre of spies was dug up again. In another article written just after the event, but not published till several weeks later, the *Straits Times* asked why "The Polite Cruiser is not Caught?". They went into a long rigmarole pointing the finger, with little subtlety, at local Dutch ports with impounded German ships. Perhaps the Dutch had failed to dismantle their wireless equipment properly? Next they turned their attention to the failure of the Royal Navy to apprehend *Emden*. They pointed out just how much havoc had been wrought by *Emden* in the Bay of Bengal with seeming impunity:

The wonder is natural that these depredations in valuable commerce, representing very large interests, should be taking place in an area of sea in which British shipping is of very great importance and value. We have an Eastern fleet, and its East Indies squadron comprises a flagship and several cruisers with a considerable number of destroyers attached. If the force was not sufficient there are the vessels of the China Squadron and the New Zealand division which could have sent cruisers to take up the chase. There are also the cruisers of the Australian fleet. We hope that the Admiralty will offer some explanation of the impunity with which the *Emden* pursues her depredations. It should surely not be beyond the power of all these warships to round up this very enterprising German commerce destroyer. If there be no other means to check the evil can not we recur to the old system of convoy, with advantage?

The doings of the *Emden* in the Indian seas convey a wholesome lesson. One cruiser of 3,600 tons carrying nothing bigger than 4 inch guns has swept the Bay of Bengal clear of shipping, sunk half a dozen British steamers and bombarded the only provincial capital which can be attacked from the sea.[43]

The next day, on 23rd September, *Emden* cruised past the French port of Pondicherry on her way south to Ceylon, but she saw no further ships and meeting up with *Markomannia* she took on some more coal. The previous night the horizon had been lit up by the burning oil-tanks in Madras and by day, the great black cloud of smoke was still visible from many miles away.[44]

Unknown to *Emden*'s crew, *Chikuma* was simultaneously making her way up to Madras from Colombo for a rendezvous with *Hampshire*. She missed *Emden* by a hairsbreadth.[45] It happened like this. Just before the attack on Madras, *Hampshire* was already steaming southwards although she had not yet reached Madras. *Chikuma*, after being delayed for a day coaling in Colombo, was steaming north to meet her. After the attack, when *Emden* stopped to re-coal at sea from *Markomannia*, *Hampshire* was just to the north, with *Chikuma* perilously close to the south. It was a very near thing. None of this was known till the ships' logs were compared many months later.

Emden now steamed south-west, around Dondra Head at the southern tip of Ceylon, past Galle and on up towards Colombo. There, von Müller could expect to find plenty of ships, but he was taking a very big risk, because Colombo was sure to have one or two warships to hand. Quite unknowingly,

Hampshire followed soon afterwards and tied up in Colombo, having missed *Emden* en route by only about three hours.[46] After coaling, Grant then set off eastwards again, heading for Aceh Head at the northern tip of Sumatra. He thought that *Emden* might cross over the Bay of Bengal once again, but in case she did not, he ordered *Chikuma* to check around Minicoi. This was the small island that Cross had passed by on his way to Penang. All the shipping lanes to the west of Colombo went past Minicoi. It was an excellent guess on Grant's part, but a bit premature.

With the benefit of hindsight, the strategy of commerce-raiding, espoused by the French *jeune école*, proved very effective, especially in the days before radar and air reconnaissance, when the limits of visibility from a big ship's masthead would be a 14 mile radius. Attacks on civilian targets were a new thing, hence the righteous indignation about the casualties in Madras. The other thing that the British ignored most of the time, was security precautions for their merchant ships and for their harbours. Responsibility for that, they thought, lay with Jerram's cruisers.

The crew of *Emden* were clearly flabbergasted by such an attitude, which lacked all common sense. Only the Australians and New Zealanders were keenly aware of the risk. They wanted complete assurances, before committing their big expeditionary force into Jerram's hands. It is quite amazing that after the Madras experience, MacIntyre, who was carrying the responsibility for Penang harbour, had learned precisely nothing. He kept all Penang's harbour lights on. It must be said that Admiral Jerram himself seems to have been unwilling, or unable, to insist upon adequate security precautions and was impatient with the Australians for their apparent squeamishness.

As already mentioned, Calcutta and Colombo Port Authorities reopened for business on 22nd September and the Madras raid followed that very evening. When the news got to the New Zealand Government, they were unimpressed by everything they heard and insisted that they had been right all along, demanding a heavy armed escort for their convoy.

Jerram hardly reacted at all to events in Madras, exasperated as he was with his own difficulties. His only comment was that *Emden*'s continued success was 'a source of great anxiety'.[47]

Churchill was incandescent. The disaster in Madras was absolutely the last thing he needed. He telegraphed the First Sea Lord, Prince Louis of Battenberg, saying:

Three transports are delayed in Calcutta for fear of *Emden*. I am quite at a loss to understand the operations of *Hampshire*'s Captain [Grant] to catch the *Emden*. What happened to *Yarmouth*? … Her movements seem entirely disjointed and purposeless … we must without further delay take measures which will give reasonable prospect of a decisive result. It is no use stirring about the oceans with two or three ships. When we have got cruiser sweeps of eight to ten vessels, ten to fifteen miles apart, there will be some good prospect of bringing *Emden* to action.

I wish to point out to you most clearly that the irritation caused by an indefinite continuance of the *Emden*'s capture will do great damage to Admiralty reputation.[48]

W.S.C.

Clearly Churchill was unable to understand why Jerram had not thought of doing sweeps. Before aircraft reconnaissance and radar, ships could remain in visual contact with each other at roughly 10 (nautical) mile intervals or even more, if their masts were high enough, so 10 ships (any old ships) strung out in a line could do a sweep 100 miles wide. The message was duly passed to Admiral Jerram, who was seriously unimpressed with this lecture about how to do his job. He sent a very sniffy reply to the Admiralty:

The search for *Emden* upon which *Hampshire*, *Yarmouth* and *Chikuma* are engaged has been from the beginning, conducted under the orders of Captain H. W. Grant of *Hampshire* and it is quite impracticable for me to control it.

I am furnishing Grant with all available information to assist him, but have refrained as far as possible with hampering him with too much advice. So far I fully approve the dispositions he has made as reported to me and I realise what an extremely difficult task it is to hunt down a single fast cruiser employed as the *Emden* now is. It seems probable that on several occasions one of our ships has been very close to her.

I have the honour to be, Sir,

Your obedient servant.[49]

Clearly he meant nothing of the kind (the bit about being an obedient servant), but for the moment Churchill backed off.

It was becoming clear that Jerram's style of command was to delegate matters to others with little overall strategy. He gave Grant no guidelines to follow in the hunt for *Emden,* and simply left him to it. He seemed to have no grip on proper security in the harbours and ports in his area, leaving it to the port officers to make their own minds up. This was disastrous in Madras and much worse was to come in Penang. Communications and the use of cipher were not properly addressed either. Shipping, beyond the convoys of troop transports and war supplies to Europe, was left to its own devices.

Jerram's preoccupation with providing escorts for his convoys of troop-transports and war-supplies seems to have left him no time to concern himself with ordinary merchant shipping, besides issuing some flabby recommendations about avoiding certain shipping lanes. Jerram also failed to pay proper attention to a regular detailed programme of planned maintenance for the ships under his command. Instead, he would wait till they were at a virtual standstill before giving them time for repairs.

Perhaps, he did not worry enough; perhaps he feared attracting criticism from the Admiralty. He did nothing to tighten up security for lone merchant ships in his area, because he thought the owners might complain. He was simply taking the path of least resistance. Grant, he supposed, would soon take care of *Emden.* Besides, the four French ships based in Penang had been patrolling the western Malacca Straits throughout the whole of September, so he had no worries about the Singapore – Colombo route.

Out in the Pacific, on 22nd September, the same day as *Emden*'s Madras attack, Graf Spee's squadron reappeared and attacked the French capital Papeeté in Tahiti. The action was indecisive and Graf Spee vanished once again. But Jerram now felt sure that Graf Spee was heading for South America. He must have realised that the chances of him doubling back to the Indian Ocean were exceedingly remote, especially with his dwindling supplies of coal. This soon became clear when Graf Spee's squadron was reported to be heading for Easter Island. The Australians and New Zealanders calmed down and fortunately, a serious rift with the British government was averted.[50] All they had to worry about now were *Emden* and the other lone raider, *Königsberg,* which was still at large.

Immediately after the attack on Madras, *Emden* vanished once again. Most people were optimistic, believing she would run out of coal, or supplies, or ammunition, or have broken-down engines, or something. There was no way, people thought, that she could keep this up. She had been at sea continuously since early August. Prisoners who had landed in Calcutta and Rangoon described the ship as being in an appalling state of untidiness. Surely she would soon limp into some neutral port to remain impounded for the rest of the war – which they thought would not last much longer anyway. So things in the Bay of Bengal were quiet again and the trade route between Colombo and Calcutta was reopened.

No sooner had restrictions on the movements of merchant ships been lifted than *Emden* suddenly reappeared, capturing ships around Colombo.[51] Four more ships were sunk and two more captured. *King Lud, Tymeric, Ribera,* and *Foyle* were all sunk between 25th and 28th September, whilst the steamer *Gryfevale* and the collier *Buresk* were captured.

To describe these events from *Emden*'s perspective, gives a clear idea of the hopelessness of British security. After *Emden* had captured *King Lud,* their next prize demonstrated the sheer audacity and bravery of von Müller's tactics. *Emden* managed to sail so close to the port of Colombo, which was well illuminated by searchlights, that the captain was able to watch the black hull of a steamer coming out of the harbour. They decided to follow and capture her. She was showing the usual navigation lights and the chase was easy. After they had gone some 50 miles towards Minicoi, von Müller thought he was far enough from land and flashed the steamer by Morse-lamp to stop. The signal took some time to get through, but finally she stopped.[52]

The ship that *Emden* had apprehended was *Tymeric,* loaded with 4,000 tons of sugar. The exasperation of the British master and von Müller's reaction, were beautifully described by Prinz Hohenzollern, although the story came from Lauterbach. After boarding *Tymeric,* Lieutenant Lauterbach asked the ship to follow them out to sea, because if they had sunk her so close to the coast it might attract attention. Lauterbach then ordered *Tymeric*'s crew to pack their belongings ready for transfer to *Markomannia,* once their ship was far enough out to sea. The captain refused.

> The captain [was] in a rage at having run into our hands right outside Colombo and in sight of the searchlights of that harbour and he began to curse with the words 'Damned Germans!' With such a fellow the short way was the only way and Lauterbach accordingly signalled [back to us] to report these insults, and asked for permission to sink the ship at once.

This permission was granted. The English crew naturally

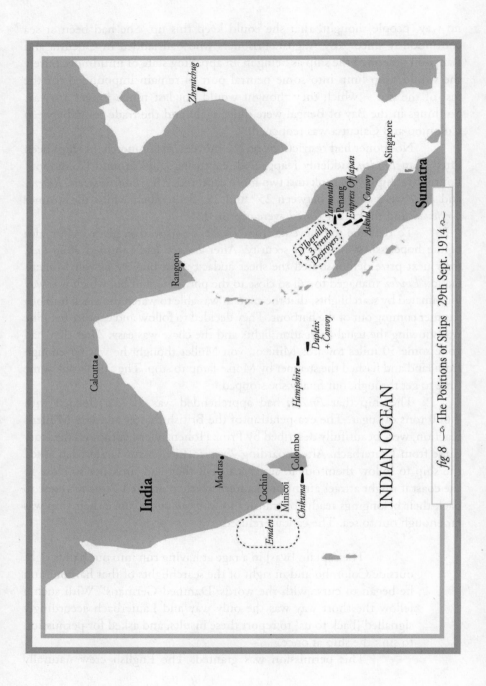

fig 8 ❧ The Positions of Ships 29th Sept. 1914 ❧

Anchor salvaged off Muka Head from 'Mousquet's' wreck. Presented to Penang Museum Jan. 1970

Esplande Road, Penang.

Esplanade Penang. Contemporary tinted postcard showing Fort Cornwallis. The tree on the left remains there to this day.

View of Penang Esplanade looking east, showing Fort Cornwallis and the harbour, the light-house and the signal-station mast. Undated photo, but roughly contemporary with 'Emden' s raid.

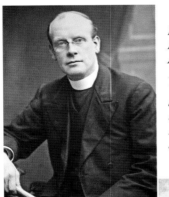

Reverend William Cross. Minister (Pastor) for St Andrew's Kirk, Penang. 1912 - 1915. Said "The Angel of Death has hovered over us". Photo by permission, United Reform Church History Society Cambridge.

Two postcards showing St Andrew's Kirk, Penang, the Presbyterian Church of Scotland, where William Cross preached. The Church has since been demolished.

THE CHINESE

Sun Yat Sen, first President of China, soon to be replaced by Yuan Shikai. Focus of warring factions in Southern China during 1914.

Yuan Shikai, President of China in Aug. 1914 at the outbreak of WWI. He was forced by the British to hand over Tsing Tao to the Japanese.

120, Armenian Street Penang. Sun Yat Sen's revolutionary headquarters in Penang in 1912. Recent photo.

Cheong Fatt Tze 'The Blue Mansion' today. Leith Street, Penang. William Cross would have been very familiar with this house.

THE FRENCH

Raymond Poincaré. French President at the outbreak of WWI. The defeat of France in the Franco-Prussian war made him deeply suspicious of Germany.

Captain Charles de Paris de Boisrouvray. Commandant of French Naval Forces, Indo-China, based in Saigon. An irascible character with little loyalty to those under his command. Died suddenly before the Saigon enquiry.

Rear Admiral Albert Huguet, Commander-in-Chief of French Naval Forces in the Far East at the outbreak of WWI. A teenager during the Franco-Prussian war, he too was deeply suspicious of Germany.

THE FRENCH

French armoured cruiser 'Montcalm'.
Rear Admiral Huguet's flagship.
Photo: Imperial War Museum Q22300.

French armoured cruiser 'Dupleix'. Commanded
by Captain Daveluy. Spent 4 weeks in Penang.

Two photos of French
destroyer 'd'Iberville', lent
to Jerram's Allied Far East
Squadron. Commanded by
Louis Audemard. Based in
Penang for several weeks.

THE FRENCH

Lieutenant Felix Théroinne.
Commander of 'Mousquet'.
Went down with his ship,
28th Oct. 1914.

Two photos of French destroyer
'Mousquet', lent to Jerram's
Allied Far East Squadron. Sunk
by 'Emden' 28th Oct. 1914.
Capable of 28 knots, could
outpace most larger warships.
Photo below by permission,
Agence photographique, Musée
National de la Marine, Paris.

THE JAPANESE

Emperor Yoshihito of Japan. Meningitis as a child left him with physical and psychological disabilities. Visited by Vice Admiral Jerram in May 1913.

Admiral Gonbee (Count) Yamamoto, previously head of the Imperial Japanese Navy. Had become Japanese Prime Minister by the outbreak of WWI. Vice Admiral Jerram offered him assistance following an earthquake in early 1914.

Below: Japanese light cruiser 'Chikuma'. Frequent visitor to Penang over several weeks. Lent to Jerram's Allied Far East Squadron. Part of cruiser squadron hunting 'Emden'.

Above: Japanese armoured cruiser 'Ibuki'. A modern ship with powerful guns. Lent to Jerram's Allied Far East Squadron. Patrolled Cocos Islands and later sent to escort Australia & New Zealand expeditionary force to Colombo.

had a grievance against their captain whose fault it was that they lost their possessions.

The captain's anger at being captured so close to the port of Colombo I could understand, and especially his anger at their naval staff in Colombo who, as the irate captain explained, had guaranteed with all certainty that the coast was clear. He had to thank his countrymen for this erroneous advice

Once again, the lack of security precautions so close to a devastating attack on Madras, can only be wondered at. The crew of *Tymeric* were duly transferred to *Markomannia*.[53]

Von Müller was playing an increasingly clever psychological game with his captives, giving the impression of invincibility if not clairvoyance. He would quietly inform the masters of the captured ships exactly when they had left Colombo and what their cargoes were. This information was nothing more than what he had read in the newspapers obtained from *King Lud*. He also made the most of the fact that *Emden*'s attack on Madras had taken place within hours of the trade route to Calcutta being re-opened. To the merchant seamen he met, it was becoming increasingly obvious that the advice they were being given by port authorities could not be relied upon in any way.[54]

Throughout her cruise *Emden* had enjoyed the advantage of strict Dutch neutrality. For much of the time the Dutch knew of *Emden*'s whereabouts, but never informed the British. It was at dawn, after the sinking of *Tymeric,* that *Emden* spotted a Dutch ship on the horizon. They feared that they would be recognised and their position betrayed. Not a bit of it. Soon afterwards they intercepted a message from an English ship, asking the Dutchman if he had seen anything of *Emden.* The Dutchman's answer, which *Emden* intercepted, ran 'For reasons of neutrality answer refused'.[55]

The capture of *Ribera, Foyle,* and *Gryfevale* followed soon after. Prinz Hohenzollern's account of the capture of *Ribera* contains what seems to be the only instance of a mistaken recollection in the book that he wrote afterwards. He reported that *Ribera*'s log described a large convoy of sixty to seventy ships in the Arabian Sea on the way across to Aden and amongst the ships, they had spotted *Askold*'s five funnels. That recollection was incorrect, because *Askold* had not even reached Colombo at that time.[56] Hohenzollern was confusing it with a later encounter with *Ben Mohr* off Minicoi, on 17th October.

But *Emden*'s last capture, the *Buresk,* was the prize they had all been hoping for. *Buresk* had a cargo of finest Welsh coal intended for Jerram's ships.

This could keep *Emden* going for ages, be kind to her boilers and make very little smoke. *Emden*'s engineers fitted *Buresk* with a good wireless, captured a while back from *Indus* (the Elysiam soap ship). She then joined *Emden* as a collier escort vessel, with a small guard of *Emden*'s crew aboard. So *Buresk* was retained and joined the near-empty *Markomannia* as a coal-tender. The crew were all professional Arab seamen, employed by the British, but they were co-operative and did a good job.

All the other prisoners were transferred onto *Gryfevale* and packed off to Colombo. When *Gryfevale* arrived in Colombo on 29th September, with prisoners from five captured ships crammed on board, it caused more uproar in the English-language newspapers.[57] For Jerram, ashore at Fort Canning in Singapore, with the telegraph chattering away, the news was grim. Maybe he did not sleep too well in his hotel billet either, with the fan whirring, because it was a humiliating story that he now pieced together.[58] Again, the idea of spies under the bed gained credibility; but now it was an 'illicit wireless station somewhere on the coast of India.'[59]

Markomannia was now emptied of her remaining coal and von Müller sent her to join *Pontoporos* off Simeulue on the other side of the Bay of Bengal. She was ordered to take her time, remaining well away from the trade routes, then cruise around till she found *Pontoporos*. Once contact was made, *Markomannia* was to transfer all *Pontoporos*' remaining coal into her own bunkers, pay off the Greek ship and her captain, and send them off to Singapore. The two German officers on board *Pontoporos,* including *Emden*'s Lieutenant Meyer, would be transferred to *Markomannia*. She was then ordered to make for a neutral Dutch port, presumably Padang, spending her allotted twenty-four hours there and delivering mail from *Emden*'s crew.

Adding everything up, that made a tally of sixteen ships captured or sunk by *Emden* since the start of the war. *Emden* and her two tenders now vanished once more, and nobody knew where.[60]

Setting out on 30th September, *Emden* headed as far south as possible, right out into the depths of the Indian Ocean to the remote Island of Diego Garcia. Although the island was a British protectorate, there was a chance that the islanders might still be unaware of the war, which had been going for only two months. Von Müller thought that in such a remote place, the island might have ships calling only every six months. So whilst *Markomannia* was plodding over 1,000 miles back to Sumatra, *Emden* accompanied by *Buresk,* was to get some long overdue maintenance.

Diego Garcia, the southernmost island in the British Indian Ocean Territory, is currently leased by the British government to the Americans as an air force base but, back in 1914, Diego Garcia was isolated and mostly self-sufficient, subsisting on coconut oil, copra, simple farming and a plentiful supply of fish from the sea.

This coral island has a huge natural lagoon which serves as a harbour. Von Müller hoped to spend some time there, doing some essential repairs and maintenance to his ship because the engines and boilers needed thorough cleaning. It is a tribute to the excellence of *Emden*'s construction, the expertise of her crew of marine engineers and the reliability of her engines, that *Emden* managed to keep going without any long breaks, for seven weeks. But if cornered, she would have to rely on her speed, and for that she would have to clean her bottom. The ship looked a mess: rust everywhere, the hull and guard-rails dented and the paint scraped off from continual coaling at sea. The ship's hull was encrusted with barnacles and sea-weed, slowing her down and using more fuel. The deck was cluttered with various stores and livestock, but the engines and guns were still in good working order.

In his usual lyrical manner, Prinz Hohenzollern described Diego Garcia as a miniature fairyland of coral banks and high palms, with a sheltered bay that could not be seen for the sea. The islanders rushed down to the harbour to see *Emden* and *Buresk*. They had not been there half an hour before a boat put out from the shore, bringing the subordinate manager of the local coconut oil company. The islanders spoke their own Creole language, but this man was educated in Madagascar and spoke French. Von Müller's mother was French and he spoke the language very well. The Islanders clearly had no idea there was a war on. Their only contact with the outside world was a three-monthly sailing schooner from Mauritius. Luckily, that was not due for a few days, so von Müller had been right.

Later, the chief manager of the company came aboard. He was not only English, but the ex-officio representative of His Britannic Majesty's Government. The representative wanted to know what a German ship was doing there and why she had such a wild appearance? Von Müller explained that they were engaged in some vast international 'world manoeuvres', and had been badly battered in a great storm. Satisfied with this explanation, the islanders plied them generously with a pig, fresh fruit, poultry and fish, offering any assistance they wished.

Meanwhile, the calm waters of the lagoon, with its crystal clear water, permitted the crew to tilt *Emden* over to one side, and then the other, so that as much of her bottom as possible could be scraped and repainted. Meanwhile, the engineers were busy sorting out the engines and boilers, whilst the rest of the crew set to repainting rusty areas. This work, including coaling from *Buresk*, was completed in three days and at the end of it, *Emden* entertained the local dignitaries on board. Unfortunately, they had to refuse a return-party ashore, but sent His Majesty's representative a present of whiskey and cigars. *Emden*'s efficient engineers also repaired the Representative's prized motor-boat, to his great delight.

> I think the Diego Garcia people never had such noble givers as guests. As thanks for all this they offered to catch lobsters for us. As our time was short we could not wait, a fact that we all rather regretted.[61]

When they left Diego Garcia, von Müller intended to head straight for Penang, but then they had another piece of luck. They intercepted a wireless message from an English ship inquiring about the security of the Colombo-to-Aden shipping lanes. The answer 'en clair' said that there was no danger and the route was safe. Von Müller also knew from questioning the crew from the ships they captured earlier, that they had been told to steer to the north of Minicoi.

This was an opportunity that *Emden* could not miss.

Chapter 6

Markomannia sunk, but There are Problems in Penang

It was on 1ˢᵗ October that Jerram received the unwelcome news from Colombo that *Emden,* having left Madras with the Burmah Oil tanks ablaze, had been at it again, this time within a few miles of Ceylon. Worse still, *Emden* had been lurking just outside Colombo harbour, where Jerram's transports with *Askold* and *Dupleix* were due. His heart must have sunk. But he gritted his teeth and decided he was not going to allow *Emden's* activities to interrupt the flow of transports any longer. *Dupleix* had already left Penang and was steaming across the Bay of Bengal towards Colombo with her French transports. She had been in Penang for almost a month and her engines had been fully serviced. Just behind them, *Askold* and *Empress of Asia,* with their small convoy, were sailing up the Malacca Straits, also heading for Colombo,[1] passing Penang Island well to starboard.[2]

Captain Cochrane in *Yarmouth* had been vainly searching for *Emden* around the Nicobars. He was back in Penang for coaling when he, too, got the bad news. Hearing that *Emden* had been so close to Colombo, *Yarmouth* left Penang in a hurry, concerned that *Emden* might pose a threat to *Askold's* convoy. Steaming at fifteen knots, *Yarmouth* soon caught up with them and accompanied the convoy halfway across the Bay of Bengal, just in case of trouble. But nothing happened, so *Yarmouth* doubled back to Penang.

Many ships were waiting in Colombo for *Askold* and *Dupleix* to provide the armed escort across the Arabian Sea to Aden.[3] Captain Grant in *Hampshire* was away, hunting around the Maldives looking for *Emden,* but he had found nothing, and was in ignorance of the latest news.

Ignoring any potential threat from *Emden*, maybe lurking anywhere out there in the Arabian Sea, Admiral Jerram telegraphed Colombo, ordering *Askold* and *Dupleix* to bash on, disregarding any threat from *Emden*. The convoy, which was of considerable size, held their breath and sallied forth out of Colombo on 6ᵗʰ October, bound for Aden. All the while, *Emden* was actually hiding away in Diego Garcia. The convoy was due to arrive in Aden on 15ᵗʰ October. In fact, everything went without a hitch and, having handed over the convoy in Aden, *Dupleix* and *Askold* were free to return to Colombo.[4]

In mid-September Captain Baron Cherkasov had brought his cruiser *Zhemtchug* from Vladivostok via the Philippines to Hong Kong, and there he stopped for a while, awaiting some French transports bound for Singapore. Lieutenant Maund now joined *Zhemtchug* as Jerram's liaison officer. They left Hong Kong on 27ᵗʰ September, just at the time that *Emden* was busy sinking ships around Colombo.[5] Heading for Singapore, they called in at Hai Phong and Saigon for coaling, picking up some extra French transports en route. On 8ᵗʰ October, with her fellow Russian cruiser *Askold* already on her way across to Aden, *Zhemtchug* arrived in Singapore with her little convoy. There they picked up two more French ships just arrived from Saigon and also bound for Colombo.[6] *Emden*'s attacks around Ceylon were now hot news. It was also the day when *Emden* and *Zhemtchug* were furthest apart. By and by, that fact became known to Cherkasov, causing him to make a serious miscalculation.[7]

Cherkasov also made another grave mistake at this point. His wife, the Baroness Varvara Cherkasova, arrived in Singapore on a private steamer.[8] It was regarded as a personal matter at the time, but was later held against him by the Russian naval authorities, who took an exceedingly dim view.

Zhemtchug was not in good shape. She had come a long way since Vladivostok, and the Commodore in Hong Kong warned Jerram that her engines were in dire need of servicing. It is not clear when she was last serviced in Vladivostok, but after the long journey south her boiler tubes were seriously clogged-up. She was consuming a lot of coal and would be unlikely to make it all the way to Colombo from Singapore without stopping for more fuel. The Commodore was uncertain how much longer she could keep going without a thorough and lengthy boiler-cleaning. The Malacca Straits and Penang, he thought, was probably the limit, and Jerram concurred.[9]

With the benefit of hindsight, it would have been better to have cleaned *Zhemtchug*'s boilers in Singapore, or even back in Hong Kong, although it would have delayed the convoy's arrival in Colombo for a week. In that way, *Zhemtchug* could have escorted the convoy direct to Colombo without stopping in Penang. *Yarmouth* would have remained in Penang, and Cochrane would have insisted on extinguishing the harbour lights. In that case, *Emden*'s mission would probably have failed. But that was not to be.

In Penang, the French destroyers continued to have problems, not just with their clogged-up boilers, but with radio communication too, referred to as 'TSF'. The local atmospheric conditions and thunderstorms around Penang played havoc with radio communication.[10] This was exactly what Jerram found in Singapore. The French destroyers were not equipped with long-range transmitters. Obstacles like hills and mountains could reduce radio reception to a whisper even nearby, and electrical discharges in the atmosphere could jam everything and even set the wireless installation on fire.

The wirelesses of *d'Iberville*, *Pistolet* and *Mousquet* had a maximum range, in ideal conditions, of sixty to seventy miles, but generally the range was far shorter than that.[11] In addition, *Fronde*'s wireless was very unreliable and usually defective. None of these smaller ships had any auxiliary power sources which could allow radio transmission to continue without the use of dynamos, so they had to have steam up to power their wireless. *D'Iberville* had batteries, but transmission was feeble without the use of auxiliary power. To transmit radio signals reliably from the inner harbour to a point south-west of Muka Head was almost impossible because, in the words of Audemard, 'a screen of imposing mountains from 250 to 850 metres were interposed between the TSF transmitters and the open sea', blocking the air-waves.[12]

Audemard therefore requested that a ship should be anchored in the northern harbour roads to act as a radio relay, transmitting out to the open sea where his destroyers were patrolling. That solution, on a larger scale, had been set up by Jerram on the Yangtze some months earlier. Audemard recommended this solution to MacIntyre, but although Daveluy did his best to support the idea, they had no success.

Besides the radio station, there was the telegraph station beside the Penang Club, staffed by the Penang Volunteer Force, which received messages from Jerram in Singapore. The British operators should, in theory, have passed relevant messages from both the radio and the telegraph stations to the French commanders, but often they did not. This should have included complete briefings about Allied ship movements, but this essential information was generally withheld, or what was given by the harbour authorities was occasionally recognised as concocted.

Captain Le Coispellier, who was later appointed by the French Navy Minister to look into this whole affair, gave this example, among many others, of poor communication:

> The destroyers were patrolling between Diamond Point [the northern tip of Acheh] and Penang without being told what to expect. On one occasion *Pistolet* was patrolling along the coast. That night, she found herself in the presence of a large number of ships which they could only approach with great caution, up till the moment when an identification signal was made by the ship *Novic*, along with a British auxiliary cruiser. They were accompanying a convoy of merchant ships and their presence should have been signalled to *Pistolet*, being within the area of their patrol.[13]

Le Coispellier went on to say that even when signals requesting identification were made to ships entering Penang harbour, they often failed to respond.[14] This lack of attention to basic security was worse than negligent; it was crass. Since the beginning of August, Penang's lighthouses had been lit up, both at Muka Head and Fort Cornwallis. The buoys to the harbour channels and the harbour itself were also illuminated,[15] just like Madras. No matter how short-sighted the policy, night-time shipping was given every possible assistance, giving commerce priority over security. Apart from cargo ships, unchecked local boats and sampans were going in and out of harbour at all hours. Any hostile group of people could have been out there laying mines.

Penang harbour was not in great shape, either. It had no shore batteries, and depended entirely upon its warships to defend it. The anchorage assigned to warships was outside the harbour mouth, towards the present container port at Butterworth. This was a good spot for a fully operational warship, but not for a ship with her boilers shut down.

Audemard, supported by his second-in-command, Castagné, had been making constant complaints about poor security to the harbour authorities. In fact, Audemard had come up with some sensible proposals.

> 1. Night-time blackout of the George Town lighthouse and channel buoys leading to the harbour.
> 2. Pilot launches at the harbour mouth from 6.00 p.m. to 6.00 a.m. to monitor any shipping movements.

3. Change of anchorage for the French warships to avoid unnecessary exposure when undergoing repairs.[16]

These three points were the most important things, although Audemard might have added a number of others. Living conditions, for example, were tough, but since Captain Daveluy's intervention two weeks earlier, those problems were now much better managed, with better rest periods for the sailors. Audemard's recommendations were later set out in detail, for the Saigon enquiry to scrutinise.

Mercifully, *Yarmouth,* with Cochrane in command, had been in and out of George Town harbour since mid-September and Audemard obtained some friendly support from him. Cochrane could immediately see the sense of what he was proposing. At first they had no luck but, in the end, MacIntyre gave in. On the first count MacIntyre demurred, but concessions were made regarding the other two requests. It is likely that Cochrane, being in the Royal Navy, finally resorted to pulling rank, giving MacIntyre a direct order. He insisted that the harbour lights be extinguished, which also meant that shipping movements at night were virtually stopped. Any small boats that came in and out would be challenged by a harbour launch, which was scheduled to patrol the harbour mouth every night.[17]

MacIntyre seems to have had greater respect for his British colleague and, from 7th October, the security for Penang harbour was greatly improved.

Grant in *Hampshire* was back in Colombo, and now ordered *Empress of Asia* to join his squadron and resume the hunt for *Emden* around Colombo and Minicoi Island, but there was no sign of her. It was around 12th October that Grant finally decided to act on a hunch and went off with *Empress of Asia* to investigate Diego Garcia. It was just about the only part of the Maldives that he had not covered. Grant had calculated that *Emden* must now clean her boilers and do many running repairs. She had to be hiding somewhere. Diego Garcia seemed the only place left, although it would take three days for him and *Empress of Asia* to get there.

The same day that Grant set off in *Hampshire* for Diego Garcia, *Zhemtchug* and her French transports left Singapore[18] and sailed up the Malacca Straits towards Penang, with the Baroness Varvara Cherkasova following later. On 14th October they arrived, and the French destroyer squadron was there to greet them. The Japanese cruiser *Chikuma*, which had so narrowly missed *Emden* at Madras, was also in Penang. She was a welcome addition to the squadron and *Chikuma* now became a regular visitor to Penang for coaling and supplies. Her Japanese sailors, alongside the French, soon became a common sight in George Town. It was intended that *Zhemtchug* should join *Chikuma* to patrol the eastern side of the Bay of Bengal, whilst *Hampshire* and *Empress of Asia* should cover the west. But *Zhemtchug* had to get her clogged-up boilers fixed, and no date for that had yet been agreed.

For the same reason, the French destroyer squadron had been forced to reduce their schedule of patrols, given the bad state of their engines.[19] A period of properly planned maintenance was urgently needed so that they could be brought back to their full operational capacity. An interval of several days had to be allocated to each ship in turn, so that they could shut everything down and have their boilers properly cleaned.[20]

Thanks to Cochrane, the level of security in Penang harbour since 7th October had been placed on a rational footing. Ships' movements were restricted at night, with a launch patrolling the harbour mouth to check any movements in and out of the harbour.

That left one major problem to be overcome. Ships entering Penang harbour, especially warships, had to start identifying themselves properly, and the French commanders needed daily schedules so they would know what ships to expect.

Unfortunately, Cochrane was leaving Penang shortly to take *Zhemtchug*'s French convoy across to Colombo. The French commanders were very concerned that the new security arrangements for the harbour would be abandoned as soon as Cochrane's back was turned.

On the day that *Zhemtchug* arrived in Penang, *Yarmouth* was temporarily absent.[21] She had been ordered to take a look down the west coast of Sumatra around Simeulue Island. The Admiralty had heard persistent rumours that a merchant ship flying the Greek flag was anchored off the southern tip of Simeulue. It was known that *Emden* had been in company with *Pontoporos* in the Bay of Bengal, and it seemed just possible that this might be her. *Pontoporos* was outside territorial waters, at a spot where the sea was shallow enough for her to drop anchor. The Dutch had two ships keeping a close watch on her, but as usual they passed no information to the British. All the British got was a rumour. That rumour was to prove correct, because the ship that the Dutch had been watching so intently was indeed *Pontoporos*.

In the early morning of 12th October, *Yarmouth* arrived at the spot, to find not one, but two, steamers. The second one was *Markomannia*, which had just arrived from the Maldives. Cochrane correctly assumed that they were waiting for *Emden. Markomannia* made a dash for Dutch territorial waters, but *Yarmouth* was too fast and headed her off with a shot across the bows. At that point *Markomannia* surrendered. *Yarmouth* took sixty German prisoners from *Markomannia* and both of the *Emden*'s officers who had been part of the prize crew on *Pontoporos*.[22]

Cochrane then sent a British prize crew aboard the *Pontoporos*, and *Markomannia* was sunk. It is not clear why Cochrane ordered this. *Markomannia* was quite a prize. She was a new collier, British built and capable of fast cruising speeds. She was in good condition, apart from some rust and dents in the hull from coaling at sea with *Emden*. She had served *Emden* unstintingly throughout the previous two months. It was a sorry end to a fine ship. Cochrane took possession of the ship's log and for the first time was able to retrace *Emden*'s exact movements since leaving Pagan. It became clear just how close Grant's squadron had been to capturing her.[23]

By sending *Pontoporos* to hang around Simeulue for too long, von Müller was indeed taking a risk; one too many, in fact. The ship was bound to be spotted by the Dutch authorities in Sumatra, and sooner or later rumours would leak out. In all this, von Müller was relying on strict Dutch neutrality. But it is likely that he regarded her recapture by the Allies as an acceptable outcome now that he had *Buresk*. At that stage of the game he may even have regarded the *Markomannia* as expendable.

Pontoporos slowly followed *Yarmouth,* and in the early morning of 16th October they were back in Penang. They caused quite a stir, especially aboard *Zhemtchug*, just freshly arrived the day before. The realisation that *Emden* might be making an early rendezvous with these captured colliers sent *Chikuma* scurrying back to the shipping lanes by Acheh. *Hampshire* was still on the other side of the Bay of Bengal, near Ceylon, but now Grant knew of the capture and was aware that *Emden* must have been contemplating a return to Simeulue at some time in the near future.

This time it was von Müller who was in the dark. He had no idea that his expected quarry, *Dupleix,* had long since gone across to Colombo and was heading towards Aden. Instead, waiting for him, were *Chikuma, Yarmouth* and *Zhemtchug*.

Penang was buzzing, and the *Straits Times* reported:

> Dawn had not yet broken yesterday (16th) when *Yarmouth* steamed into Penang harbour and took up a position just off the lighthouse with the Greek collier nestling close by her side looking

like an ugly duckling, seeking to hide herself beneath the wing of her grim-visaged, but more prepossessing-looking sister.

Signals from the cruiser soon appraised those on shore that she was on business of more than usual import and as day broke over the Island there were signs of much activity in George Town. [The Penang] Volunteers were hastily summoned for special duty and as rapidly assembled. A body of the military police marched down to the quay. At half-past eight Penang saw sixty German prisoners of war who had been captured on the high seas, marched through the streets of the town under armed guard, with a detachment of police before and behind and Volunteers on either side. The German prisoners were marched to the jail where they were placed temporarily, pending removal to Singapore.

The spectacle created a great impression in the town. To the Asiatics it was a convincing and useful demonstration of the work of the Navy. It was sound ocular proof that, though rarely seen and never heard of, they were out on the wide waters of the Indian Ocean. British seamen leading strenuous lives in order that the people of Penang may continue to pursue the even tenor of their way in tranquillity.

The prisoners numbered forty seven men and thirteen officers. Two of the Officers are Imperial German navy officers belonging to the *Emden*. All the others are the crew of the *Markomannia,* which was a Hamburg-Amerika liner.[24]

The correspondent went on to say that *Emden* was in all probability very close by because they never heard of the one ship without the other. On questioning, the captain of *Pontoporos* said he had been captured just a few days before, on Saturday 10th October and was ordered to follow *Emden*, but he did not know her present whereabouts.

This amusing account is interesting for several reasons. The reporter got the date of *Pontoporos'* capture wrong. Perhaps, for obvious reasons, the Greek captain did not want to be identified as a collaborator. The report is written in very confident tones with much British patriotic verve, clearly intended to inspire the Asiatics about British might and supremacy. The article does not make any reference to the French, who were also there, defending Penang harbour and the Straits. The writer ignored them. But pride comes before a fall, and this kind of attitude did nothing to tighten up the extremely lax security arrangements for the harbour, which were shortly to prove its undoing.

It is astonishing that the Penang harbour authorities still did not raise their level of alertness, or order lookouts, or do anything beyond Audemard's recommendations, despite this clear indication of a possible imminent attack. They knew from Colombo that *Emden* was recently active over there and she would not take long getting to the east side of the Bay of Bengal with two of her colliers apparently waiting at a rendezvous. What were they waiting there for? The prisoners who *Yarmouth* had captured, however, had little information to impart. Von Müller was a canny operator; he did not share his plans with anyone, unless and until it was absolutely necessary.

On 14th October *Pontoporos* was turned over to *d'Iberville,* to be escorted to Singapore. There, the tricky legal question of ownership and prize money would have be thrashed out. They were scheduled to leave for Singapore the next day[25] and *Pontoporos* still had over half her cargo of coal intact.

Cochrane now had the job of taking over *Zhemtchug*'s convoy from Captain Cherkasov. He had only a very short time to confer with *Zhemtchug,* but took the opportunity to speak to Lieutenant Maund, explaining some of the difficulties that the Allied warships were having with the harbour authorities. The French officers must have viewed the departure of Cochrane with dismay and now their own Audemard, was also leaving for Singapore.

It was most unlikely that Captain Cherkasov, or the captain of *Chikuma* for that matter, would have much influence on Commander MacIntyre, despite their seniority. The security of Penang harbour was once again exposed to his irresponsible practices. The moment Cochrane left Penang, the security arrangements that he and Audemard had insisted upon were recklessly dismantled.

News from the other side of the Bay of Bengal was vital if the risk of a further attack was to be properly assessed. The same day that *Yarmouth* left Penang with her convoy, bound for Colombo, *Hampshire* was nearing Diego Garcia. *Empress of Asia* got there just ahead of her. It was only then that the islanders of Diego Garcia were able to give the British the unwelcome news that they had missed *Emden* yet again. Grant's worst fears were confirmed and he had to explain, to his acute embarrassment, this sorry state of affairs to the astonished inhabitants.

Of course the news got out very quickly, to the British government's chagrin, with Churchill at the Admiralty and Louis Battenberg the First Sea

Lord thoroughly embarrassed. The press had a field day. 'High comedy on the High Seas' blared the headlines. They especially loved the story about the motorboat. In truth, the press and, to some extent, the British public were beginning to develop an admiration for *Emden* and her intrepid captain. Von Müller had acted with great consideration and old-fashioned chivalry towards his victims. The tonnage he had sent to the bottom was prodigious but, excepting Madras, nobody had died. His prisoners were treated with great politeness and respect, being sent back to the nearest friendly port as soon as it could be arranged. Captain Robinson and the *Kabinga* had even given *Emden* three cheers.

Von Müller's exemplary conduct can be explained in several ways. It was clearly in his nature to respect non-combatants with scrupulous care, and in those days wars were not expected to involve non-combatants in any serious bloodshed. The *Emden* crew also knew that they themselves would be captured sooner or later. Finally, it is important to remember the cordial relations between the British and the Germans in prewar Tsing Tao. It seems likely that von Müller may have been reluctant to fire on his British friends unnecessarily, at least not unless he had to.

It was on the same day that *Pontoporos* was being escorted into Penang that *Emden's* wireless operators intercepted the signal 'en clair', mentioned at the end of the last chapter, advising west-bound shipping from Colombo to pass 40 miles to the north of Minicoi.[26] This was too good a chance to miss, so instead of heading straight for Penang, von Müller decided that *Emden* should investigate the shipping lanes to the west of Ceylon, this time around Minicoi.

Minicoi is a small coral island with a large lagoon lying 200 nautical miles to the west of India's southern tip. Even today the island is well known to tourists and scuba-divers, with an extraordinary variety of corals. It has a resident population of about 5,000, greatly enhanced in the tourist season. A hundred years ago, however, the island was little more than a sailor's landmark on the Aden to Colombo shipping lane.

The first prize *Emden* captured was the British cargo ship *Clan Grant*. Prinz Hohenzollern described the event:

> We turned towards the ship and ordered her to stop. Lauterbach and Fikentscher were sent over and reported 'English ship *Clan Grant*'.
>
> Further reports stated that the cargo consisted of live cattle,

flour, cakes, a good quantity of other provisions and quantities of beer and cigarettes. We were not a little delighted. The positively luxurious supplies of provisions of all kinds decided our captain to give the order for the ship to follow us. In the next few days the *Clan Grant* was to be emptied as much to our advantage as possible.[27]

It seems the ship was carrying everything they could ever need; a positive treasure trove. Representatives from each of *Emden*'s departments were sent over to salvage anything they needed for their stores. Soon, *Emden* spotted more smoke, but on approaching this particular ship, the crew had great difficulty figuring out just what kind of vessel she was. She was certainly very slow.

Laughter broke over the *Emden* at the discovery that the stranger was a deep-sea dredger. Lauterbach and Schall went aboard. She was the *Ponrabbel* on her way from England to Tasmania. Lauterbach was still more surprised to find the ship's company with their things already packed and ready to leave the ship.

When the dredger's men saw the *Emden* approaching they had packed their possessions and stood by the railings ready to leave the ship. The crew were delighted by the capture. This was the second crew who had set out for Tasmania in a dredger. The first had gone down during a severe storm and the present crew, including the captain, had demanded their whole wages in advance as compensation for the danger of navigating such a small vessel on the high seas. The voyage had been bad enough and the crew had often been threatened with the fate for the first dredger. They were therefore thankful at being delivered from the danger of death by drowning and expressed without reserve, their gratitude to the *Emden*'s ship's company.[28]

The crew from the dredger settled down cheerfully in *Buresk,* along with the crew from *Clan Grant*. It was 16th October, and *Emden*'s crew would have been very depressed to learn that *Markomannia* was already sunk. But they did not find that out for a while.

The next day *Emden* stopped another ship, *Ben Mohr*. She was carrying another valuable cargo of machinery, motor-cars, locomotives, bicycles, various engines and a new up-to date motor-boat. There was no point in salvaging any of this because *Emden* was already bursting at the seams. *Ben Mohr* was sunk and the crew squeezed aboard *Buresk*.

Finding nothing more around the Colombo–Aden shipping lane, von Müller decided to try his luck further north along the Colombo-to-Bombay route. Next day they were rewarded, taking their greatest prize of all – *Troilus* of the Blue Funnel line. She was carrying a valuable cargo including copper, tin and rubber.

At this point, Prinz Hohenzollern related an amusing anecdote. On board *Troilus* were a number of passengers, and one of them soon recognised Lauterbach.

> On the deck the lady suddenly came up to him with the words 'Mr. Lauterbach! How are you?' - Speechlessness on the part of the prize officer accompanied by searchings of memory. With great vivacity the lady explained that she had spent a few days on board the *Staatssekretär Krätke*, the former command of Lauterbach's. Naturally Lauterbach could not remember her, for the big German ship carried a large number of passengers whom the captain did not especially notice. The English woman must have been impressed or pleased by Lauterbach's martial appearance for she recognised him at once. I cannot say what effect the sharpness of her memory had on Lauterbach. Like a typical Englishwoman this lady was very amused by the capture of the ship by *Emden* and particularly by Mr. Lauterbach! [29]

He added that the captain of *Troilus* gave vent to his feelings of frustration and in a fit of anger, blurted out that the English held the safest route to be thirty miles north of the Aden to Colombo shipping route. [30]

Von Müller soon made use of that valuable intelligence. Some time later, when he had calmed down, the captain of *Troilus* gave this description of Lauterbach: 'A fine big man, very tall and well-built and he was extremely nice to us.' [31] There were far too many people aboard *Troilus* to effect any transfer, so for the moment she was ordered to follow behind *Emden*. The passengers then got a fine view of *Emden* at work as they stopped their next ship.

The steamer was *St Egbert* which had left Colombo on 17th October bound for Aden, had followed the maximum diversion possible to the north of Minicoi. *Emden* was in just the right place and captured her. Unfortunately her cargo was bound for New York, so it could not be touched. Instead, she was used as another *Lumpensammler* and all the prisoners were transferred into her. Before she was sent off, *Emden* captured yet another ship, this time the collier *Exford*, which was loaded with the very best Cardiff coal.

Perhaps it is worth putting in a word here about best Cardiff coal. There were few machines in the mines in those days; mostly men and ponies. The Welsh miners dug every ton of coal using pickaxes, down on their knees or lying partly on their sides, in the tight confines and narrow seams of the deep pits of the Rhondda. This coal was the very best; but it did come at considerable human cost.

Now *Emden* had two colliers, with the very best quality coal. They had enough to last them a whole year. *Emden* had been at sea since the beginning of August and was full up with stores and equipment from *Clan Grant* and *Troilus*. She had never been so well provisioned. They took just one more ship, a brand-new one called *Chilkana*. She had an excellent wireless, so that was dismantled and transferred to *Exford*.

It is tempting to think just what might have happened if Grant in *Hampshire* had thought of going north of Minicoi at that moment. *Emden* had five ships around her: *Buresk*, *Exford*, *Troilus*, *St Egbert* and now *Chilkana*. Seven officers and sixty of her own crew were aboard these other ships. Stores and people were being transferred from one ship to another, and for a while it must have looked chaotic. But after many hours of work it was sorted out. *Exford* and *Buresk* were well provisioned, with some of *Emden*'s crew aboard both. Some Chinese stokers aboard *Exford* were willing to work, provided they were paid.

The remaining English crew from *Exford* were put aboard *St Egbert* which, crowded like a troop-ship, made for Cochin on the Indian mainland. *Troilus* and *Chilkana* were then sunk.[32]

There was much consternation when, three days later, in the early morning of 20th October, *St Egbert* put into Cochin on the south-west coast of India, bearing the news that between 15th and 20th October, she and six other steamers had been captured by *Emden,* and all within the neighbourhood of Minicoi.[33] The tally, after only five days' work, was five ships sunk, one captured and one set free with the prisoners aboard.

Troilus was incredibly well built, and the *Emden* crew had the very devil of a job sinking her. It took several hours, even after opening sea-cocks, setting explosive charges and then shelling her. *Troilus* was a great loss to the British. She was a brand new cargo ship with an extremely valuable cargo – 10,000 tons of rubber, copper and tin, valued at over £1,000,000 sterling.

Apart from being a lot of money in those days, the loss of her cargo was a setback for Britain's war effort. The *Penang Gazette* reported the loss of *Troilus* as especially worrying. 'It is difficult to understand how she [*Emden*], has succeeded in escaping detection.'

In subsequent articles, the *Gazette* commented that the value of *Troilus*' cargo was huge. A sharp rise in the price of rubber and tin on world markets was reported, and the usual theories of secret radio messages from the Indian mainland were put forward.[34] The *Gazette* later reported that: -

> The rise at Kuala Lumpur in the price of imported foodstuffs from India, owing to the activity of the *Emden,* has been severely felt by the Indian community. Indian rice and curry materials, together with vegetables, have all gone up causing a great increase in living expenses. In view of this it is probable that efforts will be made to grow locally some of the articles at present imported.[35]

The Gazette also reported an interview with Captain Archdeacon of *Chilkana*, who had been put ashore with *St Egbert* in Cochin. As she was the last of the ships to be captured, the crew missed most of the action.

> If [*Emden*] had not caught the *Buresk,* she would have had to intern herself in a neutral port owing to lack of fuel. Captain Archdeacon estimates that the loss caused by the latest raid at between £4,000,000 and £5,000,000 sterling. The captain adds that the *Emden* knows exactly the sailings of different vessels and has communication from somewhere. Other officers of the *Chilkana* state that the *Emden* has, by recent captures, obtained 14,000 tons of the best Welsh Admiralty coal. This is sufficient for twelve months.[36]

The *Gazette* then added breathlessly that one passenger believed there was a mutiny aboard *Emden*, but that was wishful thinking. Clearly, the shock had increased the British authorities' suspicions that *Emden* was being directed by spies with secret radio transmissions coming from the Indian mainland. In truth, the lack of control over their own ships' 'en clair' transmissions and their own local newspapers was as far as *Emden* ever needed to look.

It was now 20th October and, since leaving Tsing Tao at the beginning of August, *Emden* had captured or sunk no fewer than twenty-three merchant ships. Now, it was time for *Emden* to disappear once again.

Jerram, meanwhile, was under pressure to provide more armed escorts. Deciding that Direction Island was not under threat, at least not for the present, he decided that *Ibuki* and *Minotaur* should be sent to Wellington to pick up ten New Zealand transports and escort them to Albany, calling in at Hobart on the way. There they were to await escort duties for the large Australian convoy.

Thus, two of Jerram's heavy cruisers were well away from *Emden*'s vicinity and Direction Island was left unguarded.[37]

Chapter 7

The Problems in Penang get worse

Back in Penang, two days before *Emden* started harvesting more cargo ships off Minicoi, the French already knew she had been active around Ceylon sinking ships left, right and centre, so it was essential that their ships should be brought back into full working order as soon as possible.

It was 13th October, and the by-now exasperated Commander Castagné delivered a formal letter to Audemard urging him to deal with the French destroyers' engines. He was a man of action, intolerant of inefficiency, and the situation in Penang had tried his patience to the very utmost.

> I need to emphasise the fact that into October after two months of uninterrupted patrols, the mechanical state of the destroyers is now far from brilliant! ... The ships left Saigon in a hurry without being prepared for service in time of war. I wish to draw the Commander's attention to the fact that they can not hope to last out ready for all eventualities unless each month, one destroyer is taken out of service completely, for ten consecutive days, in order to undergo a thorough schedule of maintenance.[1]

Castagné added that the number of useful working hours that remained in the ship's small boilers could not, at present, be wasted, with long periods spent waiting in harbour with steam up. He added that there were still major problems communicating with the Naval 'Intelligence' Officer. The

French always referred to MacIntyre sarcastically as the 'Intelligence' Officer, using inverted commas around the word 'Intelligence'.[2]

Castagné copied this letter to headquarters in Saigon, where Captain de Paris de Boisrouvray would receive it. In this way, he hoped Admiral Jerram would be put in the picture.

This was *Zhemtchug*'s first day in Penang. The next day, *Yarmouth* departed for Colombo and *Zhemtchug* took her place as the cruiser on guard. On board *Zhemtchug*, with his own cabin (a rare privilege for so junior an officer), was the young liaison officer Lieutenant Maund. His job was to brief Cherkasov regarding Jerram's orders. Before he left, Cochrane explained to Maund the arrangements in Penang, pointing out that immobile warships undergoing repairs should not be moored in the exposed outer harbour.

Cochrane added that *Yarmouth*, when she was fully operational, would normally take up a position in the outer harbour's special warship anchorage, with an additional stern anchor laid out to moor the ship broadside on. This would bring maximum firepower to bear on any intruder. The stern anchor would ensure that his ship did not swing at anchor with the tides. Any enemy warship approaching via the harbour roads would be at almost ninety degrees to his own ship when they drew level, thus making *Yarmouth* a difficult target for enemy underwater torpedoes.

Cochrane would also have explained that from then on, the harbour lights would be switched off at night and ships' movements restricted. Lieutenant Maund was then left with the job of communicating all this to the Russian Captain[3]

But orders now came from Jerram directing *Zhemtchug* to leave Penang immediately to search the Andaman and Nicobar Islands for any German warships or, more likely, other coal tenders. That meant putting off once more the need to attend to her boilers. She needed a full week to shut down all fourteen of her boilers and get them thoroughly cleaned; she was consuming far too much coal and barely able to make ten knots. The next day however, (16th October), despite the awful state of her boilers, *Zhemtchug* departed for ten days' patrol in the direction of Rangoon. She searched the Andaman and Nicobar Islands, covering the Mergui Archipelago on the return journey.[4]

The three small French destroyers were now on their own. *D'Iberville* had already left Penang, escorting *Pontoporos* to Singapore, with the prisoners sent by train under armed escort. *Pontoporos* was due for adjudication by the Prize Court in order to decide whether the British should be given any prize money for her capture. She still had a quantity of coal aboard, and that cargo was supposed to be British.

A group of naval military and civil officials awaited her arrival and went aboard when she came alongside in the Lagoon Dock. Mr. M. Rodesse, the Marshal appointed under the rules to be observed in prize proceedings had with him a writ issued by the Attorney-General against the owner. He fixed it on the mainmast.[5]

That was a curiously theatrical maritime tradition to be sure – nailing legal papers to the mainmast. The court ruled that *Pontoporos* was liable to 'condemnation' because of her collaboration with an enemy warship.[6]

There was considerable excitement over the German prisoners, mostly taken from the crew of *Markomannia*. The *Penang Gazette* quoted a report taken from the *Malay Mail*, reporting that sixty-two men belonging to the German Navy had passed through Kuala Lumpur railway station on the way to being interned at Singapore. They all seemed to accept their position philosophically, except one petty officer who actually cried, ashamed to have been taken prisoner. The article continued:

> One of *Emden*'s officers had been aboard *Pontoporos*, and the manner in which the *Emden* is alleged to have befooled a Japanese armoured cruiser is recounted. It seems that on leaving Kiao Chow the Chief Engineer rigged up a dummy funnel. A great deal of the success which has attended the *Emden* raids in the Bay of Bengal was due to the luck she experienced in tapping all sorts of wireless messages.[7]

One of *Emden*'s officers, Lieutenant Meyer, described as 'open and debonair', said that they were sorry to have sent so many ships to the bottom;

> But we had no port where we could take them and so, though we were sorry to do so, we had to send them to the bottom where we will go ourselves shortly. *Emden* should not expect a long career; sooner or later she will be sent to the bottom to keep company with the ships she has sent below herself.[8]

There were two very significant points in this report. First, *Emden*'s ruse of the dummy funnel was now made very public. Henceforth there

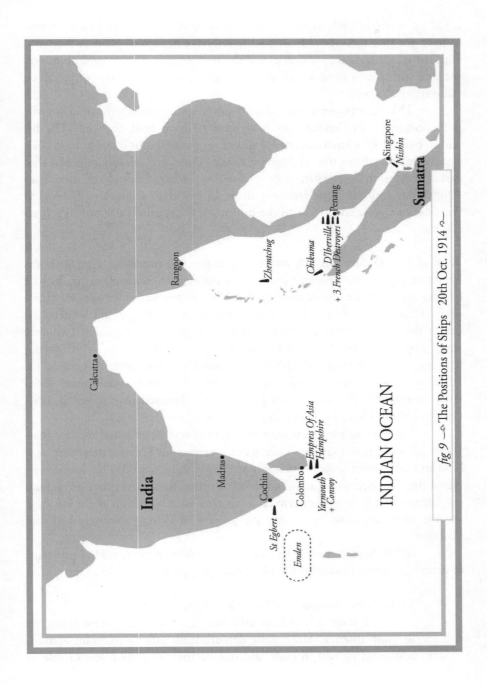

fig 9 ～ The Positions of Ships   20th Oct. 1914 ～

could be no excuse for anyone being fooled by it. Nobody in Penang seems to have got that message although it should have been very plain to the naval authorities. Perhaps they did not read the newspapers. The second point was the ease with which *Emden* gathered intelligence merely by monitoring Allied radio transmissions.

This newspaper article should have been a timely warning for the port authorities in Penang, but they seem to have paid no heed. The bit about 'befooling' a Japanese cruiser was never verified, but it could have been a recycled story from one of *Markomannia*'s crew. It probably refers to that earlier incident before Japan came into the war, when *Emden* had sailed from Tsing Tao, and two large Japanese ships dipped their colours to *Emden,* to von Müller's great surprise! But the dummy fourth funnel was not rigged up till much later.

With *d'Iberville* now on her way to Singapore, Commander Castagné was left in charge of the French squadron in Penang. It seems amazing, but he had no access to the cipher used by the Allies to transmit messages by radio. Only Audemard had that. With Audemard away, nothing could be decoded except through the Penang signal station. Castagné had complained volubly about this before, but received an emollient reply from Jerram's staff, saying that not many copies of the cipher were available. This stands to reason, but it did not excuse the exclusion of Audemard's second-in-command from vital information. If radio signals had arrived addressed to Audemard, then Castagné should have been able to read them.

On one occasion Castagné intercepted several encoded radio signals which he could not decipher. They seemed suspicious because they were very loud and came from close by; possibly an enemy ship. Next day he notified the Naval 'Intelligence' Officer and was not surprised to discover that the signals in question had been made between a Japanese merchant ship and a Japanese warship that were close by, within the vicinity of Penang. Nobody had told Castagné.

In his characteristic style, Castagné tore off a tetchy letter to Audemard to greet his return. He added the bit about the Japanese warship at the end.

To the Commander of *d'Iberville* 21ˢᵗ Oct. 1914.

I must ask you to take notice of what has been going on in your absence. Since your departure an official telegram arrived, addressed to you in code and not having the code I was unable to decipher it.

I must take this occasion to bring to your attention the following complaint which I have already made to you verbally, and which I ask you to refer to the Vice Admiral [Jerram] Commander-in-Chief of Allied Flotillas. [In your absence] the two destroyers placed under my orders and myself were unable to communicate with other ships in the allied fleet, other than 'en clair', and this is prohibited.

I must be the only senior commander at sea without the ability to decipher coded signals. On 18th October, entirely alone off Diamond Point we were receiving quantities of signals between ships. If we had understood them it would have made a big difference to our task, allowing us to avoid a serious mistake. Without our knowing anything beforehand we might have had a very inappropriate encounter with a ship at night which we did not know was in our sector, and which ought not to have been there. In the end such information could have prevented a disaster. I protest vigorously about this situation.[9]

Castagné went on to recount that on 18th October he was receiving radio signals in an unidentifiable form repeated regularly throughout the night. The following evening, when *Pistolet* was back in harbour, the same signals were picked up again, very near. Because of this, his ship spent the night at action stations.

Next day I told the Harbour Master about it. When that officer arrived at his office at 10.00 a.m., I learned to my complete astonishment that it had been a Japanese [merchant] ship in the harbour roads which had permission from Singapore to call one of their warships throughout the night. Already back in harbour and entrusted with the defence of Penang, I was the only one who had not been informed and my crew passed the night at action stations for nothing.

At my lively reaction, the Harbour-Master replied that he was snowed under with work and had forgotten to warn me! I would be very grateful if you could repeat to him what I told him verbally, to understand that the next time he fails to show me consideration when I am in the harbour, which I regard as a vital role, I will lodge immediately an official complaint against him.[10]

In his report to the Saigon inquiry, Le Coispellier raised these matters with expressions of incredulity, noting that there was invariably a busy movement of merchant ships that came and went night and day so the French squadron, which had the job of defending Penang, had absolutely no idea what was going on from one day to the next.[11]

The inability of the destroyer squadron to decipher radio messages seemed to Le Coispellier to be an extraordinary situation.

> The destroyers did not have duplicates of the code allowing [signals] to be deciphered into conventional language, so that when *d'Iberville*, the sole possessor of this code was absent, they could not decipher received signals.

> There is no need to emphasise the inconvenience of these things and the serious consequences which could have resulted for our destroyers. Jerram did not disregard this situation which he deplored, but he still could not explain his failure to attend to the cause, which was the shortage of copies of the code.[12]

It meant that things in Penang were getting increasingly tense. With the airwaves buzzing with strange signals, the French destroyers felt compelled to return to Penang more and more frequently, if only to retrieve copies of their own messages from the Penang signal station after they had been decoded. Le Coispellier summed it up like this:

> From everything that has been recounted it is clear from the evidence that the French ships did not have the resources to inform themselves of an abundance of intelligence which was kept by the Naval Intelligence Officer. Too often these resources were nonexistent or defective.[13]

The French ships were small with limited firepower and to MacIntyre they were probably insignificant, or worse still, a nuisance. Perhaps it was just a matter of language ... who knows?

Over on the other side of the Bay of Bengal, Grant in *Hampshire* was in deep trouble. *St Egbert*'s shattering news from Cochin had arrived and was all over the newspapers. These new losses, in terms of precious cargoes, were so great, and *Emden* so close around Minicoi, that he must have felt at a complete loss as to what to do. These last merchant ships had been sunk beneath his very nose. But even then, Grant did not guess just how easily von Müller had come by the information that led him to those ships. Even the most casual remarks of captured crew, such as the German-speaking Chinese stokers aboard *Troilus*, all fitted together as valuable intelligence.[14] Some newspapers blamed clandestine, unpatriotic, traitorous dogs on the Indian mainland, whilst the *Times of Malaya* blamed the Dutch.[15]

Yarmouth, with her convoy of French transports from Penang, was now just a few hours off Colombo. They arrived there in the afternoon just as the news from *St Egbert* was breaking. The French convoy was immediately halted in Colombo instead of proceeding across to Aden. *Hampshire,* along with *Yarmouth* and *Empress of Asia*, led a frantic new hunt for *Emden*. On 22nd October *Yarmouth* quickly re-coaled, taking up her station between Colombo and Minicoi. It was a forlorn hope, because *Emden* was unlikely to go back there again.

The fragment of *Emden*'s signal log that was recovered contained a note written after *Ben Mohr* was captured. The skipper told von Müller that a large convoy had been seen near Socotra with *Askold* escorting them, heading for Aden. Von Müller therefore knew that on 17th October the powerful Russian cruiser was safely out of reach. The story about the angry captain of *Troilus* blurting out that merchant ships had been asked to pass 40 miles to the north of Minicoi was there in *Emden*'s log as well.[16]

When the British captured that fragment of the log, it allowed a careful reconstruction of *Emden*'s movements on the morning of 22nd October. Grant's three cruisers were searching the waters south of Ceylon in the hope of trapping *Emden* before she could slip away. This was a good strategy and could have paid off. Grant had worked out that *Emden* would have to coal very soon and might look for another quiet spot amongst the Maldives. This time it was a very near thing indeed. Whilst *Emden*, with her two prize colliers *Buresk* and *Exford*, was rounding the southern tip of Ceylon and heading back east towards the Bay of Bengal, Grant in *Hampshire*, in company with *Empress of Asia,* was heading west from Dondra Head, which is the southernmost tip of Ceylon. They almost met, but it was not to be.

Emden stopped in the open sea and arranged for stores to be passed to *Emden* from *Exford* before sending her off to a rendezvous 30 miles north of North Keeling in the Cocos Islands. Clearly von Müller had already decided to attack Direction Island as Jerram has suspected all along. But not quite yet. He asked *Exford* to remain there till 15th November, which was a month away.

The collier *Exford* now drops out of the narrative and was not seen again till she was rejoined by *Emden* heading for the Cocos Islands.

Emden steamed off eastwards with *Buresk* following close behind. This time she was heading for the Nicobar Islands. Keeping the two ships together at night, with no lights, and only able to use a signal lamp in an emergency, was exceedingly difficult. A signal in the surviving remnant of *Emden*'s log instructed *Buresk* that 1000 metres was far too big a gap at night.

None of them realised – neither the hunters nor the hunted – that *Empress of Asia* had just passed *Emden* by a hair's breadth. At 6.30 a.m. *Empress of Asia* and *Hampshire* had been steaming in a single line a few miles apart, and *Empress of Asia* altered course to take a position 20 miles on *Hampshire*'s starboard beam.[17] This brought her course directly in line with *Emden*. When, having reached the desired position, she turned to port, she was just a few miles from *Emden*. Heavy rain squalls obscured the view and *Emden*, with her two tenders, passed as little as five miles astern of *Empress of Asia*.[18] But none of that was known till much later.

Jerram's misfortunes were quickly descending into complete disaster. When added to the earlier sinking of so many ships off Colombo, *Emden*'s recent exploits off Minicoi from 15th to 19th October were completely humiliating. They were also shatteringly expensive – seven ships sunk or captured and a king's ransom gone to the bottom. At last this evoked in Jerram some real alarm. His messages to the Admiralty contain for the first time a ring of panic. Perhaps he thought that he might experience some kind of public humiliation. Now he was calling upon the Japanese to dig him out of a hole.

> In view of the urgent need of additional ships to deal with attacks on the trade routes such as are being made by *Emden*, I represented the seriousness of the situation to the Japanese Admiralty, with a view to their sending reinforcements.
>
> In reply, they propose to form a new squadron to operate in the Indian Ocean under the command of a Vice Admiral and composed of the ships originally placed directly under my orders, with the addition of *Tokiwa* and *Yakumo*. The desired objects would thus be attained though in a different manner to that contemplated by me, and as a Japanese Vice Admiral would be senior to the Commander-in-Chief of the East Indies Station, I have referred the matter for a decision to their Lordships.[19]

Jerram then went on to admit that the shipping lanes that merchant ships were using were much too predictable. Ships would now be asked to steer more erratic courses, scattered widely on both sides of their usual track and avoiding smoke. It would have been sensible if he had also advised transmission in cipher or, better still, radio silence. The Japanese were now asking for *Hampshire* and *Yarmouth* to be, more or less, under the command of a Japanese Admiral.

Jerram's pride must have been deeply hurt. The Japanese were wanting to take their ships away from him and also asking for the best of his *Emden* hunting squadron, who were henceforward to take orders from a Japanese Admiral. It sounded as if the Japanese really had no confidence in Jerram's ability to command, or even to do his job properly. The message was clear enough. The British Admiralty actually went one stage further and suggested that the Japanese take command of all the Allied ships engaged in the *Emden* hunt on the east side of the Bay of Bengal. That was Jerram's 'side' of the Indian Ocean.[20] It is interesting to speculate that the hand of Churchill could be discerned behind that suggestion.

All of this was going to take time to arrange. For the moment, Grant had to carry on as best he could. That meant guarding the focal points where merchant shipping converged. One of these points was Ceylon, and *Hampshire* and *Empress of Asia* patrolled that area.

Zhemtchug was covering other likely hiding places around the Nicobar and Andaman Islands as far north as Rangoon. Whilst he was there, Captain Cherkasov called on the Burma Governor-General and was told that he was wasting his time up there at the mouth of the Irrawaddy. *Emden,* he was told, was miles away to the south in the Indian Ocean.[21] Unfortunately this was probably a reference to newspaper reports about Diego Garcia and, by that time, very out of date. The Governor-General may have been rather old and unused to reckoning with the speed of steamships.

It was 23rd October and *Emden* and her two colliers had not been heard of for several days. Von Müller did not know it but, far away to the east, *Emden*'s old naval base at Tsing Tao was getting a real pounding from the Japanese and the British. The *Penang Gazette* reported that:

> The Tsing Tao fortifications are strong but its fall is only a matter of time. The Japanese may be trusted to possess a thorough knowledge of the place and the quickest way of reducing it

to submission.[22]

The strategic point was Prinz Heinrich Berg, a large hill overlooking Tsing Tao, from which bombardment of the base by Allied cruisers at sea could be seen and directed. Jerram's battleship *Triumph* was there along with the Japanese cruisers *Iwami* and *Suwo*. It was the battle for this hill that was now under way. Once it was taken, the naval bombardment would soon finish off Tsing Tao, cutting off the German ships from their only base forever.[23]

Meanwhile, aboard *Emden,* there was a new air of expectation. She was steaming quietly eastwards towards her next objective – Penang. Hitherto *Emden* had pursued every wisp of smoke on the horizon in the hope of capturing another prize, and by night she chased after every light she saw. But now she did the opposite. It was essential to steer clear of every ship to avoid being discovered.

During this period of quiet, the ship needed to get fully prepared, because this would be her biggest test. In Penang she was expecting to find at least one of the large French cruisers, possibly *Dupleix,* which could inflict an awful lot of damage on *Emden.*

Keeping well to the south of the shipping lanes between Singapore and Colombo, *Emden*'s crew had several days to practise their drill. The torpedo crews, the engine-room crews and the gunners all needed daily practice, whilst the little ship's hospital had to be cleared for casualties. By day, the gunners practised on a target pulled by *Buresk,* while keeping a sharp lookout for smoke on the horizon, this time for avoidance. After dark, *Emden* cruised without lights and, although she passed one or two ships in the night, she was never spotted. At night *Buresk* followed closely in line astern, so they would not lose touch of each other in the absence of radio or lights.[24]

For *Emden*'s crew this was a good opportunity to tidy things up and make life as bearable as possible. Germans love to sing songs with a good martial beat, and the ship's band would pump out these numbers to order, raising the crew's spirits. In those days the British were much the same, although their preference was for bawdy songs from the music-halls. This brief period of tranquillity was in stark contrast to the upheavals that were going on in Penang.

It was at exactly this time that something about the need for urgent repairs to the wheezing *Zhemtchug* must have got through to Jerram. Perhaps it was Castagné's angry letter because, about a week after it was sent, the overhaul of

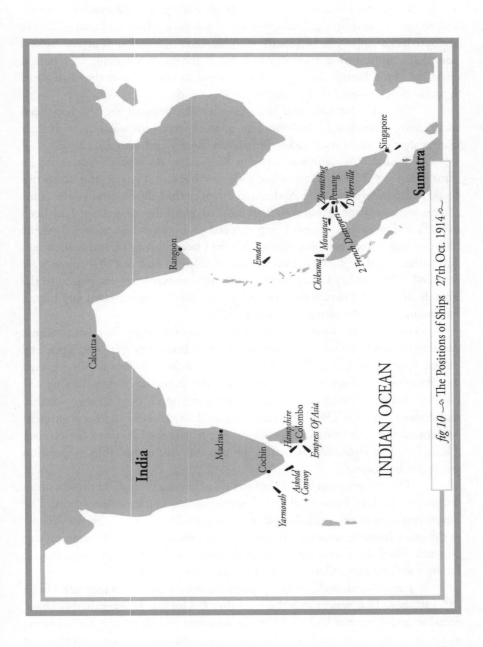

fig 10 ～ The Positions of Ships 27th Oct. 1914 ～

all the destroyers, together with *Zhemtchug,* was agreed. *Zhemtchug's* boilers and engines were thoroughly clogged up. Once she got back to Penang, Jerram granted her a full week of repairs with thirteen out of her fourteen boilers completely shut down and prepared for a thorough cleaning.[25] A radical overhaul of the French destroyers was planned to take place at the same time. A worse time to do all that could not be imagined.

On 21st October, two months after the original request had been made, leave to anchor in the inner part of the harbour for warships with their boilers shut down or undergoing repairs was finally authorised.

Whilst *d'Iberville* was away in Singapore, no repair work could be done,[26] but on 22nd October, *d'Iberville* was back in Penang and the work could begin. Only then did Audemard discover that all the arrangements for the security of Penang harbour that he had painfully negotiated had been cancelled; this, despite patrols being reduced to three destroyers only.[27] All the harbour lights were back on, just as they had been in August and September, and unrestricted night-time movements of ships in and out of Penang were resumed.[28] No further information about ships' movements was passed to the French squadron. History does not relate whether *Chikuma* fared any better, but it can be reliably assumed that she did not.

In fact, the work on the ships could not begin just yet, because Audemard was ordered to investigate a suspicious ship that had appeared in the vicinity of Pulau Weh. *D'Iberville, Pistolet* and *Fronde* all departed to investigate, leaving *Mousquet* to cover the patrol area. On leaving the North Channel, Audemard found himself confronted by a strange warship manoeuvring wildly. The ship had not hoisted any colours and for a moment Audemard thought he was under attack, but finally she identified herself over a loud hailer as Japanese.[29] Whether she was the 'suspicious' ship in question will never be known.

The investigation turned out to be a wild goose chase and the squadron did not get back to Penang till 25th October, having found nothing more. The 'suspicious' cruiser was probably Japanese, and could either have been *Chikuma* or the other Japanese warship *d'Iberville* had just encountered. Communications between Allied ships were clearly at an all-time low and it can not have helped Jerram's sinking reputation with the Japanese high command.

Jerram's orders allowing repairs to the ships were due to take effect from 25th October. That was exactly the time that *Emden* was nearing the Nicobars. Suitable arrangements had to be made to allow the ships due for servicing to tie up in the inner harbour. To begin with, MacIntyre suggested that the

French destroyers should anchor up the muddy Prai River. This suggestion was breathtakingly disrespectful because in those days the river was not dredged and they would be at the mercy of the tides in order to move in and out.[30] Under pressure, MacIntyre finally offered the French destroyers the southern part of Swettenham Pier, but he could only offer one berth.

For this reason, the two destroyers had to be tied up side by side. As *Fronde* needed urgent repairs, her boilers were shut down completely and she took the inside berth. That meant she was unable to use her guns or torpedoes, or even cast off. *Pistolet* was to be the guard-ship with her boilers at one hour's stand-by, but she was also in need of repairs with one of her engine-bearings defective and overheating due to faulty lubrication. Audemard insisted that a steam launch be put at their disposal, ready with steam up so that *Pistolet* could be towed off in a hurry if necessary. *D'Iberville* was given an anchorage close by, slightly to the south but near enough, because her wireless could no longer transmit.[31]

From now on only one destroyer would be out in the northern Malacca Straits and three in harbour. With a busy schedule of repairs, only one would have steam up, with a second at three hours' notice. The third would be shut down but ready to get steam up and cast off as soon as it was practicable. *D'Iberville* was getting a thorough overhaul; boilers, engines wireless, electrical equipment, everything – and for that she had to be entirely shut down without power, apart from a few batteries.

At the Saigon enquiry, the reason why so many ships were immobilised at once was gone into, and once again much of the blame seems to rest with Admiral Jerram. He had simply left everything far too late. For some reason he thought an attack on Penang was exceedingly unlikely, and MacIntyre agreed. Le Coispellier commented:

> The [French destroyer's engines] had been running almost without interruption, without proper inspection, for three months. After speaking to the Naval Intelligence Officer and enquiring from him if anything worrying was happening in their zone, Audemard was reassured and decided to let his chief engineer go ahead [with repairs].
>
> *Emden* was reported to be at the Chagos Islands making for the South. This reassurance was further reinforced when Jerram authorised *Zhemtchug* to stay at anchor for 7 days, inspecting and repairing her engines and cleaning her boilers.[32]

Audemard nevertheless decided to take the inner-harbour anchorage, which he did for the first time in two months. This probably prevented his ship from suffering the same fate as *Zhemtchug*.

There is an amusing insight into the maintenance of ship's equipment in the tropics. This report refers to the state of affairs in *d'Iberville* on 27th October.

> The steam-driven dynamo which supplied the power for the TSF, and the steam valve for that section, were being repaired. Hence the TSF was only able to receive [using batteries]; the role of transmission being passed over to *Pistolet*, as the destroyer on guard. Audemard then authorised the dismantling of the wireless for general inspection as well as regular disinfection.[33]

It seems that in the tropics wirelesses regularly went mouldy, which interfered with their efficient functioning. This will not be a surprise to present-day residents of Penang!

The lack of any serious effort by MacIntyre to set up better communications between the French ships and other Allied vessels is baffling. They could have used the Fort Cornwallis signal station. However, to decipher messages from Allied ships or Jerram's headquarters on the Royal Navy wavelength depended upon all the French commanders having access to the code-book. In the event, they could only communicate with each other on the French wavelength. The only conclusion that can be drawn is that the French ships, as well as the Russians, were not taken seriously. These failures were to lead to tragic consequences.

From 25th October onwards, *Chikuma* was ordered to patrol the more distant approaches to the Malacca Straits off Pulau Weh. Meanwhile, *Mousquet* and *Pistolet* were the only serviceable French destroyers available, and even *Pistolet* had engine trouble. With *d'Iberville* no longer able to use her transmitter, the patrolling destroyer had to be confined to the immediate vicinity of Penang, returning to anchor in the outer harbour each morning at 9.00 a.m.

Zhemtchug at last limped back into Penang and the servicing of her engines could begin. The ship would be immobile and not much of her fighting capability would be operational, including her torpedo tubes.

It was the usual practice throughout the navies of the world to allow shore leave when a ship was shut down for boiler-cleaning. Besides shore leave for many of *Zhemtchug*'s crew, others from *Fronde* and *d'Iberville* were given leave as well, consistent with the agreed watch-keeping rotas. Audemard felt this was very important for morale, allowing his men some brief respite from the harsh conditions they had been enduring for three months. But they still kept to the agreed watch-keeping rotas for the period of shutdown. Even those sailors who were off-watch very often slept near their machines or their guns, especially the deckhands, so they could be ready at a moment's notice.[34]

Audemard was a considerate man, as later events were to prove, and he could never have imagined that in the not too distant future this decision would be so severely criticised by his Commandant in Saigon.

The population of George Town was clearly much more worried about an imminent attack than Jerram was. The Penang pilot, William Brown, later recounted a conversation he had on the Penang quayside with one of *Emden*'s crew, captured from *Pontoporos*. He was surveying the scene of many merchant ships lying in Penang harbour:

> I spoke to a captured German Officer [possibly Lieutenant Meyer]. He had been full of confidence about the *Emden*'s ability to continue her lightning forays... 'And one day she will come here!'... He looked over the crowded anchorage.[35]

Yet Audemard allowed himself to be reassured that, for the next four days at least, there was no likelihood of that happening. In fact there was no basis whatever to commend such a lack of vigilance. Jerram could not have chosen a worse time to allow so many ships to be repaired at once. In truth, he had little option because *Zhemtchug* and the French destroyers had been seriously run down over many weeks.

There is an interesting caveat at this point. Someone, somewhere, had taken up the matter of German nationals in both Penang and Singapore. Clearly the idea of spies sending secret radio transmissions to *Emden* had really taken hold. All German nationals were to be rounded up and interned as enemy aliens. At last Captain Daveluy's concerns were being addressed. There were about thirty German nationals in Penang, hitherto merely kept under house arrest. They were now held in the Penang Club, earmarked for transport to Singapore.[36] Cross mentioned that there were others held in Fort Cornwallis, from which vantage point they were actually able to witness the forthcoming raid.[37]

However, Cherkasov was clearly unconcerned and decided to accept Jerram's offer of 7 days' shutdown. All of *Zhemtchug*'s boilers were doused, with just one left active to keep minimum power on. There was some correspondence between Lieutenant Maund and Jerram about this.[38] Jerram let Maund know that he wanted the job done faster, but Cherkasov could not do that because the Russian maintenance manual required the job to be done thoroughly using soda,[39] and that would take a week. Even if they worked night and day, six days was the minimum. This was not unreasonable, given that 14 boilers had to be done.

For the Russian crew it was in some ways worse than for the French. Their ship was larger, more comfortable and better ventilated with refrigerators on board, but now everything was shut down with only emergency power. The Russian crew were not used to tropical conditions. They had been on constant patrol and escort duty from Vladivostok, via the Philippines, to Hong Kong and thence to Saigon and Singapore with almost no respite. Those crewmen who could be spared were really in need of shore leave. Now that *Zhemtchug* was about to clean her boilers, those lucky crewmen given shore leave were ready to make the most of it.

In spite of *Zhemtchug*'s immobilisation, MacIntyre made the decision – contrary to his previous agreement – to put her back in the outer harbour.[40] This was probably because two French destroyers were already out of action and a third was patrolling out at sea. Only *Pistolet* was available to man the outer harbour but, as the Number 2 guard-ship, she had to be in close touch with *d'Iberville* because Audemard was temporarily deprived of radio communication. In fact, the only fully serviceable ship out of a total of five was *Mousquet*, and she was out on patrol to the north-west of Penang.

Nevertheless, Maund had some concerns. It may have been him who prompted MacIntyre to go aboard *Zhemtchug* and meet Captain Cherkasov, although it would have been part of his duty anyway. MacIntyre stressed that *Zhemtchug* had to be vigilant, even though he seems have been most unwilling to apply this excellent advice to himself.

Apparently Maund suggested deploying a stern anchor, as *Yarmouth* habitually used when in Penang, to hold the ship broadside on against the tide at the harbour entrance. In his letter to Jerram written after the event, Maund wrote:

> Eventually the Captain [Cherkasov] concurred and in my presence gave orders for it to be done to the Commander of the ship. I am unable to say whether the anchor was laid out, but in any case the ship was not hauled up, but lay up and down the tideway.

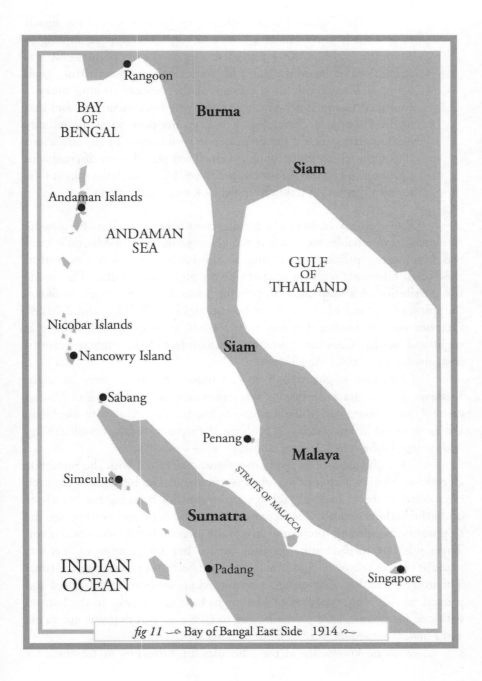

fig 11 ~ Bay of Bangal East Side 1914 ~

The Captain had previously been given a copy of the signals to be used in the event of a hostile or suspicious ship attempting to enter the harbour. Knowing what a poor system of look-out was maintained on board the ship I felt some doubt as to the alarm signals being seen, especially in the event of the weather turning misty. I consulted Commander MacIntyre and with his concurrence and that of the Captain of *Zhemtchug*, I took up my position at the military headquarters which is the first place to be informed of any suspicious ship approaching the harbour. A launch was placed at my disposal with steam up and by this means I hoped to be able to reach the ship in time to warn them, thus duplicating the look-out arrangements.[41]

The accuracy of Maund's recollections is hard to assess because he was such an unreliable witness, but the glaring omission in Maund's letter was MacIntyre's practice of keeping all the harbour lights on, as well as the North Channel, with no restrictions on night-time traffic. This made the possibility of a suspicious ship being identified exceedingly unlikely. Shipping in and out of the harbour on the nights of 26th/27th and 27th/28th October was not restricted in any way. Various ships came into Penang at night and neither Cherkasov nor the commanders of the French warships had any details of their movements.

Cherkasov might well have concluded that there were no signs whatever that an attack on Penang was either expected or likely. But Maund certainly knew about von Müller because he had been in action with *Emden* on the Yangtze and he knew that von Müller had a reputation for unpredictability and daring. Perhaps he felt safer ashore.

Thus the defence of the harbour entrance rested with the immobile *Zhemtchug*, albeit with her powerful guns still usable. Her big guns might even have done the trick, had she laid out a stern anchor bringing her broadside on to the harbour mouth. *Zhemtchug* could not use her torpedoes because the ship was immobile and four out of five of the torpedo tubes were underwater. There was one torpedo tube on deck astern, but no mention of this was made at the court martial and it may not have been in operation at the time. The irony is that had *Zhemtchug*'s port torpedo tubes been ready loaded and primed, as they were on *Pistolet*,[42] she might have sent *Emden* to the bottom with one lucky shot, hardly even having to take aim. But that was not to be, and *Pistolet*'s torpedoes were well out of range.

With no knowledge of the schedules for *Yarmouth*, or *Chikuma* for that matter, Audemard had no idea which warships, if any, were likely to come into Penang that night. In fact *Chikuma* was still patrolling off Acheh Head and might have returned at any time.

D'Iberville's position, close by Swettenham Pier, allowed her to communicate with *Pistolet* by signal lamp. She was also close enough to use semaphore, which in those days they could do as quickly as a young person taps out a text message today. Despite the lack of a wireless, quick communication between *d'Iberville* and *Pistolet* would not have presented any difficulties.

Many of *Zhemtchug*'s crew went ashore on the night of October 27th. As sailors do, they went out on the town in boisterous spirits and set about drinking the town dry.[43] This was by no means a particularly Russian thing, but somehow they could do it more thoroughly than anyone else. By late evening the launches plying to and from *Zhemtchug* were bringing the sailors back aboard.

> Those on shore-leave were in effect, completely plastered. The French sailors watching, reported that most of them were so dead drunk that they had to be tossed into the launches like so many parcels.[44]

Cherkasov, together with five of his officers including his second-in-command, Lieutenant Commander Kulibin, had gone ashore on the night of 27th/28th, doubtless believing that they were no less in need of shore leave than the crew. Cross's notes confirm that Cherkasov was booked into the Eastern & Oriental Hotel.[45] This was also confirmed in a report by the *Times of Malaya*.[46]

Earlier, the Baroness Varvara had caught the first available steamer from Singapore and whilst *Zhemtchug* was out on patrol she swept into Penang's Eastern & Oriental Hotel dressed in all her finery.[47] She later reported that her husband was rather unwell at the time he returned from patrol.[48]

By all accounts Baron Cherkasov and his wife were a remarkably devoted couple. Her arrival first in Singapore and now Penang was not unexpected as Cherkasov arranged for his wife to greet him at ports where his ship called. He would find a suitable berth for his wife on any ship that was headed in the right direction.[49] This was seriously frowned upon by the Russian naval authorities.

The Eastern & Oriental Hotel stands on the same spot today, right down by the water's edge, just to the west of Penang's outer harbour. Today the view of the harbour from the terrace of the Eastern & Oriental is partly obstructed by other buildings, but in those days you could see clear from the hotel towards the Esplanade and Fort Cornwallis. Captain Cherkasov and the Baroness had a fine view of his ship from there.

On the night of October 27th/28th Cherkasov must have noticed that *Zhemtchug* was not drawn up with an additional stern anchor. If indeed he had given the order, as Maund maintained, that would have been a serious lapse by his second-in-command. But there is no record that he was concerned about it. There was no proper organisation of watch-keepers, either, and the torpedo tubes were unloaded. Apart from half a dozen rounds each beside two of the starboard 120mm guns, the remaining artillery shells were in the store with the key hung on a nail somewhere, and impossible to find in a hurry.[50]

The way *Zhemtchug* lay at anchor that night, her bow was facing north, towards the outer-harbour mouth. Any ship coming in would have passed to her starboard side, with her 120mm guns at the ready. Only after the tide had turned in the early hours of next morning, would the ebb tide turn *Zhemtchug*'s only active guns 180 degrees, pointing directly towards George Town. *Zhemtchug*'s riding and anchorage lights were also on, besides the winking harbour lights.

Mousquet was on patrol that night, and cast off from her anchorage in the outer harbour into the waters north-west of Penang. She was due back at 9.00 a.m. the next morning to collect any communications from the signal station. Lieutenant Théroinne had no particular concerns about *Emden*. The French understood that she was far away to the south.

Catching up with what was actually happening on board *Emden,* we need to recapitulate a couple of days. At that time, *Emden*'s period of relative tranquillity was finally coming to an end. On 26th October, as she was nearing the Nicobars, there was another of those near-misses. A few miles to the east, *Zhemtchug* was cruising slowly down the Mergui Archipelago on her way back to Penang. Had Cherkasov chosen to do the round trip anti-clockwise, they would certainly have run into each other.[51]

When *Emden* reached the small island of Nancowry in the Nicobars, she dropped anchor in the harbour. As usual, the ever-romantic Prinz Hohenzollern described the scenery:

> Our ship was now lying in a bay that was perfectly beautiful.

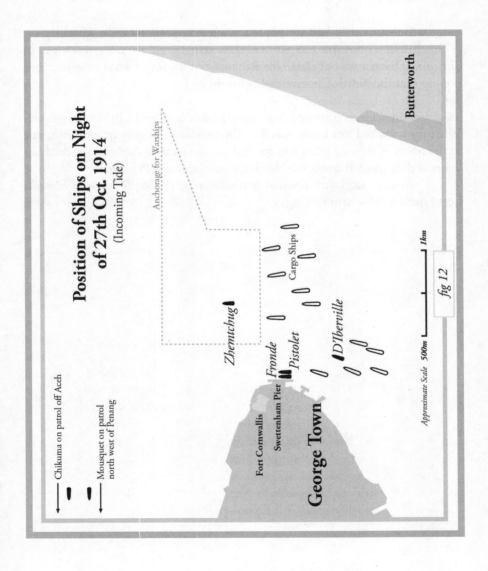

Position of Ships on Night
of 27th Oct 1914
(Incoming Tide)

Anchorage for Warships

Butterworth

Chikuma on patrol off Acch

Mousquet on patrol
north west of Penang

Fort Cornwallis
Swettenham Pier
George Town

Zhemtchug

Fronde
Pistolet

Cargo Ships

D'Iberville

Approximate Scale   500m   1km

fig 12

Nancowry harbour lies on the south side of the island and possesses fine, luxuriant, tropical vegetation, which was refreshing to look at after the long sea voyage.[52]

But now they had to repeat the whole ghastly business of taking on as much coal as possible. *Buresk* was then sent off to a rendezvous close to Simeulue. *Emden* set out alone for Penang, not knowing what to expect but hoping that the North Channel lights would be lit.

Mousquet intercepted two ships that night, a cable-layer and a British cargo ship. What the crew did not know was that *Emden* was lying quietly and unlit, just to the north of them. *Emden* had spotted the same cargo ship and watched her lights as they receded down the North Channel towards Penang.

As the cargo ship reached her anchorage the lookouts on *d'Iberville* heard her anchor-chain rattling.[53]

Chapter 8

Emden's Raid on Penang Harbour. *Zhemtchug* is Sunk

In the very small hours of 28th October, to the north of Muka Head and under cover of darkness, *Emden* lurked unseen with her engines stopped, waiting for the moment to pounce. How she got to Penang completely undetected was partly good luck and partly careful planning.

Captain Grant was still searching furiously around Ceylon with *Hampshire, Empress of Asia* and now *Yarmouth* as well. But *Emden* had simply vanished. Where could she be? Knowing that many convoys were now going across to Aden, Grant thought perhaps that *Emden* might be in the Arabian Sea. Yet the broadest of hints was unwittingly left by von Müller with *Pontoporos* and *Markomannia,* patiently waiting at a rendezvous off western Sumatra. That should have given the British, and Admiral Jerram in particular, an immediate realisation of what was afoot. Von Müller was in complete ignorance of the fact that his two tenders had been captured and that the German crew, including the 'open and debonair' Lieutenant Meyer, had been marched through the streets of Penang by a contingent of the Penang Volunteer Force. It was all over the newspapers; even the bit about *Emden's* dummy fourth funnel was broadcast far and wide, but for once *Emden* had not seen the newspapers. Had they done so, von Müller might have concluded that he was about to walk into a trap.

For the first time, the British were in receipt of superior intelligence, but completely failed to realise its significance, even though it was staring them in the face. In his famous book, *On the Psychology of Military Incompetence,*[1]

Dixon's central theme is the failure of command to act on intelligence when it runs counter to their previously held beliefs. Jerram's failure to conceive that an attack on Penang was possible – or indeed imminent – was a typical example. The civilian population was apparently expecting a raid any minute, but the behaviour of the harbourmaster showed complete scorn for such a possibility. Even Audemard allowed himself to believe that *Emden* was miles away, somewhere in the Indian Ocean. Baron Cherkasov, lulled by reassurances from the Governor-General at Rangoon, deserted his ship and went off to join his wife in a comfortable bed in the Eastern & Oriental Hotel.

So, what had been happening on board *Emden* since coaling at Nancowry? Why did von Müller plan this attack on Penang? Without doubt he chose Penang because he knew there were warships there. This was to be a real battle, worthy of fighting men of the Imperial German Navy. More than that, von Müller believed they would be trading blows with one of the most powerful French warships in the region: the cruiser *Dupleix* or perhaps *Montcalm*. Worthy adversaries.

After a few quiet days away from the shipping lanes to the south of the Bay of Bengal, *Emden*'s crew were thoroughly drilled and ready; prepared for action as never before. The advantage for von Müller was the element of surprise. The crew were by now fully aware of their destination and the very high risk they were running. Some might have wondered why they could not go on sinking merchant ships, because when the costs were counted it was far more damaging to the Allies than slugging it out somewhere with other warships. In retrospect that argument seems common sense. You have to dig deep into the psyche of young men, who have this instinct to fight and prove their strength and bravery.

Prinz Hohenzollern really got the flavour of this:

> The enthusiasm of our brave men could be seen in their eyes. The first wish of everyone in the *Emden* had always been to come up against an enemy warship. The sinking of merchantmen was quite all right, but it was no deed of arms for a man to be properly proud of. But a fight with similar weapons gave everybody satisfaction. A trial of the fitness of the ship, her officers and men. This ardent wish was to be granted and was the cause of the joy and enthusiasm of our men.[2]

Von Müller clearly believed that if his ship was to get proper recognition from the German people he would eventually have to engage in a bloody battle and hope that he would emerge victorious.

His plan was to approach Penang's outer harbour as quickly as he could, under cover of darkness, select his targets, and then make a fast exit before any opposing ships had a chance to mount an effective response. The turn of the tide and the lack of moonlight dictated the timing of the attack, which would take place just before dawn. The moon would be down some time after 2.00 a.m. and high tide would be around 5.00 a.m.

It is almost certain that von Müller knew that the harbour approaches in Penang might be lit up as they were in Madras. He would have gathered from numerous conversations with the crew members of captured ships and the Norwegian freighter *Dovre* that it had been the practice in Penang throughout August and September. It was only in the middle of October that Audemard and Cochrane finally prevailed upon MacIntyre to take some sensible security precautions. Von Müller would not have known this, but he need not have worried; directly *Yarmouth* departed for Colombo, MacIntyre had put all the lights back on and resumed shipping movements during the night.

After a day at sea, travelling south from Nancowry, *Emden* arrived off Penang at 2.00 a.m. Now the lookouts could see that the Muka Head lighthouse was illuminated, which was a good sign. If the Muka Head lighthouse was lit, then the outer buoys of the North Channel would likely be lit up also.

The moon was still up, so von Müller needed to wait at least an hour for it to set, allowing his night-time silhouette to become less distinct. On board *Emden*, final preparations were made to bring the ship to action stations, ready for the forthcoming battle. All the boilers were up to pressure and the dummy funnel in place. At 3.00 a.m. they made for the harbour roads, passing to starboard the brightly lit buoy which marked the entrance.

The harbour roads extend between the north shore of Penang Island and the mainland for a distance of about fifteen nautical miles, so that an ordinary freighter travelling at less than ten knots would take an hour and a half to complete the distance. *Emden*, travelling at fifteen knots, would take an hour to reach the outer harbour,[3] so any sighting of a ship in the roads would provide ample warning to the harbour authorities. Lauterbach, with his vast local knowledge, was very familiar with Penang harbour. According to the Penang pilot William Brown, von Müller knew the harbour too.

He was a frequent visitor to the port in prewar days and responsible for the navigation of the channel on many occasions. A popular visitor too, not just for the amazing display of flags and band-playing, with which the Germans in those days had tried to win popularity in the East, but for his brilliant kindly, gentlemanly personality.[4]

Using the charts that *Emden* had available, plus his previous experience, von Müller was prepared for the sandbars and shallows that could easily trap his ship. He also knew that warships were always anchored in the outer harbour at a special warship anchorage because he had dropped anchor there himself on previous occasions. *Dupleix,* he imagined, might be there now.

Once into Penang's outer harbour the deep channel is very narrow, with shallows on either side; even more so in those days. As they approached the 2.75-kilometre gap between George Town and Butterworth, these shallows would be the chief hazard to watch out for. He would have to make a U-turn as he got close to the narrows, and it was going to be a very tight squeeze. He also anticipated many merchant ships at anchor in the inner harbour. Should *Emden* enter too far, merchant ships would severely restrict her movements. That would be dangerous, especially if *Emden* got trapped. Prinz Hohenzollern added an interesting caveat:

If, as was easily possible, there was a torpedo boat lying in some corner it would be easy for her, during the fight, to creep unseen far enough towards the *Emden* to get in a fatal shot with a torpedo. It would be impossible to get clear even if we succeeded in sighting the torpedo boat in time.[5]

Clearly, the officers of *Emden* were well aware that there were torpedo boats in Penang harbour and would be on the lookout for them. This was another reason why von Müller had to attack when the tide was well up. He needed to give himself as much sea-room as possible. That the Germans knew all this in advance was backed up later in a conversation between some French sailors and Lauterbach. Again, there is no need to postulate secret messages passed from hidden wireless operators. British security precautions were virtually nonexistent.

The matter of tides was crucial because if von Müller took *Emden* into Penang harbour as the tide was on the ebb, the current would be flowing northwards and carry him out, giving him the best chance of a quick getaway. It was this, and the lack of moonlight that dictated the exact timing of the raid just before dawn.

In the approach to Penang Island, *Emden*'s silhouette would in all probability be spotted, even without a moon, so the dummy fourth funnel had to be rigged up well in advance. In the end, the plan depended on the fact that night-time traffic in and out of Penang was generally busy. Another ship was hardly a big surprise, least of all *Yarmouth*, which, having completed her convoy mission, could have headed back to Penang. Of course, von Müller would not have known that, but he would have anticipated some general sloppiness in the defence of Penang. His experience at Madras had reinforced that view.

As von Müller was waiting for the moon to go down, the lookouts saw, far away to starboard, the lights of the same British cargo ship that *Mousquet* had intercepted earlier, heading for Penang. Von Müller was happy to let her pass, giving the lookouts at Muka Head a false sense of security.

By 3.00 a.m. the moon had set and *Emden* was finally under way again. The next hour brought her down to the Northern Channel entrance. To the relief of *Emden*'s crew, the channel was clearly lit with its marker buoys; it was an invitation to enter and it is certain that without the lights von Müller would have thought twice about entering this area of treacherous shallows before daybreak. Clearly he knew, or had a good idea, that since the outbreak of war the lights of Penang's harbour roads were habitually turned on.[6]

The Tanjong Puchat Muka Lighthouse, now known as Muka Head, was completed in 1883.[7] It is a fine granite structure standing 795 feet above sea level. It commands a superb view for many miles out to sea and its light can be seen from 30 miles away. That vantage point gave the lighthouse crew the best possible chance to see *Emden*'s silhouette.

Some reports alleged that *Emden* was indeed spotted from Muka Head, but with her dummy funnel she was mistaken for an Allied warship,[8] possibly *Yarmouth*. This information was apparently relayed by the lookouts to the signal station in George Town. As no official notice of *Yarmouth*'s imminent arrival had ever been given, the sighting should have aroused immediate alarm and suspicion. But it did not. MacIntyre's harbour authorities knew perfectly well that *Yarmouth* was off Minicoi, hundreds of miles away, and they certainly did not expect her in Penang. But no action was taken, and no information was passed on, either to the French ships, to *Zhemtchug* or to Maund, who was at the signal station close to the harbour, awaiting just such vital intelligence.

It is hardly surprising that any reports of a warship coming into the North Channel that night, and identified by the Muka Head lookouts as *Yarmouth*, would not be documented in the British archives. Those sources could only come through the Port Intelligence Officer, MacIntyre himself. It would have reflected very badly on the British, and the harbour authorities, and could have led to MacIntyre's court martial. The French were in no doubt whatever. Here is the comment made at the Saigon enquiry:

> On 28th October at 3.00 a.m. the look-outs at the light house at Puchat [Muka Head] had signalled to the port [Fort Cornwallis] the sighting of a ship with four funnels. Of course that signal was not passed on to our ships. Nothing had changed in the course of these events. Nothing was done to positively identify the ship.[9]

The freighter that *Emden* had spotted earlier had duly arrived in Penang at 3.00 a.m., whilst *Emden* was still lurking well out to sea beyond the harbour roads. As previously mentioned, the French lookouts on *d'Iberville* reported the arrival of the same cargo ship when she came into harbour and they heard the anchor chain running out.

Pistolet was the No. 2 ship in the squadron on guard at Swettenham Pier, at the mouth of the inner harbour. All her watch-keepers were at their action-stations, including one at the stern, looking northwards over the outer harbour. The helmsman was on the bridge. The guns were loaded with supplies of ammunition at the ready. The torpedo tubes were lined up athwartships (pointing sideways across the ship), with torpedoes in place and topped up with compressed air. Verification of the residual pressure in each was made daily. Warheads and detonators were in place and primed. One boiler with hot water was ready to get up steam at one hour's notice, the other ready for firing up. The engines, as always, were tested that evening.[10] It is tragic to realise that the French were doing everything in their power to act in a thoroughly professional way whilst the harbour authorities, upon whom they relied, were doing nothing. Their exasperation can only be guessed at.

With the benefit of hindsight, it is clear that Prinz Hohenzollern's anxieties that a torpedo boat might be lurking in some corner of Penang harbour were justified. Had *Pistolet* received any warning that an unidentified cruiser, possibly with a dummy fourth funnel, was on her way down the harbour roads, she would have had ample time to get up steam, cast off and hide herself behind one of the numerous merchant ships. From there, she could dart out and deliver a probable death-blow with her torpedoes before *Emden* had time to take any evasive action. The short range of *Pistolet*'s torpedoes would not have mattered in that case.

By 4.30 a.m. *Emden* was approaching the outer harbour at eleven knots. At night, the wake of a ship usually kicks up phosphorescence, which is very visible in the dark, especially from an elevated position on land, and excessive speed might arouse suspicion. But she needed to be fast enough to escape any attack from a destroyer that might have been tipped off in advance. There are a number of small islands to the north of Penang, close to the mainland, any of which would be a good hiding place for small destroyers waiting in ambush. This was the kind of attack that the French destroyers were designed for.[11]

The Penang harbour launch approached to within 20 metres of *Emden*.[12] This little boat manned by locals – or 'natives', as Jerram called them[13] – was patrolling the outer harbour. This arrangement was one of the stipulations that Cochrane and Audemard had wrung out of MacIntyre two weeks earlier. Unfortunately, the crew of the harbour launch had no more idea than the French what ships were coming into harbour.

What happened next is not clear. One account reports that von Müller responded to a call for identification by loud-hailer saying, '*Yarmouth* coming in to anchor'.[14] Another report, allegedly from a Russian sailor, reported that later on, they too had challenged *Emden*, which replied likewise, '*Yarmouth* coming in to anchor'.[15] But there is no record of any such exchange in the German accounts and it is absolutely certain that they did not flash *Yarmouth*'s identification, which would have been the proper procedure.

Whatever happened at the outer harbour, *Emden* was allowed to pass the harbour launch without their raising the alarm. Despite advanced warning from the newspapers, her dummy fourth funnel seemed to be working and she was now approaching the warship anchorage. Von Müller whispered to his watch-keepers 'Which ships are at anchor?' Banks of mist hovering over the water created shadows between the harbour lights, making identification of ships very difficult. The one ship they were looking for was *Dupleix*. For the next 15 minutes the cruiser crept quietly about in the darkness at less than a walking pace, trying to identify a possible target.[16]

Then, at 5.04 a.m., an hour before sunrise, at 1200 metres to starboard, they finally made out the rear riding-light of what seemed to be a warship at anchor. She had more than one mast and three short funnels. Once they got to within 800 metres, the ship was finally identified as *Zhemtchug*.

Aboard the Russian ship nothing stirred. Although it was still dark, *Emden*, as required, ran her combat flags and colours up the mast-head, but with the lack of wind they hung limply in the dark, twisted around the halyards.[17]

Inside the inner harbour the three French destroyers suspected nothing, whilst the fourth destroyer, *Mousquet*, was still somewhere out there in the Straits on patrol. *D'Iberville* changed the watch at 5.15 a.m.,[18] without an inkling that *Emden* was already closing in on *Zhemtchug* for the attack. *Emden* was invisible to the lookouts even on *Pistolet*, partly because of the mist. Slowly the cruiser drew level with *Zhemtchug*. Alerted perhaps by the exchange with the harbour launch, the Russians could now see her and may have hailed her, but were unaware of any danger. Three minutes later, at 5.18 a.m., *Emden* opened fire.[19]

Down in *Emden*'s torpedo flat the crew received the order: 'Fire!!' and they released the starboard torpedo tube. There was an eleven-second pause before they heard a dull report, which was greeted with cheers, as the missile found its target. Lieutenant Levetzow watched the entire action from the bridge.

> At 380 metres we fired and the torpedo hastened to its goal. Exactly at 05.18 there was a muffled report and the Russian rose for a moment and then sank back up to her deck at the stern. At the same time the *Emden*'s starboard guns opened fire with a frightful crash. Their objective was the forecastle of the *Zhemtchug* in which were the men's flats [living quarters]. The object was to put the men out of action before they could reach their guns.
>
> It was a fearful sight. In a short time the fore part of the ship was in flames. The ship's side was pierced like a sieve and glowing with the great heat. It was indeed an awful and enthralling sight.
>
> Soon after the first torpedo had been fired the *Emden* turned sharply to port as there was considerable danger of running into the many merchant ships that were anchored close to us.[20]

Back in *Emden*'s torpedo flat, the crew had barely enough time to reload the starboard torpedo tube when the cruiser began a tight turn, heeling over onto her starboard beam. Soon after, when the ship straightened up, they received the order to load up the port torpedo tube on the opposite side of the ship.[21]

Meanwhile, chaos had erupted on board *Zhemtchug*. Once the Russian cruiser had been struck on her port side fire broke out in the after-magazine. The compartment had to be flooded, settling *Zhemtchug*'s stern further down in the water and adding a list to starboard. As previously mentioned, the tide had already turned and, moving with it, *Zhemtchug* had swung round at anchor through 180 degrees. There were only twelve shells on deck stacked beside the starboard guns, and now they were pointing towards George Town. Those heavy 120mm shells had to be dragged across the deck to the forward port gun in order to return fire. This would have taken a great deal of bravery because the gun-crews were under an intense cannonade from *Emden*. As Maund reported later to Jerram,

> Only the after gun and the No. 2 starboard gun [forward] were cleared away, the latter being on the reverse side of the ship – towards the Island, while only 12 rounds of ammunition were provided on deck – six to each gun. The ammunition for the starboard gun was transferred to the foremost [port] gun, its opposite number having been put out of action at once by a boat falling across it.
>
> It was also necessary to flood the after magazine as smoke was seen to be rising from it. Fire was opened by the *Zhemtchug* when the *Emden* had passed her and about 12 rounds in all were fired, two hits being obtained but unfortunately on the superstructure only.[22]

There are many inaccuracies in Maund's report to Admiral Jerram, partly because he was describing events that he had not witnessed himself. All the while, he was ashore by the signal station. But he knew about the problems with *Zhemtchug*'s shells from speaking to her survivors afterwards. Another controversial claim that Maund made in his report was that *Emden* was flying the British flag. Maund could not possibly have seen it, even if he had been awake, and neither could anyone else. It was completely dark when *Emden* appeared and *Emden*'s mastheads were certainly not flood-lit.

By the time the Russian gun crews were ready and opened fire, *Emden* had already passed and had ceased her firing. *Zhemtchug*'s deck was tilting at a steep angle, her guns pointing too high and unable to bear down sufficiently. In fact, *Emden* sustained no hits at all, although one or two merchant ships in the harbour did. An eye-witness later reported that it was impossible for *Zhemtchug*'s gunners to strike *Emden*.[23] Her shells passed harmlessly over the top of *Emden*, sending up great waterspouts far out towards the Province Wellesley shore, with some reaching the land to the north of Butterworth.[24]

Soon, the Russians had expended their twelve shells and there was a long, eerie, silence. The element of surprise was total and the Russians had no chance. They could only watch as *Emden* veered away, continuing her advance towards the inner anchorage, crowded with merchant ships and many other smaller craft, ready to make her turn. Had *Emden* proceeded any further she would certainly have run into these small vessels.

The Russians watched *Emden* execute her tight turn to port. By that time it was about 5.25 a.m. and the first light of dawn had not yet broken. Half an hour remained before sunrise and recognition of the unknown cruiser was still dependent upon identifying her silhouette. *Emden*'s flags were also indiscernible in the darkness.

Since the beginning of the action, the watch-keepers on board the French destroyers *Fronde, Pistolet* and *d'Iberville* had been observing these events with complete astonishment. *Pistolet* was nearest, tied up alongside *Fronde* at Swettenham Pier, whilst *d'Iberville* was almost two kilometres away.[25] There was a faint glimmer of light in the eastern sky, but insufficient to penetrate the darkness. All that could be seen of the unknown cruiser was her silhouette. From *d'Iberville* in particular, with many merchant ships at anchor, *Emden*'s silhouette could only be seen behind a forest of other masts and funnels.

The last the French had known of *Emden*'s definite whereabouts was her reported visit to Diego Garcia on 12th October. No clear information about *Emden*'s possible location had been passed to them for nearly two weeks and, very surprisingly, they were not officially told of *Emden*'s most recent activities around Minicoi,[26] although they must have heard the gossip. In contrast, they knew that *Chikuma* was round the corner off Pulau Weh and *Yarmouth* presumably across the Bay of Bengal. Either ship might be returning to Penang at any time. Both *Yarmouth* and *Chikuma* had four funnels, so it could have been either of them. *Emden* had a distinctive forward sloping bow, but that was hard to identify in the darkness, especially amongst the hulls of other ships. She also had searchlights mounted on the mizzen mast, which neither of the allied cruisers had. Other than that, it was very easy to mistake her for another ship in the darkness.

Von Müller could not possibly have known just how unprepared the French and Russians were, although he undoubtedly expected Penang harbour itself to be unprepared. Every sailor in the vicinity knew that.

The reports of various witnesses at the Saigon enquiry provide a vivid account of what they saw.

With the change of watch at 5.15 a.m. there was no indication of the imminent arrival of a cruiser to anchor. At 5.20 the watch-keeper Coeuru on board *Pistolet,* who was in the best position to see, saw the silhouette of a ship with four funnels behind *Zhemtchug*. Coeuru went immediately to the lower bridge where the officer of the watch Bourdet was, and told him calmly that *Yarmouth* had entered the roads. They manned the signal lamp ready to respond with their identification should *Yarmouth* make a signal. Reveille had just sounded on board *d'Iberville* and Coeuru had just time to return to the bridge of *Pistolet,* when suddenly a cannonade burst forth.

The first shots woke the commanders and those officers of the three ships who were not on watch. Everyone went quickly to the bridge without knowing what was happening.

After the first salvo there was a call to action stations on all the ships. The furnaces were turned up on *Pistolet* and ignited on board *d'Iberville* and *Fronde* whilst the latter two ships began to reassemble their engines.

On *d'Iberville* they reassembled their TSF with the greatest promptness. The awnings were tied up and plenty additional ammunition boxes brought to the guns.

Straight after the call to action-stations, *d'Iberville* and *Pistolet* were ready to use their artillery and *Pistolet* to fire her torpedoes. But they could not get under way before their boilers were under full pressure. That would be up to an hour for *Pistolet* and two hours or more for *d'Iberville*.[27]

For the time being they were stuck, unable to manoeuvre and vulnerable if attacked. Only *Pistolet* had any reasonable chance of getting under way. Twilight was due quite soon, but it was still very dark.

As Commanding Officer of the three destroyers, Audemard had to think quickly. His first reaction was to think the Russians had opened fire first, inadvertently mistaking an Allied cruiser for the enemy. The Russians were new to Penang and poorly briefed about ships' movements (as he was, too). Audemard initially thought the unknown cruiser was *Chikuma,* although the latter seemed to have emerged unscathed. Besides, the guns had now fallen silent, even though the unknown cruiser was still well within *Zhemtchug*'s line of fire. That clinched it from Audemard's point of view. He never guessed that the Russians had simply run out of ammunition. He assumed they had been told to be vigilant, and seeing an unexpected cruiser coming into harbour in darkness, without making any identification signals, they concluded it was an enemy ship and blasted away till ordered to stop.

From *Pistolet,* all they could see was smoke and mist hanging over the water obscuring the whole area. *Zhemtchug* was actually on fire, but the flames were not yet visible from *Pistolet.* They, too, thought that it was the Russians firing at *Yarmouth.* Castagné, in his assessment, was less charitable than the kindly Audemard. In characteristic acerbic style he turned to his second in command and said:

> The Russians are still drunk! Happily they shoot very badly ... even at point blank range![28]

Back on *d'Iberville,* Audemard was standing on the after-deck where he could best see. *D'Iberville,* like *Zhemtchug,* was swinging at anchor in the tideway, only more slowly, because she was out of the main tidal current, closer to the shore. The stern of *d'Iberville* was coming round to the north. Enseigne Muller, who was the officer of the watch and wide awake, reported to Audemard that the guns were ready to open fire. In fact, the only gun that could have made any serious impact was the 100mm gun on the forecastle of *d'Iberville.* With *d'Iberville*'s stern pointing towards the harbour mouth, the gunner had to turn the gun right round, pointing to the rear. With the ship's superstructure in the way, it created a blind arc of 60 degrees. The gunnery officer's description to the Saigon enquiry shows that during *Emden*'s first run, with the gun pivoted to its maximum, he could have fired on her from the starboard side of *d'Iberville.* But then Audemard shouted: 'Hold your fire!', exclaiming, 'It's a fatal mistake!'. Then, as the Saigon enquiry reported:

> Enseigne Muller replied, 'I don't think so. Look at the mizzen topmast. It's certainly the *Emden* and furthermore the forward funnel is false.' But in saying this he seems to have lacked conviction and Audemard disregarded him. It is also possible that Muller did not actually say this till *Emden* had already turned around and was starting back.[29]

Muller was referring to the outline of the searchlights on *Emden*'s mizzen topmast, which *Yarmouth* and *Chikuma* did not have. But it is quite possible that Muller did not make that comment till a bit later on, because after *Emden* had turned around, it was twilight and her silhouette could be seen more distinctly.

Now Enseigne Lidy, the second-in-command of *Pistolet,* glimpsing the cruiser through the mist, also thought she might be *Emden.* He was probably the first to recognise a possible false fourth funnel. Meanwhile, *Emden*'s colours were at last becoming visible, but they were still hanging limp around the halyards and could not be identified.

Because of these nagging doubts Audemard still hesitated. He still thought he could be in the presence of an Allied cruiser, responding to unforeseen aggression from *Zhemtchug.* The latter was still wreathed in a cloud of smoke which Audemard thought had come from her own guns. The firing had now ceased and everything had gone very silent. Audemard assumed that the 'visiting' cruiser was now making her way to the outer harbour where *Yarmouth* normally dropped her anchor.[30]

Audemard, more than anything else, was thinking about casualties from either of the two ships. As *Zhemtchug* was not firing, Audemard concluded that she had realised her mistake. Besides, *Zhemtchug* had made no signals. Anchored out there in the outer harbour, help could only come to them by boat. So Audemard ordered *d'Iberville*'s two whalers (large open rowing boats which could carry up to 20 men) and a dinghy to be lowered into the water immediately, under the supervision of Enseigne Tavera.[31]

Audemard then thought it best to go down to his cabin to consult his catalogue of ship's silhouettes. He was clearly uncertain about the identity of the cruiser, especially after Muller's comments. He still thought it was *Chikuma.*[32] All the while, *d'Iberville*'s gun crews were drawn up at the ready, awaiting the command to open fire.

The French destroyers now saw *Emden* make her tight turn to port, almost on her own axis. It is likely that to bring her around so sharply she had to reverse her port propeller. *D'Iberville*'s gunnery officer also watched the cruiser turn to port.[33] This concurs with the Russian account, the German account and also the German charts. It is important to emphasise this, because the British later put out a very different story.

Emden then began to retrace her steps and make for the outer harbour. As already described, her port torpedo tube was loaded and made ready for firing. For the moment, however, Audemard still believed she might be *Yarmouth* or *Chikuma,* heading for the anchorage in the outer harbour. *Zhemtchug* was still engulfed in smoke. Even at that point the French still thought it was smoke from *Zhemtchug*'s own guns.

It was probably Lieutenant Pochard, second-in-command on *d'Iberville*, who first cottoned on to what was really happening. With the arrival of twilight and with fire taking a hold, the situation on *Zhemtchug* was rapidly becoming apparent to the French ships. She was on fire. Lieutenant Pochard then exclaimed that he thought *Zhemtchug* had been forced to cease firing because she was completely disabled. One of the officers across the way, on *Pistolet*'s bridge, could also see that *Zhemtchug* was on fire, with the whole of her stern enveloped in smoke. Through the scuttles of the forward battery they could now see a fire raging, giving the impression of a ship that was already lost. Enseigne Muller was also sure that she had been badly hit because a column of yellow smoke was now rising from her amidships.[34]

Daylight was gradually breaking and the intruder was now more clearly visible. A signal between *Pistolet* and *d'Iberville* now suggested she might be Graf Spee's flagship *Scharnhorst*.[35] In fact, Castagné held to that view for quite a long while.[36]

When the first sound of gunfire awakened him, Enseigne Tavera in *d'Iberville* had darted out of his cabin onto the deck very scantily clad. He now returned fully dressed, intending to supervise the lowering of *d'Iberville*'s boats and dinghy into the water to search for casualties. He was just in time to see the cruiser open fire again. This time, Audemard no longer doubted that ever since the first salvo, he had actually been in the presence of an enemy cruiser.

At the time *Emden* opened fire for the second time, she was 1650 metres from the destroyers at Swettenham Pier and 1860 metres from *d'Iberville*. With their limited range of only 600 metres, *Pistolet*'s torpedoes were never anywhere near striking range of *Emden*[37] and their ship was still immobile. All they could do was to watch helplessly.

On board *Emden*, von Müller, manoeuvring his ship from side to side, took aim carefully at *Zhemtchug*'s port side with his underwater torpedo tube. Then came the order: 'Fire!'

> The torpedo rushed hissing out of the tube. At once there was a fearful crash which also gave the *Emden* a considerable shock. Rejoicing in the torpedo flat! We greeted the noise and the shock as proof that this shot had got home, probably in the magazine or the torpedo flat of the Russian, as the tremendous explosion was not otherwise explicable.

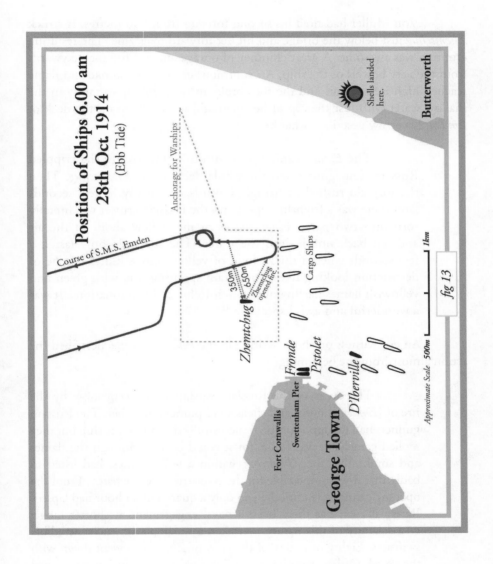

Position of Ships 6.00 am
28th Oct 1914
(Ebb Tide)

Course of S.M.S. Emden

Anchorage for Warships

350m
650m

Zhemtchug

Zhemtchug opened fire.

Cargo Ships

Fronde
Pistolet
Swettenham Pier
Fort Cornwallis
D'Iberville

George Town

Butterworth

Shells landed here.

Approximate Scale   500m   1km

fig 13

We soon received news from the conning platform[38] that the Russian had vanished, with the addition: 'We are leaving harbour'.[39]

Von Müller had fired his second torpedo from 650 metres. It struck *Zhemtchug* just below the bridge and hit her forward magazine. The resulting eruption was awesome. A great chimney of orange and red fire shot skywards from the very bowels of the ship. An enormous eruption of smoke and flame reached high into the air and the ship broke in two, sinking instantly in the shallow water with just the top of her mast still visible.[40] Up on the deck of *Emden*, Levetzow described what he saw:

> The *Emden* came up to within 700 metres of the crippled Russian. Our guns raked the whole deck of the *Zhemtchug*. Then the torpedo rushed unerringly towards the enemy. A few seconds later there was a frightful report and the Russian cruiser was literally torn into two parts. Huge pieces of metal flew about in the air and fell back noisily into the water. The spectacle only lasted a few seconds when a thick cloud of yellow smoke hid the scene of destruction looking like a mountain spouting fire, with green and yellowish flames darting out from it followed by detonations. It was a wonderful and awful spectacle.[41]

An eye-witness on shore, writing in the *Penang Gazette*, described the action almost from the beginning:

> The decks of the Russian warship were swept away by the fire of [*Emden's*] guns, and shells were pumped into her. The Russian gunners had no opportunity of successfully defending the ship but they replied gamely. It was futile, for it could be seen through the flames and smoke that the *Zhemtchug* within a few minutes, had listed so badly that it was impossible for them to strike the *Emden* … From the opening cannonade until the end only a quarter of an hour had lapsed. Rarely if ever, has there been a naval engagement at shorter range: or a calamity of this nature overtaken a warship with such incredible swiftness. Eighty or ninety of the crew of *Zhemtchug* went down with the vessel. Of her compliment of 355 men the majority were rescued but a large proportion were shockingly wounded.
>
> Several French torpedo boats were in harbour and were silent

and powerless witnesses of the hell that had been let loose. They were lying close in and like the sunken warship, had no steam up.[42]

The unfolding scene had been observed by the harbour pilot launch, which had been patrolling the South Channel, six nautical miles to the south. When the first shots were heard the launch immediately raced towards the spot as the twilight began to break. The pilot later wrote an account of the action. Inevitably, there are inaccuracies about what he saw six miles away in the twilight, but his description is vivid:

> As I drew near I could see the graceful German cruiser zigzagging northward across the anchorage and pouring murderous fire at no more than 300 yards range [it was probably twice that distance]. Just as I came within plain view of it all the *Zhemtchug* flared like magnesium and in a minute or two disappeared, leaving a great yellow cloud of smoke in the air. There was no roar of an explosion, only a mighty sizzle. Müller had used a torpedo for the death blow.[43]

The French enquiry put the interval between the first and second cannonades at seven to eight minutes[44] although the Russians estimated only five or six minutes.[45] A later German account put it at ten.[46] Whatever the precise timing, all agreed that the interval was very short. This is important because later British reports told a very different story. The Russian report also put the second torpedo at a shorter range of 370 metres.[47] However, in this instance the German report is likely to be most accurate.

By the time *Emden* had commenced her second attack, she was clearly identified as an enemy cruiser and could have been fired upon by the French destroyers if that was possible. *D'Iberville* had herself shifted position in the gathering tideway which began to pull her stern further round, pointing towards the harbour mouth. Only the 65mm gun could get a sight of *Emden* from the port side of the ship. There was a one-minute window of opportunity for that gun to open fire on *Emden* before she disappeared behind some intervening merchant ships and then behind the great eruption of smoke as *Zhemtchug* blew up.[48]

Why Audemard never grabbed that one chance to open fire is uncertain. His explanation was that he thought it foolhardy to attract answering gunfire from the vastly more powerful *Emden,* unless he himself was attacked. *D'Iberville*'s best chance of seriously damaging *Emden* had already passed when she was turning, and in the line of fire of *d'Iberville*'s powerful 100mm gun. But that weapon could no longer bear. *Emden* was now well out in the outer harbour with the distance increasing all the time, besides being hidden behind a pall of smoke. Mist still lying on the surface of the water further hampered visibility.

As Audemard did not want to expose his crew and those of the nearby destroyers to certain carnage, he decided to wait and see what *Emden* was going to do next. *Pistolet* was nearer to *Emden* and might have opened fire with her 65mm gun and 47mm cannon, but Castagné had no authority to engage the enemy without orders from his squadron commander Audemard. His small guns would have had little effect at that range anyway.[49]

But there was another factor affecting *Pistolet*. At that point she could not see *Emden* properly and, as it later turned out, *Emden* could not see her either. Unlike *d'Iberville*, *Pistolet* was moored alongside the jetty, which would have broken up her already low profile. *Emden* made her return run at 5.28 a.m. in the half-light with heavy mist still on the water. After that, the great cloud of smoke rising from *Zhemtchug* continued to obstruct *Pistolet*'s view.

Later accounts suggested that *d'Iberville* actually opened fire on *Emden*; notably an account by Lieutenant Witthooft,[50] *Emden*'s other torpedo officer. But that was based on hearsay written seven years later. He would have been several decks below in the torpedo flat when it allegedly happened. The Saigon enquiry seems to have eliminated that possibility.

Audemard's letter to Jerram, which was sent after the event and had to be officially translated, put the matter this way:

> Under these conditions should I give the order to open fire? – I did not think so – to open fire would have been for the enemy, already triumphant, but the signal for another easy victory. For us the useless sacrifice of our 300 sailors and the final annihilation of the allied forces assembled at Penang. – For all these reasons I did not hesitate in keeping silent, at the same time holding myself ready vigorously, for any attack by the enemy.[51]

Enseigne Tavera, it will be remembered, was already in *d'Iberville*'s rowing boats setting out for *Zhemtchug*. There were serious casualties in great numbers thrashing about in the water around the wreckage. He raced to the spot as fast as his crews could row. The Penang pilot and master-mariner, William Brown, takes up the story:

The *Emden*'s guns had now ceased. She continued her course for half a mile or so and stopped. I took the launch over the spot where the Russian had sunk, nosing it into a clear patch among the floating living and dead. Boats had rushed from the shore and the shipping [merchant ships in harbour]. I picked up twenty men, one of them in five pieces hanging together by threads of muscle, yet still alive. *Emden* stood off and watched while the rescued men were landed.[52]

All this commotion had awoken many people who were ashore in Penang, especially people who were close to the harbour. Those staying in the Eastern & Oriental Hotel with its terraces right down at the water's edge had a ringside seat; one of those people was Captain Cherkasov himself.[53]

The local manager of the Valvoline Oil Company, who was also an officer in the Penang Volunteer Corps,[54] happened to be staying at the Eastern & Oriental Hotel that night, and drove the hapless Cherkasov straight down to the harbour. On the same day he wrote a letter to his company headquarters in Calcutta.

> The action with the Russian cruiser commenced in the early morning at 5.20 and just off the E&O Hotel and it happened to be my night off duty in the Defensive Area. I was sleeping at the Hotel with my wife and was rudely awakened by a shell bursting just outside. To dress was only the work of a moment and to hand my wife over to the other residents and then to muster all our men for an expected landing of the enemy. The great wonder is that she did not shell the cable station. The Captain of the Russian cruiser was ashore and I had to hurry him away in a motor-car to see the last of his ship.
>
> Several shells fell close to our present offices and quite a lot went to Prai station and across Penang a distance of three miles. Several natives were injured, but no Europeans. Most European ladies are suffering from nervousness.

Another witness who was staying at the Eastern & Oriental published a lengthy account in the *Penang Gazette and Straits Chronicle,* signed simply 'F.W.E.'. He was clearly a regular correspondent and an older man, for his writing has that florid, ornate style so typical of the Victorians. But it is worth quoting some extracts, because he captures the shock and the atmosphere of the moment very vividly:

.... There was no mistaking the sound; it was the firing of heavy cannon – and at close quarters.

A Bright Flash

From my bed into the open ground of the hotel compound was but half a dozen steps. A glance in the direction of the Russian cruiser lying in the anchorage in the northern entrance to the harbour, revealed but the lights of the ship dimmed as by a haze. It was still the darkness of night, though the promise of day crowned the eastern hills of the Province with a halo of delicate light. ... [Then] there was a bright flash, apparently from the Russian cruiser and simultaneously a second – Pang! There followed a third and it seemed to me a stronger report, and a volume of smoke enveloped the warship and the lights disappeared as if extinguished.

No Panic

The Hotel grounds began to fill quickly with shadowy objects scarcely definable in the first glimpse of the dawning light. ... The Chinese servants seemed to be the first to find their tongues, but the mixed concourse of Indians soon followed suit and then came the leisurely Malay enquiry *'Apa salah?'* English voices had already exclaimed ' ... What is it? ... Is it the *Emden* come at last? ... Where is she? ... Who is firing? ... '

The Russian warship appeared – apparently all alone. 'Who's she firing at? Where is the enemy? ... ' Then in quick succession the sharp reverberating – Pang! Pang!! started again and shells and shrapnel began to fly and fall all around.

The Doomed Cruiser

... The end came suddenly and even more dramatically than the whole incident itself. In the midst of the awful rattle of battle the enveloping smoke clouds were split in twain by a huge brilliant red glare, the evident result of an explosion, yet withal a noiseless one.

The once proud Russian ship was ablaze burning to the waters edge. There were heart-rending cries and shouts of anguish as of strong men writhing in mortal agony, and a few of us thought we heard triumphant shouts from the invisible victors. For a brief spell the flaming red blaze lit up the encircling gloom but still no other boat was in view. Then it was suddenly extinguished and in its place came volume upon volume of murky black and dirty brown smoke. And as we watched, lo! – the mystery revealed itself. Out of the dense clouds of smoke arising ever upwards and upwards above the background of hills, and blotting out the soft golden roseate hues of the rising sun, sailed slowly and majestically a one-two-three-four funnelled man-of-war looming up black and formidable in the yet pale grey morning light.

When the Smoke Clouds Lifted.

As the smoke clouds lifted all that was visible of the Russian warship was the top of the mast carrying the wireless aerial and in the uncertain light of dawn, but dully reflected on the water through the haze of smoke, could be seen a struggling mass of humanity floundering about in the debris-strewn sea.

The writer rounded his article off with a description of the casualties who were brought ashore and attempts to apply immediate first aid to their injuries. Amongst the bystanders were a number of local Malays who can be seen in the accompanying photo. One of them was reported to have offered his turban and his spare sarong from across his shoulder, to be torn up and used as dressings.[55]

There were several reports that shots landed around Butterworth, and not all of them could be explained by stray shots from *Zhemtchug*, because the trajectory does not fit. It is possible that *Emden* may have fired some shells in that direction when she was making the second pass going north, but this is not mentioned in any of the French, German or British naval accounts.

Another correspondent watched the whole battle from the Crag Hotel on top of Penang Hill.

I awoke with a start and thought for a moment it was thunder, but when I heard it for the third time I realised it was not thunder and at once came to the conclusion that something was amiss down in Penang. My first thought was that Penang was being bombarded by *Emden*. Why I should have thought so I cannot say but I suppose it's because we have all read so much of the *Emden* of late. I first rushed out onto my verandah which overlooks Penang. The town lights shone up through the grey dawn and Penang looked very peaceful and at first I could see nothing untoward. I looked on for a few minutes and just then I saw a flash, and after a minute or so heard the report of a gun.

He went on to say that he could see the flash of gunfire from the two ships. He then called out to Mr. Jack Jennings, the managing director of the *Times of Malaya*, who was up there recuperating from a recent illness.

> Mr. Jennings suggested going up to our flagstaff, the highest point at the Crag. We ran together in our sarongs and on our way woke up a few of the visitors, although a good many were already on the terrace watching the fight. By this time the firing was very rapid and we now realised that we were watching a real naval battle between the Russian cruiser *Zhemtchug* and the *Emden*. All the shots seemed to be fired from the *Emden*, for we could see her broadside flashing out and I think the *Zhemtchug* only fired three shots in all. After about twenty minutes firing we saw one very vivid flash from the Russian cruiser and then a dense mass of black smoke and the *Zhemtchug* was no more. She had sunk. It was the sight of a life-time and only those on the hills and at Muka Head light-house could have seen the fight from start to finish.[56]

The correspondent was Donald Woodford, the manager of the Crag Hotel. His companion, Mr Jennings, a professional journalist, wrote:

> Now you may believe me or not, but I had a strange intuition that the *Emden* would visit Penang and one of my first remarks to Mr Donald Woodford, the manager, was that I desired an option over the 'Crag' telescope in case the *Emden* visited Penang. Mr Woodford was amused at my remark but agreed with me, that we would have a splendid view of all that happened, should the *Emden* pay her promised visit.[57]

The rest of Mr Jennings' report confirmed what Mr Woodford described. After *Zhemtchug* had sunk, other witnesses, questioned by the *Straits Echo*, were out on the Esplanade.

> There were a good many people in the streets by this time all hastening down to the sea front. We suddenly discovered that the Russian destroyer which had been lying off the Fort [Cornwallis] had sunk. There was nothing but her mast visible. Through glasses we could see a number of men in the water and wreckage floating about. The cruiser [*Emden*] was about a mile away from the destroyer [*Zhemtchug*], standing well out in the channel to the north. I saw about two hundred Russian wounded sailors brought ashore. Most of them had no clothing at all and others were very scantily clothed. They were put into motor-cars and rickshaws and taken to the hospital.[58]

The only thing the French ships could do at this stage was help pick up the survivors. Many merchant ships in the harbour were already lowering their boats to go to their assistance. A frantic rescue operation was now taking place from the shore. *Emden* was now stopped just beyond the outer harbour, watching the scene. She lingered in that area for about 20 minutes. Of what we know of Captain von Müller, he had a natural concern for survivors and he stressed, when the Germans recounted the story later, that he was satisfied that all efforts were being made to rescue the Russian sailors but, contrary to his usual practice, he made no move to assist; indeed, he would have considered it too dangerous to do so.

A writer to the *Straits Echo* said,

> The scene at the wharves from the early morning was one of intense sympathy. Everyone and anyone who had a motor came down to the rescue and the wounded were quickly transferred to the hospital. Several shocking sights were seen and operations which were necessarily performed were unavailing ... The Russians are now quartered at Tanjong Tokong House. A shell was found in Western Road and another on the golf course'. Another contributor said, 'I had the privilege of seeing a shell extracted from a wounded Russian and it is as big as the palm of your hand. Remember it is only a piece

broken off from the original shot. The man died soon after the extraction.[59]

Meanwhile, *d'Iberville*'s boats, with Enseigne Tavera in charge, had drawn level with Swettenham Pier where *Pistolet* was still raising steam, as yet unable to move off. One of the launches which had already made a trip with casualties to the shore alerted Tavera to the fact that *Emden* was still there, stopped, just beyond the outer harbour. Tavera then saw *Emden* turn and face towards them.[60] *Emden*'s guns had the range, and an attack on *d'Iberville* could be carried out easily from the safety of their position beyond the outer harbour. Fearing an imminent attack on *d'Iberville,* Tavera thought it best to turn back in case of further casualties from his own ship.

From Prinz Hohenzollern's account we know this was quite correct. *Emden* was looking for a path for her guns between the merchant ships and smaller craft that lay between them. Perhaps von Müller hoped that *d'Iberville* might cast off and move towards them.[61] We also know that *Pistolet* and *Fronde* remained quite invisible to *Emden*, otherwise she might well have tried to shell them. It is just as well that *Pistolet* did not make the futile gesture of opening fire with her small cannon at such long range, thus giving away her position. At 6.00 a.m., and 30 minutes after *Zhemtchug* was sunk, *Pistolet* was at last ready to cast off.

All of a sudden something seemed to attract *Emden*'s attention and she moved rapidly north away from the harbour, in the direction of Tanjong Tokong. *D'Iberville* was now out of immediate danger, so Tavera retraced his steps and his small boats were soon amongst the Russian survivors thrashing about in the water. For a short while Tavera and his boats were busy, joining others from the harbour and picking up survivors.

Why did *Emden* hang around for so long? In his later account, William Brown, the Penang pilot, was uncertain about von Müller's reasoning.

And still the *Emden* stood off silent. Thirty ships lay there, a harvest for her guns. Müller need only hoist a signal to them to abandon ship, then – a few shells for each on the water-level! What a victory for a commerce raider lay within his grasp far surpassing all his previous feats. We waited and wondered! The town and the harbour were at Müller's mercy! No doubt the German officers were considering the possibilities of the situation. Penang was an undefended port and Müller was, as we know from his treatment of captured crews, a man who observed the codes and proprieties of war. Probably his ignoring of the French destroyers at the wharf arose from a chivalrous desire not to harm the town. It would have been impossible to give them a salvo without damage to the buildings behind them.[62]

This was not actually correct. *Emden* knew there were four French destroyers in or around Penang. *D'Iberville* they had spotted, and indeed they had already decided to attack her before other circumstances drew her attention elsewhere. But *Emden* still had not seen any of the three small French destroyers. Had she gone back into the close confines of the harbour, any small French destroyer concealed behind a merchantman could have dispatched them with a torpedo at short range. Though *d'Iberville* was riding at anchor *Emden* had no way of knowing that she was actually immobilised.

When *Emden* made her first attacking run on *Zhemtchug* it was dark and they failed to see the two French destroyers tied up side by side, at Swettenham Pier. By the time she made her second run, going north in the twilight, *Emden*'s view of the two destroyers was obscured by mist, followed by the pall of smoke hanging over *Zhemtchug*.

As for an attack on the signal station, both von Müller and Lauterbach knew Penang well and knew exactly where the signal station was. They probably refrained from attacking it because of the need to evacuate the area first. There was also the telegraph cable station at the other end of the Esplanade, but for the moment that target would have been out of sight.

Firing had now ceased. The entire episode had lasted about fifteen minutes, starting with *Emden* stealthily approaching the Russian cruiser in complete darkness at 5.13 a.m. with no moon, and finishing with *Zhemtchug* sunk at 5.28 a.m. in the predawn twilight. At 6.04 a.m. the sun finally rose and the rescue of *Zhemtchug*'s survivors continued in the full morning light.

An interesting note, sent immediately afterwards from Maund to Jerram, listed the documents he had lost from his cabin when *Zhemtchug* went down. The Flotilla Signal Book, the Emergency Vocabulary Code, the Economic Telegraph Code, and the Secret W/T [wireless] call signs. It seems that some of these were unavailable to Castagné or the commanders of the other two French destroyers. Even a junior British officer had been given more responsibility than the senior French commanders.[63]

Upon reflection, von Müller was taking an appalling risk in raiding Penang harbour in this way. Had the harbour authorities made the slightest effort to apply reasonable security measures, then *Emden* would have been identified in the roads, an hour before she reached the harbour. *Pistolet* would have had steam up and hidden in a strategic spot, ready to dart out with a torpedo-hit. *Zhemtchug*'s big 120mm guns would also have been ready to disable *Emden* before she could loose off a torpedo.

In his memoirs, William Brown, the Penang pilot, summed things up with these observations:

> This was an instance of von Müller's great fighting skill, but at the same time there was a foolhardiness in dealing with *Zhemtchug* at such close quarters. A lucky lurch might have allowed even a *Zhemtchug* gunner a disabling shot on the unmissable target that *Emden* presented. There was a wide streak of recklessness in von Müller and finally it was his undoing. He should have realised in his fight with the Russian, so completely helpless after the first blow, that as a commerce raider he was of infinitely more value to his country than as a dare-devil battler. All the *Emden*'s worth to Germany could have been destroyed by one lucky hit in Penang harbour.
>
> The German naval officers as a class always seemed to me to be of a very high type. It has been said that the arrogance of the German Army was the reason for this. The more sensitive kind of man avoided the army and chose the new naval service open to them, the only other for most upper-class German youths. In war-time I paid special attention to the work of this rather rare German type, which to such a large extent officered the German Navy. With their imagination and gallantry they seemed to excel in a rather reckless ardour.[64]

This thoughtful analysis precisely reflects the thirst for action amongst *Emden*'s crew that Prinz Hohenzollern described before the raid on Penang harbour.

The only concern now for the people of Penang was the rescue of the casualties. At the jetty the Russian sailors were being attended to and Audemard sent a first-aid party ashore with *d'Iberville*'s doctor to help with the rescue and treatment of the casualties. Reverend Cross, by now a Penang veteran of two years standing, and a pillar of the expatriate community, was also there doing his bit, although his wife seems to have been rather less enthusiastic. He hastily jotted down his impressions the following day.

Mr. Lewis [the church-warden perhaps] got up and so did I. Then a volunteer and his motor-cycle dashed along the road. Lewis hurried into his clothes and went off. Marge [his wife] had a bad headache. The crashing went on. It was clearly shells firing at sea; a battle. What could it be? Perhaps the *Emden*? At 7.30 a.m. Mr. Lewis returned. Terrible excitement! The *Emden* disguised as a British ship with four funnels, one of them a dummy, had come into the harbour and sunk the Russian man-of-war. People were seen marching along the road with bundles of clothing. It was for the wounded rescued. We made up a bundle. With Mr. Lewis I took it down town where I met Jennings [just down from the Crag] and got some parcels with clothes and took them first to the Parish Hall. A motor carried them to the hospital where I saw the rescued Russians, all bruised and broken and bloody.[65]

Later, Cross acquired a piece of shrapnel from one of *Emden*'s shell-bursts. It remains to this day, carefully wrapped in an envelope, in his ministerial file with the following note enclosed. 'This shell piece was picked up near the race-course [now St. George's School for girls] and sold by Dr. J. B. Rose, of the War Fund. I paid $2 for this piece.'

But all of that happened much later in the day. For now, *Emden* was still hovering outside the harbour. Then something happened. It was just after daybreak and *Emden* moved northwards – fast, as if she had seen something. Indeed she had. Through the morning mist she saw, or thought she saw, a French destroyer steaming straight for her. *Emden* went full ahead into the attack.

Chapter 9

The Death of *Mousquet*

The sun had just risen and the spectators watching the action from the Crag Hotel, 750 metres up Penang Hill, were in a good position to see what happened next. After describing the sinking of *Zhemtchug*, Mr Jennings continued:

> The *Emden* certainly did not hurry away and quietly made out through the north channel on her way out somewhere off Pulau Tikus. We saw her stop and make practically a complete circle. At first we thought she was going back but she turned north again. The cruiser was about a mile away [from *Zhemtchug*], standing well out in the channel to the north. About a quarter of an hour after the last shot had been fired the cruiser turned and steamed away. She went with remarkable speed.[1]

It is not certain how long *Emden* waited outside the harbour, slowly turning a half circle and then suddenly, the full circle, but most reports, like this one, suggest 15 to 20 minutes. One witness at the Crag swore that *Emden*'s dummy funnel collapsed at this stage, only to be hoisted once again.[2] He then went on:

> Just then we saw a flash and soon after heard the report of a gun, and even saw the shells as they struck the water. The *Emden*

was firing at a small coaster making for port. She fired about seven shots and we saw every one as they struck the water, but the last one looked as if it struck the stern of the coaster. But I believe it struck the funnel and wounded an engineer; a native. The shooting here was very bad indeed. Immediately the coaster saw she was the target she changed her course and made for the land, and only then the *Emden* ceased fire having evidently seen her mistake. She must have mistaken the coaster for a French destroyer. The *Emden* then continued her journey out.[3]

What had happened was this. *Emden* was slowly turning around at a safe distance just beyond the outer harbour. Out there she felt less vulnerable, less hemmed in. *Emden*'s gunners were trying to line up *d'Iberville* in their sights, but their view was obstructed by other ships in the harbour. They were also keeping a sharp lookout for the other French destroyers which they still had not spotted. Their main fear was a sudden attack from one of these fast little ships, darting out at her from almost anywhere.

That is exactly what happened next. To the north through the mist and the early dawn light, *Emden*'s crew saw smoke and what appeared to be a French destroyer coming straight at them. The mirage effect of the sea-mist made the boat seem much larger than it actually was. The witnesses up at the Crag were high above the scene with no visual impairment. They could see very clearly that it was a much smaller boat. They were quite right about *Emden*'s poor shooting, too; her gunners were way off target. But eventually the little boat was hit, just at the moment when the mist cleared. *Emden* then realised exactly what she had been firing at. In fact, she was *Merbau*, one of the small harbour patrol boats. She made off as fast as she could for the shore at Tanjong Tokong. Unfortunately, there was some damage to the stern and the funnel of the little ship, and a Malayan engineer was wounded.[4]

From *Emden*, this was how things looked:

> We watched the new enemy from the quarter-deck. The irritating clouds of mist hindered us from recognising her. As the mysterious mist would not clear away we opened fire at about 6000 metres. In consequence of the bad mirage our shooting was not good but we were thankful when the supposed torpedo boat turned, and disclosed a small and harmless government boat. Naturally the order to cease fire was given at once. Insignificant as the little ship was she had by her appearance saved a number of ships and the

d'Iberville from destruction.[5]

But what was happening back in the harbour? The rescue effort for *Zhemtchug*'s survivors was in full swing, with many still in the water. Enseigne Tavera was there in *d'Iberville*'s boats, trying to rescue as many as he could. They were there for about half an hour. Many casualties were horribly injured and had to be hoisted into the boats before transferring them into steam launches for speedy transfer to the shore, where first aid was waiting.[6] Whilst engaged in this life-saving but grizzly work, Tavera kept a close eye on *Emden* and saw her mysterious about-turn, finally heading out to the north. Being in a rowing boat, Tavera was right down at the level of the water and could not see very far, but he continued anxiously watching. Then he saw a ship steaming rapidly towards *Emden* and the harbour, and he, too, was convinced that she was *Mousquet*.[7]

When the shooting began he could see very little, except smoke and mist, but he feared for the worst. He knew that *Mousquet* was not due to return to anchor till around 9.00 a.m., but perhaps she had been warned, or heard gunshots? Perhaps she had come back to investigate? Tavera assumed quite wrongly that *Emden* was now firing on *Mousquet* and, since the firing then ceased abruptly, followed by silence, he assumed that *Mousquet* had not only been attacked but had been sunk.[8]

Tavera and his men rowed back to *d'Iberville* at top speed to tell Audemard that *Mousquet* was lost – sunk. Tavera was not some battle-hardened veteran, and it is very easy to understand his mistake. He must have been overwhelmed by the horror of what he had just witnessed at very close quarters. Pessimism completely clouded his judgement.

It was Audemard's mistake to be affected by the same feelings. From the very beginning of this whole affair, Audemard's overriding instinct had been the saving of lives. He could not move his ship and would not be able to do so till about 7.30 a.m; that was in about one hour's time, but thankfully *Pistolet* was on the move.

At Swettenham Pier it was now 6.30 a.m. A steam launch had towed *Pistolet* off her moorings next to *Fronde,* and she was ready to go. Castagné had already come aboard *d'Iberville*, and Audemard ordered him to take *Pistolet* directly out of the harbour mouth, to the spot where he thought *Mousquet* had been sunk. Castagné was to pick up any survivors and bring them back to *Fronde* or *d'Iberville*. Thereafter, he should head out again for open water, shadow *Emden*, and attempt to make contact with any Allied cruisers in the area such as *Chikuma*. If *Pistolet* could hang on till night-fall she might mount a night-time attack.[9] It was with these instructions that Castagné went slow-ahead out of the harbour and into the North Channel, keeping a sharp look out on both sides for any sign of *Mousquet*'s wreckage or any survivors. They found none, and by that time *Emden* was already some miles away up the North Channel.

The Penang radio station was unable to transmit or receive because *Emden* was jamming the Royal Navy's wavelength, but she did not jam the French wavelength and in the subsequent action *Pistolet* was able to maintain radio contact with *d'Iberville*. The latter's TSF had now been hastily put back together and could receive messages using batteries.

Realising his mistake in shelling *Merbau*, von Müller called off the action. He set a course west by north-west, putting about seven miles between *Emden* and Penang harbour. He had become aware that a destroyer was now there, apparently shadowing her at a distance. But for the present, *Pistolet* was too far behind and moving too slowly to present a threat. It was now 6.30 a.m. in full daylight with the mist starting to clear off the water.

It was an hour and ten minutes since *Emden* had first opened fire on *Zhemtchug*. She was now heading out to sea, passing the coast of Kedah and a few small islands to starboard, while Penang Island was receding further away to port. The second Lieutenant, von Mücke, ordered the masthead flags to be hauled down and the crew released from action stations. He gave those who had been below a description of the action and the sinking of *Zhemtchug*. The crew gave three cheers for His Majesty the Kaiser.

> We gave the cheers with enthusiasm and joy. We were uplifted and refreshed by the thought that something had been accomplished for the greater glory of the Fatherland. The men were then released for breakfast and a wash.
>
> It must have been 7.00 o'clock when suddenly the order 'Clear ship for action' came. A very large ship whose flag could not be recognised had appeared on the horizon. The range was found and passed to the guns. Everyone waited for the order to open fire. At the outset everybody agreed that the stranger looked like a big auxiliary cruiser. The nearer we came however, the smaller became the ship which finally shrank into a quite ordinary merchantman. She was flying a yellow flag to show she had explosives aboard. It

was the second trick that day that the mirage had played on the *Emden*, but no harm was done.

We proceeded according to the old routine to stop her and Lauterbach and the prize crew went over. The order to sink the ship was accompanied by a message which the Captain was to pass on at the first opportunity. The *Emden* had not saved any survivors of the Russian cruiser *Zhemtchug* as there had been plenty of boats in the vicinity. The government boat had been fired on under the misapprehension that the *Emden* had to deal with a torpedo boat. The Captain of the *Emden* therefore wished to express his regrets for these facts.

Of such noble temperament was our captain.[10]

The merchant ship turned out to be the British freighter *Glenturret*. Before *Emden*'s prize crew could board the ship or pass on von Müller's message, they were hastily recalled as a very suspicious vessel with two trails of smoke had been sighted far out to starboard. It was clearly a warship. *Glenturret* was allowed to go free, to the immense relief of all on board.

Meanwhile, Castagné and the crew of *Pistolet* were still uncertain about the identity of the unknown cruiser. They had been following her at some distance into the North Channel and observed her stopping beside *Glenturret* around the position of the red navigational buoy opposite Batu Ferringhi. Then someone spotted what appeared to be Admiral Graf Spee's flag flying from the mizzen mast. Up on the bridge, Castagné signalled to *d'Iberville*, 'Scharnhorst in sight'.[11]

This shows how little the French knew about the broader picture of Graf Spee's whereabouts. At that moment, *Scharnhorst*, with Graf Spee's squadron, was halfway across the Pacific. This was a fact which Jerram knew very well, but the information was never passed to Audemard.

But *Scharnhorst* did have four funnels. So *Pistolet* sent a signal to *d'Iberville*: 'It is the *Scharnhorst*, four funnels, admiral's flag, just inspected a cargo ship and allowed it to go.'[12] As soon as she had made that signal, *Pistolet* continued sailing well out into the North Channel, determined to follow all the movements of the enemy closely, but at the same time sufficiently far away to be out of range of *Emden*'s guns. *Pistolet* kept *Emden*'s masts and funnels above the horizon but 'hull down'. The distance that *Pistolet* held would have been about seven nautical miles. Now *Pistolet* also saw the two trails of smoke and wrongly assumed the smoke trails came from two ships. Actually they

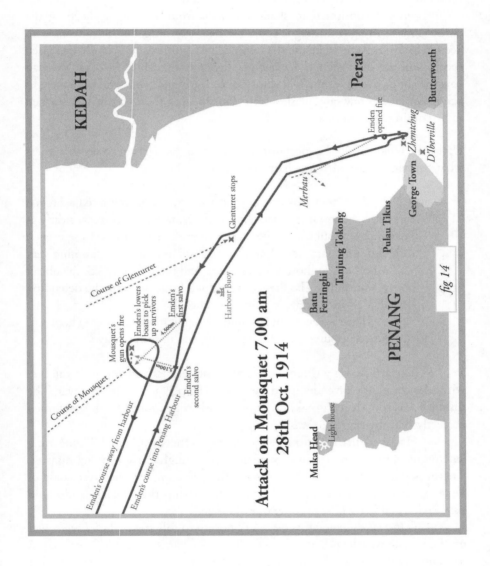

Attack on Mousquet 7.00 am
28th Oct 1914

fig 14

were coming from *Mousquet*'s twin funnels. Castagné was quite unaware that *Mousquet* was out in open water, just there. *Emden* seemed to pause for a moment. Then she headed for the two smoke trails.

Pistolet continued to shadow *Emden* from a distance, keeping the cruiser's masts in sight. Castagné could not hear anything, but his officers, with keener hearing, were adamant they could hear gunfire. So *Pistolet* increased speed, sending off a signal '*Scharnhorst* firing at two ships'.[13] After she had covered about five miles the two ships came clearly into view and both were in action. *Pistolet*'s crew saw splashes from shots hitting the water, which seemed to be coming from both sides.

Up by the Crag Hotel, the spectators could see far enough out to sea to witness what happened next with much greater clarity.

> As *Emden* was moving further out, she encountered a French torpedo boat and immediately opened fire, the range being as nearly as I can judge, about three miles. The first shell flew right over the French ship and burst far away. Again she did not appear to be shooting very well. Another shot however was nearer and finally she struck the object on the water-line. The French warship did not appear to be defending herself at all and suddenly sank by the head.
>
> The *Emden* steamed round the sinking vessel, lowered her boats and picked up survivors. Her next move was to steam away.[14]

The article was written the day after, but at that very moment the eye-witnesses could not have identified the sinking ship as a French destroyer. The distance was too great to make any positive identification. But they assumed correctly that the aggressor was *Emden*.

Had Audemard transmitted to *Mousquet* the alarm signal 'E', meaning 'enemy in sight it is dangerous to close up', she might have avoided disaster. Théroinne could have taken avoiding action, making for the west coast of Penang, waiting and watching. He had a faster ship than *Emden* and could have shadowed her whilst keeping out of range.

D'Iberville's generators were still not up to full power, but *Pistolet* was on the French wavelength and from 6.30 a.m. onwards she could have relayed to *Mousquet* the signal 'E'. Once again Audemard's judgement failed him. He was quite sure that *Mousquet* had already been sunk outside Penang harbour. Castagné simply didn't catch on, either.

Once she was out in the North Channel, *Pistolet* sent off several signals, all of which *d'Iberville* received. The curious fact is that *Mousquet* did not pick up any of them. The reason for this has never been satisfactorily explained. *Mousquet*'s wireless operator was at his post right up until the attack and for some time after, but he picked up nothing from *Pistolet*.[15]

Back in Penang harbour it was slowly dawning on Audemard that he had made another mistake. No confirmation had been forthcoming that *Mousquet* was sunk just outside the harbour and his anxieties were rising again. Over the next half-hour he sent several signals to Castagné asking if they had spotted *Mousquet* and the reply came back, 'No'.

On board *Emden*, the crew had quickly realised that the destroyer that was now steaming towards them was one of the French ones. However, the French commander, Théroinne, had absolutely no idea he was heading for an enemy cruiser. *Mousquet* hoisted the French Tricolour, but von Müller did not reply for a few minutes. Then, when *Mousquet* was well within range, von Müller hoisted the German colours and fired his first salvo, which missed, passing over the top of *Mousquet*. Prinz Hohenzollern described what happened next:

> With masthead flags flying, the *Emden* steamed at high speed towards the enemy. At 4700 metres our first salvo was fired. By turning to port our whole starboard side was brought into action. Our little enemy did not act judiciously. She did not, as would have been correct for a torpedo boat, come straight towards us. After the first salvo she turned and fled presenting us with a splendid target of her whole side.
>
> Our first salvo was somewhat high and the second fell short, but the third got home and could not have gone more exactly. The first effective salvo shot down the tricolour and found the boiler room, for huge white clouds of steam were streaming from the ship.
>
> In spite of severe disablement the enemy did not remain quiet but fired a torpedo which passed several hundred yards astern of us. Also one gun which stood forward of the conning platform was brought into action. It must have been a machine gun, for it fired with immense speed but hit nothing. Most of the shots went over us and the noise they made was like a swarm of bees.
>
> Our guns shot splendidly. After we had found the range every round told. The enemy was in bad condition. Her super-structure

was all shot to pieces and everything else as well.

After *Emden*'s twelfth salvo the Frenchman disappeared in a cloud of yellowish smoke. Our Captain therefore ordered the 'cease fire'. When the clouds cleared away the torpedo-boat was still afloat but gave no sign of being willing to surrender. The *Emden* therefore opened fire again and fired another ten salvoes with the effect that the Frenchman would never be able to move from the spot. The order was given 'Battery cease fire!' and the *Emden* approached, coming to a standstill a little aft of the torpedo boat to avoid a possible torpedo.

Meanwhile the Frenchman had plunged bows forward and gradually sank deeper, till, with her bows apparently on the bottom she stood upright in the water with her stern high above the surface. This did not however, last long and the stern vanished into the deep. Except wreckage and swimming survivors there was nothing more to be seen. [16]

Some distance away, *Pistolet*'s crew had watched the two ships firing at each other, but they could not identify either ship correctly. They watched *Emden* slowly approaching the spot where smoke lingered over the water, lowering her boats to pick up the survivors, and there seemed to be quite a lot of them. *Pistolet* then sent out the signal 'Allied ship seems sunk. Firing finished'. The cannonade had lasted from ten to twelve minutes. Prinz Hohenzollern described the scene:

> The *Emden* came up to about 200 metres from the place where she had sunk. While the masthead flags were being lowered our second cutter was lowered into the water with an officer and the assistant doctor, with bandages etc. in addition to her usual complement. The first cutter followed. With all speed we joined in the work of rescue which we naturally thought to be easy and straight-forward. We had made a mistake however, for the unwounded Frenchmen would not let themselves be rescued or taken out of the water.
>
> The reason for such a mad refusal remains a mystery to me. Probably the men had heard such bogey stories of the Germans that they would rather risk their lives in trying to swim to the neighbouring coast than fall into the hands of the 'man eating barbarians'.
>
> When the French seamen saw with what care the wounded were hoisted into the boats, they gained confidence rapidly, so that

altogether we were able to save 36 men and one Lieutenant.[17]

Emden then made off fast, first to the south, then turning west in the direction of Pulau Weh, she vanished into a rain squall. At last Castagné had positively identified *Emden,* and signalled that information to *d'Iberville*, but they still did not realise that the ship she had sunk was *Mousquet*. Castagné had tried to get *Pistolet* in close enough to identify both ships involved, but his engines did not allow him to arrive in time. By the time they finally reached the spot there was only debris floating about. They searched around for more survivors, but there were none.[18]

Pistolet was now getting serious overheating from her defective engine bearing and could raise no more than 120 revolutions. When *Emden* finally made off at 21 knots, *Pistolet* followed for a while but the mechanics from the engine-room eventually told Castagné that a main bearing on the port-side engine had finally given way. The port engine slowed and they were reduced to the starboard engine only. *Pistolet's* log reported:

> 10.07 a.m. Irreparable damage had been done whilst under way. The failure of the lubricator caused over-heating of the main-bearing and we were obliged to reduce to 13 knots, a speed we could not improve on.[19]

Emden's smoke had disappeared altogether and Castagné gave the order to abandon the pursuit.

Prinz Hohenzollern's account turns out to be extremely accurate because it tallies in almost every detail with the account given by *Mousquet's* survivors, but a couple of questions remain. Théroinne's decision to turn sharply to port could have been perceived as an attempt to run or, more likely, to bring his torpedo tubes to bear which were aimed and fired athwartships. *Emden* was still out of range, but the torpedoes were *Mousquet's* best weapon. Théroinne clearly hoped that *Emden* would close up quickly and give *Mousquet* the opening she needed.

But von Müller was too canny for that. He would have known exactly the range of *Mousquet's* torpedoes and her other armaments and stayed at a safe distance whilst pounding her with his 105mm guns. *Mousquet* had only a single 9-pounder forward and several other 3-pounders. *Emden's* third salvo hit the little destroyer hard and as the distance between them narrowed, *Emden's* gunners concentrated on destroying *Mousquet's* armaments, especially her torpedo tubes. If Théroinne had carried on steaming directly towards *Emden* he would have been unable to open fire with anything except his forward 9-pounder gun. The rapidly-firing gun described by Prinz Hohenzollern was almost certainly the starboard 3-pounder.

It is clear from the French account given below that the torpedo crews were ready and just on the point of firing when *Mousquet* was hit by a salvo. Was that torpedo ever fired? Did the Germans actually see a torpedo pass 'several hundred yards astern' or did they just see a torpedo launched towards them and enter the water? Only an inspection of *Mousquet*'s wreck could answer that question. Evidently, both ships had closed up since *Emden*'s first salvo, but it seems unlikely that they were within 600 metres. This was the effective range of *Mousquet*'s torpedoes. But the crew manning the torpedo tube was certainly taking aim, because at the very moment the order was given to fire, they were all killed by one of *Emden*'s shells.

It fell to Enseigne Tavera to narrate exactly what had happened on board *Mousquet*. He also described the care of the survivors in Sabang on Pulau Weh. They were all eventually transferred to *d'Iberville* and Enseigne Tavera took detailed verbal accounts from every one of the survivors. It is therefore a very accurate account. Tavera's final draft was written three weeks after the event because there was considerable delay in getting diplomatic clearance to fetch the survivors from Sabang. Tavera compiled all this material into a single narrative and handed it in to his commander.

This is a translation of Tavera's report. A few details, including the names of various minor players, have been omitted. The account is vivid and makes compelling reading. It must be considered the most authentic account of all. Apart from the Commandant, Théroinne, the officers are identified here as 'Monsieur', with PM, SM, QM, and 'Matelot' non-commissioned ranks in descending order of seniority.

On the bridge SM. Evinec was acting as officer of the watch and with him was Matelot Stéphan. Boxes of ammunition for the guns were ready and the torpedo tubes were pointing upwards with their covers in place. The after torpedo tube already had a torpedo in place retained by a clip. Unfortunately some of the compressed air cylinders that had been hurriedly put there temporarily hindered the aim of the after tube. The forward tube could not be turned fully, because two additional ventilation shafts had been placed there for the forward boilers. The ship was steering east by south-east at five and a half knots. She was situated about 14 miles due north of the Penang Swimming Club. The forward boiler was running and QM. Cabel with two Vietnamese stokers were on watch. The after boilers had hot water only, supervised by QM. Le Gall. At the engine-room hatch the Engineering Officer, Monsieur Bourçier, was handing over to Engineer Provost. In the engine room compartment the watch keeper was QM. Duchêne.

On seeing a warship coming from the direction of Penang, SM. Evinec warned the Commandant who immediately mounted the bridge. He laid a course for the cruiser raising the revs to 120. Ten minutes later the cruiser set a slow course towards *Mousquet,* leaving another ship [*Glenturret*] to starboard. At 06.45 *Mousquet* hoisted her colours and receiving no response after several minutes, Théroinne decided to wait for the cruiser to request identification. He was convinced that the warship in front of him was an Allied ship. It took a further 15 minutes before the *Emden* hoisted her German colours and immediately opened fire. She lay about two and a half miles from the destroyer. The first shots passed over the top of *Mousquet.*

Seeing the salvo coming from the *Emden,* Théroinne ordered everyone to action stations and ordered the radio to make the signal 'M' to alert the entire squadron. SM. Evinec made his way aft to warn the officers whilst QM. Cozic went to rouse the rest of the crew to their posts. Monsieur Bourçier, with several stokers, straight away stoked up the furnaces of the after boilers. The crew immediately fell into their battle stations by their guns and torpedo tubes.

A salvo from *Emden* hit the forward part of the ship [doubtless intended to disable the 9-pounder cannon] and the men had great difficulty maintaining their posts. The gun and the crew were put out of action. A shell then landed in the galley, seriously wounding two men. The explosion then passed through the after boiler which had at that moment four kilos of pressure. Another shell went through the radio compartment killing the two telegraphists. Monsieur Carissan and Monsieur Villedieu de Torcy climbed up on the bridge preceded by QM. Cozic, who took the helm. The previous helmsman Matelot Stéphan, being wounded, went to the flat below the bridge. SM. Mourgues, although wounded in the side by an explosion, climbed onto the bridge. Monsieur Carissan was sent to man the torpedo tubes and the Commandant gave a verbal order to

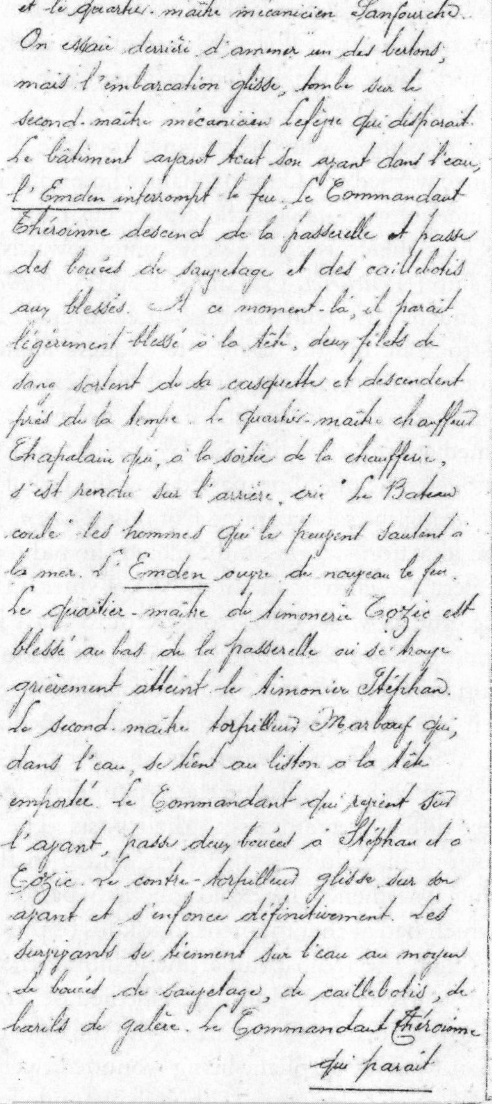

et le quartier-maître mécanicien Sansourcho.
On essaie derrière d'amener un des bidons,
mais l'embarcation glisse, tombe sur le
second-maître mécanicien Lefège qui disparaît.
Le bâtiment ayant tout son avant dans l'eau,
l'Emden interrompt le feu. Le Commandant
Théroinne descend de la passerelle et passe
des bouées de sauvetage et des caillebotis
aux blessés. A ce moment-là, il paraît
légèrement blessé à la tête, deux filets de
sang sortent de sa casquette et descendent
près de la tempe. Le quartier-maître chauffeur
Chapalain qui, à la sortie de la chaufferie,
s'est rendu sur l'arrière, crie "Le Bateau
coule" les hommes qui le peuvent sautent à
la mer. L'Emden ouvre de nouveau le feu.
Le quartier-maître de timonerie Cozic est
blessé au bas de la passerelle où se trouve
grièvement atteint le timonier Stéphan.
Le second-maître torpilleur Marbœuf qui,
dans l'eau, se tient au liston a la tête
emportée. Le Commandant qui revient sur
l'avant, passe deux bouées à Stéphan et à
Cozic. Le contre-torpilleur glisse sur son
avant et s'enfonce définitivement. Les
surnageants se tiennent sur l'eau au moyen
de bouées de sauvetage, de caillebotis, de
barils de galère. Le Commandant Théroinne
qui paraît

fig 15 — Part of Tavera's Report

increase speed. Monsieur Bourçier went down to the engine room to execute the order. Meanwhile the crew released the clip securing the after torpedo, threw the [obstructing] gas cylinders into the sea and started to remove the cover. The after 47mm gun was then loaded and opened fire.

Another salvo then arrived on board. One shell threw up a curtain of water at the water-line [witnessed from Penang Hill] and entered the crew's quarters. Explosions went off on the bridge wounding Monsieur de Torcy, who fell to the bridge floor. A shell then demolished the air intake for the forward furnace, the explosions passing through the boiler with steam rushing out via the deck hatches of the coal bunkers. The engines then stopped and Monsieur Bourçier could see that his presence was useless in the engine room, so he climbed onto the bridge. The moment he set his foot on the duck-boards some flying shrapnel sliced him in two. The remaining engine room crew, with the exception of two, came out on deck. The personnel from the after boiler room, scalded by the steam, scrambled out on deck, the first two being killed by explosions. Another sailor situated near the galley was likewise killed. The forward torpedo tube was now out of action. At the after torpedo the chief gunner QM. Heurtaux, was killed at just the moment when he said, 'and above all aim well!'.

At the starboard gun aft which had been firing, two of the crew were killed. The ship's bugler Matelot Hamon who was passing ammunition to the gunners was mortally wounded when shrapnel shattered his right arm, and QM. Duchêne was seriously wounded in the leg.

The destroyer began to go down by the bows and *Emden* came around by her stern. Monsieur Carissan left the bridge to make his way aft and was seriously wounded in the leg. [He had his left foot blown off and had open wounds in his right arm.] Monsieur de Torcy, himself wounded, came to his rescue. Explosions beside the forward torpedo tube wounded two other crewmen.

There was an attempt to bring one of the ship's boats aft but the launch skidded and fell onto SM. Lefèvre who disappeared.

The ship now had her whole bow in the water. *Emden* ceased firing and Commandant Théroinne came down from the bridge and distributed life-buoys and duck boards to the wounded. At that moment he appeared to be slightly wounded in the head with two rivulets of blood emerging from his cap and running down close to his temple. QM. Chapalain emerged from the boiler room and went back astern shouting 'The ship is sinking!'. Those men who were able jumped into the sea. *Emden* opened fire once more. QM. Cozic was wounded, and beneath the flooding bridge, seriously weakened, lay Matelot Stéphan. SM. Marbeuf, who was in the water, was holding him up by the top of his head. The Commandant returned forward and passed two more life-buoys to the wounded Stéphan and Cozic.

[It was now 7.40 am]. The destroyer slid down by the bows and finally sank. The survivors kept themselves afloat in the water by means of life-buoys and duck boards and barrels from the galley. The Commandant Théroinne, who appeared to be swimming freely at the start, was later noticed to be unconscious by the Matelot Gunner Calloch who supported him on the flag locker which had broken free. But the Vietnamese stoker Tri, who was supporting himself at the other end, let go of that piece of wreckage, which then twisted round so the Commandant and Calloch both sank. The Commandant did not re-appear. Monsieur Carissan, seriously wounded, was calling for help. So Calloch grabbed Monsieur Carissan and hoisted him onto the flag locker.

Emden now approached the survivors and, putting two launches into the water, rescued all those who were still afloat with the exception of the Vietnamese stoker Matelot Huong who, gripped with fear, slipped away from the *Emden* on a barrel from the galley.

One of the launches, learning of this, went to pick him up, but *Emden* then recalled everyone aboard. As soon as they were aboard the German cruiser, all the sailors from *Mousquet* were sent to the ship's hospital where one doctor checked those who were lightly wounded, whilst the other doctor prepared to do the serious operations.

Emden resumed her course at a speed of about 18 knots, steering westwards and then north. At the end of twenty-four hours her speed had diminished. In the hospital the doctors were operating on the gravely wounded. Monsieur Carissan asked to be operated upon last. Those who had no injury were parked on deck during the day and in the chain-locker at night. The German sailors gave them a few essentials. The *Emden* did not seem to have suffered any ill-effects from these two combats and nobody from their crew was in the hospital.

An officer of the reserve [Lauterbach] who was embarked on the *Emden* asked Engineer Provost the number of men who had been lost. In front of several men he said that the *Emden* had seen *d'Iberville* at anchorage in Penang but had not fired on her because of the presence of two cargo ships. He had not seen the other two destroyers and several Germans asked our sailors where *Fronde* and *Pistolet* were.[20]

Enseigne Tavera's report clears up a number of myths. First, it was never Théroinne's intention to make a dash for the shore. It is also untrue, as reported in some newspapers, that Théroinne had both his legs smashed and, lashed to the bridge, continued to direct his ship in that condition. Lauterbach's conversation with Engineer Provost also clears up the mystery of *Emden*'s long hesitation outside Penang harbour. They were expecting to engage destroyers. It was also the first time that *Emden*'s crew learned about the fate of their much-loved tender *Markomannia*, now at the bottom of the sea, with *Pontoporos* captured. They must have wondered why, after the capture of their tenders, Penang harbour was still lit up.

It is quite clear that von Müller knew beforehand that the French had four destroyers based in Penang. *Emden* had *d'Iberville* in her sights, but felt it was dangerous to open fire because too many merchant ships were in the way, and some might not be British. He was also unsure from which direction an unseen destroyer attack might be coming.

It also shows a certain carelessness by those responsible for the maintenance of the French ships in Saigon. Why had they installed ventilators that obstructed the free movement of *Mousquet*'s forward torpedo tube? This is doubtless the kind of thing that Castagné was referring to when he complained that none of the French destroyers had been put in proper battle-readiness before leaving Saigon and that they were urgently in need of a proper refit.

The final irony was the lack of radio communication. *Mousquet*'s wireless operators had been continuously at their posts and had heard nothing. Had Théroinne been warned, he could have slipped down the west coast of the island, and then shadowed *Emden* till a larger ship like *Chikuma* could be directed to intercept. *Mousquet* was a faster ship than *Emden* and could have done that well. Not yet having steam up, Audemard's transmitter was only capable of a very weak signal. But there was still the question as to why Audemard had not made strenuous efforts to contact *Mousquet*, either from the shore station or via *Pistolet*. In truth, he had assumed that *Mousquet* had already been sunk by the outer harbour, and that clouded his judgement. That error would later come back to haunt him.

During all this time, Maund had been busy. He was now at the cable station next to the Penang Club dispatching an urgent telegram to Admiral Jerram in Singapore, telling him what had happened. Jerram ordered all possible speed in getting the French ships moving to chase after *Emden*.

> *Pistolet* left harbour at about 7.30 a.m. but returned between 6 and 7 p.m. with her engines broken down. She had not been in action but reported that she kept the *Emden* in sight until about noon.

Apparently the harbourmaster MacIntyre, was suddenly falling all over himself to communicate Jerram's orders.

> In receipt of your telegram urging dispatch in getting under way, I accompanied Commander MacIntyre on board the *d'Iberville* and delivered its contents to the Captain. *Fronde* was under way about 9.00 am. and *d'Iberville* shortly before 10.00 am. But the latter had one engine broken down [actually dismantled] and only proceeded off Muka Head. *Fronde* had not returned the next morning, when in accordance with your instructions I left by rail for Singapore.[21]

Dr A.L. Hoops, State Surgeon and Inspector of Prisons in Kedah, reported that two bodies from *Mousquet* were washed ashore in Kedah.[22] But that was written 22 years after the event. No other account of bodies washed up from the wreck of *Mousquet* has yet been found.

There was a final twist to the tale. One sailor from *Mousquet* did get back to Penang alive. That was the Vietnamese stoker Matelot Huong, last seen floating away, hanging panic-stricken onto a barrel and refusing all assistance from the Germans. He was found later that day by some local fisherman, still clinging to his barrel, and brought safely back to Penang.[23] He was the first person to bring news, first-hand, to Audemard, reporting the fate of *Mousquet*.

Chapter 10

Counting the Cost

'This tragic action or rather this carnage' was Commander Audemard's expression of horror in his eloquent letter to Admiral Jerram.[1] In it he described the loss of *Zhemtchug* which had left 89 Russian crewmen dead. What is perhaps worse, 123 men were burned or wounded and in some cases horribly mutilated. Only 143 crew members out of 355 were lightly injured or unharmed. Amongst them was the First Officer Lieutenant Kulibin, who was ashore like his Commanding Officer Captain Cherkasov. The Baron had witnessed the appalling sight of his crewmen, or what was left of them, being brought ashore. His feelings can only be guessed at.

Audemard arranged for a first-aid party from *d'Iberville* to go ashore with the ship's doctor to do everything they could to assist.[2] A small fleet of launches and sampans, many belonging to local people, clustered around the spot and brought the survivors ashore. Every available motor car was brought to the water's edge with rickshaws and carts, anything that could convey the wounded to hospital.[3] Owing to the heat, most of the sailors had been sleeping in their underwear, whilst others were completely naked. The first of them came ashore at about 6.15 a.m. and from then on a constant stream of vehicles ran a shuttle to the hospital; 131 Russian crewmen were brought there, 96 of them injured. They were crammed in, occupying every available space and completely overwhelming the service, despite private practitioners volunteering their services.[4] The uninjured were later accommodated in Tanjong Tokong House.[5]

By the end of the day four sailors had died in hospital and dead bodies were still being washed ashore.[6] The incoming tide carried two bodies south, where they were washed up on the southern tip of Jerejak Island. They were found by fishermen and buried by the shore.[7] By the next day fifteen more bodies had been recovered, floating in the harbour, and yet more in hospital died from their injuries.[8] Four of the bodies were taken for burial at the Western Road cemetery and many local people turned out for the funeral. The volunteer force provided the military honours.

MacIntyre was also there.[9] At some level he must have realised his share of responsibility for all the carnage. Or maybe he wasn't. As reported in the next chapter, Maund sent fulsome praise to Jerram describing MacIntyre's zealous attention and 'great promptitude' for *Zhemtchug's* survivors.[10] These sentiments were later conveyed by Admiral Jerram to the Admiralty in London. 'Commander Duncan C. MacIntyre RNR, the Harbour Master, is deserving of the highest praise for his work in this connection.' The words … 'in this connection' … may have indicated slowly developing misgivings regarding the rest of MacIntyre's handiwork. The *Penang Gazette* went on:

> The Penang Volunteers lined the road and when the signal was given, the whole force marched to the Cemetery with arms reversed. Here, a large crowd was waiting with Rev. Father Duvelle and several priests from the various parishes of the settlement. The procession to the grave was a most solemn one: the coffins, which were covered by the Union Jack being carried by the survivors of the ill-fated ship and some members of 'A' company Penang Volunteers. There was only a short ceremony at the graves, a little to the left of the large cross on the Roman Catholic side, conducted by Rev. Father Duvelle, after which the remains for the unfortunate sailors were lowered to their last resting place. This done, the firing party fired their last salute.[11]

The Rev. J. H. Smith later reflected on the calamity in the *Province Wellesley Church Notes*:

> Seldom has it been the lot of landsmen to witness at such close quarters the tragedies of naval warfare as was the case this morning. Those of us who were able to witness the actual combat (if such it can be called) will never forget the display of man's vicious

anger and the terribleness of his engines of warfare. It is all beyond words; it makes little appeal to the senses as yet, because it staggers and overwhelms them.[12]

Cross, after going to the assistance of Russian casualties on the jetty, also attended the burial.

I went to the cemetery at 4.00 and waited till 5.15 when the procession came. There was an immense crowd. They were buried in the R.C. [Roman Catholic] part. Several of their wounded companions helped to bury them and a French padre officiated.[13]

Nobody knows for sure just how many bodies were eventually interred by that gravestone. Some time later two local eye-witnesses – a nun and the cemetery watchman – recollected twenty-four seamen being buried in that grave. Others were buried in an anonymous communal grave, whose location is now forgotten, or they were buried at sea in the traditional manner.[14]

For the time being, the survivors, including Cherkasov, had to remain in Penang. Many of them remained in hospital, waiting for the Russian volunteer fleet-ship *Orel*, sent from Vladivostok, to take them home. *Orel* was also ordered to salvage the guns from *Zhemtchug*. She did not leave Vladivostok till 27th December and the salvage work on *Zhemtchug* was interrupted by the Singapore mutiny. It therefore seems likely that the survivors of *Zhemtchug* remained in Penang till the end of February before they were repatriated. That was four months. It may have been a blessing in disguise, because at the beginning many would have been unfit to travel.[15]

The involvement of local people as well as expatriates over that long period, caring for stranded Russian sailors and their wounded so far from home, must have been considerable. An advertisement appeared in the *Penang Gazette* just after the tragedy:

Boots, Socks, Topis, Blankets and articles of clothing generally, are much needed by these poor men who have lost everything. If any kindly disposed persons can supply some of the above-mentioned and will send them to Chin Seng & Co Ltd, Farquhar Street, they will be forwarded by the Battalion Quarter Master Sergeant, P.V. to the Sailors' Camp.[16]

But going back to that first night at sea, the night of 28th October, the little hospital on board SMS *Emden* was also overwhelmed with French casualties from *Mousquet*.[17] Despite his evident bravado, the human cost of war, seen at such close quarters, clearly affected Prinz Hohenzollern. His account of picking up survivors gives a very clear picture of his reactions:

> The Frenchmen were carefully lifted out and taken at once to our sick-berth which is in the fore part of the ship. The poor fellows who fought well for their country, were a pitiful sight. Three men in particular were very bad. One of them I have always before my eyes when I think of his pain. The poor fellow had been hit in the stomach so that all his entrails were hanging out. It was unfortunate that the wounded had been some time in the water as it quickly aggravated their wounds.
>
> Our doctors went to work straight away. Two of the wounded had their legs shot away so that those limbs had to be amputated. The wounds were already festering, which made the doctor's work more difficult.[18]

When they were pulled out of the water, 36 of *Mousquet*'s crew were still alive. Prinz Hohenzollern went on to report various conversations between the French crew and their German guards, much of it hearsay, which doubtless came to him much later, including the myth of Théroinne's legs being blown off.[19] It lacks the methodical questioning of all witnesses that was later carried out by Tavera. That lends strong credibility to the conversation he reported between Engineer Provost and Lieutenant Lauterbach. But one of the conversations, unreported by Tavera, still has a ring of truth about it and fits in with the known facts.

Evidently some of *Mousquet*'s crewmen said they had seen a warship with four funnels heading towards Penang. They assumed it was a British warship. Even if it was not true, it was Prinz Hohenzollern's reaction that was so telling. He found it inexcusable that the French had no information about the movements of British warships and simply let a warship go by, without challenging them for identification.[20] He could not have imagined how hopelessly lax the security precautions in Penang were, or how the French had long since learned to accept that many ships came and went without giving identification and without their prior knowledge. It was von Müller's particular good fortune that *Yarmouth*'s arrival back in Penang at just that time was feasible, even though she was not expected.

Von Müller clearly knew in advance that there were other French destroyers, as yet unseen in Penang harbour, posing a threat to *Emden*. The emergence of *Pistolet*, shadowing them from a distance, confirmed it, although they guessed wrongly that she was *Fronde*. That mistake was later marked on the German charts, put together for von Müller's official report.

Prinz Hohenzollern explained that this was an important reason why *Emden* kept to the outer harbour. His comments quoted here nail the false claim by the British that *Emden* steamed straight into the inner harbour, past *d'Iberville* and beyond, before turning round.

> If we had approached the *d'Iberville*, this destroyer [*Pistolet*] could easily have cut off our exit and our destruction would have been as good as certain.[21]

Emden now disappeared into a rain squall and by the time they emerged from it, *Pistolet* had vanished. The Germans did not know that she had broken down and limped back to harbour.

Emden now set a course for the Penang–Rangoon shipping lane in the hopes of finding a merchant ship that could take the *Mousquet*'s prisoners and casualties to Sabang, the nearest neutral port. They sighted nothing that day, so they turned west towards the Nicobars. Apparently the French prisoners became agitated at this stage because they thought they were going to be left stranded on the Nicobars; so they had to be reassured.

In his usual way, Prinz Hohenzollern's romantic nature emerges in his account, waxing lyrical about the beautiful scenery around the Nicobars. He went on to describe how, during the night of 28th and 29th, two matelots, Barbaroux and Stéphan died in the ship's hospital. They were buried at sea on the 29th October at 9.00 a.m. All the officers from *Emden* and a party from their crew in No. 1 dress attended the ceremony. An armed detachment gave the military salute and the bodies were wrapped in the French flag. The Commander of *Emden* said some words in German, then in French:

> Nous prions pour çes braves, mort des blessures contractées dans un combat honorable..... [we pray for these gallant men, who died from their wounds, sustained in honourable combat].

That evening on 29th October a member of *Emden*'s crew, a native French speaker from Alsace, spoke to the survivors. (Alsace and Lorraine were annexed by Germany in the Franco-Prussian War.) They were told that they would be transferred to any cargo ship they encountered. Like all of *Emden*'s prisoners, they were asked to promise never again to bear arms for the duration of the war. The prisoners concurred.

Early next morning, at 4.00 a.m. the English cargo ship *Newburn* was apprehended. She was bound for Singapore carrying 3,000 tons of salt. Seeing that the condition of Carissan was deteriorating fast, von Müller ordered the captain of the cargo ship to make for Sabang with all possible speed.

Whilst supervising the transfer of the prisoners to *Newburn*, Prinz Hohenzollern was especially impressed by the bravery of Carissan, the only officer from *Mousquet* who was still alive.

> The severely wounded men were lashed into hammocks which made their transport easier, though the whole matter was rather difficult. The last of the ship's company of the *Mousquet* to be taken over was the officer. He returned grateful thanks for the excellent treatment given to his men in the *Emden*. We heard later that this officer died in Kota Raja [Sabang] of his severe wounds.[22]

All the survivors were transferred onto *Newburn* with the exception of the Matelot Salducci, who died during the night of the 29th/30th. He was the third to die on board *Emden*. Tavera's report to Audemard completes the story.

> The Prince Hohenzollern took the wounded to the cargo ship himself. The *Newburn* arrived at Sabang at 9.00 p.m. The Bugler Hamon died on board the *Newburn* at about six o'clock in the evening [before getting to Sabang]. When they arrived, the captain of *Newburn* signalled the mission which he had been given. The Dutch Commander Terdang came aboard the cargo ship to appraise the situation and make the necessary arrangements.
>
> Three doctors transferred the wounded to the hospital and those that were unharmed were directed towards the barracks. When they got there they were given supper, the necessities for having a wash and they were given beds. The next morning they went to the Dutch gun-boat *Serdang* [commanded by Lieutenant

van Asbech], where they were dressed in Dutch sailors' uniforms [see accompanying photograph]. Two or three hours after his arrival at the hospital Monsieur Carissan died. [He had developed gangrene and died during a radical amputation in an attempt to save his life.[23]]

Orations for him and Hamon were given on the 31st October at 5.00 p.m. All the Sabang authorities were there and all the troops were represented by armed detachments who gave them military honours. The Commander of *Serdang* gave the oration at the grave-side.

Tavera rounded off his report with a summary of the battle, emphasising that the crew of *Mousquet* had done their very best in the face of overwhelming odds, and that many of the crew, as well as her Commandant Théroinne, had shown great bravery whilst facing the terrible onslaught from *Emden.*[24]

In those days, Sabang was a busy place with a superb natural harbour. It was also used as a base for the Royal Dutch Navy. It sported a floating dock that had been laboriously towed all the way from Surabaya in Java. Sabang was also an important coaling station for Dutch, German and Russian ships which stopped by on their way to the Malacca Straits. With the outbreak of war, the neutral Dutch and their harbour authorities had no wish to offend anyone, so the management of *Mousquet*'s prisoners was a ticklish affair.[25]

The *Straits Echo* later reported that:

> The officer [Carissan] was carried to his grave by non-commissioned officers of the Dutch Army and the trumpeter [Hamon] by corporals. The coffins were covered with flowers and at the grave-side the Commander of the Dutch man-of-war gave a touching funeral oration.[26]

Léon Jaques Carissan was only 29 years old. He came from Saint-Jean d'Angely and in 1908, at just 22, was made an Enseigne de Vaisseau 1ère class. He came out to Saigon in January 1914 as second-in-command in the destroyer *Fronde*, under the command of Théroinne. Later, they both transferred to *Mousquet*. He was a popular officer who always considered his men's welfare before his own. He added strength and stability to Théroinne's command. His bravery earned him a special citation in L'ordre de L'armée. The citation ran as follows:

Seriously wounded in the battle he continued up to the last moment to do his duty with courage. Taken up aboard a German cruiser, he did not wish to be treated till all the other wounded from the crew of *Mousquet* had been attended to. He died as a consequence of his wounds, at Sabang, after having earned the admiration even of his enemies by his courage.[27]

On 5th January 1915 the Commander and crew of *Mousquet* were given a citation in L'ordre de L'armée and, after the war, the name of Carissan was given to the submarine UB99.[28]

Of the 36 who were rescued, three died in *Emden*, Bugler Hamon died in *Newburn* and Carissan died at Sabang. Thus, only 31 remained. Matelot Cannonier Calloch, who, although wounded, rescued Carissan and survived, as did the ice-cool helmsman QM. Cozic.

They were only 340 nautical miles from Penang, but Sabang was a neutral port and Penang was out of reach. The diplomatic niceties for repatriation had to be completed. International law being what it was, the Dutch had no wish to irritate the German authorities. They had to get diplomatic clearance from their own government, and presumably the German government too, before the *Emden*'s French prisoners could be released back to France. It was not until 12th November, almost two weeks after they had been brought to Sabang, that Audemard was free to leave Penang and fetch his men. By that time *Emden*, too, had met her fate.

It was under very different circumstances, therefore, that Audemard set out in *d'Iberville* to collect the survivors from *Mousquet*.[29] On the way back he drafted a report to his immediate superior in Saigon: the irascible Captain Charles de Paris de Boisrouvray.

In his report we can see that he had been impatient with the slowness of the diplomatic process. But his gratitude to the Dutch in Sabang was touching and genuine. Throughout this whole saga Audemard always comes across as a very humane man and his state of mind is very obvious in this report. His report, starting off in stilted official tones, gradually gives way to feelings from the heart.

Commandant,

I have the honour to provide you with the report on the mission I have just carried out in Sabang on the order of the Minister, with a view to repatriating the survivors from *Mousquet*, disembarked in this port on 30th October by the English steamer *Newburn*.

Upon the arrival of *d'Iberville* in front of Sabang on 14th November at 7.00 a.m., an officer from the Dutch gunboat *Serdang* came to enquire the purpose of our visit. He apologised for being unable to authorise us to anchor within the port because of his government's regulations to maintain the neutrality of the Netherlands, a copy of which he supplied me with.

My intention was to limit my stay as much as possible in Dutch waters. I asked the officer to make a report to the local authorities, to the effect that I wanted to accomplish my mission that same evening, and cast off immediately afterwards.

Around 9.00 a.m. I received a visit from the administrator of Pulau Weh and from the Naval Commander, who placed themselves with great politeness at my service, to take the necessary steps, authorised by the governor of Sumatra, with a view to obtaining immediate repatriation of our men. They did not mention any previous orders that had been received on this matter even though [as it turned out] they could have told me many days before that our men were actually free to go.

I knew from private correspondence which reached our sailors in Penang with what touching care the authorities of Sabang, civilian as well as military, rallied round the survivors of *Le Mousquet*. I can express in the name of the latter their deep gratitude and in the name of the Department, their deepest thanks for giving such compassionate help and for the material things which were so generously given to our men. In addition I want our thanks to be conveyed to those who gave our sailors that died in Sabang such a moving testimony, by accompanying them to their last resting place.

I will add in conclusion that the expenditure of all kinds occasioned by the stay of our sailors will be settled via the Consul, as far as the amounts can be known.

The formalities for rapid repatriation were done in the way that I had hoped by the Civil Administration. At 2 o'clock, the launches of the port conveyed to *Le d'Iberville,* twenty-eight sailors of *Le Mousquet,* accompanied by as many Dutch from the crew of *Serdang,* who were kept to make an escort for their French Comrades; a testimony to their good-will.

Soon after, *d'Iberville* got under way, we were saluted by the cheers of the Dutch sailors lined up in front of Sabang. With the Dutch colours at the head of our mizzen mast we broke out the signal 'with thanks'. At the same time I relayed a signal by TFT to the Sabang radio station giving my thanks and expressions of gratitude to the Civil Administrator, the Naval Commander and the other civil and military authorities.

During that short stay in Dutch waters I tried so far as I could to do my duty as dictated by the particular circumstances of my mission. But it seemed to me that we should not leave it at that. *Mousquet*'s victims were unanimous in their appreciation as beneficiaries of Dutch hospitality. The moral support of our sailors, disembarked without sustenance in a strange country, affected by events which had befallen them and weakened by their wounds; the attentions of the Commander of troops and the Naval Commander provided them with everything they lacked. Finally the dedication and care conscientiously given to the wounded by the Dutch doctors; all these acts of international solidarity given with such generosity and solicitude should merit more than simple thanks.[30]

He then went on to recommend various official distinctions that he thought should be awarded to those who provided help to the *Mousquet* crew. He makes special mention of Dr Blankenberg, the army doctor at Sabang hospital. As three of *Mousquet*'s survivors were considered too badly injured to travel, they had to remain in Sabang hospital for a while longer. The final tally of *Mousquet* survivors was 31, plus Huong which makes 32, whilst the dead numbered 43.

The finger of blame for the disaster in Penang was already pointing at the French and, with *Emden* destroyed just ten days later, the British Admiralty were no longer interested in pursuing the matter. The Far East, so far as they were concerned, was now a closed book with the Japanese firmly in charge. Jerram had got off exceedingly lightly.

On 13th November an advertisement appeared in the *Penang Gazette*.

A picture of the *Emden* will be on view tonight at the George Town Kinematograph. The Slide illustrates the cruiser steaming out of Penang Harbour after the sinking of the Russian warship on October

THE BRITISH

Britain's King George V in coronation robes. King of United Kingdom during WWI. Grandson of Queen Victoria, cousin of Kaiser Wilhelm II of Germany and Tsarina Alexandra of Russia.

The British Royal family belonged to the German House of Wettin, as well as Saxe-Coburg and Gotha. By 1917, the British royal family's German origins became such a liability that George V changed the family name to Windsor.

THE BRITISH

Right: Admiral Prince Louis von Battenberg. Photographed here when still a Commodore. British First Sea Lord at the outbreak of WW1. Commanded Vice Admiral Jerram. He was a German prince married to a granddaughter of Queen Victoria. Family name changed to Mountbatten. Prince Philip, husband of Queen Elizabeth II, is his grandson.

Left: Vice Admiral Sir Martyn Jerram. Commander-in-Chief, China Station at the outbreak of WW1. Photo: Imperial War Museum HU64343.

Below: 'Triumph'. British Battleship in Jerram's Far East Squadron. Assisted Japanese in the capture of Tsing Tao. Oct. – Nov. 1914.

Left: 'Minotaur'. British armoured cruiser, with powerful 9.2 inch guns. Served as Vice Admiral Jerram's flagship when he was at sea.

THE GERMANS

Kaiser (Frederick) Wilhelm II von Hohenzollern. Full length portrait of Kaiser Wilhelm aged 30 commissioned by his grandmother Queen Victoria to commemorate his visit to Britain in 1889. She bestowed upon him the honorary rank of Admiral of the British Fleet, as seen here. The Royal Collection © 2009 Her Majesty Queen Elizabeth II.

THE GERMANS

Admiral von Tirpitz. German Navy Minister at the outbreak of WW1. Persuaded the German Government into an arms race with Britain, building many battleships. This later proved to be a ruinous waste of money.

Vice Admiral Maximillian Reichsgraf (Count) von Spee. Commanded the German East Asiatic Squadron at the outbreak of WWI. A shy but popular officer, greatly admired by Vice Admiral Jerram. Went down with his ship and both his sons, at the Battle of the Falklands.

German armoured cruiser 'Scharnhorst'. Graf Spee's flagship. 'Emden' was mistaken for 'Scharnhorst' by the French Commander Castagné in the Penang Harbour battle, owing to 'Emden's dummy fourth funnel.

THE GERMANS

German light cruiser 'Emden'. With the outbreak of WWI, she soon became a legend, as a daring commerce raider in the Indian Ocean. Over three months in late 1914, she evaded all Admiral Jerram's efforts to capture her. She sank 'Zhemtchug' and 'Mousquet' at Penang. Photo: Imperial War Museum Q69359.

Right: Karl von Müller. Commander of 'Emden'. Shy, but very daring. Renowned for his chivalrous treatment of prisoners and extreme courtesy, nevertheless responsible for the deaths of many Russian and French sailors, and ultimately by not surrendering, the deaths of many of his own crew. Photo: Imperial War Museum Q45324.

Above: Lieutenant Helmuth von Mücke. 'Emden's' second-in-command. Gifted with exceptional leadership qualities, his epic escape to Constantinople with the landing party from Direction Island, made him famous throughout Germany. Photo: Imperial War Museum Q45322.

THE GERMANS

Lieutenant Prinz Franz Joseph von Hohenzollern. Nephew of Kaiser Wilhelm II and Second Torpedo Officer on 'Emden'. Fired the torpedoes that sank 'Zhemtchug'. Later given the task by von Müller of writing up the narrative of 'Emden's exploits.

Left: Lieutenant Julius Lauterbach. 'Emden's prize officer in the German Imperial Navy Reserve. Seconded from the merchant service where he was master of 'Staatssekretär Krütke' of HAPAG lines. Made a daring escape from prison camp in Singapore back to Germany.

This picture is signed in his own hand-writing, using the name 'Lauterbach-Emden'. All the surviving officers of 'Emden' were given the privilege of using the name 'Emden' by the Kaiser.

Kapt-Julius Lauterbach-Emden.

Portrait of Tsar Nicholas II as a young man. Married Alexandra, carrier of the haemophilia gene from her grandmother Queen Victoria. The disease emerged in their son Alexei. Rasputin attended Alexei as a healer.

Above: Tsar Nicholas II of Russia on the left and King George V of Britain on the right, just before WWI. Their similarity is striking.

THE RUSSIANS

Right: Baron Ivan Alexandrovitch Cherkasov. Captain of 'Zhemtchug'. Court-martialed in Vladivostok, sentenced to three and a half years imprisonment and stripped of all his titles. Fought with bravery and distinction as a common sailor in the Caucasus. Later reinstated.

Left: Russian light cruiser 'Zhemtchug'. Torpedoed by 'Emden' and blew up, before sinking in Penang harbour, just before dawn on 28th Oct. 1914, with great loss of life.

Two photos of the Russian Armoured cruiser 'Askold'. Well known because of her five tall funnels.

At the outset of WWI, 'Zhemtchug' and 'Askold' were lent by the Russian navy, with their Russian crews, to Admiral Jerram's Allied Far East Squadron.

28th. Tonight's performance will be under distinguished patronage.

A more sombre note was struck on 18th November. In the Church of the Assumption in Penang, a requiem mass was held for the victims of the *Mousquet*. Many local dignitaries were there in the congregation, including MacIntyre and many French people. The altar was draped in black with the French flag beside the British Ensign. The catafalque in the aisle was draped with the French Tricolour and wreaths. The service was conducted by Father L.M. Duvelle, priest of the church.[31]

When Audemard sailed to Saigon with *Mousquet*'s survivors, the whole strategic situation in the Far East had changed. At last, with *Emden* gone, the crew could relax and *d'Iberville* was scheduled to undergo her long-overdue refit. *Fronde* and *Pistolet* remained behind in Penang for a while, with Castagné in charge.[32] The mood was one of great relief and life went back to normal.

The war was now a distant event over in Europe, but Audemard's troubles were just beginning.

Chapter 11

Accusations Begin and the British Massage the Facts

The Reverend William Cross was outraged. In his opinion the entire tragedy was down to negligence. Negligence by people in positions of trust and responsibility. People who should have known better. His sense of responsibility trumped every other moral principle, and the dereliction of responsibility was the blackest of sins.

The day after the raid on Penang harbour, he collected his thoughts and put them down on paper. He was absolutely candid. There is no jingoistic patriotism here, no denunciation of the 'Hun' playing dirty tricks, which peppered the newspapers later on. He cast a critical eye over the whole tragedy and nobody escaped his searching questions.

Sifting through all the facts he had been able to muster, he enumerated key questions that had to be answered. It was quite characteristic of him that the emotional reaction of the moment was not enough. He had a very analytical mind and this he immediately brought to bear. Here are his comments put down in the form of notes for a letter, although no addressee is given.

Notes of a letter re. condition of things in Penang. Oct. 28th 1914.

The events of yesterday have brought things to a crisis. It is high time civilian public opinion voiced itself in Penang. Although very elaborate preparations have been made we appear to be without the slightest effective protection against the enemy.

All reference to what has happened, or is happening in Penang, is excluded from the newspapers, but there are too many sinister rumours going about and too many unexplained facts existing, for us to keep silent any longer.

The attack that was made upon the ships in the harbour yesterday ought not to have been possible. Everyone knows that such a danger was imminent. Someone has been guilty of gross and criminal negligence. The negligence has cost several lives. Four of those who were sacrificed so carelessly were buried yesterday. Many lie wounded in the hospital. Scores are lying drowned in the sunken Russian vessel in the harbour. It appears as if no one had any idea what to do.

We have the right to demand that the present state of things should be remedied, for in this grave matter we are all concerned. The Authorities in Singapore and at home should be clearly informed of what our condition is: so that if the men that hold the responsible military positions are not able to do their work, they must give place to better men. The following are questions that demand an answer.

1. Is it true that 27th was pay-day for the crew of the battleships that were in the harbour, and that the men were allowed to come ashore?

2. Is it true that the sailors were seen drunk on the shore and in the streets of Penang that day?

3. Is it true that the Commander of the Russian ship was not around at the time the enemy entered our harbour and attacked, and that he spent the night of 27th in a hotel in Penang instead of at the post of duty?

4. Is it true that the British officer stationed as interpreter and British representative on board the Russian vessel, also spent the night of 27th on shore, instead of at the post of duty?

5. Is it true that the French torpedo boats were quite unready for any attack: were actually moored to the harbour: had no steam up: did not get steam up till some hours after the attack?

6. Is it true that the enemy ship came right into the Straits and near the harbour unchallenged: that no question was asked by any patrol on watch: that she was merely allowed to pass because she looked like *Yarmouth*?

7. Is it true that no look-out [Penang] Volunteers were stationed who might have given the alarm: and that no look-out

Volunteers were stationed on the night of 28th [sic]?

8. Is it true that during the attack, the Germans who were interned in the Fort were permitted to clamber up on the Fort Cornwallis to see what was happening: a point from which they might easily signal to the enemy?

These are but a few of the questions that ought to be asked and answered. The sad thing is that they must be answered in the affirmative and all these things are true.[1]

The British authorities' attempt to muzzle the press was particularly foolish and the news soon broke in Singapore. The *Times of Malaya* ran an editorial complaining about this:

The extraordinary thing however, is that while in one part of the Colony the Press were not allowed to publish any account of the *Emden*'s daring raid, in another part of the Colony not only were the papers allowed to publish the report, but they were actually supplied with the information.[2]

Cross's observations all came out in the French enquiry, but it is doubtful whether he ever saw his criticisms vindicated in Penang.

To answer his points, the security arrangements in Penang were indeed abysmal. This was the fault of MacIntyre, who was not only the Harbourmaster, but also the Intelligence Officer responsible for keeping the local commanders properly briefed. These shortcomings should also include Jerram's failure to monitor MacIntyre's activities properly. The lack of precautions against an attack must have been known to Jerram at some level, and MacIntyre must have assumed the Admiral's tacit approval. Both of them must have believed that the needs of commerce had to be given a clear priority over security.

Not for the first time Jerram's policy seems to have been one of delegation, followed by inertia and inattention. And it was not just negligence. Captain Cochrane of *Yarmouth* and Commander Audemard had negotiated some important guidelines regarding ships' movements at night, with the North Channel and harbour lights extinguished. As soon as *Yarmouth* sailed, MacIntyre reversed these decisions without consultation. He should have been court-martialled for it.

The lack of a proper system of lookouts on shore manned by members of the Penang Volunteers is extraordinary. Their regular day and night motorcycle patrols along the coast as far as Batu Ferringhi had in fact been stopped just a few days before *Emden*'s raid.[3] The Penang Volunteer Force was a venerable institution set up during the Napoleonic wars. After war broke out, they were billeted at the Penang Club and members were paid $1 per day.[4] Their particular task at that time was the defence of the all-important cable station on North Beach to the west of Fort Cornwallis.[5] As a respected semi-professional organisation[6] they were the obvious choice to act as lookouts as well.

Penang Island has a high ridge of hills along its entire length, and excellent vantage points exist that enable lookouts to see far out to sea in any direction. The eye-witnesses at the Crag Hotel, who watched the attack on *Merbau* and later *Mousquet,* demonstrated what excellent vantage points were to be had. Even at night, the silhouette of a ship in the North Channel would be spotted, unless it was exceptionally dark.

There is some evidence that the lookouts manning the Muka Head lighthouse actually saw *Emden*'s silhouette, but were fooled by the four funnels. They allegedly mistook her for *Yarmouth,* but if *Yarmouth* was due in early that morning, why didn't anyone know? Had they no identification codes? Had they no wireless? Clearly no effort was made to keep vital people informed of ships' movements.

Cross was shocked to discover that without prior knowledge a warship could arrive in the harbour, unannounced and unchallenged pretending to be *Yarmouth,* and be apparently above suspicion. And this was at a time when the entire civilian population of Penang were fearful of an attack. Only the Harbourmaster seems to have known who was coming in and out at any given time and he was apparently 'too busy' to pass the information on.

The unprepared state of the warships was also the direct result of Jerram's decisions. Knowing that *Emden*'s colliers had just been captured at a rendezvous nearby, why did he choose that moment to allow three out of five warships in harbour to be shut down for repairs? The answer is that he had no alternative because all of the warships based in Penang were so overdue for repairs that they could barely function. Those repairs should have been done long ago, if he had paid attention to what he was being told. In the end, the repairs had to be carried out come what may. Jerram personally authorised the dismantling of the boilers in *Zhemtchug,* whilst acknowledging the same needs for *d'Iberville* and *Fronde.* He was perfectly well aware that they would likely be immobilised at the same time. Clearly, he did not take the possibility of an imminent attack seriously.

It cannot be wondered at, therefore, that Cherkasov had also taken the matter very lightly. The irresponsible conduct of the Russian captain, and his failure to prepare his ship properly in case of attack, was indeed reprehensible and his crew paid a terrible price. Cherkasov, too, paid a heavy price at his later court martial. But it must also be said that nothing in the arrangements in Penang harbour would have led him to believe that an attack was even a remote possibility. Since his return from Rangoon the harbour and the North Channel had been fully lit up and such lookouts and patrols as there were, seemed happy to let anything pass. Apparently, it was unnecessary for him to be informed in advance of any ships' movements even at night.

MacIntyre may have come aboard *Zhemtchug* and he may, or may not, have asked Cherkasov to be vigilant. Unfortunately, Maund's report to Jerram is the only source we have to go on, and it is so full of inaccuracies and concocted stories that everything in it has to be doubted.

Finally, there is the question of the Germans in Penang. This is part of the broader issue of security which particularly exasperated Captain Daveluy of *Dupleix,* even though some Germans in Penang had actually become naturalised Englishmen and even joined the Penang Volunteers.[7] The remaining German nationals were eventually interned, but it was a long time before that was done. Daveluy's critical letter to Jerram has already been quoted. In the same letter he added:

> Is it possible that our [French] destroyers were at the mercy of a large colony of Germans in Penang? Effectively, *Emden* knew about their presence without doubt, and the positions they were occupying, because they had already been in Penang for two months.[8]

Daveluy was partly right. *Emden* did know about the French destroyers and also about his own cruiser *Dupleix*, but von Müller had no need to go to such lengths to obtain that information. It was common knowledge amongst the crews of the ships *Emden* captured, some of whom were quite indiscreet.

In the event, Cross's call for an enquiry fell on deaf ears. For very obvious reasons, the last thing that the British in Penang wanted was an enquiry, because their irresponsibility was all too evident, even to a local clergyman like Cross. It is tempting to speculate that Maund, who knew *Emden* and von Müller's reputation for daring on the Yangtze, did feel some real apprehension and may have felt safer ashore.

The following Sunday, four days after the raid, Reverend Cross mounted the pulpit of St Andrew's Kirk and launched a stinging attack on Penang's lack of preparedness. One has to imagine the scene. In the days before microphones, preachers developed not just powerful voices, but practised a dramatic rhetorical style, which is rarely seen today outside the vast churches of the United States.

He was never a man to mince his words, but he was sailing very close to the wind. This was wartime and any criticism of his own side could be seen as unpatriotic. But this brave, austere Scot gave vent to his feelings. It comes to us as fresh today as it was a hundred years ago. The church would have been packed, because Cross was no ordinary clergyman. His congregation must have been shocked by the bluntness of his speaking. Yet looking at his words today, it is clear that he avoided making direct accusations towards the British harbour authorities. For that you must read between the lines. His criticisms of the drunkenness and dissipation of the sailors ashore would have gone down well and directed blame towards the Russians. But his target is clearly much wider than that, and much closer to home.

Here among ourselves the places of duty are set, the work of guarding the community against the enemy's attack was allotted. The community trusted that the men in the places of duty would be faithful. What has happened ought not to have been possible. Everyone knew that such a danger was imminent. The event did not come without warning. The chances of its occurrence were discussed openly among us. The certainty of its attempt, the uncertainty of its approach, the necessity of constant watching, all these elements were commonplace in our minds. We have been hurled for a brief hour into the front battle line. The deep funeral bells are tolling. The Angel of Death has hovered over us. We heard with quivering hearts the beating of His gloomy wings. He came upon us unawares. He found us sleeping. We have failed and now men lie wounded in the hospital, men lie dead in the sea.

A failure ought to teach us something. This is not a thing to be covered up and forgotten. The responsibility for demanding that the matter be sifted rests upon us all. If there has been negligence it ought to be tracked down. If there has been incapacity it ought to be removed: and those who are not able to do the necessary work must give place to better men. If there has been guilt it ought to be punished. No doubt there will be those who will try to hush the matter up, who will try to tone down its ugly and disgraceful features. That must not be allowed.

Therefore, I am taking it upon me to speak with absolute plainness about the significance of what has happened. The public responsibility for demanding an enquiry so that the truth may be made known, may lie upon the shoulders of others.

For any man to pretend to be a patriot during these days and then to allow himself in any sense to become morally careless, either because he is too self-centred to be bothered, or because his business interests are involved, or because his brain is dulled with alcohol and his heart bemused with the love of pleasure, is to run very close to the risk of becoming a traitor to the interests he ought to protect.[9]

In this angry sermon, which was very long, Cross hammered home his message that people in positions of authority who did not act with a profound sense of responsibility towards those who depended on them were guilty of the worst kind of sin.

Making an implicit attack on the authorities responsible for the defence of Penang, he pointed to an attitude of carelessness and hinted at commercial interests taking precedence over safety. His uncompromising stance against alcohol and drunkenness was not unusual in ministers of the Free Presbyterian Church. In his case such disapproval had been a part of his message since his earliest days as a minister. It was hardly surprising, therefore, that the binge drinking of the Russian sailors, ashore on pay-day, would have aroused his indignation.

But his anger went far beyond that. He was especially incensed that the authorities in Penang had actually tried to muzzle the press, at least until they found that the news had broken in Singapore. He quite rightly supposed that such censorship was an attempt to avoid criticism and had little to do with the public interest.

The reasons Maund gave for staying ashore by the signal station were indeed quite valid. For sure, he could not rely on the Russian lookouts, given the chaotic arrangements for watch-keeping that were later confirmed at Cherkasov's court martial. But he also knew that the harbour authorities made little or no effort to pass on important intelligence anyway; a problem that the French had been battling with all along. This would have been communicated to him both by Cochrane in his handover meeting with *Yarmouth,* and the French officers who he spoke to. It must be remembered that Maund was a fluent French speaker and the French would not have been slow in coming forward with this information.

A systemic failure of adequate leadership, and a cavalier disregard for those sailors trying to defend Penang and the northern Malacca Straits, was abundantly clear. For all his obsessive preoccupation with drunkenness, Cross's questions were pertinent and unanswerable.

To get some clues into the workings of Jerram's mind, it is important to understand his attitudes and his priorities. To be fair, he was dealing with the movements of a large number of ships over a vast area. He was charged with bringing to Europe, in the shortest possible time, a veritable armada of cargo ships and troop transports from India and Indochina as well as New Zealand and Australia. He also had to keep a sharp eye out for German merchant ships interned for the duration of the war in neutral places like the Philippines. Graf Spee and his powerful Pacific squadron had to be watched, and his Japanese allies had to be supported in their invasion of Tsing Tao. The matter of *Emden* was simply an irritant that he hoped would go away. When accused of incompetence his rather pompous retort to Churchill said it all.

It is, or at least was, a common failure amongst those who spent their lives in the military, to underestimate the importance of the media, except as organs for state-controlled propaganda. They tended to regard the media as servants that had to be kept under control. But Churchill was first and foremost a journalist and he realised the appalling effect that the ongoing *Emden* saga was having on the British reputation at home and abroad. It made a laughing stock of the British Navy and it was a far bigger story than Jerram's interned merchant ships, or his French transports, or even his frozen meat. He just never grasped it.

He was content to delegate the whole *Emden* business to Grant in *Hampshire* and saw no point in concerning himself further with the matter. The sinking of a few merchant ships amongst so many was to him mere piffle and, besides, von Müller could be relied upon to ensure no loss of life. British merchant ships were doing very well indeed out of the war, and nothing should deter them from doing whatever they wanted. He did pass on some Admiralty directives to merchant ships regarding security, such as avoidance of certain shipping lanes and not making radio transmissions 'en clair', but when these guidelines were ignored he just shrugged it off instead of enforcing them.

In addition, he made no attempt to link up the patrols of the French ships stationed in Penang with Grant's squadron hunting for *Emden*, or they would never have mistaken *Emden* for *Yarmouth*. Apart from the inefficiency, it was a waste of valuable ships. He once commented that French ships were too slow, but that was certainly not true of the French destroyers. Provided they were adequately maintained they were faster than anything else. His complete unconcern that three out of four French commanders could not even decipher coded messages intended for them is absolutely extraordinary. 'We are short of copies', he said.

Situated as he was in Singapore, his inattention to the defence of Penang, a major port on the Straits Settlements, is strange. Perhaps he had never visited Penang. A lesser man than von Müller could have wreaked havoc by bombarding the town, the signal station and the merchant ships in the harbour. But von Müller had his principles regarding the protection of civilians and non-combatants and he stuck to them.

The French enquiry, which was convened late the following January, gathered a wealth of verbal and written reports from dozens of witnesses, and we have them to thank for much of the detail that is known. It is on record for anyone to see. On the British side, all that has been discovered are contemporary newspaper reports from a smattering of eye-witnesses and a single report to Jerram from Maund, a junior liaison officer from one ship. No report from the harbour authorities was found in the Admiralty archives, nor any report from the dozens of witnesses who were aboard the merchant ships in the harbour. These ships were mostly British with watch-keepers aboard. The French had no access to them as witnesses, but the British Admiralty, and indeed the newspapers, could have recorded their eye-witness accounts. Why didn't they? Were they told to avoid the media as their patriotic duty?

Maund's account dated 1st November was sent to Jerram four days after the event. Jerram also had the official translation of Audemard's report, but that came after he had drafted his own report and hence does not figure in it. He seems to have been unconcerned about significant differences between the two accounts, particularly regarding the movements of *Emden* in Penang harbour, yet no supplementary report was found in the files. Audemard's report, although brief, does not differ in any important respect from the accounts given to the Saigon enquiry.

So far as British accounts of the raid are concerned, the rot set in right away. Maund first reported how things were in *Zhemtchug*, with MacIntyre coming aboard to meet with Captain Cherkasov. He then goes on to describe the raid itself:

On 28th October, at about 5.15 a.m. the *Emden,* flying British colours and a flag, the nature of which is uncertain at the fore, painted a dark grey similar to our ships and fitted with a dummy fourth funnel, entered the harbour of Penang by the North Channel. The patrol launch, conceiving her to be a British man-of-war allowed her to pass without giving the alarm.[10]

This is the only report that states that *Emden* was flying British colours. It seems very probable that this was yet another recycling of that story of *Emden* 'befooling' a Japanese ship. The Admiralty Monograph which was written later, had another version of that story:

A prisoner, taken from a ship by the *Emden* in October, reported being told by her officers 'on seeing a Japanese cruiser approaching, *Emden* promptly hoisted the British Ensign, whereupon the Japanese saluted and passed on.'[11]

There seems to be no other report of this incident, and its authenticity is therefore very suspect, coming as it does third, or even fourth-hand. Nothing of the kind is reported in Prinz Hohenzollern's account, but you would not expect that anyway. But the tale took on a certain resonance amongst the conspiracy theorists who would never believe that *Emden* could succeed, except by playing 'dirty' and flouting the international rules of warfare.

None of the eye-witnesses reported seeing *Emden* flying a British flag, neither did any of the French sailors, who were going mad trying to see what flags *Emden* actually did have, even after broad daylight had broken. There was no wind and *Emden*'s flags would not fly. Instead, they hung limp around the halyards.

Some eye-witnesses speculated that *Emden* might have been flying the Japanese flag, or even the Russian flag,[12] and both those versions were reported two days later in the *New York Times*.[13] One witness said, 'It was stated that she was flying the Russian flag, but I could not see her flag and she had obviously come in during the night.'[14] The *Times of Malaya* also reported that *Emden* was flying the Russian flag.[15] So, the only source of the idea that *Emden* was flying the British Ensign comes from Maund. Yet most of the books that have been written since, record this as a fact without questioning its authenticity. Of what we know of von Müller, he was scrupulous about the rules. There was nothing in international law about a dummy funnel and, although he left it

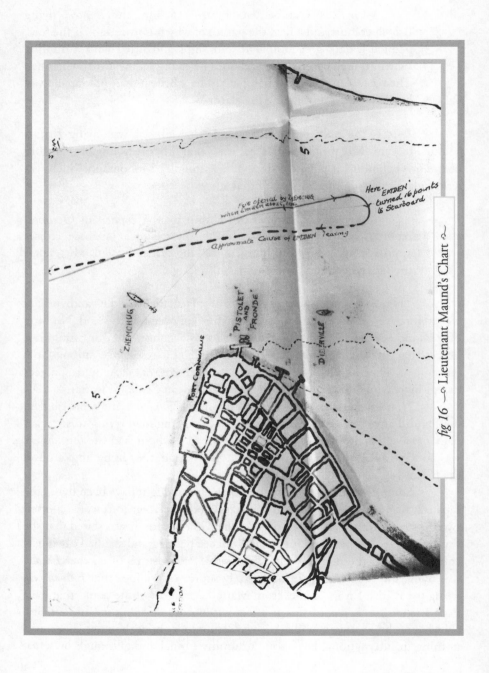

fig 16 ∼ Lieutenant Maund's Chart ∼

to the last minute, both when attacking *Zhemtchug* and *Mousquet,* he always hoisted German colours before opening fire.

Finally, Maund complained that *Emden* was painted 'British' grey. It was wartime and all the German warships were painted grey.

So in that paragraph, Maund is clearly 'massaging' the facts to make it look as though *Emden* was successful only because she was playing 'dirty'. This, he believed, was a sufficient excuse for the failure of harbour security to challenge her. Why was the pilot launch not informed if *Yarmouth* was indeed expected? If it was *Yarmouth,* why didn't she flash her proper identification signal? These questions he completely avoided.

On the next page, Maund's report descends into farce.

> The *Emden,* having passed clear of the *Zhemtchug,* turned 16 points during which time MacIntyre went alongside the *Zhemtchug* in his launch and did all in his power to exhort the men to greater exertions at the guns.[16]

Even if MacIntyre had a house right down by the jetty, he would still have to waken, get dressed, run down to his launch (which would have full steam up) and go out to *Zhemtchug* which was over a kilometre away, all in the space of a few minutes. One thing is certain, and all witnesses agree, that the time between the first and second cannonade was short. The witnesses at the Eastern & Oriental Hotel were woken by the first cannonade and had spent very little time standing on the terrace before the second cannonade started. Reports vary, but average out at ten minutes.[17] This means that *Emden* turned round immediately after the first cannonade in order to get in her second run in the shortest possible time. Had MacIntyre done what he claimed, and run up alongside *Zhemtchug* after the first cannonade, beating his fists on the sinking hull of the great cruiser and 'exhorting the men to greater exertions', *Emden*'s second torpedo and the terrific explosion that followed would probably have blown him to smithereens.

What follows is a serious misrepresentation of the facts intended to show that the French were guilty of cowardice:

> From the chart accompanying this report it will be seen that during the time that *Emden* was turning she was abreast *d'Iberville* and had already passed the French destroyers, *Pistolet* and *Fronde,* who were lying alongside each other at Swettenham

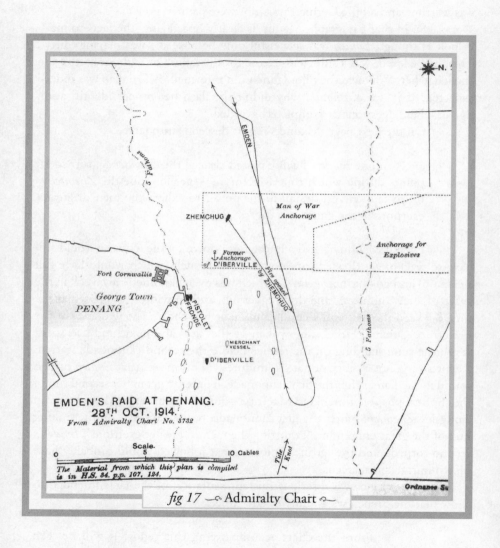

EMDEN'S RAID AT PENANG.
28TH OCT. 1914.
From Admiralty Chart No. 3732

Scale.
0 — 5 — 10 Cables

The Material from which this plan is compiled is in H.S. 84. p.p. 107, 124.

Tide 1 Knot

fig 17 ❦ Admiralty Chart ❧

Pier. None of these ships opened fire on *Emden*.[18]

This was clearly wrong. Given all the other facts it could not possibly have been true. Unfortunately, it quickly became official and the French were blamed for cowardice. Partly because the French enquiry was not held in English, the truth, as far as the British were concerned, was safely buried.

The chart that accompanied Maund's report was a scruffy affair (Fig. 16), and failed to mark any of the merchant ships that were moored there. *Emden* would have needed to negotiate them in order to reach the spot where she allegedly turned, never mind all the smaller craft that would have been in the way also. It shows *Emden* going far into the inner harbour to a point well beyond the mooring of *d'Iberville*. In those days the waters in that part of the inner harbour would have been quite shallow and hazardous for a large warship like *Emden* to make a turn. *D'Iberville* herself was built for shallow waters and had a draught of only three metres, less than half that of *Emden*.

The official Admiralty chart (Fig. 17)[19] shows some merchant ships that have been put back into the picture, but in this version *Emden* passes all of them to starboard and heads for the shore at Butterworth, well to the south of *d'Iberville*. Again, that would have brought her into shallower water where the number of small boats would have increased greatly. *Emden* is then shown turning to starboard, which contradicts all the eye-witnesses and the German accounts as well.

According to the German chart[20] and supported by the French records, *d'Iberville* was 1866 metres from *Zhemtchug*. Using that as a guide, it puts *Emden*'s turning point 2600 metres to the south of *Zhemtchug*. Including the turn, this would represent an excursion of over 5000 metres between the first and second cannonade. That is almost three nautical miles.

It would have been impossible for *Emden* to negotiate this at anything but very slow speed, given all the ships and boats crowding the harbour. Ships have no brakes and the bigger the ship, the greater the distance to slow down. So a speed of three knots would be all that could be allowed under those cramped conditions. But even if she had been steaming at five knots, she would have to come to an almost complete stop to execute the turn. At that highly optimistic estimate the whole excursion would still require forty-five minutes, which would far exceed the known interval between the first and second cannonade.

The German as well as the Russian[21] records put the first torpedo strike at 5.18 a.m. According to the British chart the second strike would have to be at 6.03 a.m. at the very earliest. That was after sunrise. All the witnesses report that the second cannonade was in twilight with an outside limit of 15 minutes after the first. The German account put the times at 5.18 a.m. and 5.28 a.m., respectively. Ten minutes exactly.[22] The official Admiralty map copied from Maund's report to Jerram is obviously concocted. Like the one published later in the *New York Times*, it is not even an approximation to the known facts.

The purpose of the chart was to mislead people into supposing that *Emden* was well within range of *d'Iberville*'s guns as well as *Pistolet*'s torpedoes. In the latter case the chart still puts *Emden*'s minimum distance from *Pistolet* at 1000 metres, which was still out of range of her torpedoes, with many other ships and smaller craft in the way.

Maund finished off this dodgy report with the following:

> Commander MacIntyre acted with great promptitude both in conveying the contents of your telegram [ordering an immediate search for *Emden*] to their destinations and in conjunction with the local authorities did everything in his power for the survivors, with the result that the wounded were rapidly conveyed to hospital where those wounded were suitably and comfortably housed without delay.[23]

Doubtless he felt that all this praise for MacIntyre was enough to exonerate him from any further culpability. Did the two of them collude in writing this dishonest report?

Having received the report from Maund, Jerram's own version to the Admiralty was based entirely on this single source. Once again, Jerram's lack of appetite for scrutinising things in a critical way allowed these dismal fabrications to become official. In his letter to the Admiralty, after the attack on Penang harbour, he had this to say:

> I much regret having to report the loss of the Russian cruiser *Zhemtchug* and the French destroyer *Mousquet* under the following circumstances. Penang is used as a coaling base for the ships operating against *Emden* on the Eastern side of the Bay of Bengal and also for the French gunboat *d'Iberville* and the three French destroyers *Fronde, Mousquet* and *Pistolet*, employed in patrolling the vicinity of Penang.
>
> *Zhemtchug* arrived there on 26th October having searched the Mergui archipelago and requested permission to clean boilers and

make good defects to main engines, stating that she would be ready for sea by 2nd November. This I approved.

Jerram then described the positions of the ships, without offering any explanation as to why an immobile warship should be anchored in the outer harbour and two destroyers lashed together side-by-side at Swettenham Pier. He went on:

> There was also an unarmed patrol launch near the northern entrance manned by natives, but with a pilot on board.

Based upon the report he had received from Maund, he then described *Emden*'s appearance in Penang harbour.

> About 5.15 a.m., just at daylight, *Emden* approached the harbour by the Northern Channel. She was flying British colours and a flag at the fore, the nature of which could not be distinguished. She was painted dark grey similar to a British ship and had a dummy fourth funnel. *Mousquet* presumably had not sighted her and the patrol launch, conceiving her to be a British man-of-war, let her pass without giving the alarm.

He then described the sinking of *Zhemtchug* and *Mousquet*, with some inaccuracies, but consistent with Maund's account. He then added:

> Their Lordships will observe that I have confined myself as far as possible to the facts connected with the deplorable loss of *Zhemtchug*.
> If she had been a British ship, I would naturally consider it my duty to investigate and report as to whether any lack of preparation against a surprise attack had contributed to the loss of such a favourable opportunity to inflict damage on the *Emden*, combined with such disastrous results on herself. This aspect of the matter will doubtless be enquired into by the Russian Authorities.
> The same remarks also apply to the French vessels in harbour none of which had steam up; the two destroyers being lashed together alongside the pier. But as yet I have not yet received a report from the French Commander so I express no opinion.[24]

What is interesting about this report is what it reveals about Jerram's attitude towards his own position as the overall Allied commander. Starting with the beginning of the report, he describes Penang as a coaling station. That was true and Jerram clearly saw Penang in those terms. No mention is made of it being a well-populated island of nearly 150,000 full of British subjects who were supposed to be protected.[25] It is likely that the defence of Penang from Jerram's point of view was a military matter and had nothing to do with him. In the narrowest sense, perhaps that was right. But the defence of the harbour and its ships was very much his concern and he does not acknowledge that at all. He also clearly separates the French ships from the squadron hunting for *Emden*. What did he think their endless patrols were for?

There is something slightly snide about his comment that the harbour patrol boat was crewed by 'natives', as if they were ignorant and therefore could not be expected to recognise *Emden*, or *Yarmouth* for that matter.

He says that he approved *Zhemtchug*'s shutdown for several days without any reference to his reasons for believing it was a good time to do so. His attitude seems to have been 'that was their affair'. And finally, he does not admit that the arrangements for the French ships 'none of which had steam up' had been discussed previously. The two destroyers lashed side-by-side was the decision of his own Harbourmaster, against French advice, yet he says nothing. It is as if anything to do with the French ships was completely out of his hands.

He boldly states that 5.15 a.m. was daybreak, in order to support the theory that her 'British Colours' could be clearly seen. It was night-time and dark, with no moon, and he knew it. How could he expect the Admiralty to swallow such transparent nonsense? But it seems they did, or perhaps they just chose to. For those more used to living in temperate zones, the transition from complete darkness to daylight in the tropics is surprisingly swift.

Finally, he fails to question how a warship of any description could enter Penang harbour, unexpected and unchallenged, with all the channel buoys lit, and allowed to pick off the first ship they saw? In truth it would have mattered little if *Zhemtchug* had been drawn up with a stern anchor as suggested, or even with Cherkasov aboard. She could not have used her underwater torpedoes because they could not manoeuvre the ship. For sure, they might have landed some shells on *Emden*, but *Emden* had the element of surprise and we know that she was expert at blasting another ship's armaments and gun-crews before they could retaliate. This is what happened later to *Mousquet*. But it was in no way the fault of *Zhemtchug* that she was unable to identify *Emden* in the dark in so short a time, when that ship had just been allowed into the harbour unchallenged. Jerram makes no mention of the fact that ships of all kinds came and went without those defending the harbour being informed.

Jerram suggested that von Müller was cheating. He had painted his ship grey (whatever next?), hoisted a dummy funnel and was flying British colours. Jerram's unwillingness to hold an enquiry because no British ships were sunk speaks for itself. Had not *Emden* been destroyed ten days later, he could have been in very hot water indeed. In fact, the Japanese had written him off already.

What followed next is an example of how fact can be stranger than fiction. An unknown correspondent sent an article to the *New York Times* written on 29th October and allegedly describing the raid on Penang.[26] It was written in such a way as to put Maund's concoctions in the shade. This was a truly vicious article, so gross and so full of fabrications, that anyone in Penang could have seen through it immediately. But its purpose was to exonerate the British and put all the blame on the incompetent Russians and the cowardly French. The *New York Times* was doubtless chosen because the US was an English-speaking country, allegedly neutral and therefore supposedly free from partiality or bias:

> It was on Wednesday morning that the *Emden,* with a dummy fourth funnel and flying the British Ensign, in some inexplicable fashion sneaked past the French torpedo boat *Mousquet* which was on patrol duty outside and entered the outer harbour of Penang. Across the channel leading to the inner harbour lay the Russian cruiser *Zhemtchug.* Inside were the French torpedo boats *Fronde* and *Pistolet* and the torpedo-boat destroyer *d'Iberville*. The torpedo boats lay beside the long government wharf while the *d'Iberville* rode at anchor between two tramp steamers.
>
> At full speed the *Emden* steamed straight for the *Zhemtchug* and the inner harbour. In the semi-darkness of the early morning the Russians took her for the British cruiser *Yarmouth* which had been in and out two or three times during the previous week and did not even query her. Suddenly, when less than 400 yards away, the *Emden* emptied her bow guns into the *Zhemtchug* and came on at a terrific pace with all the guns she could bring to bear in action. Then, when she had come within 250 yards, she changed her course slightly and

as she passed the *Zhemtchug*, poured two broadsides into her as well as a torpedo, which entered the engine room but did comparatively little damage.

Took Everybody by Surprise

The Russian cruiser was taken completely by surprise and was badly crippled before she realised what was happening. The fact that her Captain was spending the night ashore and that there was no one on board who seemed capable of acting energetically, completed the demoralisation. She was defeated before the battle began. However, her men finally manned the light guns and brought them into action.

In the meantime the *Emden* was well inside the inner harbour and among the shipping. She saw the French torpedo boats there, and apparently realised at once that unless she could get out before they joined in the action, her fate was sealed. At such close quarters the range was never more than 450 yards, and their torpedoes would have proved deadly. Accordingly she turned sharply and made for the *Zhemtchug* once more.

At the time she had been in the harbour, the Russian had been bombarding her with shrapnel, but owing to the notoriously bad marksmanship prevalent in the Czar's navy had succeeded, for the most part, only in peppering every merchant ship within range. As the *Emden* neared the *Zhemtchug* again both ships were actually spitting fire. The range was practically point blank. Less than 150 yards away the *Emden* passed the Russian and as she did so, torpedoed her amidships, striking the magazine. There was a tremendous detonation paling into insignificance by its volume all the previous din; a heavy black column of smoke arose and the *Zhemtchug* sank in less than 10 seconds while the *Emden* steamed behind the point to safety.

No sooner had she done so than she sighted the torpedo boat *Mousquet*, which had heard the firing and was coming in at top speed. The *Emden* immediately opened up on her thereby causing her to turn around in an endeavour to escape. It was too late. After a running fight of twenty minutes the *Mousquet* seemed to be hit by three shells simultaneously and sank very rapidly. The German had got a second victim.

The inaccuracies in this report are blatant, but the message is clear. The Germans were super-efficient but tricky, the French were treacherous cowards, and the Russians were muddle-headed, slothful incompetents who couldn't shoot. The comments about the French ships are especially reprehensible. The writer gives the impression that *Mousquet* was just outside the harbour and, through inattention, let the German ship slip in. The arrival of *Emden* in the harbour was therefore their fault. Once within the harbour, the Germans suddenly saw the other French torpedo boats which nevertheless failed to open fire, even though *Emden* was a sitting duck at close range. So the failure to sink *Emden* was again the fault of the French. And finally, on leaving the harbour after sinking *Zhemtchug, Mousquet* first approached *Emden*, then tried to run away as soon as she was fired upon.

It is clear from eye-witnesses, from Hohenzollern's account and from the French enquiry that none of this is true. *Emden* entered the harbour at very slow speed, and was allowed in by the Penang harbour launch. *Yarmouth* had departed nine days previously with the French transports, bound for Colombo. Clearly she could not possibly have come into Penang three times the previous week.

The course taken by *Emden* was nothing like the one described in this article and she was never even close to being within range of *Pistolet*'s torpedoes. As for *Mousquet,* she was at least 15 nautical miles away, maybe more, and well over the horizon.

Fig. 18 shows the illustration accompanying the article. The destroyers are depicted tied up in line at Swettenham Pier, which is incorrectly placed. *Emden* is seen manoeuvring around merchant ships anchored in the inner harbour. This would be both difficult and hazardous for such a large warship. Hohenzollern made it quite clear that entering the inner harbour was never an option for *Emden*. But this infamous article gets worse.

The Chivalrous von Müller

It was here that the chivalrous bravery of the *Emden*'s captain, which has been many times in evidence throughout her meteoric career, was again shown. If the French boats were coming out, every moment was of priceless value to him. Nevertheless, utterly disregarding this, he stopped, lowered his boats and picked up the survivors from the *Mousquet* before steaming on his way.

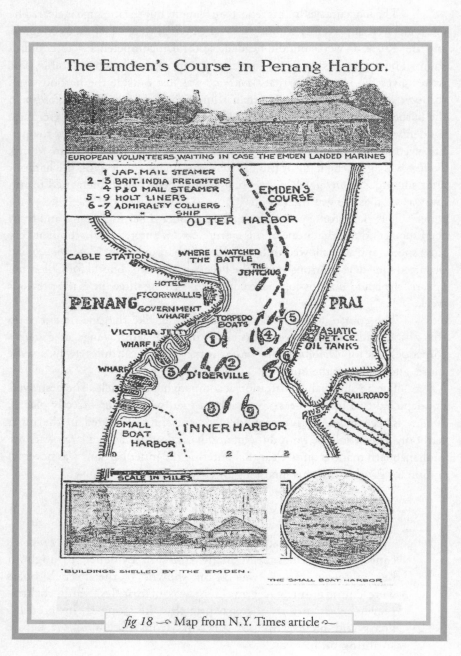

The Emden's Course in Penang Harbor.

EUROPEAN VOLUNTEERS WAITING IN CASE THE EMDEN LANDED MARINES

1 JAP. MAIL STEAMER
2 - 3 BRIT. INDIA FREIGHTERS
4 P&O MAIL STEAMER
5 - 9 HOLT LINERS
6 - 7 ADMIRALTY COLLIERS
8 " SHIP

EMDEN'S COURSE

OUTER HARBOR

CABLE STATION

WHERE I WATCHED THE BATTLE

THE JEMTCHUG

HOTEL

FT. CORNWALLIS

PENANG

GOVERNMENT WHARF

PRAI

TORPEDO BOATS

VICTORIA JETTY

WHARF I.

ASIATIC PET. Cº. OIL TANKS

WHARF

D'IBERVILLE

RAILROADS

RIVER

SMALL BOAT HARBOR

INNER HARBOR

SCALE IN MILES

"BUILDINGS SHELLED BY THE EMDEN.

THE SMALL BOAT HARBOR

fig 18 ⤳ Map from N.Y. Times article ⤳

The English here now say of him admiringly 'He played the game'.

All of this is a complete fabrication. *Mousquet* was many miles from the harbour when *Emden* sank her, and nobody knew it for certain till the Engineer Huong (he of the barrel) was brought back to Penang by fishermen the next day. The witnesses at the Crag saw the action well out to sea, but it was too far away for them to identify the destroyer. Von Müller risked nothing in picking up the *Mousquet*'s survivors. He was brave, but not foolhardy. True, *Pistolet* had them in sight and was shadowing them, but she was too far off to be a threat. Again, Hohenzollern's account is very clear on this point.

The correspondent of the *New York Times* then gave a sensible account of the scene on the jetty, where many badly injured Russians were being attended to. But the article then sinks into such fabrications that even a hardened tabloid journalist would blanch.

Here however is an account of what occurred from an officer who saw it all from closer range and more intimate conditions, for he was on the French torpedo-boat destroyer *Pistolet*. I tell this story exactly as he told it to me. 'The captain of the *Pistolet* had invited Captain T. and myself to have a game of bridge whilst on board. His ship was lying alongside the Government wharf just inside the inner harbour. The game proved to be a most interesting one and time flew by unnoticed. Finally just before 1.00 a.m. it came to a close, but owing to the fact that our going home at that hour of the morning would mean a rickshaw ride over two miles, the Captain stretched a point and invited us to remain on board, which we did. Little did we know what our decision was to mean to us'.

He then goes on to describe how they were awakened by gunfire in the morning and, rushing onto the deck of *Pistolet*, were able to witness the shelling of *Zhemtchug* at close quarters. This can not be true. *Pistolet* was the guard-ship under one hour's notice to get steam up, ready to cast off. The idea that Castagné, who we know was a tough disciplinarian, would entertain two guests in his ship to play bridge at such a time is preposterous, and for a guest to stay overnight in his ship for want of a two-mile ride in a rickshaw is ridiculous. The author could have known nothing of the conditions aboard those small ships. The sleeping quarters were cramped, hot and uncomfortable, with certainly no space for two casual bridge-players. At the subsequent enquiry in Saigon, the crew of *Pistolet* were questioned at length about this allegation and not one of them had any recollection whatsoever of any guests. But the correspondent now warms to his tale. He invented *Emden*'s alleged trip round the inner harbour and then went on to say,

> No sooner had she started on her way out of the harbour however, than the din arose once more. Just at this time the French torpedo boat *Fronde* dropped back from her position alongside us and started in to take part in the mêlée with a machine gun. This caused the *Emden* to devote part of her time to us and we were made the objective of a severe machine-gun fire which owing to our position in the shadow of the pier and of the fact that the light was very poor, did little or no damage. Nevertheless it was rather disconcerting to hear the rattle of lead on the corrugated iron shed behind us.
>
> By this time the *Emden* must have known that at such close quarters, she was subject to the danger of a torpedo attack (although as a matter of fact no effort seems to have been made along these lines) and she accordingly started up the north channel towards the outer harbour at full speed, firing broadside after broadside at the *Zhemtchug*, now badly crippled.
>
> By this time, – less than 30 minutes after the first shot had been fired – the *Pistolet* had cast off, and we started across the harbour towards the place where we had last seen the *Zhemtchug* with the *Fronde* close behind us. It was slow work as we had very little steam.

This part of his story, like the last, could not be true. Steamships cannot get up steam and cast off at short notice and *Fronde,* like *d'Iberville* and *Zhemtchug*, was completely shut down. She was moored inside *Pistolet,* which could not move for another half-hour.

The writer's intention is, however, clear. He implants the idea that all the French ships were actually free to cast off and open fire on *Emden* at close quarters, yet they made no effort to use their torpedoes. It all reinforces the view that the French were cowardly and incompetent. Finally, commonsense dictates that *Emden* could not possibly have fired 'broadside after broadside' at *Zhemtchug* whilst steaming past her at full speed. The writer knew nothing about gunnery and nothing about manoeuvring big ships.

It is interesting that the eye-witness accounts published immediately after the raid are quite clear that the French destroyers did not have steam up and could not move.[27] There is no suggestion of cowardice in any of those accounts.

The reporter then describes his own part in the rescue of many Russian sailors from the water, casting himself in the role of a hero. Next, he places himself ashore taking a rickshaw to the 'outer sea wall', wherever that was. In his illustration it substitutes for Swettenham Pier.

Emden and *Mousquet* he states, were some distance from the harbour entrance but apparently still in view, with *Mousquet* running away:

> We could see the little torpedo boat *Mousquet* trying to get beyond the range of *Emden*'s guns while the shells were throwing up water all around her. The chase had kept on for 20 minutes I should say, when we saw the little craft sink by the bow.

This account seems to be muddled up with the encounter with *Merbau*. The only witnesses to the action against *Mousquet* were high up on Penang Hill and it is probably their account that enabled him to report that *Mousquet* sank bow-first. The battle with *Mousquet* happened well below his horizon, at least fifteen miles away, and it would have been impossible to see from the 'outer sea wall'. He then goes on to congratulate the German captain for his chivalry (for not shelling the town) in the most extravagant and effusive terms and ends this eulogy by saying, 'He played the game'. It is doubtful that many people in Penang saw it quite like that; and after such appalling loss of life it is doubtful that von Müller would have been very comfortable with that, either.

But our correspondent had not finished yet.

> The sad, or rather disgraceful part of the story has yet to be told. It was true that the *Zhemtchug* was caught unprepared. The Captain was spending the night ashore, her decks were not cleared, she was slow to get into action, and when she did so her marksmanship was poor. All this could hardly be excused but it becomes insignificant when we consider the case of the French torpedo boats and the *d'Iberville* whose help the *Zhemtchug* had a right to expect. Here they lay in the harbour, with fully ten minutes warning that a hostile ship was approaching, yet they allowed the ship to enter the harbour, steam around it, turn, and make her escape without so much as firing a shot when, if they had gone into action the *Emden* could hardly have escaped. The range was everything they could have desired.

What was the matter? Why did they remain silent? The answer is this: although it was a time of war, a large percentage of the officers of these ships had been allowed to remain ashore overnight. Not one of the ships had steam up. Their decks were not even cleared for action. Yet taking this into consideration it is inexplicable when two or three torpedoes from any one of them would have saved the day. The ships need not have moved an inch to have done so. The range was ridiculously short – less than 200 yards at one time. But surprise and lack of discipline and general inefficiency seemed to hold them paralysed.

The prevailing opinion here is that they did not wish to draw the *Emden*'s fire on themselves – although one did use her machine-gun toward the end of the engagement. Whatever is said however, it is impossible to get away from the fact that the French navy today sustained a blow to its efficiency that it will take a long time to wipe out. Theirs was a 'masterly inaction' caused by something that they themselves do not attempt to define. Both army and navy commanders here are one in their contemptuous condemnation of such a spectacle.

These allegations are so appalling that they are hard to digest without a rising sense of annoyance. To this day they remain as an insult to the many Frenchmen, as well as Russians, who were victims of the negligence and the incompetence of those in authority.

The last part of the article takes one's breath away. The author must have known that his allegations were untrue, yet it contains just enough credibility to take in a casual reader. It is true that Audemard, for very good reason, was reluctant to engage *Emden* unless fired upon. This was because he was immobilised and would have needlessly endangered his crew. There was little chance of damaging *Emden* with his small cannon at that range, except with a very lucky shot. He had only one opportunity to open fire with his 100mm gun, and that was before he realised that he was in the presence of an enemy cruiser. *Pistolet* had much smaller cannons, and for most of the period after the second cannonade, *Emden* could not be seen. *Emden* never saw *Pistolet* either.

There is no reason to suppose that the French ships were lacking in discipline or in any way failing to carry out proper watch-keeping or anything else, as set out in Jerram's orders. The article cleverly suggested that 'officers' (who should be setting an example) were sneaking ashore 'overnight' (for this, read the louche reputation of Penang and the alleged French obsession with sex), when they should have been on duty. Finally, out of cowardice, they had failed to go to the assistance of an Allied ship that was in trouble.

This latter accusation is designed to inflict maximum damage on the French reputation. It is one of the rules of war that allied ships must assist one another except under exceptional circumstances, such as being out of range. The idea of MacIntyre making a 'contemptuous condemnation of such a spectacle' makes one cringe with embarrassment. He, of all people, was the one most directly responsible for the entire tragedy.

It is hard to escape the conclusion that much of this article was written with the help of someone who was anxious to shift as much blame as possible away from the British. It would also have the effect of concentrating any initial enquiry away from the real culprits and onto the French. Jerram would never have considered an enquiry for a moment. He could not have escaped criticism, because of the failures and inadequacies of his leadership. Cross never got that satisfaction.

It is a well-known fact in the world of the media, that the public will always believe the first account of something they read or hear, and it takes an awful lot to reverse that first impression. The Russians and the French have been the butt of contempt and derision in every account of the raid on Penang that has since been written in English. It was Audemard's personal tragedy that he had to face these unjust accusations alone and unsupported. He had done his best in exceedingly trying circumstances and he must have felt utterly betrayed.

Chapter 12

Emden Destroyed

Within two hours of the raid on Penang, Jerram received Maund's telegram informing him of the sinking of *Zhemtchug*. He ordered immediate mobilisation of the remaining French destroyers to chase after *Emden*. As soon as *Fronde* had steam up she went from Penang to the area around Pulau Weh, with instructions to radio *Chikuma* which was patrolling nearby. Jerram also ordered the Japanese cruiser *Yahagi* to leave Singapore and join *Chikuma*. But by then, *Emden* had travelled well to the north-west towards the Nicobars looking for a suitable ship to take her French prisoners. *Chikuma* had missed her yet again.

Grant in *Hampshire,* along with *Yarmouth* and the auxiliary cruisers *Empress of Asia* and *Empress of Russia,* were still around Ceylon. Only *Chikuma* and, later, *Yahagi* were on the other side of the Bay. *Fronde* and *d'Iberville* continued patrolling the area around Pulau Weh whilst *Pistolet* was having her engine repaired.[1]

Jerram was now intensely preoccupied with getting his Australian convoy moving. This vast assembly of New Zealand and Australian ships, escorted by the armoured cruisers *Minotaur, Melbourne* and *Sydney,* was ready to leave Albany on 1st November. First, they would stop at Fremantle where *Ibuki* was waiting with additional transports. Next, they would pass close to the Cocos Islands. *Yahagi* had originally intended to rendezvous with them there, but now she was ordered up to Pulau Weh to join the hunt for *Emden*.

The Russian armoured cruiser *Askold* was back in Colombo from

Aden just the day before *Emden*'s raid on Penang. She departed immediately for Bombay, escorting yet more transports. She was then to be assigned to cover the trade route between Madras and Calcutta, in case *Emden* should strike again.[2] *Askold* provided a reliable and efficient service to Jerram's Far East Squadron from beginning to end.

Jerram reported to the Admiralty in London that the Japanese had independently assembled a considerable naval force under Vice Admiral Tochinai covering the Indian Ocean.[3] The Japanese admiral was due to arrive in Singapore on 8th November, to be joined by *Chikuma* and *Yahagi*. He would then take charge of the operations in the eastern half of the Bay of Bengal. *Nishin* and *Ibuki* would join him as soon as the Australian convoy had reached Colombo.[4] Jerram was slowly but surely being squeezed out of the way by the Japanese.

Back aboard *Emden, Mousquet*'s survivors had finally been transferred to *Newburn*, although Matelot Salducci was too badly injured to join his comrades and died in *Emden* the next night. He was buried at sea with the same honours as the other two.

Von Müller had to change his plans to rendezvous with *Pontoporos* and *Markomannia,* knowing that they were lost. This he had learned from the survivors of *Mousquet,* as well as various news broadcasts that *Emden* had begun to pick up.[5]

On 31st October *Emden* went off to find *Buresk*. She was lying quite close by, at a point to the west of Pulau Weh. It was pure luck that neither of them encountered either *Chikuma* or *Fronde*. Prinz Hohenzollern captures the tense atmosphere on board *Emden* as they searched around for *Buresk* in the dark, knowing that Allied warships would be looking for them in exactly that area.

> *Buresk* might have been captured by a hostile warship which was now lying in wait for us. There was therefore considerable excitement when, about half past four, the stern of a dark ship came in sight.
>
> As the huntsman stalks the buck, so did we quietly approach this dark and questionable object and in spite of the darkness many sharp eyes were trying to discover what the unknown ship was like. One thing we could be certain of: the ship had only one funnel and therefore might be *Buresk*.

It was the *Buresk,* God be thanked! We had our companion again. Her loss would have been a hard blow, for a well-trained companion ship is a valuable object in the open sea. She was at once signalled by Morse [lamp] to follow the *Emden* on her new course. We steamed close to her in order to exchange important news.[6]

When *Emden* was finally destroyed, a small part of her signal log, although damaged, was recovered. The exchange between *Emden* and *Buresk* which Prinz Hohenzollern was alluding to actually survives, and gives us an interesting insight into the Prince himself.

7.45 am. To *Buresk.*

Good morning! The torpedo Lieutenant is asleep and would fly at my head if I waked him. We arrived at Penang at 4.00 a.m. Were in harbour about 5.00 a.m. Only recognised *Zhemtchug* at 800 metres. First torpedo from starboard tube at three hundred metres; hit her below the after funnel. She at once settled by the stern up to the upper portholes. Simultaneously directed devastating fire on her deck and crew's quarters. She looked like a sieve. Went about, in passing to port fired a torpedo. Tremendous explosion. Fore-part torn away. Two minutes afterwards when smoke had cleared away, ship had disappeared. Fire was opened on us from *Zhemtchug* and elsewhere, but we were not hit. Then recognised *d'Iberville* in harbour. On going about to fire, what appeared to be a torpedo-boat came in full speed towards her [us?]. Opened fire, turned and recognised as a Government steamer.[7]

The signal went on to describe the sinking of *Mousquet.* Once again this signal confirms that *Emden* never entered the inner harbour and only spotted *d'Iberville* after the second cannonade when she slowly turned round just beyond the outer harbour. Where the shots from 'elsewhere' were coming from has not been ascertained. *Emden* and *Buresk* then proceeded slowly down the west coast of Sumatra at a stately nine knots.

This was 1st November and, unknown to them, Admiral Graf Spee's squadron had scored a resounding success when they met the British Admiral Cradock in the Battle of Coronel off the coast of Chile. It was the first time that a British battle squadron had suffered a defeat since before the Battle of Trafalgar.

That very same day *Emden* also had something to celebrate. They were exactly three months out and during that time their engines had done ten million revolutions. They had steamed 30,000 nautical miles and consumed 6,000 tons of coal. The performance of *Emden*'s engines had been quite remarkable, nurtured by the tender care and maintenance of chief engineer Oberingenieur Ellerbroek and his team; and still nobody had caught her. Two days later *Emden* found a quiet spot off Pagai Island near Padang, and coaled once more from *Buresk*. The ships were visited by a Dutch representative to ensure they returned outside the three-mile limit. They treated him to a whiskey and soda and *Emden* then sailed to the Sunda Straits where she hoped she could capture a few more ships.[8]

There was not a single ship to be seen, which properly speaking was a result of our own activity. We had made the Indian ocean as unsafe as possible. We came to the well known volcano Krakatoa. The whole thing looked like a great hollow tooth.[9] From the Dutch wireless station we heard that the English ship *Newburn* had run into Khota Raja [Sabang], with the survivors from *Mousquet*,. We were glad to hear that the wounded had been brought to safety.[10]

To the south-west of them, but not far away, the collier *Exford* appeared at her rendezvous. She had been waiting since 30th October at a point forty miles north of the Cocos Islands,[11] after detaching from *Emden* in the Bay of Bengal. Now Lauterbach took command of her.

Despite the tremendous risk involved, von Müller had at last decided that he should disable the signal station at Direction Island. It was such an obvious target that Jerram, he thought, would certainly have a cruiser waiting for them; but if von Müller was successful, he would continue his war on shipping around Socotra Island by the Horn of Africa. This covered the shipping lanes between Colombo and Aden. Aden was a British base, but most of the western seaboard of Arabia belonged to the Ottoman-Turks who had just come into the war on the side of Germany. This made a big difference, because should *Emden* be cornered, she could run for a Turkish-controlled port.

So *Exford* was detached once more, to await *Emden* at a rendezvous on the western side of the Indian Ocean, in the Gulf of Aden.[12] Thus *Emden* and *Exford* became widely separated once more. *Exford,* with Lauterbach in command, never saw *Emden* again. The final capture of *Exford* took place long after *Emden* herself was destroyed.

Emden then set off for Direction Island in the Cocos group, with the collier *Buresk* following behind. As mentioned before, Direction Island in the Cocos was where various transoceanic telegraph cables surfaced. Places like this were used to make cable-junctions and to boost the signal strength. The Cocos Islands were on the path between Perth and Colombo, as well as Zanzibar and Calcutta. Cables from Mauritius, Batavia, and Australia all met there. There was also a tall radio mast. If *Emden* could sever the cables, especially the one to Australia, and blow up the radio mast, then this would cause great problems for the British and their allies.

The target was so obvious that Jerram had definitely seen it coming. After all, only a few weeks earlier he had demolished a similar German radio station on Yap Island in the Pacific. Von Müller fully expected to find the Island heavily guarded and was prepared for a fight.

The Cocos Islands comprise two atolls, North Keeling, a small island to the north and South Keeling, a group of islands encircling a big lagoon. The biggest of the South Keeling group is South Island, which is now an Australian naval base. Direction Island lies on the north side of that group.

The Cocos were originally settled in 1820 by an English 'adventurer' Alexander Hare, who settled on South Island with a private harem and a large collection of slaves. There he made a living, trading copra and other products from the coconut plantations. Exhausted no doubt from dissipation and idleness, Hare eventually made way for John Clunies-Ross, a sea captain from the remote Scottish Shetland Islands who had already set up another plantation on Direction Island nearby. Hare so ill-treated his slaves that many ran away to join Clunies-Ross on Direction Island. Clunies-Ross now took over the entire archipelago where, as the *Daily Telegraph* put it, 'The Scottish family of Ross reigns in lonely splendour.'[13] He even issued his own currency.[14]

The Islands were finally annexed by the British in 1857 with Clunies-Ross's son as superintendent. Notably, HMS *Beagle* once called there with Charles Darwin on board! At first the Islands were administered from Ceylon, then later transferred to the Straits Settlements.[15]

Since the late 19th century British Telegraph had employed a civilian workforce operating and maintaining the cable network and wireless installations. As the *Straits Times* reported:

> The telegraph company have erected a powerful wireless station at Cocos. Its range even in day-time is reputed to be about

300 miles. The company employ nearly 30 white men there and they must have expended several tens of thousands of pounds in the erection and the equipment of the cable and wireless stations – something approaching in amount the price of an ocean going steamer without her cargo.

The destruction of the cable station would produce most disastrous results. Delays would ensue in the transmission of messages to and from Australia and as we all know, delays are dangerous and expensive. The effect of the destruction of the wireless station at Cocos would probably be even more disastrous than the destruction of the cable station because it would almost certainly hinder or inconvenience the directing genius [?] of the Admiral at Singapore.[16]

Von Müller's plan was to land on Direction Island and wreck the installations, rather than bombard it from the sea as Jerram had done at Yap Island. He also needed to land, in order to find the underwater telegraph cables and cut them. So the evening of 8th November was spent drawing up plans for the landing party which would be led by Von Mücke, assisted by two fellow officers, Gyssling and Schmidt. Thirty seamen and fifteen technical ratings would be there, together with two men from the ship's wireless staff.

Von Müller had no idea how much danger he was in, not because of any careful defence of the Island by Jerram, but from the Australian convoy that was finally on its way towards Colombo. At last Jerram had a stroke of pure luck. On her way to rendezvous with *Exford, Emden* crossed the path of this vast convoy just 250 miles ahead of them.[17]

Knowing nothing of this, von Müller detached *Buresk* to a rendezvous 30 miles off Direction Island, to be collected when the action was over. Von Müller did, however, expect to find at least one warship on guard, and anticipated some fighting before his landing party could get to work.[18]

In fact, as already described, Jerram had grown tired of waiting and had sent the guard-ships off to Australia, leaving the telegraph chief, Mr Farrant, with instructions about exactly what to do in the event of an attack. The principal thing was to send off distress signals immediately, far and wide, before the invaders had time to wreck the installations. Being civilians and non-combatants, they were then advised not to involve themselves in any fighting. The telegraph team had rehearsed this strategy several times. As Jerram put it in a letter to the Admiralty:

The possibility of the Cocos Islands being seized by *Emden* had been constantly in my mind, although I could not possibly spare a ship to be stationed there permanently. I had instructed the cable station as to the precautions to adopt and the necessity of giving immediate warning in the event of a surprise attack, and [I] furnished it with a list of the secret wireless call signs of all allied ships in these waters.[19]

So at 6.00 a.m. on the morning of 9th November, *Emden* sailed into the little harbour at Direction Island directly in front of the telegraph station, sporting her dummy funnel. Her crew were astonished to find no guard-ship. The only ship there was the sailing schooner *Ayesha,* of the type that even today plies the routes around the Indonesian Archipelago. So the landing party were free to go ashore without a shot being fired. Nevertheless, the telegraph station had time to put their well-rehearsed plan into action, sending out a message by radio and by cable 'Foreign ship in harbour', before they were cut off.[20]

Later, the telegraph chief related what happened. The irony is that the dummy funnel led to the immediate identification of *Emden.* Had it not been for the dummy funnel she might have been confused with the other lone, three-funnel cruiser *Königsberg,* mentioned previously, which had been operating with very little success down the African coast. But as it turned out, *Königsberg* had already been cornered a week before and was blockaded up the Rufigi River in present-day Tanzania.[21] The telegraph chief on the Island described what happened next:

> Finding that the [warship's] fourth funnel was palpably canvas, I found Mr. La Nauze and instructed him immediately to the wireless hut to put out a general call to the effect that there was a strange warship in our vicinity, asking for assistance and signing our naval code. At the same time I proceeded to the office and sent services, as previously instructed, to London, Adelaide, Perth and Singapore. I personally told Singapore it was *Emden.*

Mr Farrant then described how von Mücke arrived in three of *Emden*'s boats, including a steam launch, accompanied by a well-armed landing party.

> Von Mücke, in charge of the landing party, was exceedingly agreeable. He informed me that he had landed three officers and forty men and his instructions were to destroy the cable and wireless stations. Further than this he said, they would not go and all private

property would be respected. He instructed me to collect the staff and take them to a place of safety as he was blowing up the wireless mast. Three charges had to be fired before it fell. The mainmast was considerably damaged. Instruments, engines, dynamos, batteries, etc. were all battered to pieces with huge axes, one of which I have and propose sending to you as a memento.[22]

One of the boats then went off in search of the underwater telegraph cables with the intention of cutting them. They located the Perth cable and managed with great difficulty to cut through it. Then, at about 8.45 a.m., *Emden* came in close to the shore and with flag signals and blasts on the siren attempted to recall the landing party. They rapidly put out in their boats to rejoin *Emden*.

The telegraph station crew were now free to go and have breakfast! Despite the mess, there was clearly nothing sufficiently urgent to interrupt their morning meal. But scarcely had they got to their houses than shouts were heard, reporting that a big warship was coming towards them over the horizon belching black smoke with all boilers at full pressure. Even with binoculars they could not identify the ship because there was so much smoke, but they made her out to be a four-funnelled cruiser. *Emden* had raised her anchor and was now steaming fast towards her, leaving the landing party behind, stranded in their cutters.

Aboard *Emden*, things had been hotting up. The lookouts had spotted the smoke on the horizon and at first assumed it was *Buresk*. Soon, however, it became clear that it was a British warship. It was actually the armoured cruiser HMAS *Sydney*, one of the escorts for Jerram's convoy from Fremantle. The convoy had reached the vicinity of the Cocos islands at precisely the same time that *Emden* had chosen to attack the radio station. Such a coincidence was quite extraordinary.

It was *Melbourne* that actually intercepted the S.O.S. call from Direction Island just before 7.00 a.m. when she was just 55 miles away. HMAS *Sydney*, under the command of Captain Glossop, was sent to investigate and set off at full power. Two hours later they sighted smoke and, finally, *Emden*.[23]

On board *Emden* it was clear that there would be no time to bring the landing party back on board so they left them behind in their boats. *Emden* steamed at full speed into the attack and a furious battle ensued.

Standing up in their boats, the landing party watched *Emden* as she opened fire, with her early shots hitting the target. Those shots killed three and wounded sixteen of *Sydney*'s crew. But *Sydney* was faster and her new 152mm guns were more powerful, ensuring that she could keep just out of range, whilst landing her own shots at will.[24] It took *Sydney* longer to find *Emden*'s range but, once they got it, *Sydney* started shooting with devastating effect.

The landing party watched as the two ships slowly continued north till they were barely visible, but the fighting still continued. *Emden* lost a funnel and then a mast, followed by another funnel, and soon she was burning astern as well, with steam escaping. The battle became totally one-sided, yet *Emden* continued gamely, zigzagging her way towards North Keeling Island, steering only with her engines.

As *Emden* was now out of sight, von Mücke's landing party were forced to return to Direction Island. Coming ashore once again, they hoisted the German flag and, gathering the telegraph crew together, told them they were under martial law. The telegraph crew were not allowed to make any attempt to communicate with the Allies. Von Mücke then explained that if *Emden* did not return, his landing party was going to take the schooner *Ayesha* to make good their escape. For this they would need all sorts of provisions and these were taken out to the schooner in *Emden*'s cutters, towed by the steam launch. They took with them mattresses, pillows, cutlery, plates, the greater part of the station's distilled water, a dinghy and as much food as they could lay their hands on. It was 6.00 p.m. when they had finally completed the task and still no sign of *Sydney* or *Emden*, or *Buresk* for that matter. But they realised that *Emden* was finished and it was time to leave.

Back on board *Sydney* at North Keeling, it was clear to Glossop that *Emden* was sinking and endeavouring to beach herself. The action had lasted about an hour and forty minutes.[25] Glossop called off the attack and ordered *Sydney* to go after *Buresk*. But before *Sydney* could capture her, the crew had opened the sea-cocks and then took to the lifeboats. The crew, most of whom were British, were then taken on board *Sydney*.

As the day wore on, *Sydney* went back to North Keeling where *Emden* had finally beached herself. Some of her survivors were seen trying to get ashore, but the waves were too rough. Still, as *Emden* was showing no sign of surrendering, *Sydney* opened fire again.

While this awful battle was being drawn out to its grizzly conclusion, an entirely different and much less harrowing drama had been unfolding on Direction Island. In the gathering dusk the German flag was broken out at *Ayesha*'s fore-peak and, after three hearty cheers on both sides, the German crew hoisted the sails. Just after 6.00 p.m. they departed into the night

Armed only with candles, the telegraph crew then rummaged about amongst the wreckage of their equipment. They located some bare essentials and finally managed to make contact with Batavia since that cable had not been cut. 'We were tired out, working with candles in the midst of chaos and broken glass, so we told Batavia to watch for us at daylight.'[26] Meanwhile, they had rigged up a primitive signalling device, and managed to get through to Singapore, reporting that they had no lights and everything was smashed. 'Will get an instrument up by daylight.'[27] They waited till next day and then got through to Singapore once again. Despite all the damage, communications were re-established with remarkable speed, thanks to the ingenuity of the telegraph engineers.

Aboard *Ayesha* the German crew, under the command of Von Mücke, took a close look at the vessel they had just captured so that they could decide what to do next. They had about two weeks' worth of supplies from the base at Direction Island. The civilian staff on Direction Island had actually assisted them. They even gave them a little tobacco and took some photos which can still be seen today. Von Mücke had three officers, six petty officers, 41 sailors, a steam launch and two cutters. They were well armed with four maxim machine guns, with 2,000 rounds of ammunition each, as well as 29 Mauser rifles with 60 rounds each. Each officer and seven ratings had Mauser pistols with 24 rounds each.

Ayesha was only eight years old and in good condition. She was used for trading between Batavia and the remoter islands around the Indonesian Archipelago. She had a sextant and a log. It was the start of an incredible adventure that eventually saw von Mücke's party safely back to Germany. German sailors in those days, as they are today, were trained to handle sailing ships as well as steamships. They were practised in the art of sailing a 'square rigger' and could manage *Ayesha* competently.

Ayesha had got away by nightfall, but *Emden* still had not surrendered. *Sydney* remained close by, waiting, having no idea that von Mücke's landing party had escaped. As things turned out, *Emden*'s crew were forced to spend the night aboard the wreck of their ship in absolutely appalling circumstances, with nothing to eat or drink. There was no chance of attending properly to the wounded, either, and several of them died in the night. Prinz Hohenzollern's detailed account of the action provides a harrowing account, worse than the *Mousquet*, because it was not till next day that the wounded were rescued.[28]

At daybreak the next morning, *Sydney* was still lying off North Keeling, waiting for *Emden* to surrender. It seems that *Emden* would have given up much earlier but they were unable to communicate this to *Sydney*.[29] For reasons that Prinz Hohenzollern later explained, they wanted to call off the action, but without technically surrendering.

Seen from Glossop's side there was no sign of a surrender, so he decided there was nothing more he could do. He left *Emden* in her miserable state and took off towards Direction Island, intending to clear up von Mücke's landing party. Two of *Sydney*'s boats arrived in the little harbour showing a white flag, but they were too late; the landing party had already left. The Australian lieutenant in charge was utterly astonished.

They took the telegraph chief aboard *Sydney* so that he could make his report to Glossop. Reassuringly, he said that *Ayesha* was old, rotten and leaked like a sieve. Whether Glossop believed him or not is uncertain.[30] Perhaps the telegraph crew just wanted to cheer him up. But Jerram certainly believed it. As usual, Jerram hoped the problem of *Ayesha* would just go away.

> It seemed possible that the Schooner *Ayesha* might proceed westwards. I think it is just possible that the *Ayesha* may never be heard of again. I am informed that she makes four feet of water a day when sailing and that both her pumps are out of order.[31]

Returning to matters on board *Sydney*, Glossop had more pressing concerns. He explained to the people on Direction Island that *Emden* still had not surrendered but had lain there on the reef all night in a complete shambles. Something had to be done, so he asked for the loan of the Direction Island doctor and any assistants, plus any medical stores they could muster. He then set out for the wreck of *Emden*. After some confusing signals to *Sydney*, *Emden* finally unfurled a white flag.

Glossop replied with a signal which, despite its formal tones, was presumably flashed by Morse-lamp. It has become a classic of its kind.

> I have the honour to request that in the name of humanity you now surrender your ship to me. In order to show how much I appreciate your gallantry I will recapitulate the position.
> 1. You are ashore three funnels and one mast down and most guns disabled.
> 2. You can not leave this island, and my ship, intact.

In the event of your surrendering, in which I venture to remind you is no disgrace, but rather your misfortune, I will endeavour to do all I can for your sick and wounded and take them to a hospital.

I have the honour to be, sir,
your obedient servant,

Captain Glossop.[32]

Glossop then sent his cutters across to the wreck of *Emden*. Prinz Hohenzollern remarked that the Australian sailors handled the boats very well in the heavy swell, and took the wounded into the boats with great care. Glossop sent his personal gig over to rescue von Müller who, like Prinz Hohenzollern, was miraculously unhurt. It was now November 10th.

At the final count, 134 people – over one-third of those on board, lost their lives. Of the remainder, 21 were seriously wounded, 44 escaped with light wounds and 117 were unhurt. Looking at the photographs of *Emden* after the battle it is a wonder that anyone survived. Had von Müller surrendered earlier he might have saved many more lives. *Emden* and her crew were by now in a pitiful state.

Prinz Hohenzollern's explanation was this. They could not surrender because it was dishonourable. A ship with any gun still working, he argued, cannot surrender. So, when they could no longer fight they should have been taken prisoner. The white flag was their only a way of showing they were ready to be captured. It was a nice point of honour, but actually cost many lives.

It was almost impossible to get about *Emden*'s decks owing to the mass of tangled ironwork. After a night on deck, many of the survivors' wounds were already infected and in some cases they were already fly-blown.[33] The wounded were taken aboard *Sydney*, where they were attended to in the ship's hospital. It was only next day that the doctor and his assistants from Direction Island were put ashore again and *Sydney* set off to rejoin her convoy.

The team on Direction Island then went out in a boat and managed to locate the severed ends of the 'Perth' cable, effecting a temporary splice. Communication was re-established in the afternoon.

Sydney was now on the way to Colombo carrying 182 of *Emden*'s crew, and *Hampshire* was there at Colombo to meet them. Grant and von Müller met up for the first time since they had watched their men playing football together in Tsing Tao. As old friends they compared notes, amazed to discover just how close they had come to each other in the hunt. Von Müller would also have learned that on 7th November, just the day before *Emden* foundered, their beloved German naval base at Tsing Tao, upon which so much money and effort had been lavished, had surrendered to Japanese and British forces. Japan hung onto Tsing Tao till the end of the war and for many years after. No German naval base was ever established again in the Far East.

Emden's story was at an end, but *Ayesha*'s story was just beginning. *Ayesha* was actually in good shape with a full set of sails in her locker. Her pumps were working and she was not taking on too much water. In fact, she was perfectly seaworthy. Von Mücke decided to make for Padang on the west coast of Sumatra because there was a German consul there. Von Mücke thought he would try to come to some arrangement with the Dutch. A sailing ship is not only slower than a steamship but, when sailing into the wind, it cannot steer a direct course but has to tack from side to side. *Ayesha* was therefore going to take some time to reach Padang. In fact it took them three weeks. On the way they ran into a fierce storm which tested *Ayesha*'s seaworthiness to the limit. It was also a severe test for the skills of an inexperienced crew, going aloft and handling sails in a gale. It says a great deal for their professionalism as sailors that they pulled through.

Land was sighted on 23rd November and a Dutch Navy destroyer came out to identify the schooner. As a German ship, she would only be allowed the regulation twenty-four hours in Padang. The Dutch then escorted her into the harbour. There were many Germans residing in Padang and the crew of *Ayesha* were given a hero's welcome. The exploits of *Emden* had already become a legend and, after due consideration, the Dutch authorities allowed *Ayesha* to remain for twenty-four hours. Jerram finally discovered to his discomfort that *Ayesha* was still active.

> The Schooner *Ayesha* which, as previously reported, left the Cocos Islands on the evening of 9th of November with the armed landing party from *Emden,* arrived at Padang (Sumatra) on 28th of November and sailed the next day.
>
> Owing to our not having a consular representative at Padang it is difficult to get news from there and it was not until the evening of 2nd December that I heard from H.M. Consul-General at Batavia of the *Ayesha* having been there.[34]

In fact, von Mücke had arranged for fresh provisions to be brought aboard *Ayesha,* courtesy of the German consul. Various efforts to find a German ship that might be permitted to leave harbour came to nothing. There was one German collier, *Choising,* impounded in Padang and given the chance, she was planning to run the blockade. She was their only hope.

So *Ayesha* was forced to leave Padang at the end of her allotted 24 hours, but now she had ten live pigs aboard! She waited outside the three-mile limit, hoping for *Choising* to appear so that *Ayesha*'s crew could board her as passengers. On 29th November, after *Ayesha* had been sailing around in circles for four days, a rowing boat came out to meet her at 2.00 a.m. There were two Germans officers aboard frantically trying to get back to Germany, but hitherto prevented from doing so. *Ayesha* finally sailed off slowly towards the west.

What they did not know was that *Exford* was very close at hand. Lauterbach, having almost run out of supplies and suspecting problems with *Emden*, had brought *Exford* back from the Gulf of Aden and was now nearing the coast of Sumatra, hoping to make for the Dutch port of Pagan (not to be confused with Padang). For the second time, Jerram was in luck. He had sent *Empress of Japan* and *Himalaya* to scout around the coast of Sumatra in the hope of apprehending *Ayesha.* They failed to find *Ayesha,* but on 11th December, *Empress of Japan* ran into *Exford* about 25 miles south-west of Padang and captured her. Jerram reported that:

> They took out of her the German prize crew, viz. 1 Lieutenant R.N.R. [Lauterbach], 2 Warrant officers and 14 men belonging to *Emden,* who have been landed as prisoners of war at Singapore.
>
> *Exford,* manned by a prize crew from *Empress of Japan* has been brought to Singapore where she will discharge her cargo of which only a small amount has been used for her own steaming: she will then be discharged from Admiralty Service.[35]

But Lauterbach was not finished yet. He was soon to reappear as a player in the Singapore mutiny.

During the search, nothing was seen of *Ayesha.* Jerram then went on to say that *Ayesha* had almost certainly been sighted by a British steamer in the area going east. He speculated that *Ayesha* had attempted to go westwards, but had been driven back by westerly gales. In that instance his theory was quite correct.[36] On 14th December a force nine gale suddenly struck *Ayesha,* and the inexperienced crew began to lose control with damage to the rigging. When things finally calmed down, *Choising* miraculously appeared, having successfully run the blockade at Padang. They took *Ayesha* in tow to the lee of the Palai Islands due south of Padang. The *Ayesha* crew, her boats and all their arms and ammunition, were transferred to *Choising*. *Ayesha* was then sunk.

Choising herself was not in good shape and could hardly make eight knots. However, with no necessity to refuel, *Choising* crept right across the Indian Ocean to the mouth of the Red Sea without being spotted by any Allied ships. She landed at Turkish-controlled Hodeiddah in Yemen and there von Mücke's crew unloaded their boats, together with all their guns and ammunition. It was now well into January.[37]

The rest of the story was an epic of heroic proportions which has been told and re-told and became part of German folklore. Von Mücke wrote a book about it and more than one film was made. Suffice it to say that von Mücke's crew made their way up the Red Sea, partly by boat and partly on camels, harassed all the way by Bedouin tribesmen hostile to the Turkish-Ottoman occupation. This was Lawrence of Arabia territory where von Mücke's party had to cope with armed guerrilla fighters and frequent betrayal by those they took to be their allies. Miraculously they reached El Ula, where they found some Turkish representatives and completed their journey by rail, reaching Constantinople on 23rd May 1915. The *Emden* detachment was the only German military formation in World War I that returned from overseas to rejoin the fray.[38] It had taken nearly seven months, and during all that time they only lost three men. The leadership skills and the intelligence of von Mücke have rarely been equalled.

Back on the Island of North Keeling things were not yet quite over, as the wreck of the *Emden* teetered on the edge of the corral reef. The sloop *Cadmus* was sent from Singapore to make a thorough search of *Emden*'s wreck whilst it was still possible, in order to retrieve any papers and strong-boxes that might have been left aboard. It was a difficult task because the heavy swell made the job of boarding her particularly tricky, balanced as she was on the reef and likely to slide off at any moment, especially when the tide was up. The crew of *Cadmus* did get aboard, but only for two days. They found that most of the papers were destroyed or badly burned, but a few documents were retrieved, including the fragment of *Emden*'s signal log already quoted. Just in case the escaped crew in *Ayesha* should attempt to retrieve them, items such as small arms and ammunition were removed as well.[39]

Back in Britain, the news of the final loss of *Emden* was greeted with jubilation. For Jerram it was a great relief because the seas in his part of the world were now cleared of enemy warships. *Sydney's* success gave him respite from continued criticism and he avoided any embarrassing enquiry. He contented himself with being magnanimous.

> I should like to place on record the honourable manner in which the captain of *Emden* has conducted his operations during the two months he has been at large in the Indian Ocean. His scrupulous care to avoid unnecessary inconvenience to the passengers and crew of captured merchant ships has been exemplary.[40]

Chapter 13

A Mutiny in Singapore and Lauterbach Escapes

Julius Lauterbach – Master of Hamburg-Amerika Line's cargo ship *Staatssekretär Krätke*, Lieutenant in the Imperial German Navy Reserve and Prize Officer of SMS *Emden* – was a prisoner of war.

It was now mid-February 1915 and he had been a prisoner for two months. When *Exford* was taken down to Singapore in mid-December,[1] Lauterbach and the other members of *Exford*'s prize crew joined the prisoners who had been captured earlier from *Pontoporos* and *Markomannia*.

It had been a bad time for the German Navy. On 8th December Graf Spee's squadron was heading back to Germany via the South Atlantic and suffered a crushing defeat in the Battle of the Falklands. All of his squadron was sunk by the British Navy, except for two ships. The two great battlecruisers *Scharnhorst* and *Gneisenau* were sunk and Graf Spee and both of his sons went down with their ship. Countess Spee lost her husband and both her sons all on the same day; an unbelievable tragedy.

By then the British had decided to intern all the German nationals from the Straits Settlements inside Tanglin camp in Singapore. There were over 300 of them.[2] The civilians were in a separate barrack block, with a small house for the deck officers of *Emden*'s escort vessels. As he was the most senior German officer there, the best billet, a small detached bungalow in the prison compound, was given to Lauterbach.

Lauterbach was an old China hand and well known to everyone in Singapore. For Singaporeans he was an entertaining, genial, teddy bear of a man who was everybody's friend. It is hardly surprising, therefore, that when he arrived in Singapore as a prisoner of war, he was given a rather warm welcome by the local Europeans, and encouraged to tell all about *Emden*'s celebrated exploits in the months before she was destroyed.

Before World War I the Germans in Singapore had become the life and soul of the Singaporean expatriate community, with many social events centred on the Teutonia Club (later to become the Goodwood Park Hotel). The success of this club had been so great that it overshadowed the nearby British Tanglin Club which was almost deserted, with its buildings in a state of dilapidation. One can almost imagine the cobwebs. The Germans, however, were a hospitable and gregarious lot.[3]

To set the scene, one needs to bear in mind what was described in earlier chapters. The free port of Singapore was regarded by the Germans as the best location for sea-freight business in the Far East. They were on good terms with the local British, even though there was keen commercial competition. Their big merchant fleet relied on foreign ports for services, much of that provided by the British and, so long as Germany remained on good terms with everyone, it was a very cost-effective strategy. It was an early example of 'out-sourcing'.[4] As mentioned previously, German entrepreneurs and their agents had an excellent commercial education[5] and many Chinese merchants preferred to transport their goods in German rather than British ships.[6]

At the outbreak of war, the local British had rather mixed feelings about curtailing the Germans. Up until the attack on Penang harbour, German businessmen had been allowed some flexibility in their movements around Singapore. Many were staying at the Teutonia Club. Herr Diehn, the director of one of the biggest German trading firms, Behn, Meyer & Co, was free to go about the town and visit his office.[7] This was exactly the kind of slackness in security that the French Captain Daveluy, of *Dupleix,* had been complaining about in Penang.[8] Now, at last, Daveluy's worries had been addressed and all German nationals were in Tanglin, along with Julius Lauterbach.

Lauterbach had been twiddling his thumbs for six weeks and was absolutely determined to escape. To that end he persuaded some other prisoners, including Herr Diehn, that they should dig a tunnel. Although the camp was well lit at night, he noticed that some areas were in shadow and would be suitable for digging. On 27th January he and his pals started to dig. They worked every night, but without the right tools progress was slow even though the soil was sandy. The tunnel also had to be wide enough to contain Lauterbach's perspiring bulk. Each day the entrance to the tunnel was covered with turf and the guards never noticed. It was later reported by the Singapore Governor, Sir Arthur Young, that by Monday 15th February the tunnel was so near completion (then 17 metres long) that Lauterbach and his friends would almost certainly have broken out the next day, had not other events overtaken them.[9]

After they had been painstakingly tunnelling for two weeks, Lauterbach and his little group became aware that talk of mutiny was in the air. But they could not be certain of it. British sepoys of the 5th Native Light Infantry were posted as guards at the prison camp. Theirs was a regiment from the British Indian Army which had only recently arrived in Singapore. They were due to depart for Hong Kong on 16th February. On 13th February, in anticipation of that, the 5th Light Infantry had been relieved of guard duties at Tanglin, their place being taken by volunteers from the Johore Military Forces.

As Lauterbach recounted later, the sepoys had already began to suspect a trick. They would be sent, they believed, not to Hong Kong but to the European front. Being the kind of man he was, Lauterbach gossiped with his guards all the time, listening to their grievances. He recollected two guards in particular: Sergeant Imtiaz Ali and Ismail Khan.

Imtiaz Ali, 'a magnificent-looking, tall, black-bearded sepoy', used to seek out Julius Lauterbach in his bungalow, clearly hoping to recruit him to their cause. He was doubly dissatisfied because a recent promise of promotion had failed to materialise. Lauterbach simply went along with his grumbling and mutinous threats, hoping that it might in some way assist his own escape. Lauterbach later recollected these conversations:

> Every day, I conversed with the Indian noncommissioned officers who had been entrusted with the immediate surveillance of the prisoners. 'Sergeant' as I always called him, was the senior non-com. (NCO) and as such, had the run of the stockade at all hours. As the weeks went on he came more and more frequently to my bungalow in the night, usually with a subordinate or two. We would chat for hours. At first they merely wanted to hear about the exploits of the *Emden* and then gradually our talk passed on to other matters … I was on excellent terms with Sergeant and his brothers.[10]

Lauterbach then went on to say that Imtiaz Ali was convinced that his regiment were going to face certain death at the European front, and discussed his plans for a mutiny. Not surprisingly, Lauterbach thought this might turn to his advantage, so he gave him plenty of encouragement. He emphasised the awful nature of the war in Europe.

> The English will never tell you what is happening to your men. They wouldn't dare. Your Indian regiments in France have lost nearly all their men. It is very cold in France. Your brothers in the Punjab cannot stand that kind of climate. The English newspapers say that the Indian soldiers are dying bravely in battle, mowed down by German machine-gun fire. They die like sick dogs.[11]

The mutineers felt they had to act fast. At 3.00 p.m. on 15th February they seized their ammunition carts, already packed up for Hong Kong, and broke out of their barracks. About 100 mutineers marched up to Tanglin prison camp, bent on releasing the German prisoners. They opened the gates to the compound and roamed through the camp, killing three British officers along with several others, including two German prisoners of war who they mistook for British.

Lauterbach later claimed that he had incited the whole mutiny, but that was just his usual exaggeration. He always loved a good yarn – that was part of his nature. Clearly, his only concern was to escape back to Germany and he simply made use of any gullible sepoys who came his way. So, it can safely be assumed that the Germans were not the masterminds behind the sepoy break-out.

But Lauterbach and Diehn would not have been surprised by the mutiny, and they would have been ready to seize any opportunity for an escape. But it is doubtful whether they shared their plans with the civilian prisoners. An interesting account from a comparatively neutral standpoint was written much later by Sho Kuwajima, in his book, *The First World War and the Asia-Indian Mutiny in Singapore*.[12] Two Japanese hairdressers, Imamura and Onda, who worked in the civilian part of the camp, said that the Germans they were in regular contact with were completely taken by surprise.

Now that the mutineers had arrived at the camp, they soon spotted the huge figure of Lauterbach and surged around him. As he later wrote:

> They hoisted me onto their shoulders and ran out shouting 'Here is our leader'. One of these fanatical fellows jerked off his turban and jammed it over my ears. I must have looked like a drunken

sultan. His comrades cheered but I didn't. Not me. If I should be caught by the British in that turban and as the acclaimed leader of the mutineers, I should have made a fine target – tall and broad – for a firing squad. Moreover, a German officer does not fight without his uniform or in the ranks of mutineers. At least, he doesn't unless he is a renegade.[13]

He might also have added that any prisoner of war joining a mutiny would be guilty of a capital offence!

But this is where the mutineers' plot began to unravel. They believed that the Germans would join their insurrection with Lieutenant Lauterbach in command. They would capture the whole Island of Singapore and hand it over to the Germans. But Lauterbach had no such plans and refused to give his support. Without adequate leadership, nor any remaining sense of purpose, the mutineers were reduced to killing as many British as they could, soldiers and civilians alike.

In Tanglin camp a British hospital attendant, Paul Bray, was watching from the verandah as these chaotic events unfolded. One of the German prisoners urged him, 'You had better make yourself scarce. They are coming up.' Bray withdrew to the ward and a German patient suggested that he should change out of his khaki trousers. He changed into whites to match his shirt. Some mutineers came clattering into the ward, questioning patients to see if any were British. For Bray it was a hair-raising experience. He sat there, not looking up and continuing to apply a dressing to a patient. The other patients watched apprehensively and waited for the sepoys to ask Bray the fateful question about his nationality. Surprisingly, they did not. It was just afterwards that two Germans rushed into the hospital to tell Bray that two of their number had been shot and needed urgent attention.[14]

Governor Sir Arthur Young was in a bad spot. The Singapore police were unarmed, apart for a detachment of 200 Sikh guards armed with rifles. That left a few professional soldiers attached to the Singapore batteries and a rag-tag collection of Volunteers – essentially civilians acting as part-time soldiers. Sir Arthur declared martial law and took immediate steps to mobilise almost every able-bodied European man on the Island, regardless of their nationality (except the Germans). He also included many civilian Japanese who worked on the Island. Somehow, he supplied most of them with rifles. Ex-patriot women and children were evacuated to the safety of the ships in harbour.

As soon as Brigadier General Ridout, the General Officer Commanding Singapore, got word of the mutiny he dashed out, directing his wife to phone Tanglin camp where the German prisoners were being held. The mutineers were shooting the guards, and his wife got through just in time to hear the shot that killed Lieutenant Love-Montgomerie as he was taking her call.[15] Meanwhile, in Alexandra Barracks, their Commanding Officer Colonel Martin was under siege in his own house.[16]

Clearly, there was some collusion between the mutineers and Lauterbach's group of would-be escapees. Mioru Fujii, the Japanese Consul, reported to Kato, the Japanese Foreign Minister, that Diehn and some of the Germans 'did not show any surprise when the mutineers attacked'. Later that day 'they swiftly equipped themselves for the journey and received arms'.[17]

This small group of eleven prisoners, who made up Lauterbach's party of escapees, had risked their necks to get away. The party consisted of Lauterbach himself with other *Emden* prize crew members from *Exford*. It seems probable that one or two from *Markomannia* came along with them too. There were also two German businessmen, including Herr Diehn.

Not long after the mutineers had left the camp, Bray bumped into Lauterbach, who spoke to him in a low voice and said, ' I hope there will not be trouble between you and the *Emden* men tonight. You must try to keep quiet.' At the time, Bray did not understand what that was all about. It is now clear that Lauterbach had already made an agreement with the mutineers and he didn't want Bray to raise the alarm. The great majority of the German prisoners had no inclination to escape, anyway; indeed, they sheltered some British subjects, like Paul Bray. They were anxious to show that they had given no assistance to the mutineers whatsoever. In his evidence to the later court of enquiry, a Dr P. Fowklie said this:

> The majority of the Germans were frightened for their own safety and they were consistently very solicitous for the safety of those Britishers who found their way into the camp. Some of them remarked to me, 'What is to become of us? There is no one to take charge of us! We will be killed!' and other such expressions.[18]

However, the mutineers did return that evening with arms for Lauterbach's party of escapees and, in the ensuing chaos, Lauterbach and his small party of Germans succeeded in making their daring escape. Somehow or other Lauterbach had got a hold of some money; he may have had an account in Singapore and been allowed access to it. His party of escapees quickly made their way down to Pasir Panjang under cover of darkness and, after some haggling, managed to hire a fishing boat with a crew of Singhalese boatmen. Fourteen hours later they reached Karimun Island off Sumatra, a distance of about 25 nautical miles. This belonged to the Dutch, so they were safe.[19]

By nightfall the final count at Tanglin was three wounded and fourteen dead. Trained troops were urgently needed to put down the mutiny, and the navy was called upon to save the day.

Jerram had to provide urgent assistance. All his warships, bar one, were far away. Looking out over the harbour from Fort Canning, Jerram could see that the only warship riding at anchor was HMS *Cadmus*, which had recently been searching the wreck of *Emden* for her documents. She was a small British sloop of extraordinarily antiquated design[20] which had been running errands for Admiral Jerram ever since he had arrived out East in early 1913.

Cross, who was preparing to take up a new posting with the Presbyterian Church in Singapore, came by a letter written in the middle of the insurrection. The author was a Dr Ellis, a senior officer in the Singapore Volunteers and an eye-witness to those events.

Using Dr Ellis's letter and conversations with eye-witnesses, Cross wrote a narrative of the mutiny.[21] In this he described how *Cadmus* came alongside at Tanjong Pagar and landed a party of 102 armed sailors. They eventually relieved the besieged Colonel Martin. Next morning the Singapore Volunteers took possession of Tanglin camp. Only seventeen German prisoners had escaped, and six of them came back later. Meanwhile most of the mutineers were still at large roaming all over the island.

Next day, 16th February, Jerram, displaying a presence of mind that was rare on such occasions, called for additional assistance from any Allied warships that were in the vicinity. First, he contacted the French flagship *Montcalm*. She was at sea on her way to Saigon to attend the formal enquiry that had been set up to investigate the sinking of *Mousquet*.[22]

Relaxing in his cabin that afternoon, Admiral Huguet received an astonishing wireless message from Jerram. He was informed that there had been a mutiny in Singapore and the British needed urgent help.[23] At this point the mutiny had been going on, he was told, for almost 24 hours, with some parts of Singapore virtually under siege. The irony of this would not have been lost on Huguet. It seemed that the recently vilified French Navy were now being called upon to dig the British out of a hole.

Huguet ordered *Montcalm* to make an immediate about-turn. The vast French cruiser slowly came around. Down in the depths of the stoke-hold, in an inferno of heat, scores of sweating stokers stripped to the waist shovelled ever more coal into the immense row of furnaces, with the roar of the blowers fanning the flames and drowning their curses. *Montcalm* then headed back to Singapore at full power with black smoke belching from all four funnels.

Saigon now had a new commanding officer, Captain Fatou. He was the new Chief of the French Naval Division for Indochina. When he arrived from Marseilles to take over command at Saigon, Fatou must have been quite unprepared for what happened next. On Tuesday 16th February Saigon began to intercept fragments of radio messages passing between *Montcalm* and Jerram in Singapore.[24] The first one that Fatou was able to decipher was at 8.30 p.m., from Jerram to *Montcalm*. In those days most admirals were 'sea-borne' and not land-based, as they tend to be nowadays. Admiral Huguet, as the senior French flag officer in the Far East, could act without immediate consultation with Saigon.

The first signal that Fatou intercepted from Jerram was very alarming, apparently requesting assistance from a detachment of armed men:

> Please inform me time of arrival and how many men armed with rifles can be landed, also whether you have any machine guns suitable for shore service.

Fatou must have been stunned and quite at a loss to comprehend what was going on. Two hours later, came:

> You can enter the roads at any time during the night. Pilot will meet you off Peak Island.

Three-quarters of an hour later, Huguet radioed back to Jerram in Singapore offering substantial reinforcements:

> *Montcalm* to Admiral. We shall be at moorings between 8.00 and 9.00 a.m. and can land 130 men just with rifles. Also a section of 25 men with rifles and two machine guns and another of 24 men with rifles and two field guns. Altogether, 7 officers and 173 men, 7 petty officers and 180 rifles. You should send tugs.

This was quite a force to be sure, and proved to be the largest and best-equipped professional unit that went to Jerram's assistance. In the small hours of 17th February, Jerram replied:

> Tugs will be sent for the landing party as soon as you anchor in the roads. Field guns not to be brought but I would be glad of their signal to be deferred.

Montcalm duly arrived back in Singapore early on the morning of 17th, with the mutiny entering its third day. The French sailors were quickly disembarked. *Montcalm* landed 150 armed men who immediately went off in motor vehicles to the Selatan district. That evening, the Japanese cruiser *Otowa* came in and landed another 100 men.

As *Montcalm* was the first ship on the scene, apart from *Cadmus*, their presence was crucial in halting the mutineers. With the arrival of the Japanese, 250 armed sailors and marines were on the mutineers' tails. They soon retreated and scattered, forming many small sniper groups that had to be hunted down one by one. This enabled the ex-patriot women and children to come ashore in reasonable safety, to be cared for in guarded hotels which could better provide essential food and shelter.

The Russian volunteer fleet-ship *Orel* was in Penang, carrying out work on the wreck of *Zhemtchug*. Her divers were busy salvaging guns and other fittings from the wreck when, on Wednesday 17th February, she received an urgent summons from Jerram to go at full speed to Singapore to help quell the mutiny. She immediately set out, arriving on the evening of Thursday 18th. She landed a party of 50 armed marines who at once set off to secure Alexandra Barracks, where the sepoy regiment had been stationed.[25]

The same day, Huguet telegraphed his first report to Saigon, asking for *d'Iberville*, *Pistolet* and *Fronde* to come to Singapore right away. Captain Fatou realised that he had to act quickly and on his own initiative. As the formal inquiry into the sinking of *Mousquet* had to follow the due process of French naval law, Fatou could not release the destroyers without the permission of the Convener, Captain le Coispellier. In view of the seriousness of the affair, le Coispellier released them as soon as he could, albeit after a short delay.

Quoting from Dr Ellis's letter, Cross takes up the story, describing how matters were developing in Singapore with the arrival of reinforcements from the Japanese:

> On Friday evening 19th a second Japanese warship (*Tsushima*)

came in and landed more men. Tomorrow we expect to arrive 600 Territorials from Rangoon. They were sent off in the fastest ship directly they heard the news.

Dr Ellis was now sure that the mutineers hadn't a chance, given the array of forces that were now ranged against them. Describing the scene on that day he wrote:

> The mutineers are still all over the place in batches of 2 and 4, etc. sniping; as in this wooded locality they are difficult to round up. From 30 to 40 Europeans have been killed, mostly civilians. What we think was, they meant to kill the guard at Tanglin and the Malay States Volunteers, and then arm the Germans and assist them in taking the Town. But the Germans wouldn't have it: thought it not good enough: were funked[26] by two of themselves being shot. Of the 300 German prisoners unguarded through most of the first night, only 50 or 60 broke out. All but 17 of these returned to the camp next morning. They [the escapees], included Herr Diehn chairman of the Behn Meyers company. They got to Pasir Panjang and by boat to the Karimun Islands. Mr. Dalton a barrister, was shot dead by our own people by mistake.

Dr Ellis's scorn of the German prisoners' cowardice, in refusing to join in the mutiny, was silly. The Germans in Tanglin were almost entirely civilians who had hitherto enjoyed very good relations with the local British. At the time, almost everybody believed that the war would be over very soon, and life would go back to normal. Why should they take up arms against the British, upon whom they had always relied for essential services? Besides, they had no common cause with the mutineers' grievances and two of their number had already been shot. It was the mutineers they feared, not the British. It has often been said that Singapore might have been taken by the Germans and the course of history changed forever. But that ran completely contrary to the aspirations of the local Germans.

The rather bellicose tone which can be sensed in that account betrays Dr Ellis' general mind-set. The mutineers were all treacherous dogs who deserved to be hanged and the Germans were wimps, evidenced by his use of the derogatory word 'funked'. He was clearly a man who didn't care to analyse the issues. To be fair, he had just been shot at, and his family placed in grave danger, therefore such anger is to be expected. In such a mood, racial prejudices are most likely to show. Cross was clearly unhappy with Dr Ellis' next remarks, putting them firmly in inverted commas.

> All the allies were out after the mutineers. It is a lesson to them and the Mohammedans here and elsewhere that they have no friends. I do hope they wipe out the lot of them and don't take too many prisoners.

Most of the mutineers were rounded up by Friday 19th February. For this the British were indebted to the large contingent of French and Russian sailors who secured Alexandra Barracks, plus a considerable number of armed Japanese from the cruisers *Otowa* and *Tsushima.*

Meanwhile, the French destroyer squadron from Saigon had finally departed for Singapore with Castagné in overall command. Audemard had to stay behind because he had been suspended from his command. *D'Iberville* was therefore under the acting command of his number two, Lieutenant Pochard.[27]

In spite of Captain Fatou's best endeavours, the French destroyers did not arrive on the scene till the mutiny was more or less over. *D'Iberville, Fronde* and *Pistolet* arrived on Tuesday 23rd, just as *Montcalm* was leaving. Castagné sent a signal to Saigon from *Pistolet,* confirming that all three destroyers under his command were in Singapore and the situation was much calmer. It had taken a week to bring the insurrection fully under control.

Fatou was anxious that the French destroyers should remain in Singapore for as short a time as possible. He instructed Castagné to negotiate with Jerram for their speedy return to Saigon because the court of enquiry was still continuing its deliberations.

After only two days in Singapore Lieutenant Pochard, the acting commander of *d'Iberville,* suddenly developed a fever and had to be hospitalised. So, when all three French destroyers set out for Saigon on 27th February, Pochard was left behind. At that stage a small ship like *d'Iberville* must have been running rather short of officers! Any questions that the Saigon enquiry needed to put to Pochard had to be handled by the French Consul in Singapore.

Lauterbach, Herr Diehn and the other German escapees who had got away from Singapore on the first night reached Sumatra just as the French destroyers were arriving in Singapore. Quite a remarkable feat, really. Herr

Diehn sent a cheeky postcard to Sir Arthur Young saying 'arrived safely!'[28]

The ring-leaders of the mutiny were tried by court martial and forty-seven were condemned to death. They were executed publicly by firing squad at Outram Road in March. The *Straits Times* reported that an enormous crowd of more than 15,000 people turned out to see the spectacle. Transportation for life was awarded to sixty-four of them and seventy-three were given prison sentences.[29]

The causes of the mutiny have been widely written about over many years. Standards of leadership by the British officers were poor, and the sepoys did not trust them to tell the truth about where they were going next. Nowadays the mutiny tends to be seen in the context of a nascent anti-colonial resurgence, supported by the Ghadar Party which was based in the US and committed to ousting the British from India.[30] But that argument seems shaky. Why were the mutineers so keen on handing Singapore over to the Germans, yet another imperial power? A German called Herr Hanke, in Tanglin camp, was given to painting portraits as a hobby and, seeing one he had done of the Kaiser, a sepoy called Taj Mohammed saluted it. 'Are you mad?' Herr Hanke exclaimed. 'He is my king!' replied the sepoy.[31]

It is noteworthy that the mutineers never seem to have made any attempt to recruit native Singaporeans either, concentrating instead on recruiting the German prisoners in Tanglin to their cause. The reaction of the native Singaporeans to the mutiny was quite singular. A large proportion were Chinese, and the Singapore Volunteers amongst them were off duty for Chinese New Year. The acting Colonial Secretary, M.G. Maxwell, described their reaction to the mutiny as follows:

> The native population of Singapore was quiet through [sic]. Chinese, Malays and Tamils pursued their ordinary vocations as though nothing unusual were occurring. No crowds collected and so far from there being any panic, there was amongst the Chinese in particular, all through the town and country districts, an imperturbability which amounted to unconcern. The natives of Northern India showed no sign of any sympathy with the mutineers.[32]

As for Lauterbach, his whole career was larger than life. His period as a prisoner in Singapore and the circumstances of his escape were a pinnacle to an extraordinary career. His escape to Germany across Java, China, the Pacific, the US and finally to Germany is an epic tale of adventure which has been told many times. But there is no need to embellish the story, as so many did, including Lauterbach himself. The known facts are entertaining enough.

Immediately after their escape, British ships were searching for the fugitives everywhere, stopping many Dutch merchant ships, hoping they had spotted a fishing boat answering to their description. The British printed off hundreds of pamphlets promising a reward of $1,000 per person for their capture. But to no avail.[33]

Once they reached Padang, Lauterbach and his companions were welcomed by the German Consul. When news of this got out, the British upped the reward money to $5,000. A tidy sum. Undeterred, Lauterbach took passage on a local merchant ship, landing first in Batavia and thence to Surabaya, where he seemed to have some very useful contacts. Lauterbach's best chances always lay in the sea-ports, where he had friends and people who owed him favours. It was also said that he had girlfriends all over the place who were invaluable in helping him to hide from the authorities. They even provided him with disguises; at least, that is what he claimed, and it was probably true.

In Surabaya he assumed a new identity and obtained a forged passport in the name of H.W. Johnson, a Swedish subject. He was determined to get back to Germany by going east, not west. To the west lay too many British territories and the war was raging. To go eastwards was going to require immense patience, but China, South-East Asia and the western Pacific coast were his old stamping grounds. He had lots of friends there.[34]

After many amazing adventures Lauterbach reached Copenhagen and then on to Germany to a rapturous hero's welcome with a brass band playing. He was presented to High Admiral Tirpitz and then to the Kaiser himself. It had taken him 11 months to get home. During that time the war had evolved into something appallingly brutal with terrible loss of life, and nobody seemed to know how to stop it.

Chapter 14

The Saigon Enquiry

The Singapore mutiny interrupted the Saigon enquiry which was trying to get to the bottom of the sinking of *Mousquet* and *Zhemtchug*. From the outset, Audemard had pressed for this enquiry, believing that the French had been unfairly blamed by the British. In time, after the scurrilous article in the *New York Times* had been published, the need for an enquiry received official support from the French government.

The enquiry opened just ten days before the Singapore mutiny, but the events that led up to it had been going on since November of the previous year.

When *Zhemtchug* and *Mousquet* were lost, the news quickly arrived in Saigon and landed on the desk of Captain de Paris de Boisrouvray, the Commandant of the French naval base at Saigon.

De Boisrouvray would have been well aware of the problems that affected the French patrols. They included the angry letter he received from Castagné in June the previous year, complaining about Théroinne's shortcomings as the commander of *Mousquet*.[1] He also knew that all four ships had sailed from Saigon at the beginning of the war without first having a refit, or making them battle-ready. Since arriving in Penang they had kept up a punishing schedule of patrols and, after three months of this, Castagné had written a formal letter of complaint to Audemard, which de Boisrouvray had received, with a copy sent to Jerrram. De Boisrouvray knew that the ships had become unreliable, their boilers were clogged up and their bearings worn. They were long overdue for a proper refit. When *d'Iberville* finally got back to Penang after escorting *Pontoporos* to Singapore, followed by a wild goose chase over to Pulau Weh, they were forced to deal with the problem. With two ships temporarily immobilised and *Pistolet* crippled by a faulty engine-bearing, patrol duties from 25th October onward had to be confined to the area immediately to the north of Penang Island.

What de Boisrouvray thought about the lack of security in Penang has never been recorded. No letters from him on the subject are to be found in the files, but he would have read Audemard's letters of grave concern and Daveluy's as well. He must have been well aware of the lack of co-operation by the Penang harbour authorities. Perhaps he just chose to ignore it. Perhaps, like Jerram, he was too preoccupied with escorts for his ships because many French transports from Indo-China had to be taken across to Colombo. His immediate commanding officer, Admiral Huguet in *Montcalm*, was miles away across the Pacific, mopping up German colonies and chasing Graf Spee's squadron. Huguet was therefore in no position to comment. Perhaps de Boisrouvray did not want to be troublesome to Jerram, who was in overall command.

After the news of *Mousquet*'s loss, it must have been with a sigh of exasperation that de Boisrouvray awaited the reports from Audemard. He had probably decided already that heads must roll.

On 20th November Audemard arrived at Saigon in *d'Iberville*, bringing with him from Sabang all the survivors of *Mousquet*, except the three who had to stay behind in hospital. *D'Iberville* went into dock straight away for a refit and Audemard was left to submit his reports to de Boisrouvray. These were the reports that he and Tavera had been writing on board *d'Iberville* as they steamed back to Saigon from Sabang. They also included the other report by Audemard to Jerram about the sinking of *Zhemtchug*.

De Boisrouvray immediately sent these reports off to the French Navy Minister in Paris. As the mail-boat was on the point of leaving, he penned a hurried covering letter.

De Boisrouvray was a man who tended to shoot first and think later. His first impulse was to divert any possible criticism away from himself because his own position was by no means secure. He had gone along with everything the British harbour authorities in Penang had done or not done. He had systematically ignored all the problems that his local commander had carefully enumerated in his letters. In the matter of Audemard's concerns, there is nothing on file to suggest that de Boisrouvray took any action whatever. He remained entirely passive and allowed Jerram to deal direct in the matter through his 'Intelligence' Officer Commander MacIntyre, who was supposed to liaise directly between Jerram and the ships in Penang.

Around the time of *Emden*'s attack on Penang harbour, Graf Spee's squadron was already well out into the Pacific, and the only other threat was the lone commerce raider *Königsberg,* which was operating off the coast of Africa. That meant that *Emden* was the only ship in the Indian Ocean that posed any immediate threat. Yet there was no link-up between the French destroyer squadron in Penang and the squadron of cruisers, including *Chikuma.* This does not appear to have bothered de Boisrouvray. The matter of poor TSF communications and the lack of code-books for the French commanders elicited no apparent reaction from him either; at least there seems to be nothing in the files.

It is tempting to suppose that he considered an attack on Penang so unlikely that he refused to give the matter his attention. This view was not shared by the people of Penang.

So now, he hit on the first thing he could find in order to pass on the blame. The obstruction of the torpedo tubes on the deck of *Mousquet* seemed like a promising area. In the case of the after torpedo tube, this was caused by some compressed air cylinders on deck, beneath the torpedo tube. This was quickly dealt with by simply throwing the cylinders overboard. Not much time wasted there. The pivot for the forward torpedo tube was partly obstructed by ventilation shafts installed in Saigon. *Mousquet*'s crew could hardly be blamed for that. Besides, as *Emden* carefully remained out of range of *Mousquet*'s torpedoes, they could be only be launched in the wild hope of a lucky strike.

To suggest that *Mousquet* and her crew were not properly prepared was clearly nonsense. Nevertheless, de Boisrouvray reported this as his conclusion. He may well have been prejudiced by the reprimand he had issued to Théroinne a few weeks earlier. Now, de Boisrouvray had this to say:

> I have come to the conclusion that *Mousquet* was not properly ready for action, and I have made an order to remind all the ships which are under my authority in time of war, that all means of attack and defence should be constantly at the ready.[2]

This was all bluster. The part about constant preparedness was a preposterous generalisation. Such demands could not possibly be met. In wartime especially, the normal day-to-day running of ships over several months required regular maintenance, with the ship's boilers and engines shut down. This should have been properly planned with authorisation endorsed by de Boisrouvray, but apparently it was not.

The same day, de Boisrouvray sent off a kinder letter, telling the Minister that he had submitted his heartfelt thanks to Sabang via the French Consul in Batavia, acknowledging all the help that had been given to the survivors of *Mousquet*. He hoped that the three men who had to remain in hospital in Sabang would be sent to Saigon as soon as possible. He also asked the French Consul to reimburse any money that had been lent to *Mousquet*'s crew.

Assurances came back from the government of the Dutch East Indies to their Consul in Singapore, but without offering to defray the costs involved!

> We were called upon to deliver a duty of simple humanity by shouldering the costs of the stay of those sailors in Sabang. Similarly the costs of the hospitalisation and other things. We also provided somewhere for the sailors to stay before repatriation, and we will continue providing for the three patients who were still in treatment.[3]

De Boisrouvray then sent word via the French Consul in Singapore, thanking the Dutch Government once more for their generosity and trusting that the men still in Sabang would continue getting the treatment they needed He also sent a letter to the Navy Minister, Victor Augagneux, in France, asking for various honorific distinctions to be given to key people in Sabang.

A citation in the French Fleet's daily orders was put in, acknowledging the heroic conduct of *Mousquet*'s crew, citing especially Commander Théroinne: 'who disappeared with his ship having fought up to the last minute to save the lives of his sailors without thinking of his own safety', and Enseigne Carissan, who 'died of his wounds in Sabang having heroically supported his Commander during the combat and when rescued by *Emden,* insisted upon being operated upon last'. Also Gunner Calloch who, 'wounded in the foot, yet despite his wounds tried to save his commander from the wreck and succeeded in supporting Monsieur Carissan until the *Emden* launches arrived'. Finally, QM. Cozic 'who remained at the helm on the bridge throughout the combat and showed tremendous 'sang froid' despite being wounded twice'.[4]

For the last two, Calloch and Cozic, the military medal was requested. The citation then goes on to recommend various awards to other members of the crew.

About two weeks later, after de Boisrouvray had reflected a little, he must have realised that it was a bad strategy to make disparaging remarks about dead heroes. Perhaps somebody had pointed that out to him. Somewhat pompously, he retracted his previous statement:

> By the last mail-boat I sent you two reports provided by the Captain of *d'Iberville* about his mission to Sabang and the loss of *Mousquet*. These reports were conveyed to me the moment the post was departing and I could only enclose a hurried communication.
>
> Commander Théroinne perhaps did not take all the precautions as laid down but he died so heroically that I have not the heart to reproach him. Knowing nothing of the bombardment in Penang he saw a warship with four funnels come out of the harbour. He could not have had any idea that the latter was the enemy. He was quite confident about what was in front of him and was then riddled with shots, without having any chance to mobilise his means of defence.

That communication is quite telling. De Boisrouvray was unsurprised that a warship could exit from Penang harbour without the French having any idea whether it was friend or foe. Actually, there was nothing in Tavera's report to suggest that *Mousquet* was within sight of the harbour, anyway. Both *Emden* and *Mousquet* were out in the open sea and Théroinne could only have seen a warship coming from that general direction. The idea that they were within sight of the harbour probably came from the infamous *New York Times* article. De Boisrouvray then goes on to reassure the Minister that he absolves *Mousquet* of all blame.

> Although they only knew [that they were confronted by an enemy ship], from the actual start of the battle, it is certain that all on board *Mousquet* did their duty heroically, firing without hope right up till the destroyer was engulfed.[5]

By this time, de Boisrouvray had hit upon a fresh and softer target to blame in the form of Audemard, whom he had just been interrogating.

> One thing that could have saved *Mousquet* was a TSF transmission from Penang telling them of *Emden*'s presence. I asked Audemard why he had not made that signal. He replied that of the three ships moored in Penang, none had steam up and when I indicated my astonishment, that he had not organised a watch, he

added that the crew were very exhausted and he needed to give them a complete rest. I believe that under those conditions Commander Audemard has neglected his duty as the commander in overall charge. *Emden* would certainly have attempted to jam the signal but there was one convention composed of the simple letter 'E' which only meant one thing 'Enemy in sight, it is dangerous to close up' The *Mousquet* would have understood and could have looked for cover behind the islands to the North of Penang.

De Boisrouvray was clearly being disingenuous. He knew perfectly well that *Fronde* and *d'Iberville* could no longer put off servicing their engines and boilers, including the dynamo providing current for *d'Iberville's* radio transmitter, and both MacIntyre and Jerram had stated that there was no immediate threat from *Emden*. He knew that *Pistolet* was at an hour's notice to get steam up and was ready. He knew that arrangements for watch-keeping had been modified for the period the ships were immobilised in the inner harbour. Why this sudden attack of astonishment? There is nothing to suppose that watch-keeping as stipulated was not carried out with proper efficiency. No lack of vigilance was evident from any of the three French ships that were in the harbour. Within the limits of visibility they saw everything that could have been seen from where they were.

Nevertheless, de Boisrouvray was determined to suspend all three commanders with disciplinary action pending. His remarks bore an uncanny resemblance to some of the opinions reported in the *New York Times*. Had de Boisrouvray been listening to some unpleasant anti-French tittle-tattle? Did this come from Guy Maund's report; or the British harbour authorities?

In truth, Audemard's description of *Zhemtchug's* attack is rather vague and imprecise in its details. He supplied a rough chart with his report which traced *Emden's* path in Penang harbour, but it shows *Emden's* first pass steaming away from *Zhemtchug* at much too wide an angle to bring her torpedo tubes to bear. On that trajectory, *Emden* would have to come to a virtual halt and turn at least thirty degrees to starboard, before firing her first torpedo. From Prinz Hohenzollern's account as *Emden's* torpedo officer, and from the German chart, we know that Audemard's illustration was incorrect. But Audemard himself did not witness that part of the action, anyway. Only the watch-keepers did, and they could only see dimly through the darkness.

Audemard then shows *Emden* turning to starboard and re-passing *Zhemtchug* at much too close a range. This error was corrected at the Saigon enquiry by the eye-witness Enseigne Muller, who was on watch and wide awake from the beginning. He clearly described *Emden* turning to port. In truth it was only after a very detailed enquiry in Saigon that the various pieces of the puzzle were put together, and a clear picture emerged. Audemard, already in shock, was in no state to do such painstaking work just after the attack. He hurried on deck after the first cannonade and his impressions of *Emden*'s early movements were hindered by the darkness, the sea-mist and then the smoke.

The second report that de Boisrouvray sent to the Minister about the sinking of *Mousquet* was completed by Audemard's Enseigne, Tavera. That report is excellent, but Tavera was not under the same pressure as Audemard.

A close examination of de Boisrouvray's letter also reveals some clear non sequiturs. If the ships had no steam up, how could they transmit TSF signals to warn *Mousquet*? How could any reorganising of watches make the slightest difference? *D'Iberville*'s batteries allowed her wireless to function as a receiver but could not provide the necessary power to transmit. What was missing was arrangements by the harbour authorities to make good the deficiency. De Boisrouvray avoids that question completely. Instead, he endeavours to implant the idea that Audemard was guilty of some wanton dereliction of duty by allowing his ships to be unprepared in a most disgraceful way.

This was a very serious allegation which carried the threat of a court martial. De Boisrouvray also implanted the highly damaging suggestion that Audemard encouraged his crew to abandon their proper duties as watch-keepers. It is very easy to see how this line of questioning could have happened. When he was interrogated by de Boisrouvray about why alternative orders for watch-keeping had been put in place, Audemard may well have added that his crew were exhausted. His concerns for his men always trumped everything else. One can just imagine the gleam of triumph in de Boisrouvray's eye as he moved in for the kill. Audemard was not the kind of man who would have retorted that he was simply carrying out recommendations endorsed by Jerram. With his ship completely shut down including the TSF, a full complement of watch-keepers throughout the ship made no sense. But the watch-keepers on deck and at the guns were certainly at their posts.

But the matter of the TSF transmissions still remains. Had Audemard taken a different course of action, using *Pistolet*'s transmitter when she had steam up, he might just have got through to *Mousquet* in time. His mistake was to believe Tavera when they rowed back to *d'Iberville* in the whalers, reporting that *Mousquet* had been sunk in the outer harbour. Audemard even sent *Pistolet* to pick up the survivors. But he was wrong. *Mousquet* at that time was well out in the open sea with time to respond. The second mystery is why *Mousquet* did not receive *Pistolet*'s transmissions about '*Scharnhorst*'. There were at least three of them, and *d'Iberville* received them clearly at a time when *Pistolet* was actually much nearer to *Mousquet*. *Pistolet* was transmitting loud and clear and *Mousquet*'s wireless operators were at their stations. That cannot be doubted. Why did neither *d'Iberville* nor *Pistolet* receive *Mousquet*'s transmission 'M'? Was there a mix-up of wavelengths? This seems the most likely answer.

It appears that Audemard's assumption that *Mousquet* was already sunk prevented him from taking urgent measures to contact her by other means. *Emden* was jamming the Royal Navy wavelength, but not the French wavelength. In the end it was probably this piece of misjudgment that allowed the French naval authorities to nail Audemard and blame him, at least in part, for the loss of *Mousquet*. But that did not happen for a little while yet.

For the next three weeks Audemard remained in Saigon whilst *d'Iberville* was being refitted. We can only guess at his feelings at that time, realising that his Commandant was determined to fasten all blame for the loss of *Mousquet* upon him and his Penang squadron.

By 17th December *d'Iberville* was ready for sea and, on the orders of Jerram, she left Saigon for Singapore. Audemard was probably very relieved to get away from Saigon for a while.

De Boisrouvray had been agitating to recall *Pistolet* and *Fronde* to Saigon so that Castagné and Baule could answer for their sins. When he got around to it, Jerram recalled both of them from Penang[6] and they arrived promptly in Singapore the following day. Now that *Fronde*'s boilers were fixed and *Pistolet*'s bearings were done, these fast little ships were working well. After they had tied up and coaled, the crew had the chance of an evening ashore. They had not seen Singapore in over three months and it must have been a welcome change.

The two young French commanders called in on Admiral Jerram at his headquarters.[7] Jerram and his staff were still in Fort Canning with the telegraph close at hand. Jerram made no reference to the disciplinary charges that were to be brought against the commanders. It is very likely that he had, as yet, no idea what de Boisrouvray was up to, and would probably have been very surprised.

By coincidence, this was the very day that *d'Iberville* and Audemard also arrived in Singapore after a three-week refit in Saigon. Audemard must have been in despair about the attacks that de Boisrouvray was making on his competence, as well as his integrity as a commander. He must have shared this with Castagné and Baule, who would have been deeply shocked.

All three ships left Singapore on Monday 21st December. At midday; *d'Iberville* left for Borneo, joining *Empress of Japan*. They were searching for *Ayesha* which, so far as they knew, was still at large with a well-armed German crew aboard, sufficient to capture an undefended merchantman. In fact *Ayesha* had been scuttled by her own crew just a week before, but Jerram did not know that. *D'Iberville*'s job was to guard the little British North Borneo port of Tawau in Sibuka Bay which was an important coaling station and entirely undefended.[8] *Pistolet* and *Fronde* then sailed for Saigon, with their commanders, anticipating rough treatment at the hands of their Commandant.

On 23rd December at 8.00 p.m., they were anchored at Cap Saint-Jacques at the entrance to the Dong Nai River. Cap Saint-Jacques is the old French colonial name for the peninsula at the southern end of Vietnam. The following morning, on Christmas Eve, they arrived in Saigon after the long run up-river in daylight.

No sooner had they arrived than they were astonished to discover that their peppery, bad-tempered Commandant, Charles de Paris de Boisrouvray – had dropped dead. Perhaps it had all been too much for him.[9]

But that was not all. Had *d'Iberville* been in Saigon, Audemard, despite possible disciplinary measures pending, would have had to assume acting command of the station. In the event, Audemard was in North Borneo, whilst the two big cruisers *Dupleix* and *Montcalm* were miles away. To his complete surprise, Castagné found himself the most senior officer there and had to assume command till mid-January. Without hesitation he made immediate arrangements for the two destroyers to be thoroughly serviced.

Castagné was made of altogether sterner stuff than Audemard, and immediately sent off a telegram to the Navy Minister, informing him that he had assumed command in Saigon. He then set about repatriating various officers, including *d'Iberville*'s doctor, who was currently in Singapore, and appointed two Enseignes as acting commanders of *Fronde* and *Pistolet*. He would have been fully aware of the disciplinary procedures that the deceased de Boisrouvray had been trying to mount against him and his fellow commanders, but he just carried on regardless.[10]

On 7th January Monsieur Aubert of the Justice Division of Fleet Services in Paris made his report to the Navy Minister, Victor Augagneux. He accepted de Boisrouvray's version of things, but added further assumptions about the squadron's unpreparedness. There seems little doubt that he had received a translation of Maund's report to Jerram. That report clearly showed *Emden* steaming right past all three French destroyers well within range of their guns, if not their torpedoes. This is an extract from Aubert's report:

> Concerning the reports from Capitaine de Vaisseau Commandant de la Marine en Indo-Chine [de Boisrouvray] dated 21st November and 3rd December it is clear that *d'Iberville*, *Fronde*, *Pistolet* and *Mousquet* were not ready for combat at the time when the German cruiser *Emden* entered Penang and sank the cruiser *Zhemtchug*. The watch-keepers on board these various ships were not sufficiently organised. None of the ships tied up in port were under steam and in addition the alarm signal was not made by TSF to *Mousquet*. Under the circumstances I judge, like the Commandant, that Captain Audemard had failed in his duty of overall command.
>
> The reports that the captain of *d'Iberville* sent to the Commandant did not contain any precise details about the destruction of *Zhemtchug* by the *Emden*, or the manner in which the French warships were placed. It does not allow any precise understanding of the part played by each commander.
>
> I therefore ask the Minister that instructions should be given to the Commandant [de Boisrouvray] to issue an order against Captain Audemard and the commanders of *Fronde* and *Pistolet*, conforming with article 273 of the naval code of justice.

Aubert then went on to quote the relevant sections of the code and the punishments that should follow:

> '... [they should therefore] be punished by dismissal from the command of any part of the Naval forces of the Empire [for failing to] attack and engage with an enemy, equal or inferior in force, or to help a French ship or an ally pursued by the enemy, or to engage in combat; or not to have done so, in the event that they had not been given specific instructions or serious reasons ...'
>
> If the Minister approves this point of view I request him to endorse the present report with his signature.

The signature of Victor Augagneux duly appeared with a handwritten postscript stating: 'Approve, but probably impose as an immediate measure the replacement of Audemard.'[11]

Effectively, this meant that the suspension of Audemard had to be acted upon right away. Yet in the legal arguments which Aubert set out there was one serious flaw. The information that the Justice Department had not yet considered was 'specific instructions or serious reasons' as to why all the ships apart from *Mousquet* were unprepared. This would have been sufficient in law to exonerate all the defendants. Even the alleged unpreparedness of *Mousquet* was a very dubious claim. But the report sent by de Boisrouvray had deliberately withheld all the circumstances leading to the immobilisation of the French warships in Penang, although these decisions had been tacitly approved by Jerram himself.

Next day, a telegram sent from Victor Augagneux to the Commandant in Saigon repeated Monsieur Aubert's recommendations, giving a disciplinary order against all three Commanders including Castagné. But with de Paris de Bousrouvray's decease, Castagné was now acting in his place. Frantic efforts had to be made to find a new Acting Commandant for Saigon as well as a new Commander for *d'Iberville*. Finally, a directive was made from the 'Direction Militaire des Services de la Flotte' dated 10th January and signed by four very senior officers.

In Saigon there was a transport-frigate called *La Manche* with a comparatively large complement of officers. Incidentally, one officer who had previously served in *La Manche* was Enseigne Villedieu de Torcy, who was transferred to *Mousquet* and sadly lost his life. The commander of this ship was Commander Couraye du Parc, who held the same rank as Audemard and Castagné, although junior to both of them. He must have been rather taken aback to find himself suddenly promoted to the position of acting Commandant of the French Navy in Indo-China.

But the Minister may have been developing some personal misgivings about the whole thing. He also realised that, legally, Couraye du Parc would not have sufficient seniority to enforce the order against Castagné anyway. The order to suspend Audemard right away from his command had been made on 7th January and was endorsed by Augagneux himself, so that had to stand. But for the time being at any rate, Castagné and Baule were not yet suspended. Moreover, as Audemard was away in Borneo he was still in command of *d'Iberville*. In a rather coy piece of incredibly convoluted prose Augagneux added:

> It is up to you as the officer holding the information in the report, to decide if there are grounds or not to pronounce judgement … If the necessary legal elements needed to carry this out are not available in Saigon then the matter should be referred to the Naval Préfect in Toulon.[12]

Very wisely, Couraye du Parc took no further action and there he remained until the arrival of the substantive Commanding Officer Captain Fatou, who left Marseilles on 10th January to take up this new post. This was the man who, almost as soon as he arrived, was drawn into affairs concerning the Singapore mutiny.

The question now was what should be done about *d'Iberville* when she returned? The French naval authorities decided that Audemard should be temporarily replaced by his second-in-command, pending the final confirmation of Audemard's dismissal. 'In any case', they said, 'when Audemard returns he must remain ashore in Saigon awaiting the full enquiry which he himself has now set in motion.'[13]

From this letter it becomes clear that Audemard had succeeded in getting the naval authorities to arrange a formal enquiry. He must have been deeply hurt, not just by the lack of support from the British, but their misrepresentation of the facts in order to cover up their own irresponsible behaviour. He must have felt that an enquiry was his only hope of vindication.

It was at this point that the scurrilous article in the *New York Times* came to light officially, although it had been doing the rounds for a while. It was believed by most people to be the definitive eye-witness account of what had taken place in Penang. The French government now realised that without a proper enquiry these allegations would go unanswered, and the Battle of Penang would go down forever as an ignominious slur on the French Navy and the French people. In a long letter dated 12th January, the Minister for Foreign Affairs – no less – contacted the Navy Minister.

> I am sending you in this envelope various extracts from the *New York Times* which were sent to me from the French Ambassador in Washington …
> I must hope that the details given in the American newspaper are not completely accurate and the impression gained the next day at the heart of this article, also enclosed, is severely exaggerated.

What he was saying was that the allegations that were made against the French 'at the heart of the article' demanded a response; otherwise the reputation of the French would be permanently damaged.[14]

It is worth wondering why de Boisrouvray had seemed so set upon smearing the reputation of his own side. One must suppose that at some level he realised that the French squadron had been given a very raw deal in Penang, deprived of the wherewithal to do their job properly. They were treated in a derisory way, snubbed, ignored and humiliated. How was de Boisrouvray going to account for this appalling treatment which finally led to such a heavy loss of French and Russian lives? Whatever serious lapses in vigilance and discipline the Russians might be accused of, there is no getting away from the fact that they really did not have a chance.

Did de Boisrouvray seriously think that by hanging Audemard out to dry he would himself escape any censure or any responsibility for the tragedy? Was the attitude towards the British by everyone concerned too craven? Hitherto, the only people with real seniority who had been seriously critical were Captain Cochrane of *Yarmouth* and Captain Daveluy of *Dupleix*. The written warnings from Audemard and Castagné about the Harbourmaster and his foolish arrangements would probably never have seen the light of day but for the Saigon enquiry that followed. They would certainly have been copied to de Boisrouvray. We know that he had time to study Castagné's complaints about *Mousquet*'s profligate consumption of coal the year before, and responded to it in his characteristically sharp manner (modified shortly afterwards). He would certainly have had time to respond to something as grave as the entire defence of Penang. But he did not – or, if he did, the evidence has not yet been found.

The mild-mannered Admiral Huguet now appeared over the horizon in *Montcalm*. As Graf Spee's squadron had finally been sunk off the Falkland Islands, there was no German presence left in the Far East. He must have hoped that he could bring a little commonsense to bear. He immediately set to work on things that were happening in Saigon. In a letter he sent to the Navy Minister he clearly calls for calm and a rethink about the battle in Penang, citing Audemard in particular. It is uncertain just where he was on 19th January, because the letter was headed 'on board *Montcalm*', but most likely it would have been in Singapore, where Huguet needed to confer with Jerram.

D'Iberville was also back in Singapore, and Huguet had the unpleasant task of telling Audemard that he was no longer in command of his ship. She was to be taken over by his second-in-command Pochard. In fact that was impossible because Pochard, as recounted in the previous chapter, was ill and had been admitted to hospital in Singapore. The next in line was Enseigne Tavera, but he did not have enough experience. Thus, for the time being, Huguet was forced to transfer his own gunnery officer from *Montcalm*. This clearly peeved him a great deal and he asked for his gunnery officer to be returned to him as soon as possible.

In a telling remark which summed up his view of the whole affair, Huguet added:

> I finish by letting you know that Admiral Jerram, Commander of the English Naval Division in China and the allied forces, testified on two occasions that he was extremely satisfied with Capitaine de Frégate Audemard, his intelligence, his way of working and the services he has given.[15]

And that was the truth. Forever the reasonable man, Audemard had done his best intelligently and diplomatically. Jerram, for one, was not going to point any finger of blame at him. The order of 'non lieu', relieving Castagné and Baule of their commands, was never confirmed and never carried out.

The French Navy Minister, Victor Augagneux, was now in no doubt that the Saigon enquiry should go ahead as soon as possible. It was to be conducted by an authorised commissioner of the Government reporting to the Commandant Captain Fatou. The Commissioner was a very senior officer, Captain Le Coispellier of the French Naval Reserve, who was a lawyer. The enquiry got under way on 5th February and Le Coispellier was right in the middle of examining the witnesses when he was interrupted by the Singapore mutiny. As described in the previous chapter, several of his witnesses were called away at short notice, delaying his deliberations somewhat.

The French enquiry was constituted with remarkable speed and was the only enquiry into the circumstances surrounding the Battle of Penang. Its deliberations carried on till early March. It was meticulously conducted by Le Coispellier in the traditional French inquisitorial style, and addressed to Fatou as Commandant in Saigon.

It is to that enquiry, added to the information from (genuine!) eye-witnesses, plus the German accounts and charts, that we owe such an accurate reconstruction of events in Penang harbour and *Emden's* movements. Although Le Coispellier was not required to address the wider issue of the British security arrangements in Penang harbour, the question was unavoidable and cropped up in many places. For this reason, Le Coispellier made reference to it right away in his opening preamble, an excerpt from which is quoted here;

> It is certain, for example, that if the requests of Audemard regarding the extinguishing of lights to the anchorage had been taken into consideration and if the English authorities had given satisfaction regarding entry by day and night to the anchorage, the *Emden* could not have entered Penang so easily. And if they had come in at a prohibited hour, there would have been much less chance of misidentification of the cruiser which presented itself.
>
> Similarly, the senior commander [Audemard] over the course of two months, never reached an agreement around the issue of the anchorage which allowed allied cruisers not to make identification signals. If there had been, then there would certainly have been much greater significance attached to the arrival of the cruiser on October 28th, in the small hours of the morning, having not made any such signal. That would certainly have raised legitimate concerns.[16]

The report itself does not include the full transcripts taken from all the witnesses, but only the relevant bits. But it runs to nearly fifty pages, summarising many interviews. The crew of all four ships, such as were available in Saigon, and their commanders, were all interviewed. Cross-checks between witnesses' statements were carefully compared for inconsistencies and contradictions. Le Coispellier then drew up his conclusions thus:

> Right away I distance myself with all my power from the accusation against the three accused of allowing themselves to be taken by surprise by the enemy.
>
> After everything which I have said above, about the roster of watch-keepers made in all three ships on the night of 27th/28th October, and the way action-stations were carried out from the first gun-shots, I do not think anyone could sustain such an accusation.
>
> And the accusation of not going to the assistance of an allied warship engaged in combat: I distance myself right away from that accusation so far as Castagné and Baule are concerned.
>
> If indeed they had acted in defence of *Zhemtchug* when attacked by *Emden*, the commanders of *Pistolet* and *Fronde* had to await orders from Audemard. They could not have engaged in combat except on a signal from their Commander or under instructions they

had previously received. They never received a signal ordering them to open fire and never received an order through any other means enjoining them to do so.

Le Coispellier now asked the question, could *Pistolet*, have given help to *Mousquet*?

> If, after casting off from George Town, the commander of *Pistolet* had gone to the assistance of *Mousquet* which he believed was already sunk, and when he was informed that the cruiser [*Emden*] was engaged in a fresh combat: given circumstances that were out of her Commander's control [her engines], I believe *Pistolet* still could not have arrived in time to intervene. It follows that Castagné cannot be held to blame any more than Baule.

The fact that *Emden* was well out of range of *Pistolet*'s torpedoes at all times was clearly established, and required no further comment. Le Coispellier then goes on to the more tricky question of whether Audemard could or should have tried to open fire on *Emden* from *d'Iberville*. Although the window of opportunity was very small, he knew *d'Iberville* could have opened fire. This is what he concluded:

> So it only remains to examine the case of Audemard, the officer commanding the French squadron who alone, according to procedures laid down in 1910, could order the French ships to open fire in support of *Zhemtchug*.
>
> That eventuality never presented itself urgently to Audemard, except at the moment that he was certain of being in the presence of an enemy cruiser; that is to say when she opened fire for the second time. At that moment, *Emden* was 1630 metres from the destroyers and 1866 metres from *d'Iberville*.
>
> The gunnery officer stated that after the unknown cruiser turned and opened fire the second time, she had already escaped the field of fire of her [*d'Iberville*'s] 100mm gun. The latter could only have hit the German cruiser with two 65mm guns and two 47mm guns, whilst *Pistolet* could have hit her with one 65mm and two 47mm guns.
>
> I do not hesitate to say that it would have been foolish to

engage in combat with such [feeble] means, where one could only hope to get an acceptable result by chance, given the distances that were involved.

Le Coispellier then went on to speculate why *Emden* first steamed north away from the outer harbour and then, why did she turn around?

There are two things here. The first is this. Had *Emden* abandoned *Zhemtchug* because she was out of action, and simply scornful of such insignificant enemies as still remained [the French destroyers]? Did she continue her course into open water without worrying about any other intervention?

Or secondly, should she turn to engage adversaries over which she had a crushing superiority of artillery and the advantage of mobility, but *choosing her own distance* [author's italics] and the spot at which to shoot at them with complete protection from their shots?

Clearly the second theory is the correct one. As well as having *d'Iberville* in their sights, *Emden* was indeed looking out for other French destroyers, but had failed to spot them. That was confirmed in the remnant of *Emden*'s signal log recording the conversation with *Buresk*. That is why they were so quick to fire on *Merbau*. So Le Coispellier's conclusion was correct. *Emden* had decided to open fire on *d'Iberville* from a safe distance outside the harbour and clear of any possible ambush. The range of her 105mm guns gave her safety and a clear advantage. Next, Le Coispellier agrees with Audemard that to actually invite or draw *Emden*'s fire, without first being attacked, would have been reckless, given *d'Iberville*'s extreme vulnerability.

If, therefore, Audemard had opened fire on the enemy cruiser, he would have doomed to certain destruction the units he was in charge of, without being of any help to *Zhemtchug*. He did not think he could take on that responsibility and he was right. We now know that in effect, *Zhemtchug* had been fatally damaged already since the first torpedo.

[When] *Emden* opened fire again, *Zhemtchug* disappeared amongst the flotsam after an explosion that would not have allowed the French ships to continue firing effectively, because the enemy was hidden behind a pall of smoke.

They were only able to fire with guns [65mm] which would have given no more than superficial scratches, for a maximum period of 46 seconds for *d'Iberville,* and 68 seconds for *Pistolet.* Allowing 4 seconds to take aim, that would have been 42 seconds for *d'Iberville* and 64 seconds for *Pistolet.* The target then disappeared behind the cargo ships.

Besides, I estimate that to have opened fire in these conditions would undoubtedly have risked the loss of the French ships without bringing any useful help to an ally who was entirely disabled.

Le Coispellier then states categorically that there was no credible evidence to conclude that Audemard was at fault.

For all these reasons I believe that Audemard had good reasons, about which he is questioned in the text, not to go to the help of *Zhemtchug* when she was engaged with *Emden,* and furthermore this principal accusation against this senior officer must be ruled out. I believe there are no grounds upon which to pronounce a lapse of judgement.[17]

In his report he also addresses the problems with TSF communications and points out that *Mousquet,* unaccountably, did not appear to have received *Pistolet*'s TSF transmissions. But he did not address Audemard's failure to try all other means to contact *Mousquet,* saying only that Audemard was certain that *Mousquet* was already sunk. This criticism was left unanswered.

The results of this enquiry were forwarded by telegram to the Navy Minister on 19th March, with the following comments from Saigon. The signature is not clear, and it is a numbered 'copy of the original', but it almost certainly originated from Captain Fatou.

The commissioners of the Government have scrupulously studied all the circumstances for the Penang affair. A great deal of work. It established perfect vigilance in all the French ships and their call to action stations. After the first cannon shots during darkness there was uncertainty about the identity of the cruiser which was mistaken for an ally up to the second cannonade, a minute before *Zhemtchug* exploded. At that moment *Emden* was too far away [for

Pistolet] to launch a torpedo and beyond the range of any effect from light artillery. To open fire under those conditions could have brought about the loss of a French ship without any chance of bringing help to *Zhemtchug*.

This affair has concluded with a suspension. I withdraw the general suspension and propose that Audemard and therefore Couraye du Parc [previous Acting-Commandant in Saigon] are reinstated back to their respective commands.[18]

Audemard must have been mighty relieved and prepared to return his old command. But he was not out of the woods yet. The Ministry in Paris still had to endorse the decisions taken in Saigon. In Paris it was duly referred to the Minister, with a somewhat enigmatic covering letter stating that: 'The ordinance of suspension has been lifted concerning the affair of *d'Iberville* in Penang, and Audemard who is available in Saigon, may return to Paris by the next mail steamer.'[19]

It seemed that he was not to get his command back. Instead, he was to be posted elsewhere. It was clear, however, that no further action would be taken regarding the other two commanders. Castagné and Baule remained in command of their respective ships. But Audemard was required to return to Paris. He was moved on, but there were no further disciplinary measures.

This caused some initial confusion and it was not till 4th May that the matter was finally laid to rest. In a final, *final*, letter to the Director of Fleet Services marked 'confidential', the Ministry explained:

> The Minister has decided to maintain the measure taken against Audemard who has already been relieved of his command. No order has been given in relation to the other officers involved in the affair. I think, under these conditions, that the affair should be considered entirely closed and that no particular sanction be taken vis-a-vis the officers receiving an ordinance of suspension, except that concerning Audemard.[20]

Audemard was neither publicly disgraced nor dismissed from the service; instead he was given an administrative job in Paris. Clearly, Augagneux thought, after all the damaging publicity that accompanied the first reports of the battle in Penang, it would be best to remove the French Commander from that sphere of operations.

He may have been right. Audemard, as mentioned at the beginning of this story, was not a young man, nor was he in the best of health. He had a record of many periods of sick-leave with recurring bouts of malaria.[21] In fact, he retired at the end of the war. Knowing his character, he would have consoled himself that by avoiding a futile gesture of derring-do, exposing the location of the two French destroyers that *Emden* had not seen, he probably saved the lives of many in his squadron. But he must have asked himself for the rest of his life whether he might have been more effective in saving *Mousquet* from her tragic fate.

Chapter 15

Baron Cherkasov's Court-Martial

The fate of Baron Cherkasov took longer to decide. After the Russian Volunteer Fleet-ship *Orel* returned to Vladivostok there was little Cherkasov could do but wait for his court martial. This was held in Vladivostok in August 1915. Both Captain Cherkasov and Lieutenant Commander Kulibin pleaded guilty.[1]

Cherkasov was accused of failing to comply with the orders of Admiral Jerram and failing to keep a regular rota of watch-keepers. It is questionable whether he did fail to comply with Jerram's orders, since those orders were simply to shut all his ship's boilers down and clean them. But in such a long string of indictments, that is a mere detail. He was also charged with failing to arrange a change of watches amongst the gun-crews at night. He also left the torpedo tubes unloaded and unmanned. Cherkasov pleaded guilty to all those charges.

The indictment went on to say that he had allowed the *Zhemtchug* to lie in the open roadsteads fully lit and with only one man on look-out. He apparently allowed strangers to visit the cruiser and move freely all over her. People later claimed that some of them were prostitutes, but that rumour was never substantiated. 'Visitors' could refer to anyone, such as the alleged guest aboard *Pistolet*. Reverend Cross would certainly have mentioned it in his notes had any such scandal had been brought to his attention.

The court martial found that arrangements for watch-keeping were totally inadequate for a ship in a state of high alert, but it has to be said that this reflected the general state of things in Penang harbour. Like other ships, apart from the French, her riding lights were on. They had posted a lookout and the gun-crews were drawn up, although only twelve rounds of ammunition were immediately available.

The torpedo tubes were not prepared for action. This was also mentioned in the French archives, but it was understandable given the fact that *Zhemtchug* was immobilised and having her boilers cleaned. It was not possible to use underwater torpedo tubes without having steam up to manoeuvre the ship. *Zhemtchug* carried one deck-mounted torpedo tube at the stern,[2] but it is not known if that weapon was in service at the time.

Then there was the question of inappropriate radio messages. Referring to an earlier occasion, the Court noted that when the cruiser was in the Philippines checking for enemy merchant ships, Cherkasov sent a radio message to *Askold* giving his exact position without putting it in code. This was a serious breach of security for which there was no excuse.

In late October *Zhemtchug* had visited the Andaman Islands for coaling. This was just after *Zhemtchug* had handed over the convoy of French transports in Penang to *Yarmouth,* and had then set off in search of *Emden* or her tenders. It was also the time when the Governor-General of Rangoon told him that *Emden* was nowhere near the area he was searching.[3] Captain Cherkasov had apparently gone ashore on one of the Andaman Islands with five of his officers, spending the night there. As was the case in Penang, *Zhemtchug* was fully lit. In addition the gun-crews were not standing by and the torpedo tubes were unloaded. On that occasion the ship was not immobilised so it was a more serious lapse. Cherkasov was aware that *Emden* had been in that area more than once, but seemed quite confident that there was no present risk. It is very ironic that just two days after he had left the area, *Emden* arrived at Nancowry in the Nicobar Islands to coal from *Buresk,* in readiness for her attack on Penang harbour. That was not far to the south of the spot where *Zhemtchug* had been anchored.

Once back in Penang, all *Zhemtchug*'s boilers were dismantled bar one, to keep emergency power on, and all the shells and cartridges were returned to the store except the twelve rounds which were on deck.[4] Cherkasov then went ashore at about 6.00 p.m. to join his wife in the Eastern & Oriental Hotel. He did not return till he arrived at the jetty in the early hours of the next morning to see the wreck that had once been his ship, with so many casualties on the jetty.

The court martial took an exceedingly dim view of Cherkasov's habit of allowing his wife to accompany him 'during the cruise'.[5] He corresponded with her by letter and telegram and he used Russian Navy facilities to do this.[6] Cherkasov also claimed that he was unwell, which in those latitudes was not too surprising, and this was supported by his wife.[7]

The Petrograd newspapers reported that the court martial was held in public. Sentence was passed just over nine months after the sinking of *Zhemtchug*. Both Cherkasov and Kulibin were to be stripped of their civil rights, deprived of all decorations and be dismissed from the Imperial Service. Cherkasov was to lose his title of Baron and be jailed for three-and-a-half years. Kulibin was sentenced to jail for one-and-a-half years.[8] It must have been a prolonged and devastating humiliation for both of them.

By any standards, the sentence passed on Cherkasov was savage, but the scale of the disaster which had overtaken his ship was such that only an exemplary punishment would satisfy public outrage. Cherkasov made no attempt to defend himself and seemed to welcome his humiliation which was witnessed so publicly. Feelings of self-reproach must have completely overwhelmed him.

There can be no doubt that *Zhemtchug* was decidedly unready and was never called to action-stations. But that only begs the question as to why she was in such a state of unreadiness and caught by surprise. In spite of Cherkasov's numerous failures as a commander, it is also true that *Zhemtchug* had only a few moments in which to identify the unknown cruiser as an enemy and then open fire. Even if she had been at full battle-readiness this would have required lightning-fast reactions.

Conditions on board *Zhemtchug* would have been insufferably hot, especially for a Russian crew not acclimatised to the tropical heat. Hence many of the men were sleeping on deck in their underwear, as the French did. Even those gunners who were not on watch were probably sleeping beside their guns anyway. Had they received warnings of an unknown cruiser making her way towards the harbour, things might have been very different. That would have given the gun-crews time to muster and load their guns quickly, ready to fire, with other men bringing extra ammunition out on deck. Even twelve rounds from *Zhemtchug*'s big guns could easily have crippled *Emden*, which was only a lightly armoured cruiser.

Had *Zhemtchug* been drawn up across the harbour mouth with a stern anchor, she would have been better able to shoot at *Emden*, had the look-outs identified her approaching. She would have presented an altogether trickier target for *Emden*'s torpedoes. Given that *Zhemtchug* was lying up and down the tideway in the harbour mouth, she was probably in the worst possible position for such an attack, and *Emden* could take aim with ease.

In his letter to Jerram, Maund reported a conversation aboard *Zhemtchug* between himself, MacIntyre and Cherkasov. During this conversation Cherkasov was advised to draw up a stern anchor. He added that the order was passed on to the 'ship's commander' (presumably Lieutenant Commander Kulibin) in his presence.[9] But there seems to be no confirmation of this conversation on the Russian side. Maund's report was so full of confabulations intended to whitewash MacIntyre, that everything in it has to be doubted.

We know that Cherkasov was staying at the Eastern & Oriental Hotel where he had a good view of his ship. Even at night with her riding lights on, he would have seen that his order for a stern anchor had not been carried out. To disobey a captain's order in this way would be a very serious offence and it is curious that there was no mention of it at the court martial. Was it possible that Cherkasov was shielding Kulibin or did that conversation with Maund never happen?

But the inescapable conclusion is that neither Cherkasov nor his fellow officers took the risk of an attack from *Emden* at all seriously. And why should they? Cherkasov had already been assured in Rangoon that *Emden* was a thousand miles away, south of Ceylon in the Indian Ocean being chased by *Hampshire* and other cruisers. Jerram himself had decided that an attack on Penang at that point in time was so unlikely that he allowed *Zhemtchug* and two French ships to dismantle their boilers for cleaning, together with a much-needed general service.

No amount of battle readiness and sobriety on *Zhemtchug* could have prepared her for an attack by an enemy cruiser that was simply allowed to sail right into the outer harbour at night without giving her identification signal, unchallenged; with the lighthouses and the North Channel buoys lit and the harbour lights on.

Much has been made of the fact that many of *Zhemtchug*'s crew had been ashore the evening before and had got thoroughly drunk. This story has been repeated in every book that was ever written on the subject. But such behaviour by sailors ashore was by no means unique, and it did not necessarily follow that the whole ship was thereby disabled. Reverend Cross made much of the sailors' drunkenness, but it must be remembered that all his working life he waged a private war against alcohol.[10] He also saw drunkenness as a particularly British vice. Anyone with experience of the British Navy a few decades ago would know that such scenes were quite usual. When the crew had a 'run ashore' the ship would routinely send out a patrol armed with batons to stop the fights and escort the drunks back to the ship. In the days of daily rum rations, the whole ship had to function every afternoon with the entire crew mildly inebriated. In the case of *Zhemtchug*, those who remained on board that night were probably sober enough. The French comments about the drunken Russians are also not surprising given that French drinking habits have always been different.

One of the Russian sailors reported that *Emden* was hailed by *Zhemtchug*'s lookout and identified herself as *Yarmouth* before hoisting the German colours and opening fire. But it was probably too late, anyway. There was no time. *Emden*'s gunners constantly practised and, if conditions were right, they were very accurate. As they drew level with the ship their first target was the main armament on *Zhemtchug*'s deck, starting at the stern. They did not miss and, after their first torpedo struck, smoke was seen rising from the after magazine, so that the compartment had to be immediately flooded. Both of these factors led to *Zhemtchug* settling by the stern up to the after-deck and taking a list to starboard, tilting her guns up in the air and making it impossible for them to bear down on *Emden*. The derision that has since been heaped upon the Russian's gunnery never takes this into account.

In Vladivostok, Cherkasov's court martial did not consider the conditions prevailing in Penang harbour at the time of the attack. What they focused on was the preparedness of the ship and, above all, Cherkasov's fitness to command. On both counts, Cherkasov was found wanting. The charges read out against him included various references to what was deemed to be his irresponsible personal conduct well before the battle in Penang, and it has to be admitted that he consistently displayed an extraordinary lack of professionalism. This kind of attitude had indeed been endemic amongst the officer-class in Russia for many years, even before the humiliating defeat of their fleet by the Japanese at Tsushima.

It is ironic that Cherkasov's speciality was gunnery, and there is no reason to doubt his competence in this field. Indeed, his expertise was about to be put to better use.

Baroness Varvara Cherkasova was deeply distressed by the harsh sentence of the court, believing quite correctly that the lack of proper vigilance by the Penang harbour authorities had not been sufficiently stressed. This, she argued, was partly to blame for the catastrophe. No sooner was the sentence passed than she started to lobby various important people for his sentence to be commuted. She wrote to the Navy Minister:

To his Excellency the Navy Minister.

From the Baroness Varvara Cherkasova, wife of the Captain Baron Ivan Alexandrovich Cherkasov, condemned by the Naval Court.

My husband Baron Ivan Alexandrovich Cherkasov, found guilty by the court in Vladivostok for the destruction of the ship entrusted to him, has been sentenced to a hard and serious punishment. He has lost everything, despite honestly recognising his mistakes. I am asking your excellency, because of his long fighting service, to commute his sentence without degrading him by relegation to the lowest ranks and sending him off to the battlefield to expiate his guilt with his blood, for the Tsar and his motherland.

Vladivostok 12th August 1915.[11]

The reason for this outburst was her husband's determination to do exactly that. Rather than serve a prison sentence, he was determined to join in the war at the lowest rank, and go to the front. He even wrote to the Tsar himself, and this extraordinary letter remains in his file. Starting off in that stilted and highly formalised style of address that was reserved for the Tsar, Cherkasov went on to make this request. Instead of going to prison he wanted to go on fighting.

The Court ... has sentenced me to be expelled from the Navy and after being deprived of my baronial title and civil rights to be imprisoned for three and a half years. So, I ask your Imperial Majesty a great favour.

In the execution of the court's decision, I ask them to further downgrade me to the very lowest rank in the army or the navy within my speciality of artillery so that in our struggle against the enemy, I can wash away with my blood the disgrace that now lies within me. The blood through which my family has been serving your Most August House since the time of Peter the Great.

There is something here slightly akin to the turbulent emotions of Winston Churchill at roughly the same time. He felt so guilty and wretched

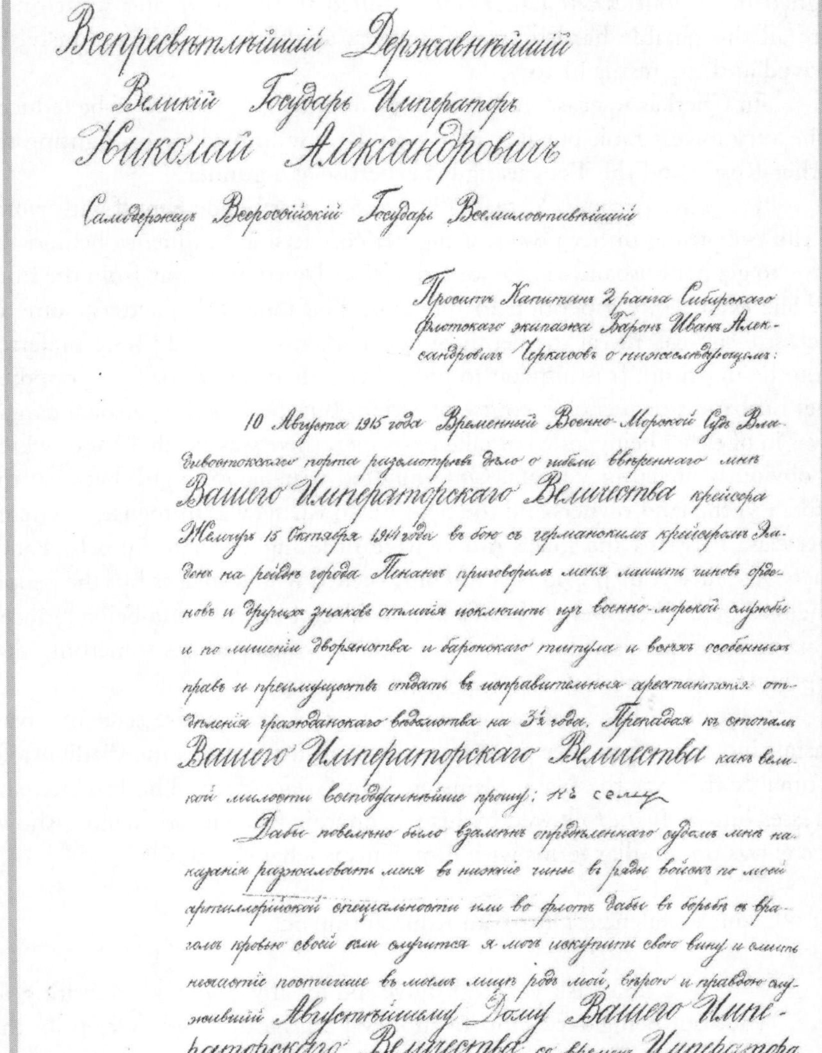

Всепресвѣтлѣйшій Державнѣйшій
Великій Государь Императоръ
Николай Александровичъ
Самодержецъ Всероссійскій Государь Всемилостивѣйшій

Проситъ Капитанъ 2 ранга Сибирскаго
флотскаго экипажа Баронъ Иванъ Александровичъ Черкасовъ о нижеслѣдующемъ:

10 Августа 1915 года Временный Военно-Морской Судъ Вла-
дивостокскаго порта разсмотрѣвъ дѣло о гибели ввѣреннаго мнѣ
Вашего Императорскаго Величества крейсера
Жемчугъ 15 Октября 1914 года въ бою съ германскимъ крейсеромъ Эм-
денъ на рейдѣ города Пенангъ приговорилъ меня лишить чиновъ орде-
новъ и другихъ знаковъ отличія исключить изъ военно-морской службы
и по лишеніи дворянства и баронскаго титула и всѣхъ особенныхъ
правъ и преимуществъ отдать въ исправительныя арестантскія от-
дѣленія гражданскаго вѣдомства на 3½ года. Предавая къ стопамъ
Вашего Императорскаго Величества какъ вели-
кой милости всеподданнѣйше прошу: из селу

Дабы повелѣно было взамѣнъ опредѣленнаго судомъ мнѣ на-
казанія разжаловать меня въ нижніе чины въ ряды войскъ по моей
артиллерійской спеціальности или во флотъ дабы въ борьбѣ съ вра-
гами кровью своей бы служить я могъ искупить свою вину и смыть
нѣкоторое позорище въ моей лично родъ мой, вѣрою и правдою слу-
жившій Августѣйшему Дому Вашего Импе-
раторскаго Величества со времени Императора
Петра Великаго. Городъ Владивостокъ 14 Августа 1915 го.

fig 19 ⟶ Cherkasov's letter to the Tsar ⟵

after the failure of his 1915 Dardanelles Campaign, in which so many of Admiral Jerram's Australian expeditionary force lost their lives, that he resigned from politics altogether. He enrolled in the army and went on to share all the terrible hardships and dangers at the front. Miraculously, he survived and the rest is history.

In Cherkasov's case, rather than go to prison, he wanted to be reduced to the very lowest rank possible that would allow him to go on fighting for Mother-Russia and the Tsar, using his expertise as a gunner.

His wife, Baroness Varvara Cherkasova, was beside herself with worry and did everything in her power, using her contacts and influence behind the scenes, to get her husband's sentence reduced and keep him away from the front line. She even wrote a petition to the Tsar. The tone of her letters, some of which still survive, reveal the depth of her despair – she would have preferred him to be in prison. It is difficult to judge her state of mind, being so opposed to her husband's own chosen course of action. But, besides the personal danger he was in of either being killed or taken prisoner, there was another factor which was obviously affecting Varvara. One hundred years ago the gulf between the aristocracy, the land-owners and the peasants in Russia was immense. To many upper-class Russians the lower orders were little higher than animals. Land-owners, just fifty years previously, not only owned whole villages but the people in them as well. These were the serfs. So, the idea of her husband being reduced to the status of mere serfdom – cannon fodder – was perhaps something that this proud and beautiful woman just could not accept.

Amongst her correspondence is a letter addressed to Ivan Konstantinovich when her husband was still in prison in Vladivostok. Presumably this was the Navy Minister, Ivan Grigorovich. The fact that she addresses him as Ivan, followed by his patronymic (the father's name), shows that she was on familiar terms with him. This is what she says:

Your excellency, Dear Ivan Konstantinovich

I must ask you to forgive me for my boldness in writing to you, but being very short of money I am hardly able to keep up the personal struggle on behalf of my husband.

I will not bore you with the details of my husband's career as an officer and a commander. All I can say is that he served irreproachably for 23 years and always had brilliant recommendations. So, for an ordinary person like me it is impossible to understand how such a

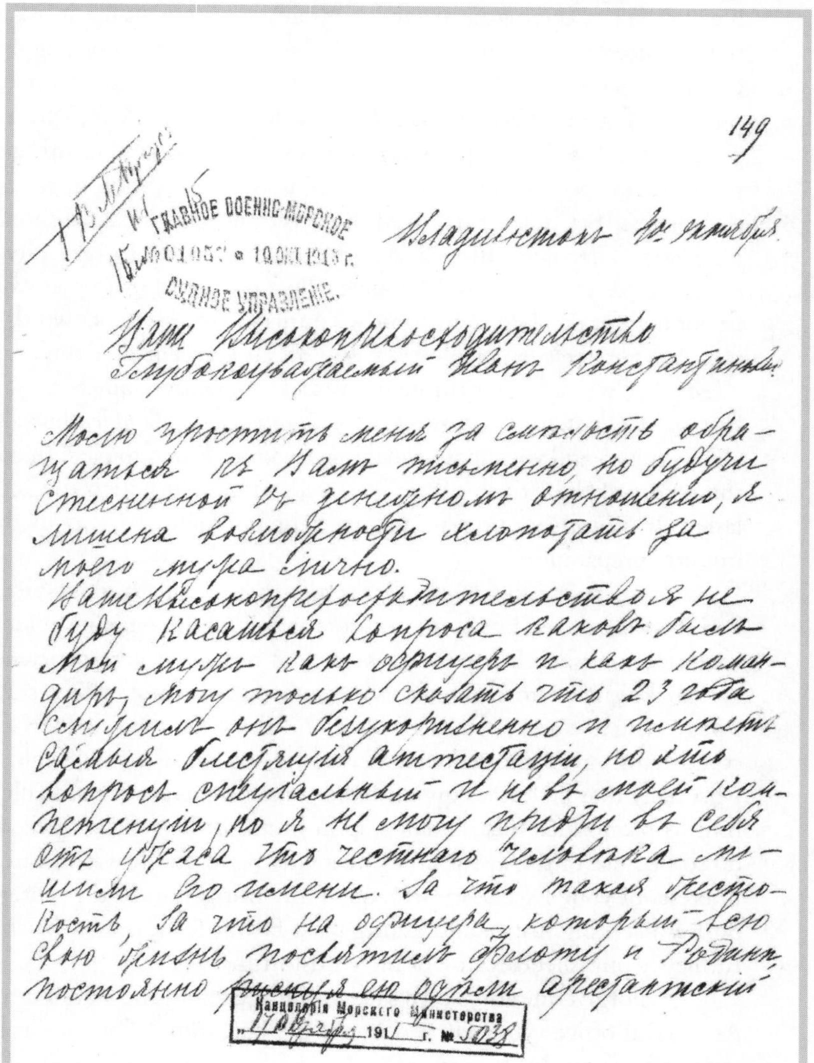

149

Главное Военно-Морское Судное Управление. № 01957 10 ОКТ 1913 г.

Владивостокъ 20 сентября

Ваше Высокопревосходительство
Глубокоуважаемый Иванъ Константиновичъ

Молю простить меня за смелость обращаться къ Вамъ письменно, но будучи стесненной въ денежномъ отношеніи, я лишена возможности хлопотать за моего мужа лично.

Ваше Высокопревосходительство я не буду касаться вопроса каковъ былъ мой мужъ какъ офицеръ и какъ командиръ, могу только сказать что 23 года служилъ онъ безукоризненно и имеетъ самыя блестящія аттестаціи, но это вопросъ спеціальный и не въ моей компетенціи, но я не могу придти въ себя отъ ужаса что честнаго человека лишили его имени. За что такая жестокость, за что на офицера, который всю свою жизнь посвятилъ флоту и Родине, постоянно [illegible] одеть арестантскій

Канцелярія Морского Министерства „17“ Октября 1913 г. № 5038

fig 20 ~ First page of Varvara's letter to Navy Minister ~

person should be completely deprived of his name and status. What could be deserving of such cruelty to an officer that has devoted all his life to the Fleet and his native land, constantly putting his life at risk and now reduced to wearing prisoner's clothes as if he were nothing but a criminal, a swindler or a thief? Why has my husband been so shamefully punished for a military mistake? I appeal to your Excellency's heart to petition the Tsar in order to soften my husband's fate and mitigate this punishment, perhaps by transfer to the military detention quarters in the fortress. Let him be deprived of everything but do not dishonour his name. The state of my husband's health is awful so take pity on him. We see you as our only chance where one word from you would be enough for the Tsar to mitigate his punishment. My God, words fail me. As your Excellency knows, it was all an accident that the cruiser *Zhemtchug* was lost, not through any lack of alertness but because on first sight the enemy ship was not recognised as the *Emden* but as an allied cruiser, and with that protection she was allowed to pass. In court the report of the British officer was read out and although the action lasted 20 minutes, our readiness to fight only allowed two to three minutes preparation.

There are documents that certify that my husband was unwell and this was agreed by the prosecutors as well as those giving evidence against my husband. My God! Who does not have these deficiencies and make such errors? The public prosecutor did not expect such a savage sentence and is shocked by it and the Chairman of the Court could hardly read the sentence because it was so severe. He told me personally that he knows my husband well and it was very difficult for him to pronounce this sentence upon him, but he was compelled to do so because of the awful times we are living in and it was not in the interests of your Excellency to request any mitigation of the sentence. So I am seeking justice and asking for a favour for a person has been ruthlessly punished because of mere misfortune.

Forgive me for God's sake and understand the state I am in. As a naval officer yourself you know the hardships of service at sea, each officer your brother-in-arms. Intercede for him and do not allow this mockery towards an officer and a gentlemen. You have rights and you have powers. Where can I search for justice and protection? I am in despair and losing my mind but I trust in your mercy and sense of justice. Please respond to these entreaties and protect us. The Lord will bless you and give you long years of health and happiness if you can act successfully in this awful problem. I beg of you, help.

With a deep belief in your sense of mercy,

With my sincerest respect for you,

The Baroness Varvara Cherkasova.[12]

Vladivostok. October 4th 1915.

In another letter, sent on 10th October, Baroness Cherkasova even wrote to the Tsar, pleading that her husband was tricked by *Emden* posing as *Yarmouth*.[13] Finally, she sent off a letter to the Navy Prosecutor, pointing out that Admiral Jerram himself authorised the shutdown of *Zhemtchug*'s boilers and that no security precautions were taken in Penang harbour.[14]

But Varvara's pleas fell on deaf ears, partly because her husband was still determined to assuage his guilt on the battlefield. His request was allowed, although he was not let out of prison till March 1916.[15]

He was given the rank of a common sailor and sent to the Caucasus to join the Urmiyskaya flotilla, where Russia was fighting on a second front against her old adversary, the Turkish Kurds.[16] The Caucasus was not a good spot to be in because the Kurds did not always treat their prisoners well. Sailors, like marines, could fight on land, and Cherkasov so impressed everyone with his bravery and his gunnery skills that he was awarded the St Geogiy's decoration for heroism.

The lack of proper leadership from the ruling elite was one of the factors that led to the July Revolution. Once that got started, the government and the entire administration were brought down. In April 1917 an immediate Russian amnesty with Germany followed. Their war had came to an end and by that time both sides had virtually fought themselves to a standstill.

Miraculously, Cherkasov survived. In June, Ordinary Seaman Ivan Cherkasov, still in the Caucasus, had his case reviewed. But the court took a dim view and refused to consider any restitution of his former status. In fact, they especially criticised his wife, apparently seeing her as some kind of viper.

Cherkasov had his case reviewed once again in July 1917. This time he was more fortunate. At a meeting of the Siberian Flotilla in Vladivostok, it was decided that, owing to his bravery and excellent service in the Caucasus, he was to be reinstated as a Commander in the Russian Navy with his titles returned to him.[17]

Following the October Revolution he continued to serve in the Black Sea Fleet, and throughout the civil war he fought on the White Russian side. In 1919, with the provisional government now in exile, they maintained a semblance of legitimacy and Baron Cherkasov was appointed to Istanbul as naval attaché to Baron General Vrangel, serving the very Turks he had just been fighting.

In 1921 he went into self-imposed exile in Paris, where he lived for the next twenty years. He died in Paris on 11th March 1942 and was buried in the St Geneviève cemetery. He was 68 years old.[18]

What happened to the Baroness Varvara we do not know. Perhaps she got lost somewhere in the civil war, as so many did. There is no sign of her in the St Geneviève cemetery.

The awful irony is that Ivan Cherkasov lived just long enough to watch the German Army parading through the streets of Paris and to hear of the German army marching through Russia. It must have broken his heart.

Chapter 16

Loose Ends

The Germans

Emden

Emden's wreck had many photographs taken at the time, but she was then abandoned to her fate, slowly sliding backwards down the reef and under water. The remains of the wreck are still there a few metres down, but the seas around North Keeling are rarely calm and diving is difficult.

Karl von Müller

The injured survivors from *Emden* were treated in Colombo, and as luck would have it they were able to return to Germany much earlier than the rest. Guarded by soldiers, the remainder were taken with the great Australian convoy to Port Said in *Orvieto* of the Orient Line. During the voyage, von Müller gave Prinz Hohenzollern the task of writing up the account of *Emden's* campaign in the Indian Ocean. The book that Prinz Hohenzollern later published was largely based upon this report, which was written immediately after the event. Here are some comments he made about the time they were in captivity.

[Fregatten]Kapitän von Müller had already begun to put together all the news about the *Emden*. This was necessary as our log-book was burnt soon after the fight so that it would not get into enemy hands. One could while away many a weary hour with such official literature and it was pleasant to return in thought, to our gallant and beloved *Emden*.

Once the great convoy reached Port Said at the northern end of the Suez Canal, they stopped and were ordered to remain in Egypt. This was because Churchill had decided that they should join the campaign against Ottoman-Turkey in the Dardanelles. Prinz Hohenzollern remarked:

> At this, the Englishmen cursed frightfully as they would have been glad to spend some time in old England. This was understandable for most of these men had been in the colonies since their youth and were therefore very anxious to get home. Through Turkey joining the German side the original plans were altered. I am of the opinion that a large part of these men only enlisted in the hope of seeing home once again, for there was no general military service in England.

The *Emden* prisoners were then transferred to *Hampshire* under Captain Grant, and there they stayed in Port Said, awaiting further instructions.

> It was noticeable that we were among members of our own profession. The whole tone was far warmer. That we were received so cordially by the *Hampshire* was especially remarkable as this ship had been detailed to chase us.
> Our accommodation was very good indeed. The English Captain had completely abandoned his cabin to us. We could go on deck any time which was very pleasant at sea and in good weather.

Finally they set sail for England when a radio message arrived, ordering *Hampshire* to remain with the Mediterranean Fleet, docking at Malta. There, the *Emden* officers were held in Verdala Barracks, and the rest went to Fort Salvatore. They were imprisoned there for the next four years till the end of the war. The accommodation was not particularly good and von Müller worked tirelessly to improve the conditions for his men.

The difference between the navy and the army met the eye and the ear at once. The hearty friendship of our professional fellows was missing now. Coldness and hardness were already noticeable in the tone of the Army officers.[1]

In 1916, von Müller received the news that he alone was being transferred to England. On 8th October he was taken to England in HMS *London*. On the journey he was given no freedom whatever. He was then transferred to the German prisoner of war camp in Sutton-Bonington, near Nottingham. Suffering with a bad chest and recurring bouts of malaria, he was transferred to neutral Holland in January 1918, as part of an exchange of prisoners. There, he received treatment and was finally repatriated to Germany before the end of the war.

The story of *Emden* has now passed into German naval folklore and the fate of the key officers involved with *Emden* has been extensively written about elsewhere.

On 21st March 1918, von Müller was given Prussia's highest award, the Blue Cross 'Pour Le Mérite'. After the war he was often asked to write his memoirs, but declined to do so. The loss of so many members of his crew weighed heavily upon his conscience, and for the rest of his short life he devoted himself to the welfare of the survivors. He was promoted to Captain, and the photograph of him in Captain's uniform is shown here. It was taken after the war and shows how much he had aged in those last few years. He died on 11th March 1923.

Hellmuth von Mücke

After his amazing adventures; escaping with his crew all the way to Constantinople, von Mücke quickly gained great notoriety in Germany. After the war he wrote a book about it, which was soon made into a film. But he got involved with German nationalist politics and fell into disfavour with the Third Reich administration. He was given a very minor role in World War ll and finally died, an exceedingly grumpy old man, in 1957.

Franz Joseph von Hohenzollern

The story of Prinz Franz Joseph von Hohenzollern, the Kaiser's nephew, had a sad end as well. During the Third Reich Hitler managed to flatter him into joining the National Socialist Party. He acted as an ambassador for the party, presenting to the outside world the aristocratic face of German politics. Before World War II he joined Himmler's SS, but as the war progressed his loyalty began to waver and he was finally expelled from the SS before the war had ended. He died in obscurity in 1964.

Julius Lauterbach

After his escape to Germany, Julius Lauterbach went on to serve very actively in the Baltic. By now he was something of a folk hero and he wrote a book about his exploits, although it was prone to exaggerations. After the war, he settled in San Francisco and established a successful shipping business of his own, thus avoiding the rise of National Socialism in his native Germany. He died after Word War II.

Of all the key people involved in the battle in Penang Harbour, Lauterbach must be regarded as the most successful. All the enterprises he undertook, even a late marriage, seemed to work out and his wife was still living in Cologne in 1982.[2] He remained popular, successful and irrepressible to the end.

The essential difference between Lauterbach and his Commanding Officer von Müller is captured in a reported conversation between him and Captain Isdale, Master of *Ribera*. As *Emden*'s prize officer, Lauterbach was the first to board the captured merchantman. When Isdale asked him what *Emden* would do if they were discovered by an Allied warship, he replied, 'We shall run like the devil! We are not built for fighting!'[3]

Kaiser Wilhelm II

Prinz Hohenzollern's famous uncle also had a sad end. Even before the war ended his subjects began to rebel, urged on by the revolution in Russia and the futility of the war. By the time the Armistice was concluded on 11th November 1918 he had been forced to abdicate and went into exile in the Netherlands. There he lived out the rest of his days in the quiet opulence of his private mansion, Huis Doorn. Although he was violently anti-Semitic he did not approve of Hitler's regime. He died in June 1941 during the German occupation of the Netherlands. He was 82.

The French

Mousquet

On 8th December 1969, 55 years after she was sunk, the *Straits Echo* announced that a salvage operation was taking place on the wreck of *Mousquet*.

> A twelve-man salvage team is now engaged in recovering a French vessel sunk 10 miles off Muka Head during the First World War. The leader of the team, Mr. H.R. Leishman 28, said today that the salvage operation was to recover semi-precious metals like copper and brass for re-sale locally.
>
> 'A ton of scrap copper may fetch up to $3,000 and this is a profitable venture' he said. Mr. Leishman said that his team worked for a local company engaged in recovering scrap metal from old sunken ships around the coast of West Malaysia. His divers were school-leavers, strong swimmers, former divers and fishermen aged between 19 and 28.

Two months later the *Echo* published a progress report with the surprising news that human remains had also been brought ashore from the wreck by the divers. They also recovered two anchors.

> A half-ton anchor of a French destroyer Mousquet will be donated to the Penang Museum. Two anchors were recovered from the ship. The anchor is about 5½ feet high and is made of cast iron. A similar anchor from the same ship is intended for an historical organisation.

Skeletons

> A representative of the company Mr. Ooi Peng Khoon, said that both anchors were still in good condition, considering that they had been in the sea since Oct. 28th 1914. The salvage company also recovered some bones and skeletons. A French ship will be coming here in a few months to take the bones back to France for proper burial.
>
> An old Lewis gun was also salvaged but it was too corroded

to be presented to the Penang Museum or for anyone else for that matter, said Mr. Ooi.

'We have been trying to obtain an old anchor for some time' Mr. Low Hun Leong, Curator of the Museum said. He thanked the firm for donating the anchor and he said that it would be of tremendous educational value for the people and children of Penang.[4]

Three days later, the museum announced that the anchor would be re-conditioned, treated with anti-rust paint and displayed in some suitable location.[5] At first it was in the front hall of the museum under cover but latterly was placed outside in the courtyard where it now stands.

On 20th October the same year, the French frigate *Amiral Charner* called in at Penang and the remains of *Mousquet's* crew were taken from the Cathedral of the Assumption in Penang where they had been kept[6] and conveyed to the French naval base at Nouméa in New Caledonia. There, the French navy constructed a fine memorial and on 28th October each year, a service of remembrance is held.

A steam pressure gauge and the brass dial from *Mousquet's* engine-room telegraph were brought up and presented to Dato' Anwar Fazal who was then Secretary of Penang City Council. They are in his possession to this day. A second repeater-dial from the engine room telegraph finally found its way to Paris, and is to be found in the Maritime Museum at Trocadéro.

Louis Audemard

After retiring, Louis Audemard seems to have gained an amazing new lease of life. Well into middle age, his health improved greatly, he got married and devoted the rest of his long life to writing beautifully illustrated books about traditional sailing craft in the Far East. His illustrations are meticulous, as one would expect from a professional hydrographer, but also exceedingly artistic. Clearly this sensitive man had hidden depths. He finally died at the ripe old age of 90.

Jaques Carissan

Enseigne Carissan was buried along with bugler Matelot Hamon at Sabang on Pulau Weh at the northern-most tip of Acheh, Sumatra. Later, the remains of Hamon were removed elsewhere but Carissan's grave remains. The little

Christian cemetery lies on some high ground above the beautiful harbour which is now a quiet backwater. The island is mainly known nowadays for its excellent scuba-diving. The graveyard is very well tended and Jaques Carissan's grave is the most prominent. The people of Sabang all know their French sailor and children play about among the gravestones, shaded by large trees. It is nice to think that Carissan is not forgotten, at rest in his tropical paradise.

The Australians and New Zealanders

Once they had reached the Mediterranean, the Australian and New Zealand expeditionary force was directed to the ill-fated offensive against the Turks in the Dardanelles. That was to prove one of the great tactical disasters of World War 1, with massive loss of life. It led to the defeat of the government and Churchill's resignation as First Lord of the Admiralty.

The British

Martyn Jerram

In 1915, the defence of the Far East Station was eventually handed over to the Japanese and most of the British ships were withdrawn to the Mediterranean or the North Sea, and Jerram along with them. In September 1916, despite his evident shortcomings, Vice Admiral Martyn Jerram was awarded the KCMG (Knight Commander of the Order of St. Michael & St. George).

At the Battle of Jutland he headed the Second Battle Squadron in his flagship *King George V*, alongside Admiral Jellicoe who commanded the British Grand Fleet. It was a bloody battle between the giant Dreadnought battle-ships of the British and the German navies. The outcome was indecisive but Jerram, as ever, emerged unscathed, despite some criticism from Admiral Jellicoe.

He retired at his own request as a full Admiral at the end of the war in 1918, ceasing all duties a year later. He lived on for many years in comfortable retirement and died in 1933 at the age of 75. Indeed, he led a charmed life.[7]

Guy Maund

Guy Maund had a colourful career. Despite, or maybe because of, his efforts to blame the French for the carnage in Penang, he received praise for his contribution. It is said in his service file that he took measures "in an advisory capacity whilst *Zhemtchug* was at Penang, which were highly creditable to his sense of duty and he rendered most valuable services in looking after survivors" (which no doubt he did).

He was placed on the retired list at his own request in 1920 and transferred to the Merchant Navy. His early service record described him as "capable in all respects with real brains and ability. Any amount of tact, and handles officers and men very well." Whilst a young cadet at Royal Arthur he was noted to be "very good at French, German and with fair modern Greek."

In World War ll, he re-enlisted in the Royal Navy and with the acting rank of Captain, was given the job of liaising with the Russian naval and civil authorities in north Russia. He was the Senior British Naval Officer in Archangel. He was awarded the DSO in 1940 and came away with the Order of the Red Star from the grateful USSR.

But a distinguished career has never been a guarantee of probity and in 1949 he was arrested and convicted of larceny in a German court. Their Lordships at the Admiralty took a 'very serious view' of this, and even considered depriving him of his pension. But in view of his excellent service record he was let off with a written warning, entered into his service record.[8]

Duncan MacIntyre

Commander MacIntyre continued as Harbourmaster in Penang till the end of the war and then retired, aged only fifty. He survived for another 18 years and died in London on 1st April 1932 aged 68. Obituaries in the local newspapers[9] made no mention of the Battle of Penang or the part he played in it.

William Cross

William Cross moved to Singapore in 1915, taking up the post of Minister for the Presbyterian Church at the top of Orchard Road. Before he left Penang, the *Penang Gazette* gave him a sterling write-up. An extract is quoted here:

> His influence extended far beyond the confines of his own

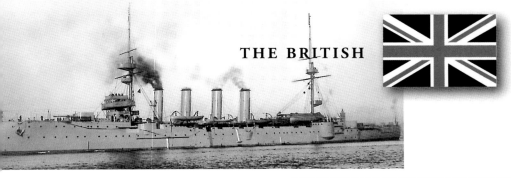

THE BRITISH

Above: British light cruiser 'Hampshire'. Commanded by Captain Grant, leader of squadron hunting for 'Emden'. Photo: Imperial War Museum Q38999.

Right: British light cruiser 'Yarmouth', commanded by Captain Cochrane. Frequent visitor to Panang. 'Emden' mistaken for 'Yarmouth' in Penang raid. Photo: Imperial War Museum Q21960.

Below: Postcard of Eastern & Oriental Hotel, roughly contemporary with 'Emden's' raid. The sinking of 'Zhemtchug' was witnessed from this terrace which remains there to this day.

Left: Top of 'Zhemtchug's mast sticking above the water of Penang harbour.
From William Cross's Ministerial file.

Above: 'Zhemtchung's survivors, with hardly any clothes, are given first aid on the quay-side. Note the motor-car number plate P1. Possibly the Governor's car. Unidentified magazine photo in William Cross's Ministerial file.

Survivors from 'Zhemtchug' in Penang Hospital.

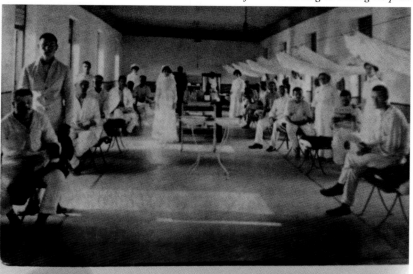

В госпитале г. Пинанга раненые моряки с крейсера «Жемчуг» (1914 г.)
(Изд. не установлено, 1914 г.)

THE FRENCH

Above: Piece of shrapnel from one of 'Emden's' shell-bursts. Picked up near Penang race-course. Purchased by William Cross. William Cross's Ministerial file.

Above: Artist's impression of 'Mousquet' under attack from 'Emden.' Note 'Emden's' 4 funnels. Photo by permission, Agence Photographique, Musée National de la Marine. Paris.

'Mousquet's' survivors, apart from three crewmen still in hospital. Photographed in Dutch uniforms at Sabang, Pulau Weh, Sumatra. Photos from Charles Merien. His grandfather 'Mousquet's' carpenter, bearded, first left.

Enseigne Jaques Carissan. Died from his wounds in Sabang Oct. 1914. Later decorated for bravery.

THE AUSTRALIANS

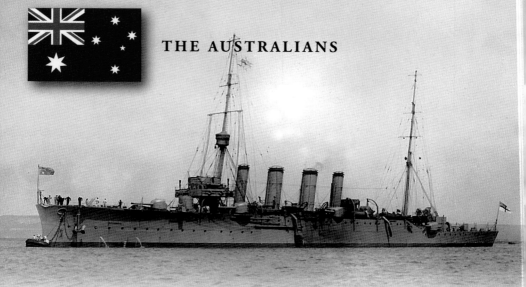

*Australian armoured cruiser HMAS 'Sydney'.
Responded to SOS call from Direction Island
and destroyed 'Emden' 8th Nov. 1914.
Photo: Imperial War Museum Q21817.*

*Two views of 'Emden's' wreck, beached on reef at
North Keeling Island. Viewed from deck of 'Sydney'.
Photo below: Imperial War museum Q22743.*

*Left: British sloop 'Cadmus'. Ran many errands for
Jerram. Searched 'Emden's' wreck for documents and
helped quell Singapore mutiny.*

THE GERMANS

Direction Island. Lieutenant von Mücke's landing party evacuate and take command of 'Ayesha'.

Right: 'Ayesha' in full sail. Photo: Imperial War Museum Q22717.

Constantinople. After many adventures Lieutenant von Mücke brought his entire party, with the loss of only three men, to Constantinople (Istanbul), and thence back to Germany. Von Mücke is the tallest officer on the left. Photo: Imperial War Museum Q64246.

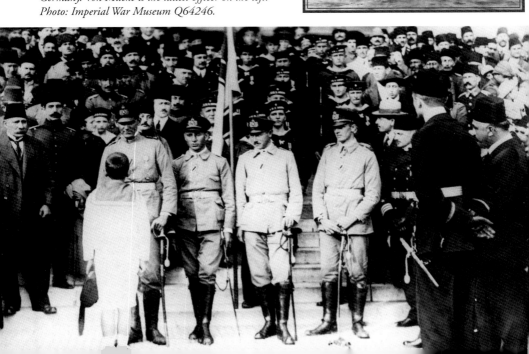

THE RUSSIANS

Above: Russian Grave and Memorial to 'Zhemtchug's' dead. Western Road Cemetery, Penang.

Right: Roll of honour to 'Zhemtchug's' dead.

ПОГИБШИЕ МОРЯКИ КРЕЙСЕРА
Жемчуг
15 (28) ОКТЯБРЯ 1914г.

Above: Russian Naval personnel honour their dead at Western Road Cemetery Penang. Annual Remembrance. 28th Oct.

Right: Graveside Commemoration. Two of 'Zhemtchug's' crew, were washed up on the shore of Jerejak Island, Penang.

THE FRENCH

Above: Sabang Harbour 1904 crowded with ships. Sabang was a busy Dutch coaling station just west of the Malacca Straits.

ICI REPOSE
L'ENSEIGNE de VAISSEAU
Jacques CARISSAN
MORT POUR LA FRANCE
LE 28 OCTOBRE 1914

Far left: Enseigne Jaques Carissan's grave, Sabang. It is well tended and any local person will take you there.

Plaque on Carissan's grave.

Nouméa, New Caledonia. Annual Remembrance service on 28th October, for 'Mousquet's' dead. Inscription reads: "The remains of the crew of 'Mousquet', sunk in combat at Penang in 1914 and returned to France in 1970."

The Blue Cross 'Pour le Mérite', awarded to Captain von Müller, Prussia's highest military award.

Above: Dato' Anwar Fazal, Penang. With items salvaged from 'Mousquet' and presented to him in Jan. 1970.

Above: Von Müller as a Captain after WW1. He has aged tremendously since the previous photo and died just three years after this photo was taken.

Right: Repeater dial from 'Mousquet's engine-room telegraph.

Left: Steam pressure gauge from 'Mousquet'.

church. There is hardly any section of our varied community that has not benefited from his work... those who have been privileged to sit under him have heard the Christian faith expounded to them in inspiring sermons with a wealth of imagery that would be difficult to excel.[10]

The *Penang Gazette* added that he was instrumental in setting up the Penang Athenaeum and was its first chairman. He remained in Singapore throughout World War 1, and helped to set up the YMCA which stands next to the Presbyterian Church. On returning to UK in 1921, he immersed himself in good works, particularly amongst the Jewish community. Even in old age he was still doing part-time work, his old zeal and energy still there, although somewhat diminished. He died in 1950 aged 82, at the end of a successful and highly productive life. Despite his austere outlook; his warmth, sincerity and commitment brought him both love and loyalty wherever he went.[11]

The Russians

Zhemtchug

Following the salvage of *Zhemtchug*'s guns by *Orel* early in 1915, various additional salvage operations were carried out over the years. This was partly to obtain valuable metals, and partly to flatten the wreck's superstructure so it presented less of a hazard in those shallow waters. A Singapore syndicate dived on the wreck in 1932[12] in the hopes of finding bullion aboard, but none was found. Throughout March and April 1934[13] a Japanese salvage company did major work. They dismantled much of the superstructure and brought her two massive bronze propellers ashore which were worth a great deal.[14] Explosive charges were also used, reducing the wreck's profile so it no longer presented any significant hazard to shipping.[15]

The Russian naval authorities have always paid their respects on an annual basis, at the grave-side of their fallen countrymen at the Western Road Cemetery in Penang. This is arranged on 28th October, each year, in commemoration of the occasion.

In 2004, some funding was provided from the Russian Government and the grave of the two *Zhemtchug* sailors buried on Pulau Jerejak was properly cleared and landscaped. Today it stands as another quiet memorial to that terrible day in 1914 when so many Russians lost their lives.

Epilogue

Reverend William Cross Gives a Talk

Twelve weeks after the tragic events in Penang, William Cross gave a lecture to the Penang Athenaeum. The venue he used was the Masonic Hall, although Cross himself was not a Free-Mason. For those readers who are interested in the power that ideology has over politicians, it makes compelling reading, not least because it reveals how ideas, born in the rarefied intellectual spheres of philosophy, may be warped and bent by politicians to justify all manner of evils.

Before coming to Penang, Cross's arguments would have been well rehearsed in the many 'conferences' he held in London, where the politics of the day – anti-Semitism and the rise of Germany's power – would have been high on the agenda. In these noisy debates, confronting sceptics, atheists and idle on-lookers, he offered his opinion that only Christian values offered any meaningful alternative to the philosophy of Nietzsche, which gripped certain members of the German elite and many others too, even in Britain, with the idea of the 'Übermenschen' – the 'Super-race'.

In this talk, he tackles head-on the eighteenth century philosophy of 'The Enlightenment'. Scotland was one of the main centres for this way of seeing the world in which reason and observation alone, must inform man's beliefs. David Hume and Adam Smith were amongst the great Scottish philosophers of the day and their ideas spread all over Europe and the United States. That philosophy dominated many of the early men of science, like Erasmus Darwin, the grandfather of Charles Darwin.

William Cross grew up in this intellectual environment where beliefs and ideals had to withstand the test of reason. He applied reason to the ways in which people seized upon the Enlightenment to trash Christian values. Even if the reader is not a Christian, Cross's arguments are persuasive. He makes no attempt to discredit the Enlightenment. On the contrary he accepts much of what it contains. What he sets out to show is that plausible though they are, these ideas can never provide a complete answer. Worse, the conclusions of the Enlightenment philosophers had long since been debased and corrupted by politicians, who found within them a justification for their own odious conduct, first in France during the 'reign of terror', and many years later, numbers of intellectuals and politicians in the rest of Europe.

It is rather chilling to see how Cross takes the development of Nietzsche's ideology to its logical conclusion, predicting where it will lead. The full realisation of that did not take place in Germany and elsewhere for another twenty years, but in this we can see how far-sighted Cross was.

His most compelling observation is that you cannot kill an idea, nor can you forcibly control people's thoughts. Only civilised debate can achieve that. His plea for reasserting democracy, and particularly Christian values is unlikely to appeal to everyone, but his arguments and observations really go to the heart of things.

Here are selected excerpts from his talk which was given on Monday 18th January 1915, and reported the following day in the *Penang Gazettte & Straits Chronicle*.

What has caused the war? Some suggest that the war is the result of failed diplomacy. No doubt it is interesting, although it is a trivial thing, to trace the petty manoeuvres of subtle Ambassadors, but we have concentrated our minds too much on persons, the Kaiser, the British Ministers, the Russian Grand Dukes.

When we get away from the occasion, to the real causes, we find that in the heart of the war only two peoples are concerned – the Germans and the British – and though all the others got their disputes settled, and retired from the field, these two would have to go on till one or other went under. With them, it is not a war for a settlement, for a re-arrangement of political relations, but a war for life and death.

The war would not end if the Kaiser disappeared, or if a new Government came into power in Britain. On our side we are not fully conscious of this yet. They know it in Germany. To the Germans this is not the game of an individual, but the uprising of a nation. The Kaiser is but a symbolic head and voice of his race. Militarism, or whatever name you give to the Germanic movement, is not a temporary or local flush of the spirit: it is resolute attitude of a Soul: it is the firm form of an Ideal. Spiritual movements like this may be conscious, only in the minds of a handful, but they have their home in the groping instincts of the race. It is the growth and meaning of a spiritual ideal that I wish to put before you. Out of this, arise the real causes, out of this will flow the permanent effects of the war.

Nietzsche.

Thoughts came from Nietzsche's brain like burning lava from a volcano; now in a stream that made a volume, now in single red-hot stones that simply filled a line or a page in his notebooks. His crowning work 'Thus spake Zarathustra' was published in 1885. It is said that every German officer carries a Zarathustra in his pocket. In 1889 the overwrought brain gave way. The lamp of Nietzsche was shattered. The brightest intellectual light in Europe lay in the dust. He was taken to an asylum. On August 25th 1900 aged 45 years, he died.

Boldness and sincerity and strength are the chief characteristics of his work. He has been called 'the greatest European event since Göethe'. No writer of modern times had anything like so stimulating, yet so disturbing an effect, upon thought and life. He is the supremely active influence of our time. Everywhere, you come across his formative ideas.

He was a Poet and sang the song of Power. One can see heraldings of his ideas in Montaigne, Emerson, Disraeli, Ibsen, Carlyle and Blake. These made bold journeys towards the South Pole, but Nietzsche gets there. He is the incarnation of the world's unrest. 'One must have chaos within' he cried, 'to enable one to give birth to a dancing star.' So he gloried in the chaos. It was a promise of a higher world.

Deliberately he set himself the gigantic task of criticising, to the last shred, every accepted moral idea of his age. The idols this iconoclast set out to break, are what humanity has hitherto called its most sacred ideals. 'I know my destiny' he said. 'There will come a day when my name will recall the memory of something formidable – a crisis the like of which has never been known on Earth, a profound clash of consciences, the passing of a sentence upon all that before, had been believed hallowed. I am not a man. I am dynamite.'

He came up against hoary conventions. Rules of morality went down before him as a house of cards before a battering ram. That conventional Christianity, which was but a traditional veneer of respectability, and that namby-pamby Christianity which has become so soft and sentimental that it looks as if continuously fed on a diet of boiled hymn books, he abhorred with his whole soul. If he had done little else for us, other than the banishing of these shams, he deserves our reverent gratitude. In striking at conventions, unfortunately, he also struck realities.

Self-Sacrifice.

The conventional thought – Christian and Social – upon which almost all our higher morality is based, is the thought of self-sacrifice. We take it for granted that self-sacrifice is the supreme virtue. Two opposites are before us – self and the other. The other may be society, our country, a Great Cause, Christ, God. Whatever the other is, it has been assumed that the other is greater than the self, or at least that to sacrifice self for the other is the greater deed.

Nietzsche calls this absurd. We assume that if one saves others and himself he cannot save, therein is supreme goodness. But says Nietzsche the other may be selfish, worthless, degenerate, why not reverse the thought? Why should not the other do the sacrifice? Why not sacrifice the multitude for the few sovereign spirits? Are we not standing on our heads when we sacrifice a man of genius for a mass of mediocrities? Nature knows nothing of this absurdity. She selects the fittest for survival. Granted that self-sacrifice is a good thing, why limit it to the strong individual? You say, sacrifice yourself. That is as much martyrdom as the other is.

It is clear that a limit must be set to the thought that sacrifice in itself is a virtue. The truth is sacrifice may become a crime, and Christianity is based upon that crime. Behind this religious sanction of self-sacrifice is nothing but the mob's instinct of self-preservation. Nietzsche astutely points out that Christianity arose amid the slave population of the Roman Empire, and therefore welcomes the slave morality, which sacrifices the one supreme soul for the many. But too much unselfishness always overleaps itself and spoils life. How often children are spoilt by the indiscriminate sacrifices of the mother? How often communities are ruined by indiscriminate charity! Do too much good for a person, and you do harm, not good. Give too much, and you feed the spirit that gets too much. The self-denying person tends to become the selfless person. A deficiency in personality afflicts the race. Thin, meek, obliterated persons, who have no value for earth or heaven, take the place of strong men.

Nietzsche asks daringly 'why is a man better who is useful to others, than one who is useful to himself?' The answer is, only because, and if, others are of more value and higher. But suppose others are of less value. Surely then, he who serves himself, may be better, even if he does so, at the expense of others. The reasoning is cold-blooded, but who can gainsay it? Too much Pity is dangerous. Pity may imperil something valuable: it may destroy your brother's soul. Ideals are always exacting and hard. To reach them men must be strong. No one has the right to destroy his brother by kindness and sacrifice. Save your brother by flinging him into the sea. Better he drown than never learn to swim. Improve your orchard by excluding trees that come diseased and maimed from the nursery. What we should aim at is not the propping up of weak specimens, but the production of good specimens.

Nietzsche's Great Idea. The Superman.

All this thought culminated in the idea of the greater man, the superman. Hitherto man has been accustomed to think of himself as the crown, an end of creation. That, in the light of evolution, must be given up. Man must be something that must be surpassed. Who would say that the men we know are a justification of the long centuries? They are poor creatures. What is really great in man today is that he is a bridge, not a goal. What may be loved in man is his power of transition. Man is but a rope, flung across a precipice, connecting animal and superman. The definite aim of this generation should be to create a race of men capable of entering fully and yet more fully, into the glorious life of which this mighty earth is possible. Only so, can the long bloodstained centuries be justified.

Nietzsche wanted men to accept responsibility for themselves and their future. When he contemplated the long millenniums of evolution, it irritated him that we had only got so far. The movement of evolution must have an end. Here, of course, is struck a foundation principle. What is the end, purpose, meaning in evolution? Religion says, To glorify God. Nietzsche crushed that aside. What is the long evolution for? An end is essential. Otherwise there is nothing save chaos. The end is the production of a type, superior to man, to evolve a superman.

One could sacrifice gladly all the present humanity, to assist a higher species than man to come into being. So the aim of every real reformer should be, not the preservation of the present race, but the surpassing of the present race. Whatever takes us the least little bit forward on the road to the superman is justifiable.

Power.

We can see now whither Nietzsche would lead us. For him the primary characteristic of all ascending life as revealed in nature is Power. That which has power has the promise of higher things. Power must root itself in will. It must be a will to power. We shall never drift into superman. Here Nietzsche renounces materialism. His is spiritual thought. Evolution has tended to mislead mankind into thinking things move onward by an irresistible fate.

Not so! Man's will is the one point where the vicious circle is broken. The superman must be willed, prepared for, bred. He has not existed yet. We cannot describe him. We can only get hints.. He shall be strong. The Church has tried to lead mankind to a higher type, but the Church's higher type is a race for another world, not for this world. Therefore the Church has been the Arch-traitor of humanity. Superman is not present man writ large, it is a new species, a new creation. He will be endowed with new faculties, new moralities, new modes and consciousness. Now let us take this thought in.

Evolution.

Carry your mind back to that dim time in the history of this planet, when the human, according to the evolutionist theory, was dawning over the dark realm of animal life when there began to appear instances of apes of a higher intelligence. For a thousand generations this went on. Gradually the human emerged: a being emerged that was ape-like, but was not an ape. He was a super-ape, and infra-man: more than ape, less than man. Gradually this being, separated himself from apes. He despised apes. He felt the beating and call of a life that was higher. Had he been able to speak our language, he would have called it a 'diviner' life.

As ages still rolled on, the distinction of this separated being became more and more empatic. At last he whom we now call 'Man' awoke to know that he was man. He went on developing. He made laws. He established customs. He built cities. He evolved civilisations. He is ourselves, today's crown of creation.

Now asks Nietzsche, is that the end? By no means. The process is going on, and will go on. We are still evolving. A yet higher being is possible. Man must become superman, as ape became super-ape.

What then, does this imply? The moment we have said 'superman' we are beyond good and evil. The conventional laws of morality do not apply. If I am a superman, or have in me the seed of a superman, is it not incumbent upon me to preserve that precious deposit? Why should I hesitate to crush out the lower men who hinder me? Nay, a thousand mediocre men are no more to one superman, than a thousand apes are to one super-ape i.e. one man. Is a man justified in slaying a thousand apes or rats or leopards to secure his own life? Certainly.

In relation to the beasts, he is beyond Good and Evil. Nietzsche applied that thought boldly. In relation to ordinary mediocre men, the man with the sacred seed of the superman in him, is beyond good and evil. The ordinary laws of morality do not apply. He is beyond the Ten Commandments. He can repudiate all bargains or treaties based upon these commandments. They are but scraps of paper.

Do you see where we are? It is when we consider this Nietzsche, an idea of getting beyond Good and Evil, that certain very strange and dark things become clear. It has been assumed by us all that Germany gave her whole case away when she pooh-poohed a solemn treaty as a scrap of paper, and when the German Imperial Chancellor on August the 4th said: 'We are compelled to override the just protest of the Belgian Government. The wrong that we are committing we will endeavour to make good as soon as our military goal has been reached. We are under necessity and necessity knows no law.'

That seems a flagrant abandonment of all moral life. But in the light of Nietzsche's teaching we can understand it. What then shall we do? I asked an intelligent man this question the other day, and he unhesitatingly replied: 'Do! We ought to go one better and shoot them! The Germans who believe such monstrous doctrines must be crushed. We must get a bigger army: we must enforce military rule amongst ourselves and see to it that all who think such monstrous thoughts are ended.' Alas, that would not settle the business. There are thinkers amongst ourselves who have imbibed the Nietzschean thought. Professor Cramb is one of them. To go one better than the Germans is merely to continue in our own lives and cherish in our own bosoms the viper we desire to slay. We shall never gain anything by merely going one better than the Germans. We must first understand why the Germans should think themselves to be right. We are up against a big thing. And it will not do to fling out at it wildly and blindly. No one can put an end to a thought.

German Culture.

Germans then, have appropriated the discovery of the superman to themselves. They take it as a prophecy of themselves. When the poet sang of Power, the Germans said, 'he sings for us. This trampling of weak things is what we feel in ourselves. Hitherto we have been ashamed of it. We did not know it was culture. But if the poet sings it, and nature exhibits it, why should we shirk our destiny and refuse to do it?' No one will deny that the Germans have a right to the prophecy. German culture is not a thing to mock at. We are all steeped in its influence. In all the departments of human energy, in religion, music, science, social endeavour, military and industrial discipline, Germany easily holds a first place. We need not grudge them this. Their riches are the world's treasure.

But out of their intellectual achievements has come the world's danger. The corruption of the best is the worst. The Germans have taken the high thought of Nietzsche and made it the handmaiden of low ambition. They have interpreted with a material mind things that are spiritual. They have taken the holy vessels of the holy temple and drunk wine in them. The superman, and all the arguments that might justify him, have been taken as justifying them. The will to power – has taken the place of Love. Step by step with the growth of their culture has arisen the dream of world domination. They assume themselves to be the chosen race, with a destined mission for the world. They would make the German mind and the German genius prevail everywhere. For 40 years they have been in the wilderness gathering strength for this enterprise.

All classes from the Kaiser to the peasant are obsessed with the glory of achieving the destiny of their great land. And now 'The Day' has come. The long preparation moves towards fulfilment. The chosen people have come forth to seize their Promised Land. Well, we shall see, what we shall see.

A Clash of Ideals.

At last we are able to see what the War really means, and what issues are at stake. It is a clash of Ideals. Although the war seems to come like a bolt from the blue it is in deepest truth the inevitable outcome of long gathering clouds of a storm. There are no bolts from the blue. Readers of von Bernhardi know this, and they know how the German mind justifies the war. 'A good war' said Nietzsche 'hallows every cause'. Life is conflict. The violent take the kingdom of heaven by storm. Paradise is under the shadow of swords. Conflict is the essence of real life - not only one element, but the indispensable and essential element.

There are three things that Germany has forgotten. Forgetting these things, she has been misled by the very spirit in her that was great. Germany finds herself hemmed in by her physical borders. She is in need of new markets, new colonies. The necessity of her life drives her forth to conquer the world. You might as well ask fermenting wine to abstain from bursting the old wine-skins, as ask a nation with powers such as they possess, to keep tamely within their borders. Germany before the war was an apostle of culture. The champion of civilisation. The world, no less than Germany, had come to a crisis in its history. Civilisation was bankrupt. Only a new spirit could save mankind. The new spirit it was imagined, slept in the German cocoon. Therefore, as Professor Cramb said, it became Germany's destiny, her ideal, to impart her culture, that her new religion of valour to mankind might not be lost, and progress come to a standstill.

The Necessity for the War.

The movement of the world's progress demanded the supremacy of Germany. The supremacy of Germany involved the disturbance of the European balance of power. Herein lay the secret and sacred necessity for the war.

The war then is a life and death struggle between two empires. That was known in Germany from the beginning. It became clear to the whole world, not many days after the war broke out. For a whole generation, there has been steadily instilled into the German mind, the idea that the British Empire was ready to fall to pieces on its own weight and age. Britain, having tasted the sweets of Empire, was destined to give place to a better nation. Degenerate and gorged with greedy wealth, softened to luxury and indulgence, continually craving for peace, because he was too fat and cowardly to fight, the man was to give way before Superman.

Vital Civilisation at Stake.

I venture, however, to say that even greater things are at stake than the fate of Britain. Bound up with that fate, held in that earthen vessel, is the great political idea and treasure which we imperfectly gather up and express in the word Democracy. It is not a happy word, but it will serve to indicate the happy truth. Democracy stands for the broad brotherhood of mankind. That is the precious fact and hope which is being swamped in the rising flood of Pan-Germanism. Nietzsche and the dominant elements of the German race renounced Democracy. To them there is only one chosen people upon Earth. Other people are not brothers. They are barbarians or apes, or degenerates, hinderers of the advancing culture, fit to be governed and drilled, that is all.

The renunciation of democracy, as the basis of our political relationships, is implied in militarism. Von Bernhardi makes that clear. Militarism is a deliberate reversal of the progress which humanity has been making for a hundred generations. In that evolution of society, which has produced Western civilisation, the movement has been outward as well as upward. Society has advanced in democratic feeling as well as culture. Broader and broader has become the basis of political and social life. From slavery to serfdom, from serfdom to Craft Guilds, and the free cities in the

14th century, through peasant revolts and bread riots of the 16th century, by way of English and French revolutions, upon the shoulders of industrial upheavals; slowly and painfully democracy has arrived.

At last there has appeared among the ideals of mankind the conception, that those who toil have a right to be reckoned, that small nations have inalienable rights, that backward peoples ought to be nursed into liberty by those that assume domination over them; that the links of real Empire are forged by personal freedom, that there is a liberty that makes men loyal. 'This conception', says Prof. Henry Jones, 'is the greatest discovery made in political practice since the Greeks evolved the civic state.'

The Future.

As for Nietzsche, we welcome him too. Though he fought Christianity with his utmost strength, and though he glorified in the name of Anti-Christ, he built more than he knew. By his intensity of criticism, he has forced us to acknowledge truths we were neglecting. By the sheer thoroughness of his intellectual probing, he has stamped out materialism as a possible explanation of life. Will, is the secret of the world.

The tragedy of Bernhardi, and all his school, is that they have made this spiritual thought the slave of selfish ambition, and treated humanity as the mere prey of those who could be most violent and most astute. Our fathers would have called that the mind of the Devil.

Yet we may be calm, and gladly acknowledge the gift of Nietzsche's mind, even though in him, we see the ultimate source of all this havoc. Give even the Devil his due. Only by doing so, can we overthrow him. He has done Christianity an incalculable service. He has cleared the field of thought. We now see what the only spiritual alternative to true religion is. The war that will end war is never waged with physical weapons. Only when the nations put off the old military mind, and put on the new Christian mind, can real peace come. The world will not be at peace until it deserves peace, the hopes of that new mind lies in the Christian future. It is far enough off yet, but it is the world's dream, even in the midst of the world's horror, and all good men desire it.

Notes

Chapter 1: Rev. Cross Goes to Penang

1. *Straits Echo*, 28th Jan. 1970, p. 2.
2. 'Minister'—term used in the Presbyterian church for pastor or clergyman.
3. 'Kirk'—Scottish word for church.
4. Cross, Ministerial file, 1911 magazine cutting: 'Conferences'.
5. Tarek (1995: 46). Quotes W. L. Langer.
6. Cross, Ministerial file, undated handwritten note.
7. Cross, Ministerial file, handwritten note, 19th May 1912.
8. Khor and Khoo (2004: 171, Table 11.2).
9. Ibid.: 2–4.
10. Greer (1956: 108).
11. The principles of free trade were British government policy under Gladstone's Liberal Party administration.
12. Fairbank et al. (1973: 453–460).
13. Ibid.: 556.
14. Howe (1996: 172).
15. Fairbank et al. (1973: 740).
16. Golding (1917: 196).

Chapter 2: Saigon and the China Station

1. Hoyt (2001: 3).
2. Naval Staff Monograph, p. 34.
3. Marder (1978: 39).
4. Navy List, 1914.
5. Dartmouth College Archives, telecommunication Sept. 2009.
6. Maund, Service file.
7. Ibid.
8. Liste de la Flotte, 1914, États-Majors embarqués, pp. 296–297.
9. French Navy correspondence. Notice sur les bâtiments ayant porté le nom de *Mousquet*.
10. Audemard, Service dossier.

11. Le Coispellier, *Rapport du Commissaire du Gouvernement,* p. 8.
12. Liste de la Flotte, 1914, p. 341.
13. Jane (1914).
14. *Fronde* = catapult.
15. *Pistolet* = pistol.
16. *Mousquet* = musket.
17. Liste de la Flotte, 1914, p. 357.
18. Le Coispellier, *Rapport du Commissaire du Gouvernement,* p. 28.
19. Wardroom = officers' mess on a ship.
20. Hough (1969: 87).
21. Admiralty Corresp'dence, ADM 137/1014, Jerram, 29th Aug. 1913, p. 3.
22. Collier = coal cargo-ship, equivalent to a modern-day oil tanker.
23. Commander = Korvettenkapitän in German.
24. Taylor (2007).
25. Hohenzollern (1928: 59).
26. *Straits Times*, 14th Nov. 1915, p. 9.
27. Admiralty Correspondence, ADM 125/62, Jerram, 11th May 1913.
28. Ibid., 29th May 1913.
29. Ibid.
30. Ibid., 25th July 1913.
31. Ibid., 31st July 1913.
32. Ibid., Sir John Jordan, 1st Oct. 1913.
33. 700 miles = 1120 km.
34. Admiralty Correspondence, ADM 1/8376/109, Jerram, 23rd Sept. 1914.
35. Ibid., ADM 125/62, Jerram, 15th Dec. 1913.
36. Huguet, Service dossier.
37. Naval Staff Monograph, p. 33.
38. Ibid.
39. *Hong Kong Gazette*, 8th May 1914.
40. Admiralty Correspondence, ADM 125/62, Jerram, 5th May 1914.
41. *Minotaur.* His usual flagship was *Triumph,* which was undergoing an extensive refit.
42. Admiralty Correspondence, ADM 125/62, Jerram, 16th July 1914.
43. Not the famous Russian composer, but a near relative in that very naval family.
44. Admiralty Correspondence, ADM 125/62, Jerram, 16th July 1914.
45. Ibid.
46. Théroinne, Service dossier.
47. French Navy correspondence. Notice sur les bâtiments ayant porté le

nom de *Mousquet.*
48. Roche (2005: Vol. 2).
49. Registre historique de la correspondance intéressant, Pistolet, pp. 584–586.
50. Ibid.
51. Ibid.

Chapter 3: War. The Dominoes Fall

1. Admiralty Correspondence, ADM 137/11, Jerram, 30th July 1914.
2. Ibid., Commodore Hong Kong to Admiralty, 4th Aug. 1914.
3. Naval Staff Monograph, pp. 8–9.
4. Admiralty Correspondence, ADM 137/34, Jerram, 12th Aug. 1914.
5. Ibid., ADM 137/11, Commodore Hong Kong, 8th Aug. 1914.
6. Jane (1914).
7. Russian State Navy Archive, Fond 406, Inventory 3, File 1151 pp. 496–502, & Inventory 9, File 4585, pp. 2–11.
8. *Evening News,* 6th May 1914 & 6th Aug. 1914.
9. Admiralty Correspondence, ADM 137/34, Jerram, 12th Aug. 1914.
10. Ibid.
11. Admiralty Correspondence, ADM 137/11, Receiver General, Suva to Marine Paris copied to Admiralty, 12th Aug. 1914.
12. Ibid.
13. Naval Staff Monographs, p. 45.
14. Hohenzollern (1928: 24).
15. Ibid.: 30–31.
16. Tarek (1995: 150–151).
17. Admiralty Correspondence, ADM137/11, Special Telegraph, Peking, 5th Aug. 1914.
18. Hohenzollern (1928: 15).
19. Naval Staff Monograph, p. 46.
20. Ibid., p. 45.
21. Admiralty Correspondence, ADM 137/11, Statement, Japanese Minister of Foreign Affairs, 10th Aug. 1914.
22. Ibid. ADM 137/11 18th Aug.1914.
23. Ibid. 21st Aug. 1914.
24. Naval Staff Monograph, p. 46.
25. Golding (1917: 195–196).

Chapter 4: The Hunt for Graf Spee

1. Naval Staff Monograph, p. 48. The Minister's ironic reference is to Puccini's tragic opera *Madame Butterfly,* which is set in Japan.
2. Naval Staff Monograph, p. 46.
3. Van der Vat (1983: 34).
4. Naval Staff Monograph, p. 46.
5. Ibid., p. 45.
6. Admiralty Correspondence, ADM 137/34, Jerram, 23rd Aug. 1914, p. 6.
7. Ibid., ADM 137/11, Jerram, 24th Aug. 1914, p. 2.
8. Naval Staff Monograph, p. 55.
9. Jane (1914).
10. Hohenzollern (1928: 23–24).
11. *Penang Gazette* (weekly mail edition), 12th Nov. 1914, p. 1306.
12. *Straits Times,* Thursday 26th Nov. 1914, p. 2.
13. Hohenzollern (1928: 52–56).
14. Naval Staff Monograph, p. 61.
15. Hohenzollern (1928: 55).
16. Admiralty Correspondence, ADM 137/11, Intelligence Officer S'pore, 29th Aug. 1914.
17. Ibid., ADM 137/34, Jerram, 3rd Sept. 1914.
18. Corbett (1938: 283).
19. Hohenzollern (1928: 59–61).
20. Ibid.: 61.
21. Ibid.: 58.
22. Ibid.: 51.
23. Ibid.: 65.
24. Ibid.: 66.
25. Le Coispellier, *Rapport du Commissaire du Gouvernement*, pp. 8–9.
26. Admiralty Correspondence, ADM 137/34, Jerram, 29th Aug. 1914.
27. Naval Staff Monograph, p. 61.
28. Ibid., p. 62.
29. Le Coispellier, *Rapport du Commissaire du Gouvernement*, p. 8.
30. Van der Vat (1983: 84).
31. Admiralty Correspondence, ADM 137/11, Jerram, 5th Sept. 1914.

Chapter 5: Jerram Hunts for *Emden*

1. Morse code: using dots and dashes, flashed by signal-lamp or audio for radio and telegraph.
2. Hohenzollern (1928: 68–70).
3. *Penang Gazette* (weekly mail edition), 30th Sept. 1914, p. 1159.
4. Ratings = non-commissioned ranks.
5. Hohenzollern (1928: 113).
6. Ibid.: 68–70.
7. Naval Staff Monograph, pp. 62–63.
8. Hohenzollern (1928: 87).
9. En clair = plain language, not encrypted.
10. Naval Staff Monograph, pp. 61–62.
11. Hohenzollern (1928: 89).
12. Laskars = sailors from the East Indies.
13. *Penang Gazette* (weekly mail edition), 9th Oct. 1914, p. 1160.
14. *Straits Times*, 3rd Oct. 1914, p. 4.
15. Hohenzollern (1928: 91).
16. Corbett (1938: 297).
17. Naval Staff Monograph, p. 65.
18. Admiralty Correspondence, ADM 137/34, Jerram, 15th Sept. 1914.
19. Naval Staff Monograph, p. 64.
20. Corbett (1938: 282).
21. Naval Staff Monograph, p. 65.
22. Admiralty Correspondence, ADM 137/11, Singapore to Admiralty, 16th Sept. 1914.
23. Le Coispellier, *Rapport du Commissaire du Gouvernement,* p. 12.
24. Cross, Ministerial file, handwritten notes, 28 Oct. 1914.
25. Le Coispellier, *Rapport du Commissaire du Gouvernement,* p. 10.
26. French Navy Correspondence, Daveluy to Admiral Jerram, 20th Jan. 1915.
27. Admiralty Correspondence, ADM 137/11, Jerram, 18th Sept. 1914.
28. Ibid., 15th Sept. 1914.
29. Hohenzollern (1928: 94–95).
30. Naval Staff Monograph, p. 67.
31. Corbett (1938: 297).
32. Hohenzollern (1928: 96).
33. Mole = sea wall providing shelter at the entrance to a harbour.

34. Hohenzollern (1928: 100–103).
35. *Penang Gazette* (mail edition), 25th Sept. 1914, p. 1132.
36. *Penang Gazette and Straits Chronicle*, 25th Sept. 1914, p. 5.
37. *Penang Gazette* (mail edition), 25th Sept. 1914, p. 1131.
38. Hohenzollern (1928: 103).
39. Naval Staff Monograph, p. 68.
40. Hohenzollern (1928: 103).
41. *Penang Gazette* (mail edition), 29th Sept. 1914, p. 1230.
42. *Straits Times*, 5th Oct. 1914, p. 12.
43. Ibid., 26th Oct. 1914, p. 10.
44. Hohenzollern (1928: 104).
45. Naval Staff Monograph, pp. 68–69.
46. Corbett (1938: p. 298).
47. Admiralty Correspondence, ADM 137/34, Jerram, 1st Oct. 1914, p. 3.
48. Van der Vat (1983: 74).
49. Admiralty Correspondence, ADM 137/34, Jerram, 1st Oct. 1914, p. 3.
50, Naval Staff Monograph, p. 76.
51. Admiralty Correspondence, ADM 137/11, Jerram to Singapore, 16th & 17th Sept. 1914.
52. Naval Staff Monograph, pp. 73–74.
53. Ibid., p. 104.
54. Ibid., p. 69.
55. Hohenzollern (1928: 115).
56. Ibid.: 121.
57. *Penang Gazette* (mail edition), 30th Sept. 1914, p. 1149.
58. Naval Staff Monograph, p. 75.
59. *Penang Gazette* (mail edition), 30th Sept. 1914, p. 1169.
60. Naval Staff Monograph, p. 76.
61. Hohenzollern (1928: 132–137).

Chapter 6: *Markomannia* Sunk

1. Admiralty Correspondence, ADM 137/11, 1st Oct. 1914.
2. Starboard = the right-hand side of the ship looking forwards.
3. Naval Staff Monographs, pp. 75–76.
4. Admiralty Correspondence, ADM 137/34, Jerram, 16th Oct. 1914.
5. Ibid., 1st Oct. 1914.
6. Naval Staff Monographs, p. 80.

7. Admiralty Correspondence, ADM 137/11, Jerram, 17th Sept. 1914.
8. Buyakov et al. (2004: 12, 55, 76).
9. Admiralty Correspondence, ADM 137/11, 17th Sept. 1914.
10. Le Coispellier, *Rapport du Commissaire du Gouvernement*, p. 14.
11. Naval Staff Monographs, p. 80.
12. Le Coispellier, *Rapport du Commissaire du Gouvernement*, p. 14.
13. Ibid., p. 12.
14. Ibid., pp. 12–13.
15. Ibid., p. 10.
16. Ibid.
17. Ibid.
18. Admiralty Correspondence, ADM 137/34, Jerram, 10th Oct. 1914.
19. Le Coispellier, *Rapport du Commissaire du Gouvernement*, p. 9.
20. Ibid., p. 11.
21. Naval Staff Monographs, p. 80.
22. Ibid., pp. 80–81.
23. Ibid.
24. *Straits Times*, 5 Oct. 1914, p. 2.
25. Admiralty Correspondence, ADM 137/34, Jerram, 16th Oct. 1914, p. 3.
26. Hohenzollern (1928: 137).
27. Ibid.: 140–141.
28. Ibid.: 142.
29. Ibid.: 148–149.
30. Ibid.
31. *Times of Malaya*, 5th Nov. 1914, p. 9.
32. Hohenzollern (1928: 159).
33. Naval Staff Monograph, p. 83.
34. *Penang Gazette* (mail edition), 24th Oct. 1914, p. 1247.
35. Ibid., 29th Oct. 1914, p. 6.
36. Ibid., 6th Nov. 1914, p. 2.
37. Admiralty Correspondence, ADM 137/34, Jerram, 10th Oct. 1914.

Chapter 7: Problems in Penang Get Worse

1. Le Coispellier, *Rapport du Commissaire du Gouvernement*, p. 11.
2. Ibid.
3. Admiralty Correspondence, ADM 1/8365/7, Maund to Jerram, 1st Nov. 1914.

4. Ibid., ADM 137/34, Jerram, 16th Oct. 1914.

5. *Penang Gazette & Straits Chronicle,* 21st Oct. 1914, p. 2.

6. *Straits Times*, 9th March 1915, p. 7.

7. Ibid., 19th Oct. 1914, p. 9.

8. Ibid.

9. Registre Historique de la Corresp'dance intéressant, Pistolet, pp, 604–605.

10. Ibid.

11. Le Coispellier, *Rapport du Commissaire du Gouvernement,* p. 12.

12. Ibid., p. 13.

13. Ibid.

14. Naval Staff Monograph, p. 85.

15. *Times of Malaya*, 26th Oct. 1914, p. 9.

16. Hohenzollern (1928: 121).

17. Starboard beam = abreast of *Hampshire* on her right-hand side.

18. Naval Staff Monographs, p. 85.

19. Admiralty Correspondence, ADM 137/34, Jerram, 26th Oct. 1914, p. 2.

20. Naval Staff Monograph, pp. 87–88.

21. Russian State Navy Archive, Baroness Cherkasova, 7th Nov. 1915, Letter to Russian Navy Prosecutor, Vladivostok, File 1785, pp. 156–159.

22. *Penang Gazette* (mail edition), 4th Sept. 1914, p. 1065.

23. *Straits Times,* 26th Nov. 1914, p. 2.

24. Naval Staff Monograph, p. 89.

25. Admiralty Correspondence, ADM 1/8365/7, Jerram, 1st Nov. 1914.

26. Le Coispellier, *Rapport du Commissaire du Gouvernement,* p. 12.

27. Ibid., p. 9.

28. Ibid., p. 10.

29. Ibid., p. 9.

30. Ibid., p. 11.

31. Ibid., pp. 10–11.

32. Ibid., pp. 34–35.

33. Ibid.

34. Ibid., p. 13.

35. Blain (1940: 211).

36. *Penang Gazette* (mail edition), 24th Oct. 1914, p. 1254.

37. Cross, Ministerial file, handwritten note, 28th Oct. 1914.

38. Admiralty Correspondence, ADM 1/8365/7, Maund to Jerram, 1st Nov. 1914.

39. Washing soda = a cheap, commonly used cleaning agent.

40. Le Coispellier, *Rapport du Commissaire du Gouvernement,* p. 17.
41. Admiralty Correspondence, ADM 137/34, Maund to Jerram, 1st Nov. 1914.
42. Le Coispellier, *Rapport du Commissaire du Gouvernement,* p. 15.
43. Ibid., p. 23
44. Farrère et Chack (1928).
45. Cross, Ministerial file, handwritten note, 28th Oct. 1914.
46. *Times of Malaya,* 31st Oct. 1914, p. 8.
47. Buyakov et al. (2004: 12, 55, 76).
48. Russian State Navy Archive, Baroness Cherkasova, 7th Nov. 1915, to Russian Navy Prosecutor, Valdivostok, File 1785, pp. 149–150.
49. Russian State Navy Archive, Cherkasov, Aug. 1914, Vladivostok, Inventory 1 File 1785, pp. 167–168.
50. Farrère et Chack (1928).
51. Naval Staff Monograph, p. 89.
52. Hohenzollern (1928: 166).
53. Le Coispellier, *Rapport du Commissaire du Gouvernement,* p. 20.

Chapter 8: *Emden's* raid on Penang

1. Dixon (1976).
2. Hohenzollern (1928: 168).
3. Ibid.: 171–172.
4. Blain (1940: 218).
5. Hohenzollern (1928: 170).
6. Farrère et Chack (1928).
7. Victoria Government Gazette, 16th Nov. 1883.
8. Harper and Miller (1984: 17).
9. Le Coispellier, *Rapport du Commissaire du Gouvernement,* p. 13.
10. Ibid., p. 15.
11. Hohenzollern (1928: 172).
12. Ibid.
13. Admiralty Correspondence, ADM 1/8365/7, Jerram, 1st Nov. 1914.
14. McClement (1968: 122).
15. *Penang Gazette* (mail edition), 28th Oct. 1914, p. 1274.
16. Huff (1994).
17. Hohenzollern (1928: 175).
18. Le Coispellier, *Rapport du Commissaire du Gouvernement,* p. 20.
19. Huff (1994).

20. Hohenzollern (1928: 175).

21. Ibid.: 176.

22. Admiralty Correspondence, ADM 1/8365/7, Maund to Jerram, 1st Nov. 1914, p. 3.

23. *Penang Gazette* (mail edition), 2nd Nov. 1914, p. 1273.

24. Blain (1940: 213).

25. Le Coispellier, *Rapport du Commissaire du Gouvernement*, p. 28.

26. Ibid., p. 20.

27. Ibid., pp. 20–21.

28. Farrère et Chack (1928).

29. Le Coispellier, *Rapport du Commissaire du Gouvernement*, p. 23.

30. Ibid.

31. Ibid., p. 26.

32. Ibid.

33. Ibid., p. 28. Also Buyakov et al. (2004: 68).

34. Le Coispellier, *Rapport du Commissaire du Gouvernement*, p. 27.

35. Farrère et Chack (1928).

36. Le Coispellier, *Rapport du Commissaire du Gouvernement*, p. 27.

37. Ibid., p. 28.

38. Conning position. Warships have a gun direction platform situated as high as possible on the superstructure, from which gunfire or torpedo fire can be aimed or directed.

39. Hohenzollern (1928: 173–174).

40. Huff (1994).

41. Hohenzollern (1928: 177).

42. *Penang Gazette* (mail edition), 6th Nov. 1914, p. 1273.

43. Blain (1940: 212).

44. Le Coispellier, *Rapport du Commissaire du Gouvernement*, p. 31.

45. Buyakov et al. (2004: 67).

46. Huff (1994).

47. Buyakov et al. (2004: 65–66).

48. Le Coispellier, *Rapport du Commissaire du Gouvernement*, p. 28.

49. Ibid., p. 42.

50. *Singapore Free Press & Mercantile Advertiser*, 7th Feb. 1931, p. 17.

51. Admiralty Correspondence, ADM 1/8365/7, Audemard to Jerram, 4th Nov. 1914, p. 4.

52. Blain (1940: 212–213).

53. Cross, Ministerial file, handwritten note, 28th Oct. 1914.

54. *Straits Echo* (mail edition), 26th Nov. 1914, p. 1630.

55. *Penang Gazette & Straits Chronicle,* 2nd Nov. 1914, p. 7.

56. *Straits Echo* (mail edition), 5th Nov. 1914, p. 1523.

57. *Times of Malaya*, 30th Oct. 1914, p. 9.

58. *Straits Echo* (mail edition), 5th Nov. 1914, p. 1524.

59. Ibid.

60. Le Coispellier, *Rapport du Commissaire du Gouvernement,* p. 35.

61. Hohenzollern (1928: 177).

62. Blain (1940: 213–214).

63. Admiralty Correspondence, ADM 1/8365/7, Maund to Jerram, 1st Nov. 1914, p. 5.

64. Blain (1940: 214, 215, 218).

65. Cross, Ministerial file, handwritten note, 28th Oct. 1914.

Chapter 9: The Death of *Mousquet*

1. *Straits Echo* (mail edition), 5th Nov. 1914, p. 1524.

2. *Penang Gazette* (mail edition), 6th Nov. 1914, p. 1276.

3. *Straits Echo* (mail edition), 5th Nov. 1914, p. 1524.

4. *Penang Gazette* (mail edition), 6th Nov. 1914, p. 1273.

5. Hohenzollern (1928: 178).

6. Le Coispellier, *Rapport du Commissaire du Gouvernement,* p. 32.

7. Ibid., p. 36.

8. Ibid.

9. Ibid.

10. Hohenzollern (1928: 178–180).

11. Le Coispellier, *Rapport du Commissaire du Gouvernement,* p. 36.

12. Ibid.

13. Ibid., p. 37.

14. *Penang Gazette* (mail edition), 6th Nov. 1914, p. 1274.

15. Le Coispellier, *Rapport du Commissaire du Gouvernement,* p. 35.

16. Hohenzollern (1928: 181–183).

17. Ibid.

18. Le Coispellier, *Rapport du Commissaire du Gouvernement,* p. 32

19. Registre Historique da la correspondance intéressant, Pistolet, pp. 607–608.

20. French Navy Correspondence, Tavera to Audemard, 19th Nov. 1914.

21. Admiralty Correspondence, ADM 1/8365/7, Maund to Jerram, 1st Nov. 1914, p. 5.

22. *Straits Times*, 26th May 1936, p. 10.

23. Forum, Section 2, p. 6.

Chapter 10: Counting the Cost

1. Admiralty Correspondence, ADM 1/8365/7, Audemard to Jerram, 3rd Nov. 1914, p. 6.

2. Le Coispellier, *Rapport du Commissaire du Gouvernement*, p. 41.

3. *Straits Echo* (mail edition), 5th Nov. 1914, p. 1523.

4. *Straits Times*, 22nd Nov. 1915, p. 10.

5. *Straits Echo* (mail edition), 5th Nov. 1914, p. 1523.

6. *Straits Times*, 30th Oct. 1914, p. 10.

7. Ibid., 30th July 1969, p. 6.

8. *Penang Gazette* (mail edition), 6th Nov. 1914, p. 1274.

9. *Singapore Free Press & Mercantile Advertiser*, 2nd Nov. 1914, p. 10.

10. Admiralty Correspondence, ADM 1/8365/7, Maund to Jerram, 1st Nov. 1914.

11. *Penang Gazette* (mail edition), 6th Nov. 1914, p. 1274.

12. Ibid., p. 1275.

13. Cross, Ministerial file, handwritten note.

14. www.liveinternet.ru/users/seamermaid/post96897432/

15. Admiralty Correspondence, ADM 1/8365/7, Jerram, 31st Dec. 1914.

16. *Penang Gazette* (mail edition), 6th Nov. 1914, p. 1277.

17. Hohenzollern (1928: 184).

18. Ibid.: 183–184.

19. Ibid.: 186.

20. Ibid.: 185.

21. Ibid.: 188.

22. Ibid.: 196.

23. Forum, Section 2, Rapport, Solcard, Médecin 2ème Classe, p. 14.

24. French Navy Correspondence, Tavera to Audemard, 19th Nov. 1914.

25. Moreau (1926: 106–108).

26. *Straits Echo* (mail edition), 12th Nov. 1914, p. 1558.

27. Carissan, Service dossier.

28. Forum, Section 1, p. 25.

29. Admiralty Correspondence, ADM 1/8365/7, Jerram, 27th Nov. 1914, p. 3.

30. French Navy Correspondence, Audemard to Commandant, Saigon, 20th Nov. 1914.

31. *Penang Gazette* (mail edition), 18th Nov. 1914, p. 1337.
32. Admiralty Corresp'dence, ADM 1/8365/7, Jerram, 27th Nov. 1914, p. 3.

Chapter 11: Accusations Begin

1. Cross, Ministerial file, handwritten note, 28th Oct. 1914.
2. *Times of Malaya*, 2nd Nov. 1914, p. 8.
3. *Straits Times,* 22nd May 1936, p. 3.
4. Ibid., 7th Aug. 1914, p. 10.
5. *Singapore Free Press & Mercantile Advertiser*, 3rd Dec. 1912, p. 12.
6. Ibid., 12th Aug. 1914, p. 10.
7. Khoo (2006: 20).
8. French Navy Correspondence, Daveluy to Jerram, 20th Jan. 1915.
9. *Penang Gazette & Straits Chronicle,* 2nd Nov. 1914, p. 4.
10. Admiralty Correspondence, ADM 1/8365/7, Jerram to Admiralty, 3rd Nov. 1914.
11. Naval Staff Monograph, p. 74.
12. *Straits Echo* (mail edition), 3rd Dec. 1914, p. 1668.
13. *New York Times*, 30th & 31st Oct. 1914.
14. *Straits Echo* (mail edition), 26th Nov. 1914, p. 1630.
15. *Times of Malaya,* 29th Oct. 1914, p. 9.
16. Admiralty Correspondence, ADM 1/8365/7, Maund to Jerram, 1st Nov. 1914.
17. Buyakov et al. (2004: 67).
18. Admiralty Correspondence, ADM 1/8365/7, Maund to Jerram, 1st Nov. 1914.
19. Naval Staff Monographs, Admiralty chart No. 3732, 1922, *Emden* in Penang.
20. German charts (no index number), reproduced by kind permission of Penang Museum Library.
21. Buyakov et al. (2004: 10 & 61).
22. Huff (1994).
23. Admiralty Correspondence, ADM 1/8365/7, Maund to Jerram, 1st Nov. 1914.
24. Admiralty Correspondence, ADM 1/8365/7, Jerram, 3rd Nov. 1914.
25. *Singapore Free Press & Mercantile Advertiser*, 29th Apr. 1911, p. 6.
26. *New York Times,* 20th Dec. 1914, p. 8.
27. *Straits Echo* (mail edition), 5th Nov. 1914, p. 1523.

Chapter 12: *Emden* destroyed

1. Admiralty Correspondence, ADM 1/8365/7, Jerram, 3rd Nov. 1914, p. 7.
2. Ibid., p. 6.
3. Ibid., pp. 3–5.
4. Naval Staff Monograph, p. 96.
5. Ibid., p. 98.
6. Hohenzollern (1928: 197–198).
7. Naval Staff Monographs, p. 93.
8. Ibid., p. 98.
9. Krakatoa was the largest recorded volcanic eruption in modern times, filling the upper atmosphere with fine ash which drifted around the globe, and set off huge tsunamis which killed many people.
10. Hohenzollern (1928: 201–202).
11. Corbett (1938: 380).
12. Hohenzollern (1928: 204).
13. *Daily Telegraph,* editorial, 11th Nov. 1914.
14. www.historyofnations.net/oceania/cocos.html
15. en.wikipedia.org/wiki/Cocos_(Keeling)_Islands.
16. *Straits Times*, 13th Nov. 1914, p. 8.
17. Corbett (1938: 380).
18. Hohenzollern (1928: 203–205).
19. Admiralty Correspondence, ADM 137/34, Jerram, 13th Nov. 1914, p. 1.
20. Hohenzollern (1928: 206).
21. *Straits Times*, 12th Nov. 1914.
22. Ibid., 25th Nov. 1914.
23. Admiralty Correspondence, ADM 137/34, Jerram, 13th Nov. 1914, p. 2.
24. Corbett (1938: 382–383).
25. Ibid.: 383–384.
26. *Penang Gazette & Straits Chronicle,* 27th Nov. 1914, p. 2.
27. *The Times,* 14th Nov. 1914.
28. Hohenzollern (1928: 206–239).
29. Ibid.: 239.
30. Ibid.
31. Admiralty Correspondence, ADM 137/34, Jerram, 27th Nov. 1914, p. 2.
32. Van der Vat (1983: 114).
33. *Penang Gazette & Straits Chronicle,* 27th Nov. 1914, p. 2.
34. Admiralty Corresp'dence, ADM 1/8365/7, Jerram, 17th Dec. 1914, p. 1.

35. Ibid., p. 2.
36. Ibid., p. 3.
37. Van der Vat (1983: 125–139).
38. Ibid.: 178.
39. Admiralty Corresp'dence, ADM, 1/8365/7, Jerram, 13th Nov. 1914, p. 1.
40. Ibid., p. 3.

Chapter 13: Mutiny in Singapore

1. Admiralty Correspondence, Jerram, 17th Dec. 1914, p. 2.
2. Harper and Miller (1984: 18).
3. Johnson (1955: 40).
4. Tarek (1995: 14–15).
5. Ibid.: 20. Cites *Straits Times*, 6th Aug. 1915, p. 1875.
6. Ibid.
7. Turnbull (2009: 125).
8. French Navy Correspondence, Daveluy, 20th Jan. 1915, Letter to Jerram, copied to French Navy Minister.
9. Kuwajima (1988: 68).
10. Ibid.: 62.
11. Harper and Miller (1984: 36).
12. Kuwajima (1988: 61).
13. Harper and Miller (1984: 65).
14. Ibid.: 61.
15. Ibid.: 59–60.
16. Sareen (1995: 14–15).
17. Ibid.: 61.
18. Kuwajima (1988: 67).
19. Harper and Miller (1984: 69).
20. Scott (1919: 37).
21. Cross, Ministerial file, handwritten narrative of Singapore Mutiny, 15th Feb. 1915.
22. Le Coispellier, *Rapport du Commissaire du Gouvernement,* pp. 4–8.
23. French Navy Correspondence, Fatou. The whole of the French correspondence reported here, including Jerram's communications, is held in a single file labelled 'First file. The Singapore affair, and its repercussions on the Penang enquiry'.
24. French Navy Correspondence, Direction Militaire des Services de la

Flotte, 1914, Report.

25. Sareen (1995: 14–15).
26. Funked = cowardly avoidance.
27. Le Coispellier, *Rapport du Commissaire du Gouvernement,* pp. 4–8.
28. Harper and Miller (1984: 70).
29. *Straits Times,* 26th March 1915. The execution of twenty-two renegades.
30. Sareen (1995: preface).
31. Harper and Miller (1984: 63).
32. Kuwajima (1988: 69).
33. Dijk (2007: 323–324).
34. *Penang Gazette,* (mail edition) 22nd Oct. 1915. p.1508.

Chapter 14: Saigon Enquiry

1. Registre historique de la correspondance intéressant, Pistolet, pp. 584–586.
2. French Navy Correspondence, de Boisrouvray, Report to the Minister, 21st Nov. 1914.
3. Ibid.
4. Ibid. Fatou. ? Feb. 1915. Incomplete document.
5. Ibid., de Boisrouvray to Navy Minister, 3rd Dec. 1914.
6. Admiralty Correspondence, ADM 1/8365/7, Jerram, 31st Dec. 1914, p. 2.
7. French Navy Correspondence, Castagné to the Navy Minister, 16th Jan. 1915.
8. Admiralty Correspondence, ADM 1/8365/7, Jerram, 31st Dec. 1914, p. 2.
9. French Navy Correspondence, Report to Minister from Monsieur Aubert, 7th Jan. 1915.
10. Ibid., Service de la Flotte à Commandant la Marine en Indo-Chine, 8th Jan. 1915.
11. Ibid., Direction Militaire des Services de la Flotte, Rapport au Ministre, 10th Jan. 1915.
12. Ibid., Service de la Flotte à Commandant la Marine en Indo-Chine, 8th Jan. 1915.
13. Ibid., Direction Militaire des Services de la Flotte, Rapport au Ministre, 10th Jan. 1915.
14. Ibid., Le Ministre des Affaires trangères à Monsieur le Ministre de la Marine, 12th Jan. 1915.
15. Ibid., Contre-Amiral Huguet à board *Montcalm,* Commandant La Division d'Extrème Orient à Monsieur le Ministre de la Marine, 19th Jan. 1915.

16. Le Coispellier, *Rapport du Commissaire du Gouvernement,* preliminary notes.

17. Ibid, pp. 42–44.

18. French Navy Correspondence (illegible signature), 19th March 1915. Copy of telegram No. 9, Saigon to Marine à Paris.

19. Ibid., Vice Amiral, Chef d'État Major Général de la Marine pour la Direction Militaire des Services de la Flotte, 25th March 1915.

20. Ibid., Pour Monsieur le Vice Amiral Directeur Militaire des Services de la Flotte, 4th May 1915.

21. Audemard, Service dossier.

Chapter 15: Cherkasov's Court Martial

1. Russian State Navy Archive, Inventory 1 File 1785, pp. 1–164.

2. Jane (1914).

3. Russian State Navy Archive, Inventory 1 File 1785, pp. 156–159.

4. Admiralty Correspondence, ADM 1/8365/7, Maund to Jerram, 1st Nov. 1914, p. 3.

5. Buyakov et al. (2004: 12, 55, 76).

6. Russian State Navy Archive, Inventory 1 File 1785, p. 167.

7. Russian State Navy Archive, Baroness Cherkasova to Senior Navy Prosecutor, Valdivostok, 7 Nov. 1915, Inventory 1 File 1785, pp. 156–159.

8. *Penang Gazette,* 22nd Nov. 1915, p. 9.

9. Admiralty Correspondence, ADM 1/8365/7, Maund to Jerram, 1st Nov. 1914.

10. Cross, Ministerial File, Articles and notes.

11. Russian State Navy Archive, Prosecutor, Vladivostok, 7th Nov. 1915, Inventory 1 File 1785, pp. 138–139.

12. Ibid., pp. 149–150.

13. Ibid., p. 155.

14. Ibid., pp. 156–159.

15. Buyakov et al. (2004: 146).

16. Russian State Navy Archive, Inventory 1 File 1785.

17. Buyakov et al. (2004: 104, 146).

18. *Parisian Messenger*, Paris, No. 14 (13th Sept. 1942), obituary.

Chapter 16: Loose Ends

1. Hohenzollern (1928: 259–266).

2. Van der Vat (1983: 192).

3. *Times of Malaya*, 10th Oct. 1914, p. 9.

4. *Straits Echo*, 28th Jan. 1970, p. 2.

5. Ibid., 31st Jan. 1970, p. 2.

6. *Straits Times*, 15th Oct. 1970, p. 3.

7. Jerram, Service File.

8. Maund, Service File.

9. *Singapore Free Press & Mercantile Advertiser,* 2nd Apr. 1932, p. 11; and *Straits Times*, 2nd Apr. 1932, p. 11.

10. *Straits Times*, 8th May 1915, p. 5.

11. Cross, Ministerial file, Obituary and other papers.

12. *Straits Times,* 16th Nov. 1932, p. 2.

13. *Singapore Free Press & Mercantile Advertiser*, 9th March 1934, p. 1; 22nd March 1934, p 6; 24th Apr. 1934, p. 12.

14. *Straits Times*, 23rd Apr. 1934, p. 13.

15. *Singapore Free Press & Mercantile Advertiser,* 31st March 1934, p. 2.

Bibliography

Primary Materials

Admiralty General Correspondence. China Station. May 1913–Dec. 1914. National Archives, Kew, London.

Audemard, Louis T. CC7 4è Moderne 7 dossier 189. Service Historique de la Défense, Château de Vincennes, Paris.

Carissan, Léon Jaques. CC7 4è Moderne 24 dossier 11. Service Historique de la Défense, Château de Vincennes, Paris.

Cross, W. Ministerial file. United Reform Church History Society. Westminster College. Cambridge.

De Paris de Boisrouvray, Charles. CC7 4è Moderne 61 dossier 6. Service Historique de la Défense, Château de Vincennes, Paris.

Forum. Internet. 'Pages d'Histoire: Marine", pp. 14–18: *Mousquet*: Contre-torpilleur. French Navy Correspondence, 1914-15. Guèrre d' Orient, Cote SSG1 Carton 1 1Mi501. Archives Centrales de la Marine, Service Historique de la Défense, Paris.

Huguet, Albert L. CC7 4è Moderne 23/2 dossier 2459/660. Service Historique de la Défense, Château de Vincennes, Paris.

Jerram, Thomas Henry Martyn. ADM 196/87. National Archives, Kew, London.

Le Coispellier, Saigon 12 March 1915. Rapport du Commissaire du Gouvernement à Capitaine de Vaisseau Fatou, Commandant la Marine en Indochine. Guèrre d'Orient, Archives Centrales de la Marine. Cote SSG1 Carton 1 1Mi501. Service Historique de la Défense, Château de Vincennes, Paris.

Liste de la Flotte, 1914, Division Navale de l'Indo-Chine,1914, pp. 296-297, 338-339, 340-343, 356-357, 368, 369. Service Historique de la Defénse, Château de Vincennes. Paris.

Maund, Guy. ADM 196/53 & 196/145. National Archives, Kew, London.

Naval Staff Monographs, Historical Fleet Issue: The Eastern Squadrons, 1914, April 1922, Volume 5. ADM 186. National Archives, Kew, London.

Registre historique de la Correspondance intéressant, le personnel et le matériel du bâtiment, 30 Juin 1912 à 14è Sept 1915, pièce no. 6: *Pistolet*, Cote

SSY 412, Service Historique de la Défense, Château de Vincennes, Paris.
Russian State Navy Archive, Navy Ministry. Baron Cherkasov Ivan Alexandrovich, including service records. RGA VMF Fonds 406 & 407.
Théroinne, Félix. CC7 4è Moderne 70 dossier 7 & 3535 dossier 5. Service Historique de la Défense, Château de Vincennes, Paris.

Published Works

Blain, W. (1940), Home is the Sailor: The Sea Life of William Brown, Master Mariner and Penang Pilot, London: Hurst & Blackett.

Buyakov, A. M., Kritskiy, N. N. and Shugaley, I. F. (2004), Last Battle of the Cruiser *Zhemtchug*. Vladivostok: Far East State University Press. (In Russian)

Cheeseman, H. R. (July 1951), 'St Andrew's Presbyterian Church, Penang 1851–1951', St Andrew's Outlook, 101.

Corbett, J. S. (1938), Naval Operations, Vol. 1: To the Battle of the Falklands, December 1914, 2nd edn, London: Longmans Green.

Dijk, Kees van (2007), The Netherlands Indies and the Great War 1914–1918, Leiden: KITLV Press.

Dixon, N. F. (1976), On the Psychology of Military Incompetence, London: Jonathan Cape.

Fairbank, J., Reischauer, E. and Craig, A. (1973), East Asia: Tradition and Transformation, London: George Allen & Unwin.

Farrère, C. et Chack, P. (1928), Combats et Batailles sur Mer, Paris: Imp. Flammarion.

Golding, H. (1917), Wonder Book of the Navy, London: Ward, Lock.

Greer, R. (1956), A History of the Presbyterian Church in Singapore, Singapore: Malaya Publishing House.

Harper, R. W. E. and Miller, H. (1984), Singapore Mutiny, Singapore: Oxford University Press.

Hobhouse, H. (2002), Seeds of Change: Six Plants That Transformed Mankind, London: Pan Books.

Hohenzollern, F. J. (1928), *Emden*: My Experiences in SMS *Emden*, translated from German, London: Herbert Jenkins.

Hough, R. (1969), The Pursuit of Admiral von Spee, London: Allen & Unwin.

Howe, C. (1996), The Origins of Japanese Trade Supremacy: Development and Technology in Asia from 1540 to the Pacific War, Chicago: University of Chicago Press.

Hoyt, E. P. (2001), The Last Cruise of the *Emden*, Guildford, Connecticut:

The Lyons Press.

Huff, P. G. (1994), SMS *Emden* (1909 bis 1914): Schicksal eines kleinen Kreuzers, Kassel: Hamecher.

Jane, F. T. (1914), Jane's Fighting Ships, London: Sampson Low, Marston.

John's Maritime History Society – German steamships – Book 1. http://maritime-history-one.webs.com

Johnson, A. (1955), The Burning Bush, Singapore: Dawn Publications.

Keegan, J. (1999), The First World War, London: Pimlico.

Khoo, Salma Nasution (2006), More than Merchants: A History of the German-Speaking Community in Penang, 1800s–1940s, Penang: Areca Books.

Khor, N. and Khoo, K. S. (2004), The Penang Po Leung Kuk: Chinese Women, Prostitution and a Welfare Organisation, MBRAS Monograph 37, Kuala Lumpur: Malaysian Branch of the Royal Asiatic Society.

Kuwajima, Sho (1988), 'First World War and Asia: Indian Mutiny in Singapore (1915)', Journal of Osaka University of Foreign Studies, 69: 23–48.

Marder, A. J. (1978), From the Dreadnought to Scapa Flow: The Royal Navy in the Fisher Era, 1904–1919, Vol. 3: Jutland and After, May 1916– December 1916, New York: Oxford University Press.

McClement, F. (1968), Guns in Paradise: The Saga of the Cruiser *Emden*, Toronto: McClelland & Stewart.

Moreau, H. D. (1926), Les Escales Maritimes. Le Port de Sabang (Indes Néerlandaises), Paris: Librairie Maritime Internationale.

Navy List (1914), London: HMSO (printed J.J.Keliher & Co. Ltd.).

Padfield, Peter (1974), The Great Naval Race: The Anglo–German Naval Rivalry 1900–1914, London: Hart-Davis, MacGibbon.

Roche, Jean-Michel (2005), Dictionnaire des Bâtiments de la Flotte de Guèrre Française, de Colbert à Nos Jours, Imp. Rezotel-Maury Millau.

Sareen, T. R. (1995), Secret Documents on Singapore Mutiny, 1915, New Delhi: Mounto Publishing House.

Scott, Sir Percy (1919), Fifty Years in the Royal Navy, London: John Murray.

Tarek, Abd. El-Hamid Ahmed Amin (1995), Anglo-German Rivalry in the Malay Peninsula and Siam, 1870–1909, PhD thesis, University of Malaya.

Taylor, J. M. (17 May 2007), http.//www.historynet.com/karl-frederich-max-von-muller-captain-of-the-emden-during-world-war-i.htm.

Turnbull, C. M. (2009), A History of Singapore 1819–2005, Singapore: NUS Press.

van der Vat, D. (1983), The Last Corsair: The Story of the *Emden*, London: Hodder & Stoughton.

Index

Names & Places